The MIND
behind
the GOSPELS

Reference Library of Jewish Intellectual History

Herbert W. BASSER

The MIND
behind
the GOSPELS

A Commentary
to Matthew 1–14

Boston
2009

Library of Congress Cataloging-in-Publication Data

Basser, Herbert W.
The mind behind the Gospels / Herbert W. Basser.
    p. cm. — (Reference library of Jewish intellectual history)
Includes bibliographical references and index.
ISBN 978-1-934843-33-8 (cloth) — ISBN 978-1-934843-34-5 (pbk.)
1. Bible. N.T. Matthew — Commentaries. 2. Rabbinical literature —
Relation to the New Testament. I. Title.
BS2575.53.B38 2009
226.2'07 — dc22
            2009026385

ISBN 978-1-934843-33-8 (cloth)
ISBN 978-1-934843-34-5 (pbk.)

Book design by Ivan Grave

Published by Academic Studies Press in 2009
28 Montfern Avenue
Brighton, MA 02135, USA
press@academicstudiespress.com
www.academicstudiespress.com

CONTENTS

ABBREVIATIONS

General

b.	Talmud Bavli
LXX	Septuagint
m.	Mishnah
M.T.	Masoretic Text
t.	Tosefta
y.	Talmud Yerushalmi

Hebrew Bible

1Chron.	1 Chronicles
2Chron.	2 Chronicles
Dan.	Daniel
Deut.	Deuteronomy
Eccles.	Ecclesiastes
Exod.	Exodus
Ezek.	Ezekiel
Gen.	Genesis
Hab.	Habakkuk
Hag.	Haggai
Isa.	Isaiah
Jer.	Jeremiah
Josh.	Joshua
Judg.	Judges
Lam	Lamentations
Lev.	Leviticus
Mal.	Malachi
Neh.	Nehemiah
Num.	Numbers

Obad.	Obadiah
Prov.	Proverbs
Ps.	Psalms
1Sam.	1 Samuel
2Sam.	2 Samuel
Song	Song of Solomon (= Song of Songs)
Zech.	Zechariah
Zeph.	Zephaniah

New Testament

Col.	Colossians
1Cor.	1 Corinthians
2Cor.	2 Corinthians
Gal.	Galatians
Matt.	Matthew

Mishnah, Talmud, and Related Literature

ʿAbod. Zar.	*Avodah Zarah*
ʾAbot	*Avot*
ʿArak.	*Arakhin*
B. Bat.	*Bava Batra*
B. Meṣ.	*Bava Metziʾa*
B. Qam.	*Bava Qamma*
Beṣah.	*Betzah*
Ber.	*Berakhot*
Bek.	*Bekhorot*

'Ed.	*Eduyyot*
'Erub.	*Eruvin*
Ḥag.	*Hagigah*
Ḥul.	*Hullin*
Giṭ.	*Gittin*
Ker.	*Keritot*
Ketub.	*Ketubbot*
Ma'as.	*Ma'aserot*
Mak.	*Makkot*
Meg.	*Megillah*
Me'il.	*Me'illah*
Menaḥ.	*Menahot*
Mo'ed Qaṭ.	*Mo'ed Qatan*
Naz.	*Nazir*
Ned.	*Nedarim*
Pe'ah	*Pe'ah*
Pesaḥ.	*Pesahim*
Qidd.	*Qiddushin*
Roš Haš.	*Rosh HaShanah*
Šabb.	*Shabbat*
Sanh.	*Sanhedrin*
Šeb.	*Shevu'it*
Šebu.	*Shevu'ot*
Sem.	*Semahot*
Šeqal.	*Sheqalim*
Soṭah	*Sotah*
Ta'an.	*Ta'anit*
Ter.	*Terumot*
Yad.	*Yadayim*
Yebam.	*Yevamot*
Zebaḥ.	*Zevahim*

Targumic Texts

Tg. Ps.-J.	*Targum Pseudo-Jonathan*

Other Rabbinic Works

'Abot R. Nat.	*Avot of Rabbi Nathan*
Deut. Rab.	*Deuteronomy Rabbah*
Exod. Rab.	*Exodus Rabbah*
Gen. Rab.	*Genesis Rabbah*

Lev. Rab.	*Leviticus Rabbah*
Kallah Rab.	*Kallah Rabbati*
Midr.	*Midrash*
Pesiq. Rab Kah.	*Pesiqta of Rab Kahana*
Pirqe R. El.	*Pirqe Rabbi Eliezer*
Sipra	*Sifra*
Sipre	*Sifre*
Sop.	*Sopherim*
Tanḥ.	*Tanhuma*

Greek and Latin Works

Eusebius, *Hist. eccl.*	*Ecclesiastical History*
Irenaeus, *Haer.*	*Against Heresies*
Josephus, *Ag. Ap.*	*Against Apion*
Josephus, *Ant.*	*Antiquities*
Josephus, *Life*	*The Life*
Josephus, *War*	*Jewish War*
Philo, *Mos.*	*On the Life of Moses*
Suetonius, *Vesp.*	*Vespanianus*
Tacitus, *Ann.*	*Annales*
Tacitus, *Hist.*	*Historiae*

Old Testament Pseudepigrapha

T. Iss.	*Testament of Issachar*
T. Jud.	*Testament of Judah*
T. Levi	*Testament of Levi*
T. Sol.	*Testament of Solomon*

Dead Sea Scrolls

CD	*Damascus Document*

New Testament Apocrypha and Pseudepigrapha

Ps.-Clem.	Pseudo-Clementines

PREFACE

This book offers my interpretation of what I see as Jewish concerns embedded in the rendering of the birth and ministry of the life of Jesus of Nazareth, as presented in the first fourteen chapters of the Gospel of Matthew. The predominant (although not exclusive) method of my inquiry into the Jewish rhetoric found in Matthew's Gospel presupposes that its author selectively drew upon various oral and/or written materials that he had at his disposal. Among these are early stories told by the followers of Jesus, both during his lifetime and shortly after his death, that reflect the stories as well as the cultural context of prevailing trends in "Second Temple" Judaism as they were understood by that Jesus community.

Remnants of these Second Temple Jewish traditions now lie scattered in bits and pieces in various works. In the process of transmission, they have been constantly remolded and reshaped, added to and subtracted from, by Jewish Scribes and scholars from the Second Temple period through the fifteenth century. The more some of these traditions moved from one setting to another, with subtle, substantive changes in meaning, the more their forms solidified, standing out in contrast to the literary styles of later periods in which they were newly recorded. Consequently, we are able to compare their forms to other, untouched originals of a much earlier time.

My literary models for the transmission of the Jesus stories are the materials concerning the *Besht* (Israel Baal Shem Tov, 1698–1760) who flourished in the first half of the eighteenth century. These contain the bodies of literature that purportedly record the oral stories of the miracles, faith-healings, establishment-criticisms, and teachings to disciples of Israel Ba'al Shem Tov. One might consult *In Praise of the Ba'al Shem Tov* for illumination. These tales (*Shivhei HaBesht* in Hebrew, first edition 1815), having circulated orally for a time, were formally transcribed about fifty-five years after the Ba'al Shem Tov's death. The recent opening of archives in Poland and Russia now allows scholars to make historical evaluations, based upon the clues these stories provide about the settings in which they were produced and reproduced, of the various ways in which they were told and retold. Tales referring to currency exchange rates that accurately reflect the historical reality of eighteenth-century economic transactions almost certainly preceded, and thus are arguably more original than, those stories with nineteenth-century exchange rates.[1] Thus, we can gauge which stories are earlier and (presumably) more reliable and which give us hints that they were recast and remolded to suit the needs of later times.

The same analytical approach can be applied to Jewish Second Temple traditions that emerged in medieval times. At times, far later writings can closely reflect much earlier forms. For instance, some legal passages from Nachmanides closely match some of those found in Philo; whole sections from the works of Rabbi Moses of Narbonne (known as *Ha-darshan*) match, word for word, some of the traditions recorded in the Dead Sea Scrolls.[2] Beyond the narrower questions that revolve around discerning "parallels," however, lies the revelation of irrefutable evidence that there exists an entire literature, spanning the ages, through which the Jewish imagination has constructed vivid images to express profoundly Jewish sentiments. These expressions still exist and are preserved as part of the legacy of the Jewish "sea of learning" and provide a prism for viewing Matthew's imagery. They need not be reinvented. Furthermore, it is superfluous to concoct hypothetical interpretations of these images when uncontrived real ones actually exist, although some have been altered or "updated" in their retelling.

Change can be very slow, even inadvertent, in Jewish tradition. Present-day academies of Talmudic scholarship have much more in common with their medieval precursors than with modern educational systems. The core of the practices of religious Jews is not very different from those of their ancestors, nor is their religious vocabulary very different. It is extraordinary indeed how the words of the Hebrew Bible have exhibited such consistency through the ages. Once thought to be later than the parent texts of the LXX, the masoretic text-type of the Torah can now be seen to be of the same, if not of an earlier, date.[3]

This is the case because of the endeavors of Jewish teachers through whom these traditions have been handed down. It was their job both to recite what they had heard and to progressively systematize the body of Law and lore, integrating accretions into the formation of a seemingly seamless and organic whole — *the* tradition (singular). It is for this reason that the core of the tradition has held firm within the same forms and often in the same words from one generation to the next.[4] Otherwise, the great bulk of "the tradition" would have been too diverse and confusing to have been of any use. This process of systematization continues to this day, with new questions being asked concerning the fixed tradition and new theories being propounded in response to them. *Ex nihilo nihil fit.* The stories told in Midrash and the Talmuds and passed down by them did not come out of nowhere. They had to have had antecedents, perhaps from a variety of sources. This is also the case with the material found in the Gospel of Matthew. Its author organized and wrote down what he had previously heard and read. Certainly he added things here and there but in no way can it be said that he invented his Gospel. Preservation is not invention.

The purpose of the Gospel of Matthew is to tell the story of Jesus' life and death and his subsequent resurrection. If Matthew's author dwells on matters such as Jesus' disputes with the Pharisees or with the circumstances surrounding his birth and subsequent flight into Egypt, I assume, along with R. T. France, that this is because his sources dwell on them.[5] The sudden breaks in the structure of the narrative confirm for me France's notion that the author of Matthew used presynoptic material as a source for his Gospel. This early material is most clearly discernible in the *midrashic* forms, the legal formats and formulae, and the frequent allusions to the prophetic literature that are found in Matthew. This is why Matthew's author, who can express such vehement anger toward the Jewish leaders, the Jewish people, and the Jewish Temple, can also write so movingly in his Gospel about concepts that profoundly resonate within Jewish culture.[6]

I do not believe that the author of Matthew was a master of *derash* (a technique for substantiating a Jewish theology into the words of Scripture by repunctuating or revocalizing or utilizing other creative literary mechanisms), or that he was interested in *halacha* (Jewish Law). Rather, Matthew's author relied upon sources, whose complexities he at times did not fully comprehend, and followed them to the letter. He was also a gifted writer who interpolated his own ideas into the received narratives into his Gospel.

Perhaps the point might be made that the Gospel of Matthew seems to be too early for it to contain any evidence of the "rabbinic" forms and contents that I argue it does. Nonetheless, I contend that were we to try to construct a precursor to rabbinic oral tradition in literary form, we could not have done much better than a text like the Gospel of Matthew. The legal arrangements and forms of argumentation in Matthew are well within the range of full-fledged "rabbinism," as I have shown elsewhere.[7] The sermons in Matthew are likewise composed of interpretations current in the rabbinic literature of a later time period; they are centered on the very same biblical verses and share the same interpretive idiom. Since Jewish sources from the second through to the fifteenth centuries preserve the old oral and written traditions intertwined with new ones, so far as I am concerned whatever from these sources helps us to understand Matthew's text is welcome.

As much as I am able to, I use the earliest material available to me to shed light on the Gospel. Nonetheless, I do not shy away from using material from later compilations found in rare manuscripts whose provenance is unknown. Nor do I have any qualms about using literary formulations of late date if they are useful. The forms of literature dictate the choice of the materials I cite. I am sensitive to the forms of exegesis that fit fixed, known rhetorical methods. In any given case, the attribution of Matthew's method to the appropriate category of form, visible in rabbinic tradition, helps us find the intended meaning of his rhetoric. So when I recognize congruent forms in Matthew and in other Jewish texts, I cautiously use the latter to illuminate the former. Even if it turns out that some of this material was somehow influenced by pre-Pauline Christian sources, I would argue that such material is still a most valuable tool to unpack Matthew's earlier models. We need offer no excuse for using the Talmudic traditions at our disposal when they appear to match or share a style and structure similar to that of Matthew's text. Those who sneer at using rabbinic materials to help interpret the Gospel must either invent convoluted interpretations of their own, or else turn to and rely upon Jewish traditions from the intertestamental literature that are not nearly as close to Matthew's formulations as are the rabbinic formulations.

As a rule, I will not bore the reader with every account in Jewish literature of an angel announcing an impending birth or a king decreeing the destruction or persecution of Jewish children. Nor is it necessary to point out the long list of Jewish sources that confirm the wickedness of Herod, or each and every Hebrew Bible verse that seems to corroborate Matthew's mode of thinking. In most cases, one or two examples will suffice. I do not think it necessary to expand upon the Gospel's presentation of Jesus as a new Moses and Herod as a new Pharaoh, although some may find intertexts that would enable them to read some theological message into such an argument to be of interest. I am not concerned, for the most part, with the historical accuracy of the information found in the Gospel texts. Instead, I am interested in understanding the models upon which the author of Matthew has based his rhetoric, and explaining the reasons why the sentences in his work follow one another in the way that they do.

Some of what I consider to be the most useful and meaningful source material, essential for understanding the Gospel of Matthew, has been previously pointed out by others. Yet the real import of these sources has generally been overlooked, and the sources themselves have been overwhelmed and obfuscated when they are swallowed up by other materials of little worth. While Strack and Billerbeck's *Kommentar* can be useful, it is so cluttered with irrelevancies that it overburdens the reader to seek out the one or two worthy comments in every ten pages of this densely printed work.[8] Generally speaking, Talmudic scholars from Montefiore to Flusser give us much less of what is irrelevant than their "Old Testament" and/or "intertestamental" colleagues do. Nevertheless, their focus on parallel *content* in Jewish literature usually distracts them from the importance of parallel *style, form, and structure*.[9]

Time and again in my work, I have tried to show that existing records found in *midrashim* (Jewish homiletic interpretations), from whatever sources they are now available, inform, are informed by, and inform us about the culture upon which the presynoptic stories are predicated, which accounts for some of the odd details in them.[10] All this, again, I hope to demonstrate in the work that follows.

In all cases, I have tried to ensure that my translations facilitate the understanding of all passages I discuss, even if they occasionally vary from one other. Since all translations are interpretations, my renderings of Hebrew Bible, Greek Matthew, and Hebrew/Aramaic writings of Rabbis adjust to the requirements of the context at hand. A single passage might be translated slightly differently in different contexts. The quest for consistency in translation can sometimes obscure the meaning or significance of certain passages. I have tried to avoid rigid insistence on the consistent translation of a specific word or phrase, especially when the understanding I present here differs from that found in standard translations.

My work has very little to do with theorizing about the Gospels' influence on one another. Although it is sometimes useful to compare the phrasings in one document with those in another, or to scrutinize the manuscript variants within a single Gospel, I have tried to keep such discussions to a minimum. Unlike most Matthean scholars, I have difficulty seeing Matthew as a Jew, although I do not discount the possibility altogether. I prefer to read Matthew, as I do all the Gospels — as a retelling of a basic storyline passed down through time. Matthew's author, more than others involved in the transmission process, lets us see his cards on occasion. Even when he repeats what others also know, his presentation is more dramatic, more highlighted, more brilliant.

My method is this: I read the Matthean verse. If and when it suggests something else I've learned, I argue that there is a connection. I speculate how everything might fit together. If I like it, I write it; if not, I go on. If I find that others before me have said something similar, I either provide a citation to their work or (more likely) I discard what I have written. In general, I have tried to avoid restating what others have said, for not everything bears repeating. Many years ago Professor Baruch Halpern quoted that great fictional detective, Charlie Chan: "No barber shaves so closely he does not leave room for another barber." I see myself as that other barber, working closer to the skin, some might complain at times, even splitting hairs. In the parlance of the Rabbis, I am a gatherer of forgotten sheaves, salvaging and bringing together the leftovers of earlier gatherers. Above all, I look for handles by which to make sense of the complexity behind Matthew's simplicity. I have no idea about the dates of the sources used by Matthew and it may be that a few, even more than a few, incorporate material that predates Jesus to some extent. Of course, I do not speak of passages from Israel's Holy Scriptures, which are obviously earlier.

The Gospels in our hands seem to have originated from an older tradition no longer known. From it their authors skillfully develop a new approach to old questions with a fresh voice. This realization of adjustment of older materials requires a sophisticated reader. The New Testament takes for granted, but does not cite at length, those oral materials that would become embedded in classical Jewish literature after the formulation of the New Testament. Generally, Jewish sources explicitly cite Hebrew Scripture and then follow the citation with an interpretation. In the case of Matthew, the biblical proofs and interpretive frameworks are often hidden from the Gospel reader, but once the guiding source is located many passages take on new dimensions. The arguments that have been made for the preponderance in the Gospel of Greek rhetoric and Hellenistic imagery are undermined when the close correspondence of their idioms and motifs to those found in Jewish texts is recognized. It is essential for the reader of the New Testament to recover the interpretive triggers that lie behind the statements and stories of the New Testament. To my mind, the Christian traditions Matthew inherited were deeply steeped in Jewish interpretive strategies and methodologies, resonant in almost all of the key issues at their most basic strata.

By writing this commentary to Matthew 1–14, scene by scene, and tracing the idiom, motif, and theology, through the Jewish mind, I rediscover and expose the latent message of each passage's background material. My intention is to present to the reader an in-depth study that systematically presents the Gospel of Matthew as part of a complex of Jewish ideas that pervaded the cultural matrix of the early Jewish, Galilean, and Judean Christian communities. Within Judaism (as evidenced in core chapters in *b. Sanhedrin*), these ideas, in the ensuing centuries, gave rise to a philosophy of human legislative responsibility within a system of divinely given commandments.[11]

True storytellers never tell, they show. Michael Riffaterre uses the concept of "fictional truth" and "truthful novels" to reveal how competent storytellers create worlds for the reader to enter into by building upon images they or others have used in previous works.[12] Recognizing this allows us to judge the level of artistry in any narrative work, whether fiction, history, or sacred text. It is left to the reader to draw conclusions based upon the descriptive images the storyteller evokes. These images have both immediate lexical and also wide narrative import that is at once self-referential and also "library"-referential; that is, the images the storyteller creates in one work connect with and/or reflect images he or she has found works. For Riffaterre, a story never stands alone, but always fits into a wider context. This method of storytelling is used throughout the whole body of Jewish literature from the Bible onward, in which God is seen as the primary author of Israel's story and history.

In the following study, I base my reading of the Gospel of Matthew upon this image-connecting and/or image-reflecting understanding. A careful reader of the Gospel is able to uncover the author's motives and intentions while at the same time making connections between the images in the Gospel with other images, or "truths," presented in the Talmudic "library." Since Matthew and the rabbinic traditions sometimes draw from common early sources or derive from a shared understanding, I see no reason why these two traditions, in such cases, cannot be read together. Within each there is a common rhythm, as it were, that creates the harmonies or the constructs the counterpoints found between them. And so now I invite the reader to join me in pondering the portrayals of dialogues offered by Matthew, based on his received information and personal writing skills, in his Gospel. For me, these evoke images from the vast literary and oral Jewish tradition that I have long studied, which today is increasingly accessible both in print and electronic form.[13]

NOTES

1   See Mondshine, ed., *Shivhei Habesht,* 14. Also see Rosman, "Le-Toledotav Shel Mekor Histori," 183–84. Chapter 9 of his book, *Founder of Hassidism,* casts doubt on the historicity of the stories (sharing much in common with stories told of Rabbi Isaac Luria). I am open (although I make no claim to the historicity of the Gospels since they provide no method of verification) to seeing the Gospel as based, in part, on some actual reports by believing eyewitnesses to Jesus's paranormal faith-healings, exorcisms, and prognostications, together with eyewitness reports of Jesus' style of preaching. On the other hand, like those of the Ba'al Shem Tov (i.e., *Besht*), stories of his legendary birth and attendant revelations are undoubtedly later additions to the core stories. I. Etkes, in *The Besht,* quotes Reiner, "The transmission of [the hero's] praise is part of the ritual of this public" (229), and quotes Rosman, "Hagiography is primarily concerned with turning the exemplary life into a proof text for a position advocated in the present" (*Founder of Hassidism,* 233). Also citing Rosman he remarks, "and [additions that] describe the *Besht*'s parents, his childhood, and the manner in which he acquired his esoteric knowledge, are all linked to the *Besht*'s future role as a leader" (233). Etkes, using historical documents, letters and written accounts found in both *Besht*'s supporters and opponents, is prepared to acknowledge that much of the reported wonderworking in the tales was based actual occurrences of some kind, taken at face value by the *Besht* and those who were his devotees (223, 258). Unwittingly, the historical *Besht* brought to an end the long period of past faith-healing techniques. Through his teaching, through his actions, and through his stories his students found a new method of seeing divinity in the world. In a short time his students attributed to him the creation of a new Jewish sect, *Hassidim.* In reality, this sect was a continuation of an older sect. What was new was the founding of new types of rabbi-shamans who came to lead communities of this sect. This innovation immediately aroused the ire of the official rabbinic establishment for a considerable period of time.

2   Basser, *Studies in Exegesis,* 129ff.; Stone, "Testament of Naphtali."

3   Ulrich. *The Dead Sea Scrolls and the Origins of the Bible.*

4   David Flusser, in *Jewish Sources in Early Christianity,* remarks: "The literature of the sages began to be collected in the generation following the destruction of the Temple. Thus we can find parallels to New Testament Midrashim [HB: Flusser's designation] only in very late collections" (63).

[5] See France's introduction in *The Gospel According to Matthew*, 78.

[6] Basser, "Gospel and Talmud," 285–95.

[7] Basser, "The Gospels Would Have Been Greek to Jesus."

[8] Strack and Billerbeck, *Kommentar zum Neuen Testament aus Talmud und Midrasch*.

[9] Yuval, in *Two Nations in Your Womb* (23 n. 33), wrongly proclaims that works such as the present one show a one sided influence of New Testament on Talmud and Midrash. Detailed analysis of both literatures shows, at best, a common well-spring of unique Jewish culture. His proofs hold no substance. What serves as proof is his mistaken idea that the Talmudic assertion that "Pentecost (Shavuot) celebrates the day the Law was given at Sinai" was taken from the appearance of the Holy Spirit to the Apostles in Acts 2, fifty days after the Crucifixion, is as weak as his other arguments. M. D. Herr, in "The Calendar," has already shown that a pre-Christian source, Jubilees, alludes to the substance of the Talmudic assertion. Yet, on p. 116 Yuval, in a full turnabout, claims the link between Shavuot and the revelation at Sinai is assured after the second century B.C.E., if not earlier, and supplies scholarly references to that effect. Furthermore, Yuval's claim (*Two Nations*, 29) that Christians were completely aware of the practices and beliefs of contemporary Jews in the Middle Ages is disproved by a close reading of Church Fathers and schoolmen on Jews as shown in my work, "What Makes a Commentary Jewish or Christian."

[10] See, e.g., my "The Jewish Roots of the Transfiguration"; "Matthew 21:12."

[11] See Steinmetz, *Punishment and Freedom*. The entire book is a convincing exposition of this thesis.

[12] Riffaterre, *Fictional Truth*.

[13] I try to resist here issues of social history, feminist concerns, and details of Jewish practices where the Gospel is not dependent on them. My primary goal is to grasp important possibilities in the nuance of the narrative. If readers require more, perhaps the subsequent volume will satisfy those wishes.

ACKNOWLEDGMENTS

Regarding translation conventions: the rabbinic passages are my own; the biblical ones are either mine or generically borrowed from a variety of Internet sites. Whenever a point requires a specialized reading of Scripture, then the translation is mine. While the body of my commentary uses, in the main, a new translation of Matthew provided through the kindness of Peter Zaas, David Malone and I reworked this translation at various points. In notes and comments where precision is not the issue I again have utilized, as a matter of convenience, whatever Internet translation appeared most accessible and appropriate. The greatest of care, however, has been taken in the precise translation of the Matthew base text and the rabbinic materials. David Malone checked my own translations of the rabbinic materials against standardized published translations in order to readjust the numbering system I used, since the chapter numbers in my printed Hebrew texts were sometimes at variance with those found in the standard translations.

David Malone, my research associate, read through piles of articles and books while finely editing the first twelve chapters. The goal was to produce a unique work, as unlike others as possible. Among those who helped me generously and diligently are Howard Adelman, Dale Allison, Jacob Basser, Gail Baxter, Therese Boyd, Marsha B. Cohen, Kirsten Dane, Amy-Jill Levine, Sarah Shorthall, Ellen White, Judy Young and Peter Zaas. Special thanks are due my publisher, Dr. Igor Nemirovsky, for his diligent care. There were many others who shared ideas with me such as Steven Fine, Annette Yoshiko Reed, and Kris Linbeck, and I thank everyone for their help and encouragement. I am most appreciative for the help of the **Social Sciences and Humanities Research Council (Canada), which** funded this project from 2004 to 2008.

The MIND behind the GOSPELS

A Commentary to Matthew 1–14

My title is based on my personal understanding of early Christian materials embedded in the Gospel of Matthew and other gospels. The "mind behind the Gospels" may be taken as that collective "mind" shared by Jewish teachers from the first century (if not earlier) until the present: a mind of which early Jewish(-Christian) raconteurs were still a part. These raconteurs, unlike other Jewish students of the Torah, spread stories of Jesus, likely in Aramaic, before the earliest written Gospels were composed. The training of these raconteurs — Jewish[-Christian] students of traditions current in the Apostolic Church — was, I suspect, placed in the hands of the earliest documenters of Christian teaching.[1] They preached the news of salvation through faith in Jesus, the Christ, to the lost sheep of Israel. These missionaries, who seem to have been faith healers (Matt. 10:1), shared the same cultural outlook, the same written and oral traditions, the same "mind" as Jews in the Land of Israel, for indeed, prior to Paul, "the directors of the Apostolic Church" were Jews in the Land of Israel (Gal. 2:1). It follows that they shared the same communities as did other Jews and understood matters much as they all did. If the community had fault lines of division, so did they. What each said was intelligible to the other: agree or disagree as they might. The idiom and thought pattern of this "mind" informs, to large extent, the backdrops of the Gospels: Matthew, Mark, Luke, and John. And it is the erudite imagination of this "mind" (at times generative, at other times associative) that is the focus of my commentary.

But this stage in which early Christian missionaries still shared in the mind behind the Gospels did not last long; in fact, it did not, I submit, survive much past the generation in which these first preachers spoke. Our best evidence from the writings of Paul and Luke (namely, the Book of Acts) suggests that in the Diaspora, the Jewish elements within Christianity, were being challenged, while everywhere in Jewish circles Christian preachers who were Jews, like Paul, were not welcome. Within a very few years, the Jewish(-Christian) Gospels were readjusted by adding pro-gentile and anti-Jewish sentiments, by cutting out natural Jewish references to the centrality of Torah study and the Land. By such methods these Gospels were tailored to suit the growing numbers of gentile adherents: first in the churches of the Diaspora, and apparently later in the Land of Israel itself.[2] Gradually, in the decades close to the time of the destruction of the Temple in 70, vehement anti-Jewish tones and polemics were seeping into the earlier accounts of the raconteurs, whose final tones came to match the gut-felt revulsions of many Jewish leaders and Christian teachers toward the other soon after the year 70. The canonical Gospels, in varying degrees, reflect the hostility so that the Gospel we call Matthew has both layers brilliantly enmeshed in it. The Jewish material is thoroughly the Jewish mind of the early missionaries; the anti-Jewish material is thoroughly the mind of preachers who needed to drive a wedge between the two communities. I am well aware that other scholars see the development of the Gospel tradition and Christian split with Judaism in a radically different light than I do, placing the major split in the second century or later and they find reason to think so. If taken at face value, their readings of the situation would seriously impair some of my interpretations.[3] I do not see the Gospels' anti-Jewish material as in-house sectarian quibbling between Jews of different outlooks. For me, there is too much praise of the gentile ethic and condemnation of Jewish leaders and their customs in Matthew to see this as in-house banter.[4] In my commentary I draw attention to these passages.

I now illustrate my above account of the stages in which the early Christian communities of the first century understood, as a matter of course, the idiom of Jewish teachings that was their culture, and embraced many of them in Aramaic formulations ascribed (correctly or incorrectly) to Jesus of Nazareth.[5] My portrayal requires we accept that the Gentiles required Greek Gospels, as Jewish languages were not understood by them fully. The older Aramaic traditions now served as raw material out of which to fashion the new compositions. To appreciate the shifts in moving from the Aramaic stories to the Greek ones, we need to realize that it is advisable in rare instances to translate, that is, to retrovert passages back into a conjectured Aramaic idiom.[6] This is most suitable where the Greek texts fail to do justice to the inherent logic required to understand the passage. In moving from the Aramaic to the Greek, more than language shifts; a simultaneous bias against the Jews creeps in. I offer Matt. 12:11–12 in illustration of the point. Jesus is called upon to defend his healing of someone's withered arm on the Sabbath.

He said to them, "Which person from among you who has a single sheep, would not grasp it and lift it out, should it fall into a pit on the Sabbath! Now, how greatly does a human being surpass a sheep! So it is permitted to do good on the Sabbath."

Here the unassailable logic should logically argue, but does not in fact argue, that since one is permitted on the Sabbath to ease the pain of a sheep caught in a pit, one should certainly be permitted to ease the suffering of a human whose importance, on the scale of Creation, is much greater than that of a sheep. The necessary conclusion of such an argument is that one may benefit people, on the Sabbath, who are in pain. But this is not what Matthew tells us. His words imply that one will set aside Sabbath prohibitions where one's own interest is at stake. The owner is worried about harm coming to his property. But unless we speak of an ill human being who serves the interests of the healer more than an endangered sheep would, the logic of the passage as given in the Greek fails.

Matthew, most likely following his source, confuses the issue by speaking of a single sheep. Here is what Kevin P. Edgecomb wrote me in private correspondence:

> The language in Mt 12.11 additionally indicates that the hypothetical man only "has one sheep" (exei probaton en),[7] which I would think is also a very important point. To be so poor as to have only one sheep, the milk and wool of which would be more precious for that man's livelihood than if it were one of hundreds; [the] loss of the sheep would be a loss of not just property but livelihood. It's likely that this understanding lies behind the Mt passage, rather than the loss of one out of many sheep.

Now I agree that this is precisely what Matthew's text is telling us. Yet this scenario defeats the argument that leads us to conclude that a human deserves care, too. What gets lost in the argument is the Jewish legal principle of "relieving pain of living creatures" — if for an animal how much more so for a human! How did Matthew, whose language is usually very precise, manage to lead us astray here?

I think the simplest and most plausible answer is to be found by attributing the confusion to a mistranslation that Matthew inherited in his source material. The translator mistook an Aramaic form that is somewhat ambiguous and rendered "one sheep" where the meaning of the original likely mentioned "a sheep." In Aramaic it is conventional, but not a rule without exception, that if the sense is *one* object" the number follows the noun, but if the sense is "*an* object" the number (one) precedes the noun. There is a passage discussing the Messiah in *y. Ber.* 2:4 where the text reads: "*an* Arab passed by" (*'abr had 'arabii*). The text could conceivably be translated as "*one* Arab passed by," but in context this would not make good sense, since there are no others in the scene. If that sense was, for some reason, the intended sense, then the writer would have said *'abr 'arabii had*. It seems most plausible that the Christian translator of the sheep passage, not paying attention to the logic of the argument of relieving an animal's pain, rendered the passage with the sense that Jews commonly break the Sabbath for their own self-serving interests ("Which person from among you who has *one* sheep [*'ana had*],[8] would not grasp it and lift it out, should it fall into a pit on the Sabbath!") and paid scant attention to the logic of the passage. He thereby misconstrued the intent. The issue could not have been about the self-interest of the man — it had to be about the interest of the sheep. The sheep would likely survive until after the Sabbath in a pit but it would suffer. Now it follows that the interest of a sick person is of greater consequence and, even if he will survive the Sabbath, his suffering can be lawfully alleviated. The original likely had a reversed phrasing to that suggested above: "Which person from among you who has *a* sheep (*had 'ana*), would not grasp it and lift it out, should it fall into a pit on the Sabbath [to help it]!" Notice that the understanding that we speak of is alleviating pain, and nothing self-serving, which is evident in the conclusion of the argument: "So it is permitted to do good on the Sabbath." In this case, Matthew has an old source that was misunderstood and leads us to confusion. Of course, it is possible that Matthew slightly altered his source to make Jews look devious. In any event, the intent of the passage requires us to read "a sheep."

The above example teaches us two further things. Where Matthew has material no other Gospel mentions, Matthew may have an older source for it which he follows nearly slavishly. Also, there is strong reason to accept that Aramaic and Hebrew forms of the Gospels circulated at early times. A report by Church Fathers actually says a Gospel called Matthew was composed in one of these languages. In Annette Reed's wording (paper on Matthew): Papias in Eusebius, *Hist. eccl.* 3.39: "Matthew put together the oracles [of the Lord] in the Hebrew language, and each one interpreted them as best he could." Irenaeus, *Haer.* 3.1.1: "Matthew also issued a written Gospel among the Hebrews in their own dialect, while Peter and Paul were preaching at Rome, and laying the foundations of the Church."[9]

Matthew's Gospel lacks the dominant themes of Talmudic literature: love of Israel, love of the land, love of Torah. To my mind, the Gospels are aimed at Gentiles.[10] This raises the question of when we should argue

Jewish(-Christians) no longer considered themselves, and were no longer considered by others, as Jews. Schuyler Brown, although his study dates to 1980 and so much more has been written on the topic to date, has written a piece that deserves close scrutiny because it is typical in many ways of the studies that followed it. Essentially, he argues that once the Temple was destroyed, the gradual process of separation raced ahead into an inevitable separation. Jews needed to define themselves and their belief system to draw tight boundaries around communities that were no longer held together by the central Temple and Christian communities needed to give way to the predominance of Gentiles within their communities and break with Jewish ceremonial rituals. Brown's argument, like most other arguments, tries to avoid the glaring contradiction: Matthew (writing about 80 C.E.) seems to have incorporated post-70 Jewish traditions in his Gospel while at the same time actively encouraging Samaritans and Gentiles to form the backbone of churches no longer dependent on the (Christian) Jerusalem central command. I do not know how these two claims can simultaneously be true. For Brown, this very ambiguity is the substance of Matthew's Gospel: Matthew, on the one hand, could not oppose the mandate of his community, which was set by Peter's authority, while, on the other, this same evangelist wanted to move the community into the gentile camp to "heal divisions." The destruction and subsequent exile have been understood to show that Jews are no longer the chosen of God and the church was free to operate outside of "Jewish territory." Brown transfers his own problem with historical reconstruction to the substance of Matthew's problem that, for Brown, the Evangelist needs to work out in the final scenes of the First Gospel. To date, no theory of the parting of the ways suffices to answer all the problems. And it has even been suggested that the ways never parted and hence no need to become muddled in the conflicting pieces of evidence.[11]

While I dispute that Matthew is responsible for the Jewish content in his Gospel and that this content is largely post–70 C.E. (p. 214), and that Jesus himself abrogated kosher laws (pp. 195, 198), I accept that the break is final shortly after 70 C.E. (although, for me, Matthew writes from the gentile perspective and is clear on his position).[12] I would argue that for there to be a break, there need not have been a total abandonment of Jewish Law in all churches and therefore the ambiguity and contradictions within present-day reconstructions of "the parting of the communities" actually reflect the contradictions and ambiguity that ensued in the post-70 era. Some mystical practices known from Scripture and the Talmudic literatures, such as purity laws, might have been practiced by some groups (*Ps.-Clem. Homilies* mentions such practices—as cited in Reed's piece [*Ps.-Clem.*

Homilies] on p. 13).[13] Reed's paper raises new questions about the practice of Jewish Law in Christian communities even if the social break between the communities was already complete.[14] Acts 24:5 uses the term *Nazoraiwn* (Hebrew *Notzrim*) for Christians as a separate group (implying they are not Jews) as do the Talmudic Rabbis (*b. 'Abod. Zar.* 7b). Yaacov Teppler has provided us with a review of the material, both Christian and Jewish, pertinent to this discussion.[15] Both Justin Martyr who flourished around 140 in Caesarea (in his *Dialogue with Trypho* [is this Rabbi Tarfon?]) and Talmudic sources record a ban on Jews talking to Christians.[16] *B. Šabb.* 116b refers to this ambiguity of observance of Jewish Law in the period following the destruction of the Temple and the ensuing exile of many Jews. *B. Šabb.* 116a refers to the need to eradicate the Gospels and avoid Christian places of worship at all costs. It has become clear to me that the break was precipitated more by the rejection of scribal Law and interpretations, leading to the entire abrogation of the Torah's rituals than by ideological and theological "heresies."

The Jewish layer of the Gospel tradition was not eradicated but placed into a setting in which much of its original shine became dulled and tarnished. What I try to recover is not the notion so much of Jewish/Gospel parallels as an idea of a Jewish mind and a Jewish approach to life that lies buried beneath words and episodes in the Gospel of Matthew — a mind that I have already suggested the Gospel writer does not share. I therefore conclude that what looks Jewish in spirit is arguably genuinely Jewish since the Gospel writers hardly celebrate it. I'm not sure why it is there unless maybe the early church was genuinely a Jewish movement and its early material was preserved, even if subsequently cast into antipharisaic polemic (which I do not think it was originally). The Gospels' use of Jewish tradition mirrors what William Scott Green claimed about the use of Scripture for Talmudic Rabbis: "Rabbis did not so much write about or within Scripture as they wrote with it, making it speak with their voice, in their idiom, and in their behalf. The rabbinic interpretation of Scripture, therefore, was anything but indeterminate or equivocal." This is, to my mind, an apt description of how the Gospel tradition appropriates Jewish tradition and misappropriates it, for its own purposes. The process is natural, and responsible Jewish teachers of all times have appropriated but not misappropriated it. They never deny basic values and rooted identity markers of Israel and their laws in reinterpreting their own traditions, not only their Scriptures, to address contemporary issues and needs.[17]

The above question of how the Gospel of Matthew and the literature of the Talmuds are related introduces a number of questions. The most pressing one for me is, "What mentality framed the life of Jews in Matthew's day?" It is becoming more and more in style to speak of "competing Judaisms," "proto-rabbinism," "Temple-centric Judaism," and many other kinds of systems that would suggest our current corpus of Talmudic writings are too late to tell us anything useful about Jewish life in Matthew's day. Professor Steven Fine suggested to me privately that perhaps all of these terms derive from some kind of reconstruction of history based on Protestant views of historical development over the past century and a half. For these scholars, Catholicism broke away from some more pluralistic foundation as Catholic Fathers strove to consolidate power and authority for their form of Christianity. There was a gradual "catholicizing" that eventually won the day. What Fine suggests is that we have a "protestantization" of Jewish history.[18]

I now need to address my notions concerning the literature I use to illumine the images preserved in Matthew's writings. This literature derives from a group of teachers, we now term "rabbinic." It preserves many old traditions (attested by Josephus and the New Testament) and shows us developments in manners of biblical exegesis and reformulation and systemization of inherited legal materials. These "Rabbis," for all intents and purposes, are the very group that the New Testament writers and Josephus identify as Pharisees. I prefer the term "Talmudic Rabbis" as I see these people as major figures in a large corpus of works that I lump together under the name "Talmudic" (expressive of an approach to Law and lore exemplified in the Talmuds) for convenience rather than for precise accuracy. Throughout this book, the term "Rabbis" should be understood as referring to those masters of Jewish tradition whose literary formulations expound the documents they commonly called "Talmud Torah." They are not meant to be designated as a religious group sharply set apart from pre–70 C.E. teachers[19] or even from their later interpreters (post–500 C.E.) or indeed from the majority of their contemporaries. The literary purpose of the Talmuds and subsequent documents is, to large extent, to systematize materials passed down from teacher to student into a coherent whole through finely argued discussions of masters and students of Jewish legal traditions. The process of this systemization continues into modern times, using the same categories of thought and reference as did the Talmudic Rabbis of early times.

Should we ask how the tradition inherent in the Mishnah and Talmuds came to be, we might adopt one of three possible models. 1) Early Israelites practiced a biblical religion that became outmoded as social and political changes occurred and new forms of practices and beliefs formed in response to Hellenism and new political realities, the major one being the Destruction of the Temple in 70 C.E.; 2) the tradition unfolded naturally through intellectuals, or learned judges, working the material and refining it as time progressed; 3) There existed traditions tied to written phrases in the Hebrew Bible as well as, and alongside them, purely oral traditions (with no connections to any written Scriptures) which provided specific details of what had once been obvious to the people who cared about the Torah's injunctions.[20] All of these positions have their proponents and perhaps some mixture of the models is truer to the mark than any single one.

It should be noted that a large corpus of Law, custom, and local practice developed over time and I refer to these, somewhat anachronistically, as scribal laws or rabbinic laws in my work. There was also, in the first century if not earlier,[21] a discrete body of laws that were fixed, called "tradition of the Fathers (or Elders)," which incorporated this corpus as well as oral tradition said to be handed down from God through a chain of teaching throughout the generations. We might take note of the very many laws that the first-century writer Josephus enumerates which accord almost verbatim with the laws which the Talmuds and midrashim record in the name of authorities spanning the years 135 to 500 C.E.[22] Josephus assures us that the Pharisees are experts in the many ancestral laws that have been handed down from ancestors and not written in the Law of Moses; the masses support them (*Ant.* 13:294–97, *War* 2:162). When Josephus brags that he is the foremost scholar of Jewish Law and exegesis in his time, of which there are less than a handful like him, he speaks of knowledge of Law (*nomos*) and interpretation of Holy Writings (*hermeneusai hierwn grammatwn*). Chaim Milikowsky identifies these two enterprises (in *Ant.* 20:264–66) as referring to matters in the categories of what the Talmudic Rabbis referred to as "Mishnah" and "Midrash" respectively.[23] Josephus tells us in his *Life* (9) that he had studied Jewish learning and showed talent both in memorizing and understanding legal points. He mentions here that when he was fourteen years old, elders of the community consulted him on legal points. Talmudic Rabbis report these two modes of study (*b. Sukkah* 28b): *girsa* (memory work), and *iyun* (understanding, wisdom). In hyperbolic praise (*b. Ber.* 64a) they used terms like "Sinai [memory of the tradition]" and "uprooting mountains [understanding]" to refer to different types of scholars who had mastery in particular areas.

Talmudic literature shows no awareness that its enterprise is anything other than a continuation of long-standing traditions and accepted modes of analysis of these traditions. Some modern scholars have built arguments for gradual rabbinizations that created a new Judaism over six centuries from the time the Temple was destroyed in 70 C.E. However, the models of continuity are not easily dismissed.[24] An interesting example is that of James 2:2–4: "[if there come unto your synagogue/court...in splendid apparel, and a poor man, and say, Sit here well…stand there, or sit here beneath]." Midrash Tannaim explains Deut. 16:19, "[Judges!] Do not recognize persons: "Do not say this one is rich while this one is poor…this deserving one should sit beneath [me] and do not have it that the poor stand and that the rich sit. …God stands with the poor and not with those who oppress them." They are virtually one and the same, except one is said to be "pre-Rabbis" and the other "post-Rabbis."

Finally, if there is any question that what we have in our possession of early Jewish Law was indeed transmitted orally over long periods of time, that question has been laid to rest by the article of J. Zussman showing that Oral Torah was exactly that: Oral transmissions of Law and lore.[25]

Why then, if the materials are so ancient, is the literature of the Talmudic Rabbis so cohesive and self-referential that it appears as a self-contained culture of academic intellectuals on its own merits without much reference of its legal materials to the first century or earlier? To rephrase: the apparent originality of the documents showing us legal arguments contain their own points of reference and named authorities primarily from the second century onward, but next to nothing before that. So what is it that this literature does that is new and exciting that drove the shape of Judaism for two millennia? It seems to me, that a great deal is assumed by the framers of Mishnah and Midrash. While the "traditions" of the first century and earlier (one of them concerning vows mentioned in Matt. 15:1–2) were summarily cited as anonymous Law by consensus from antiquity, the Talmudic Rabbis stated legal positions that were subjects of debates and not consensus, allowing for speculation on the fine points that gave rise to these disputed positions.[26] This gave rise to theories of legal consistency and the Mishnah, with its listings of positions and counterpositions, led to a new enterprise of weighing arguments and developing a unified Law. To this date, many points are still debated, Law is not completely unified, and the process is one of intellectual satisfaction and religious experience in exploring the halachic universes of the Talmuds. While we have some scant evidence of legal reasoning and controversies in earlier periods both from Josephus and the New Testament, as already noted, the explanation and celebration of controversies, as far as our evidence allows, was not viewed as the goal of study but rather a means to reach definitive and expert opinion on a legal point.[27] Consensus was seen as strength. Debate was inter-party, not intra-party.[28] What also seems to be different is the manner of biblical exegesis, that Rabbis appealed to in order to justify known traditions dating from the Second Temple period. What Talmudic Rabbis supply is some innovative hermeneutics allowing for the tradition to continue and develop.[29] The "Rabbis" understood that the Torah had been designed from its very giving at Sinai to allow authorized sages in each generation to use new insights to interpret matters as they would arise.[30] One would be hard pressed to argue that such had not been the view of rulings among the pre-70 teachers as well, but Talmudic Rabbis tended to stress and acknowledge their own creativity in claiming that the results of their exegesis should be more beloved to scholars than the received dry word of unprocessed Scripture.[31] It was their particular genius to catalogue concrete laws through fine analysis in order to extrapolate their essential abstract principles. These principles could be applied to new concrete cases requiring creative solutions in the religious, ethical, and social realms.[32]

This volume does more than replace the outdated classic Strack-Billerbeck in showing Jewish forms of thinking that lie behind much of the Gospel. Unlike this latter work, I have tried to show the relevance of these forms to the meaning of the passage at hand. Nevertheless, my assertions are not very much different from their stated goals. Page vi of their introduction suggests they did not claim they were presenting a clear, definitive exegesis of the New Testament. Rather, they seem to suggest their goal was to present an understanding of the New Testament which the reader would derive from reflection upon the material found in the Talmud and the Midrash.

A list of those who wrote works collecting rabbinic parallels to the New Testament are found in the appendix to a doctoral dissertation completed in 1986 at Dropsie College, Philadelphia, titled *Paul Billerbeck as Student of Rabbinic Literature: A Description and Analysis of His Interpretive Methodology*, by Daniel John Rettberg. The literature is substantial. For my part, I do not suggest I am doing much more than bringing the sense of Matthew to life by selecting materials to show what an informed reader would derive from reflection on these materials. I do not claim anything more than is reasonable. What exists in Jewish literature, from any time period where heirs to the cultural norms of *aggada* (lesson-driven *Tanak* interpretation) and *halakhah* (legal-driven interpretation) dug profoundly into their learning, can be more helpful in uncovering deep meaning in the New Testament than the works of modern-day scholars who speculate upon what might have been in Matthew's mind. At least my material is not invented to fit my view of what I need Matthew to say. I do not merely give a parallel, as many of my predecessors do, but try to show what the parallel teaches us about the meaning of the Gospel verse at hand. In short, I have selected, from the original Hebrew and Aramaic sources at my disposal, those pertinent Jewish teachings that solved difficulties in interpretation to my satisfaction. I have tried to indicate what we can learn from the material to give us a better handle on the Gospel tradition.

Finally, in explanation of the materials I use, the reader should not become alarmed that there will be times when I cite late medieval sources where Talmudic sources of a much earlier period are sufficiently available to make the same point. The reader's eyebrows may rise several inches to note such things: "Basser, are you nuts! In chapter 14 you cite Rashi's eleventh-century commentary to a Talmudic passages to make the point those very early Talmudic passages have already made." I answer: "My preference is to use a credible course that dramatizes a familiar scene, from rabbinic times to the present, in a way that portrays the *realia* of the Gospel's picture." The same picture, in Rashi and Matthew, of the Master blessing, breaking, and distributing bread, shows us a shared culture that finds meaning in the same details. In fact, that very picture, in every detail, is still common practice today for many Jews. I will continue to argue throughout my book that in many instances where we have such close literary matches between Gospel and Talmud we cannot easily escape the conclusion we deal with more than a shared mind, we deal with an articulated tradition that predates both our Gospel and Talmudic sources. We might say that at times we have sister traditions, while at other times we have more distantly related traditions. It would not be wrong to use the term "genetic" even if the channels of transmission from Jewish Oral lore to Christian Gospel are too circuitous to even contemplate uncovering. The internal evidence for such transmission of shared mind and shared content is sharp and clear.

In the present work, I comment on the first half of Matthew's Gospel and until such time as a further volume appears, readers may rely on my published works to indicate the thrust of my thought in the second half of Matthew's Gospel.[33] My hope is that readers will not glance or skim this work, or even read it page after page. To really see into the text of Matthew using my methods, the reader must study each comment slowly and carefully until the connection between verse and comment becomes crystal clear. Only by wrestling with the rabbinic materials in conjunction with the Gospel will the reader discover that there is more in the Matthean text than could reasonably be set down in a volume. The reader is my partner in this study and the insights in the book we write together will be celebrated in the reader's appreciation of the "minds" of Matthew. I have not made the work easy but I have pointed to some lingering crumbs along the hidden path to help the lost reader travel halfway through this Gospel.

NOTES

1. I use "disciples" as the first Christians would have: first, as the immediate students of Jesus who told his story to celebrate their experience of him and second, as more general followers who pass down legal and narrative traditions they have been taught. Luke 1:1–4 mentions that Luke himself had inherited traditions, both oral and written. Some of these disciples may have become missionary-raconteurs spreading the story to attract followers to their sect. I do not go so far as Bauckham, *Jesus and the Eyewitnesses,* to suggest we always have eyewitness accounts behind the stories in the Gospel rather than literary compositions, but I do grant that the earliest history of gospel production could have been, and likely was, based (at least in part) on eyewitness testimony. Issues of sources and relationships of Matthew to other Gospels are discussed in Davies and Allison, *Matthew,* ix–xxvii. These questions are not my issues here and I note that many have speculated on these relationships on which I largely remain silent; it might well be that we lack the literary evidence to make more definite judgments with any degree of certainty. See further n. 1 to the preface.

   Matthew, living in the subsequent Gentile phase of the Church's leadership, sees Jesus as the replacement for the Law. He puts "Make disciples of all the nations" into the mouth of Jesus (28:19; see chap. 2, n. 1). In doing so he rephrases the central directive of *m. 'Abot* 1:1 to set it into a Gentile context: [Moses received the Torah from Sinai and transmitted it to Joshua; Joshua to the elders; the elders to the prophets; and the prophets handed it down to the men of the Great Assembly. They said three things: Be deliberate in judgment,] *raise up many disciples,* [and make a fence around the Torah].

2. So seems to be the common knowledge informing the story about one of these raconteurs in *b. Šabb.* 116b. This source also preserves a Gospel text similar to Matt. 5:17 in Aramaic.

3. See, e.g., the various opinions in Becker and Reed, eds., *The Ways That Never Parted.*

4. See the discussion of the various views of Jesus: Jew or Gentile, in Davies and Allison, *Matthew 1–7,* 7–30. They argue against those who see Matthew as a Gentile. I lean toward seeing Matthew as either a Gentile or, perhaps, a Jew-turned-Gentile who has abandoned Jewish tradition and the Jewish people.

5. Steven T. Katz's objections (*"Methodology* in *Basser's* Studies) to this train of thought and my answer can be found in *Review of Rabbinic Judaism* 4, no. 2 (2001): 320–43.

6. See David M. Goldenberg's critique of a suggestion I proffered and his criteria for judging the value of retroversions in "Retroversion to Jesus' Ipsissima Verba and the Vocabulary of Jewish Palestinian Aramaic." Regardless of the actual possibility of my suggestion being right or wrong, his criteria strike me as reasonable.

7   In Matthew "*hen*" is always used in the sense of "one," "the one." Nevertheless, "*heis*," "*mia*," "*hen*" seem to be available in rare instances as an indefinite article in "Koine."

8   The Syriac *Peshitta* has this word order, with "*ḥad*" following '*arb'a* to signify a single sheep.

9   Annette Yoshiko Reed sent me her essay, "Jewish Christian Evidence for the Rabbinization of Roman Palestine?" (I also thank her for making her paper "The Gospel of Matthew and/as Judaism" available to me.)

10   Matthew 21:42–43: shows us Jesus saying: "Did you never see in the Writings, 'The stone which the builders put on one side, the same has been made the chief stone of the building: this was the Lord's doing, and it is a wonder in our eyes (Ps. 118:22)?' For this reason I say to you, *The Kingdom of God will be taken away from you, and will be given to a nation producing the fruits of it*" (emphasis added). The "chief stone" refers to the gentile nations here which replace Israel, whereas in Mark 12:10, Luke 20:17, Acts 4:11, Eph. 2:20, and 1 Peter 2:7, this stone is taken to refer to Jesus.

11   Brown, "The Matthean Community and the Gentile Mission," 213, 215. See the bibliography in Becker and Reed, eds., *The Ways That Never Parted*, for the various positions on the conflicting pieces of evidence.

12   Ibid., 195, 198, 214.

13   See n. 9 above.

14   What she calls *rabbinization* might refer to decrees promulgated in 66 at the outset of the Jewish-Roman War or earlier. I am skeptical of the use of the term *rabbinization* as I am (with Reed) on the use of the term "Jewish-Christianity" pre-70, and for the same reasons: there is no evidence of any self-awareness of distinctness from the larger group of Jews that either of these people live with. Since the author of the *Homilies* speaks in the mouth of Peter, perhaps the Jewish material is to lend credence to the notion that these are the words of Peter, particularly if they were missionary tracts aimed at converting Jews. Too much about the date and provenance and audience of the *Homilies* is unknown for anyone to speculate at all or use the material constructively for historiographic purposes. Reed is aware of the pitfalls and remarks that her speculations are more to begin discussion than to close them.

15   Teppler, *Birkat haMinim*.

16   See ibid., 126–27, 252.

17   See Green, "Romancing the Tome."

18   See Fine, *Art and Judaism in the Greco-Roman World*, 55. Also see 47–81 and especially chap. 3, "Archeology and the Search for 'Non-Rabbinic Judaism'" (33–46). I thank Professor Fine for making these materials available to me.

[19] In *Life* 9, Josephus says he engaged in sophisticated legal discussions with the ranking scholars of his day: presumably requiring the same Talmudic-style analysis that we find in the legal debates in the Gospels.

[20] See my "Review of Jacob Neusner, *Four Stages of Rabbinic Judaism*" (New York: Routledge, 1999), in *Review of Rabbinic Judaism* 3, no. 1 (2000): 203–6.

[21] See Baumgarten, "The Pharisaic Paradosis." This article helps us push back the sense of *masoret* meaning "oral Law," or nonscriptural Law (even if the term is anachronistic) into Pharisaic, pre-Christian times. See further considerations of oral form versus written form in Mason, *Flavius Josephus on the Pharisees*, 241–43.

[22] See the listings in Feldman and Hata, eds., *Josephus, Judaism, and Christianity*, 37–40. See further, Feldman and Reinhold, *Jewish Life and Thought Among Greeks and Romans*, 402:17.

[23] See Milikowsky, "Josephus: Between Rabbinic Culture and Hellenistic Historiography," 159–200.

[24] See Fonrobert and Jaffee, eds., *The Cambridge Companion to the Talmud and Rabbinic Literature*. The following articles best show the variety of current positions on what is old and what is new in the teachings of the Talmudic Rabbis and current theories of rabbinization: "Rabbinic Authorship as a Collective Enterprise" (M. Jaffee); "The Orality of Rabbinic Writing" (E. Shanks Alexander); "Social and Institutional Settings of Rabbinic Literature" (J. Rubenstein); "The Political Geography of Rabbinic Texts" (S. Schwartz); "Rabbinic Midrash and Ancient Jewish Biblical Interpretation" (S. Fraade); "The Judean Legal Tradition and the Halakhah of the Mishnah" (S. Cohen).

[25] Zussman, "Torah She-Be'al Peh: Peshutah Ke'mashma'ah."

[26] Matthew 15:1–2, "Then the Scribes and Pharisees who were from Jerusalem came to Jesus, saying, "Why do your disciples transgress the *Tradition of the Elders*? For they do not wash their hands when they eat bread." B. Ḥul. 33b discusses the rationale for the hand-washing rules and *m. 'Ed.* 5:6 mentions excommunication as a sanction against one who treated the matter lightly. The *Tradition of the Elders* is part of the legacy of the Talmudic Rabbis. Again, in 15:5–6, "But you say, 'Whosoever shall say to his father or his mother, "whatever [I have] with which you might have been benefited by me is given to God"; he shall be absolved from honoring his father' — and so you have abrogated God's word for the sake of your *tradition*." *M. Ned.* 5:6 records an event in Beth Choron (in which the existence of the Temple is assumed, so the story likely dates from before 70), about a father who through a vow [i.e., "giving to God"] would be forbidden to enjoy anything of benefit from the son. In the story, a friend of the son actually wants to give to the Temple things the son tries to give the father through him. Rabbi Nissim Gerondi (to *b. Ned.* 48a) interprets *m. Ned.* 5:6 to mean that the son had taken a vow, forbidding his father all access to benefit from his property. The upshot is that the Gospel (15:5–6) is likely citing

an actual clause from the pre-70 *Tradition of the Elders* which was operative for the Talmudic Rabbis: "Whosoever shall say to his father or his mother,' whatever [I have] with which you might have been benefited by me is given to God; [a standard oath formula]' he shall be absolved from honoring his father."

27   See Bernstein and Koyfman, "The Interpretation of Biblical Law in the Dead Sea Scrolls." On 68 they discuss the harmonization at Qumran of Lev. 19:1–2 and Deut. 14:1–2 (11QT 48:7–11) but they do not mention that the Talmud *b. Mak.* 20a cites a *Baraita* in standard rabbinic form to accomplish much the same results. The Qumran Law is not precisely the same as the Rabbis.

28   See Harrington, "Holiness in the Laws of 4QMMT." See her comments on 110 and especially 128.

29   In 1987 I spent a pleasant evening with Prof. J. Zussman, the celebrated scholar of Talmud at Hebrew University, at his home in Jerusalem, telling him of places I had discovered in *midrash halachic* works that accorded with Second Temple pseudepigraphic sources. He then showed me the extensive marginalia he had written that indicated the very sources I had alluded to earlier. I was then working on "Matching Patterns at the Seams: A Literary Study," in *From Ancient Israel to Modern Judaism: Intellect in Quest of Understanding,* (Atlanta: Brown University, 1989), 2:95–118, which included some of my investigation on this matter.

30   See *Sipre Deut.* 313 (ed. Finkelstein, 335) and for the idea that each generation's leader has authority like Moses to interpret and legislate see *b. Roš Haš.* 25b.

31   *Y. Sanh.* 11:4, *y. Pe'ah* 2:4, *b. B. Bat.* 108b; *b. Naz.* 2b, *b. 'Erub.* 21b.

32   Fonrobert, "From Separatism to Urbanism." The laws in the oral tradition concerning marking boundaries in which one may carry on the Sabbath were known to the Qumanites before the Christian Era. Fonrobert demonstrates how rabbinic powers of complex analysis and abstraction of legal details were used to conceptualize social space and find new mechanisms (based on existing institutions) to enable the expansion of private space in new ways.

33   *Studies in Exegesis;* "Gospel and Talmud"; "Planting Christian Trees in Jewish Soil"; "Matthew 21:12"; "Sharing in the Divine"; "The Gospels and Rabbinic Literature"; "The Gospels Would Have Been Greek to Jesus"; "Ideas of Glory and Sonship in Hebrew Scriptures and the Gospels"; "Midrashic Form in the New Testament"; "Derrett's 'Binding' Reopened"; "The Meaning of 'Shtuth."

CHAPTER ONE

INTRODUCTION

The introductions to the chapters address important issues that demand more attention than a commentary warrants. I have tried to limit my attention to matters not widely discussed in the literature. For example, the issues of Matthew's models for his genealogy in chapter 1 have occupied a good deal of the scholarly literature that need not be repeated here. On the other hand, in the commentary to chapter 1 I include discussions of genealogical form and style in the MT and LXX that seem to inform Matthew's structure of the genealogy. In general, I avoid the theoretical issues of synoptic parallels, form criticism, and textual variants. Notwithstanding some noteworthy exceptions, this work seeks to provide new and strong oars for navigating the Gospel material afloat in the sea of the Jewish literary tradition.

In the first chapter of his Gospel, Matthew seeks to convince his audience that Jesus is the Messiah and Savior whom Israel expected. He demonstrates, by way of a theory of cyclical chronological patterns in Israel's religious history, that the years when Jesus lived marked the endpoint of that pattern. That demonstration, necessary but insufficient in and of itself, does not "prove" to us that Jesus was the Messiah — just that someone, in those days, must have been. So how do we know Jesus was the very Messiah and Savior that Israel was waiting for? Matthew shows that certain prophetic signs at his birth (and throughout his life) fulfilled ancient prophecies, signs that sufficiently "proved" that he was the divine messenger of redemption.

TRIPARTITE HISTORY

Matthew lays out a history of Israel divided into three parts: "Thus all the generations from Abraham to David were fourteen generations, and from David to the Babylonian Exile were fourteen generations, and from the Babylonian Exile to the Christ, fourteen generations" (1:17). The final verse swings from the biblical period of the ancient Hebrews to the close of an interim period and thus allows a symmetrical chronology to emerge.

Although Matthew does not give explicit meaning to the pattern he develops, attention to Jewish texts helps ascribe some meaning to it. *B. 'Abod. Zar.* 9a also divides Jewish history into three equal periods, though this text focuses on years rather than generations, and it understands history to be 6000 years in duration. After the first period, which in reference to the preformed and thus "formless" (*tohu*) world in Gen. 1:2 the Rabbis call "Chaos," the advent of Abraham indicates the beginning of the second period. Rabbinic literature understands Abraham to mark a new phase in human history, following the initial phase marked by dysfunctional human development.

According to *Gen. Rab.* 2:3, immediately following the flood, God again set in motion a plan built into nature from the beginning of creation. This text finds Abraham's appearance in history analogous to that moment when, as the wind of God hovered over the watery abyss, light first appeared (Gen. 1:2). This wind (*ruah*) was also thought to be the same wind that calmed the waters at the close of the flood.

> "And God brought to pass a wind upon the earth" (Gen. 8:1). God had said how long must the world be mired in darkness (see Gen. 1:2). May light come! For God had said, "Let there be light!" (Gen. 1:3). Of course this referred to Abraham, as Isaiah intimated, "Who has enlightened the righteous one from the East [enlighten: heh-ayin-yod-resh], [calling him to follow Him?]" (Isa. 41:2), but he really meant to say "caused him to radiate light" [radiate light: heh-aleph-yod-resh].

According to the Rabbis, Abraham is the primordial light that illumines the darkness, distinguishing good from evil and truth from falsehood. He is the transitional figure whose appearance marks the beginning of Messianic history. In another striking passage from *Gen. Rab.*, Rabbi Judah (second century) makes plain his understanding that Abraham was just such a figure and that his separateness was enshrined in his name.

> "And it was told to Abraham the Ivri" (Gen. 14:13). ...Rabbi Judah explained "IVRi" to mean that the whole world was across from him on one side and he was across from them on the other side (eIVeR) (Gen. Rab. 42:8).[1]

For the Rabbis of the midrash, Abraham had been chosen, selected from all others for a unique mission: his role in God's historical plan was to father a nation, embodying the divine presence and a process of enlightenment for all humankind. They saw the final movement of Abraham's mission in the integration of all Israelite-Jewish history, which is also the goal and end of history, in the advent of the Messianic Age.[2] For Matthew, this Messianic Age was already being realized in the first century. For the Rabbis, the eschatological age had not yet begun to occur in either the third or fourth centuries (or yet in the twenty-first).

But Matthew's pattern of generations was likely composed under the influences of biblical tradition and later Jewish speculation upon the redemptory end-times. If this were not the case, why would he bother to show us a pattern in the first place? In a tradition preserved in both *m. 'Ed.* 2:10 and *t. 'Ed.* 1:14, *Qetz* (end-time) divisions are measured in generations. The Hebrew word *Qetz*, which literally means "end," or "limit," signifies the close of a period of oppression, which is destined to end at a predetermined time.

The term *Qetz* is also found in the Bible, where it has eschatological connotations. For example, in Amos 8:2, Lam. 4:18, and Ezek. 7:2, it refers to an end of Israel's suffering and the day of tribulation for Israel's enemies. In Dan. 9:21, 11:16, 12:11, and 14:24 it refers to a predestined period of time marked by an end point that is followed by another period of time.

In both *m. Eduyyot* and *t. Eduyyot* the brief excursus concerning *Qetz* times is interpolated into a discussion of another matter. In the Mishnah the excursus is absorbed into a list of things with which a father is supposed to endow his son. It is perhaps because "length of years" is included in this list that the excursus is found therein. I italicize the sections from *t. 'Ed.* 1:14 that amplify *m. 'Ed.* 2:10. The texts are as follows:

M. 'Ed. 2:10 (Ms Kaufman, Vienna):

> . . . and with the number of generations before him, and this is the Qetz. Even though Scripture says: "And they shall serve them; and they shall oppress them four hundred years" (Gen. 15:13), and [yet] it says, "And the fourth generation shall return here."

T. 'Ed. 1:14 (reconstructed on the basis of all the available manuscripts):

> "And the number of generations are before Him [var. in Ms. Erfurt: before his sons] [at] the Qetz." — *Even though the days and hours* [var. Erfurt: "days and nights"] *are reckoned by God with hair-like precision, in point of fact he counts* [to the Qetz] *by generations, as Isaiah says: "He called the generations from the beginning"* (41:4). "And even though Scripture says: 'And they shall serve them; and they shall oppress them for four hundred years' (Gen. 15:13) [fully

cited in Ms. Erfurt], and [yet] it says: 'And the fourth generation shall return here'" (Gen. 15:16).

According to Gen. 15:13–16, cited in both texts, Israel's oppression in Egypt was to be measured in years, and the point of redemption was to occur to a specific generation, the fourth. Another rabbinic midrash, recited in the Passover *Haggadah,* states that God did indeed fulfill the *Qetz* (*vehishav et haqetz*) in the generation that returned to the Land after the four hundred years of servitude had ended. The *Haggadah* understands that the oppression, leading to the dramatic redemption, began through historical events (Israel's initial sojourn in Egypt) that were compelled (*anus*) to conform to the Word of Gen. 15:13 (*dibur*). Israel's history of oppression and redemption follows a divine script.

The *Haggadah* notes: "as a result of the pattern of *Qetz* determination, history has followed suit, for in no generation have the Jews been entirely wiped out. God has and will always interfere with every tyrant's plan [*matzileynu meyadam*] to annihilate the Jews."

The underlying assumption in these rabbinic texts discussing biblical hints of Israel's final redemption, known as *Qetz* times, is that Israel's history is divided into discrete periods, culminating in a final period of redemption. God has determined these periods, but only after the final period of redemption has come — the period of *Qetz* — will they be evident. Divisions of this kind are most often found in apocalyptic literature (either in images of hours, *Apoc. Ab.* chap. 30; or generations, Gen. 15:15; or in the seven-year periods called weeks, Dan. 9:24–27, *1Enoch* 93:1–10; or in the fifty-year-periods called the *jubilee* units, *Book of Jubilees* 4:18–19; or even in two-thousand-year periods, *b. 'Abod. Zar.* 9a). Apocalyptic thought lays out Israel's history in such a way that every unit of time, however measured, concludes with a divinely ordained event that ushers in a new era, sometimes in decline, sometimes in ascent.

The connection between the rabbinic tradition and Matthew's genealogy becomes clear. Because Matthew understands that the coming of Jesus means the coming of the end, the *Qetz*, his genealogy stops with him. Jesus represents the last generation, the generation of the *Qetz*.[3]

FULFILLMENT TEXTS

Matthew adduces prophetic verses to highlight some unexpected turn in the Gospel narrative. The uses can be divided into two forms that, while closely related, are not identical.[4] Matthew's usage of the device is sometimes (when the prophecy and fulfillment are closely related) like that used in the *Tanakh* or Hebrew Bible itself, but at other times, when the prophecy and fulfillment do not appear so closely related, his usage requires some further understanding of what fulfillment entails for him. Let us consider these two usages in some depth. In the Hebrew Bible, the fulfillment of a prophecy is often confirmed by the phrase "according to the word of the Lord," to which is sometimes added the statement that the prophecy had come "through the hand of his servant, etc." (e.g. 2Kings 14:25). On the occasions when these fulfillment passages were read aloud from the Prophets in synagogues, both the reader and the congregation would respond, "Blessed is he who fulfills his word" (*Kallah Rab.* 4:11, which likely dates to the fourth century).[5] Observing that a prophecy had been fulfilled was itself a form of praise, and the Passover *Haggadah* preserves a blessing of similar form, "Blessed is the one who keeps his promise" (Heb: *barukh shomer havtaho*). Rabbinic liturgy prescribes that the reader of the prophetic lesson should say: "Even one of your prophecies shall not be left behind to return empty (compare Isa. 55:11), for you are a trustworthy God" (*Sop.* 13:10). It is following in this biblical tradition of noting prophecy fulfillment that Matthew incorporates prophetic texts into his Gospel. We can summarize this usage of fulfillment of a prophetic sign in two ways.

Type 1

The first way Matthew uses fulfillment prophecy has a long tradition. We first meet an example of this type of usage in Matt. 2:17, "the slaughter of the innocents." We recognize this type when Matthew inserts into the narrative the prophecy that has been fulfilled through an event he has just mentioned. The characters experiencing the event are unaware of the fulfillment. As I have said, this formulation is not much different from what is found in the Hebrew Scriptures (e.g., 1Kings 13:26, 14:18, 15:29, 16:12, 17:16, 22:38; 2Kings 1:17, 4:44, 7:16), or in the Talmud (*b. Ber.* 59b states that even the appearance of hurricanes is a fulfillment of Nahum 1:9).

However, Matthew claims prophetic signs have been fulfilled even when the words of Scripture look to be addressing issues far removed from the Jesus narrative. For instance, Matthew will find that "from Egypt I called my son" (Hosea 11:1–2) is a messianic sign that was fulfilled in the life of Jesus. The original Isaian context of this verse is that Israel is not a good "son"; "son" is used to highlight that Israel (despite God's special love for him) is a "rebellious son," for the passage goes on to list Israel's heinous crimes.

However, "my son" and "out of Egypt" are sufficient signs for Matthew to claim that this verse shows that God intentionally engineered the whole flight and return of Jesus' family to fulfill necessary conditions for Jesus to be the Messiah. The signs are being fulfilled, one by one. We now summarize the more complex, second way that Matthew utilizes fulfillment Scriptures.

Type 2

In the second usage of showing fulfillment of a prophecy, Matthew makes clear an intentional effort was made by a character to fulfill a biblical verse by closely attending to its wording. An unusual meaning is assigned to the verse and it is this meaning that Matthew intends us to see. Accordingly, Matthew in 2:15 notes that the angel of God acted *in order to fulfill* to its fullest detail a prophecy entailing an unusual understanding of "virgin" (a possible sense of the verse in Greek, as in LXX Gen. 34:3–4, and possibly in ancient Hebrew as well). This type of fulfillment is exemplified for us in *b. Ber.* 57b: a certain rabbi upon entering Babylon took dirt up into his turban and then threw it aside, in order to fulfill Isa. 14:23 ("'I will sweep her with the broom of destruction,' declares the Lord Almighty"); and to *b. Šabb* 150a, which states that Nebuchadnezzar, while riding on a lion, tied a serpent to its head, in order to fulfill Jer. 27:6 ("Now I will hand all your countries over to my servant Nebuchadnezzar king of Babylon; I will make even the wild animals subject to him"); also see *b. Yoma* 38a, which insists that clean bread was never served to the family of those who baked the Temple show-bread (one might suspect them of having stolen some of it for personal use); the practice literally fulfills Num. 32:22, which speaks of being clean (an idiom for free from obligation) before God ("and the land is subdued before the Lord; then after that you shall return and be *clean* of obligation to the Lord and to Israel, and this land shall be your possession before the Lord"). The Talmuds record many such fulfillments performed in strange ways by characters who read certain words hyperliterally. To fulfill a verse according to its every nuance was considered an act of piety.

A text from the *y. Šeqal.* 6:3 reveals that "fulfill" (Heb: *leqayyem*) is often taken to refer to a hyperliteral reading of a scriptural rule or prophecy. The passages describes how King Solomon melted a thousand gold talents to make one very large single bar of gold from which to make the vessels for the Temple in order to fulfill Exod. 25:39, which, if taken literally, can be understood to mean that all the vessels in the Temple must be made from a single ingot of gold: "It shall be made, with all these utensils, out of a talent of pure gold."[6]

> *The book of generations of Jesus Christ,[7] the son of David,[8] the son of Abraham.* (v. 1)

Matthew 1:1 briefly outlines the genealogy that follows as well as introduces the subject of that genealogy through its two most prominent figures: Jesus Christ, son of David, son of Abraham. Matthew understands that the name "Jesus Christ" is also a title — "Jesus, the Christ" — as the conclusion of his genealogy makes clear (1:17). The term *christos* is the Greek translation of the Hebrew *mashiah*, which means "anointed one" or "messiah" (LXX Dan. 9:25–26). The Qumran scroll 11QMelch (ii:9–13) speaks of "the Anointed of the Spirit [*mashuah haruah*], of whom Daniel spoke."

The term *mashiah* referring to a redeemer understood as foretold in the Prophets is unequivocally found only in literature postdating the Hebrew Scriptures. Although these Scriptures never refer to any future redeemer by the single term "the Messiah," for the Gospels as for the Talmudic Rabbis, the term (with no further added qualification) is already well known as a title. Its sense of "anointed" became subsumed by connotations of redemption. Rabbinic notions of Israel's messianic redeemer are roughly the same as Matthew's. Indeed, both the Rabbis and Matthew prefer the title "son of David" to describe the Messiah, and both also understand that a redeemer had been foretold by prophecy.[9]

The genealogy's structure duplicates biblical language and form. "Book of Generations" — in Greek, *biblos geneseos* — signifies an account of an important genealogy. Although *geneseos* is singular in form, *biblos geneseos* is how the LXX translates the Hebrew plural *sefer toledot* of Gen. 5:1 (compare 2:4), which introduces Adam's genealogy. But whereas in Genesis what follows *sefer toledot* is a list of the descendents of Adam, in Matthew what follows *biblos geneseos* is a list of Jesus' ancestors. Thus Matthew's genealogy employs the pattern of the brief genealogy of Isaac (25:19), which lists only ancestors (or in this case one ancestor, Abraham).

"Jesus" is the anglicized form of the Greek *Iesous*. In the LXX (e.g., Deut. 32:44 and numerous other places) Yehoshua (Joshua) is called Iesous. In uncensored versions of Sanhedrin 107a–b in the Babylonian Talmud, Jesus is called *Yeshu*. It is difficult to know if this designation is based simply on the dropping of the final "s" from the Greek name, or if the name was shortened (scribally by dropping the final ayin) from more original Hebrew/Aramaic texts that called Jesus Yeshua.[10] For the name "Yeshua" see Neh. 8:7.

Beginning the genealogy with Abraham, Matthew suggests that what came before was of little account. The Talmudic Rabbis would agree. *M. 'Abot* 5:2 states that the ten generations between Adam and Noah, and also the ten generations between Noah and Abraham, "provoked [God] continually," so that He withheld his bounty from these generations and instead bestowed it on Abraham.

Rabbinic comments on Gen. 37:1 suggest that they understood the biblical listing of genealogies to be analogous to searching for jewels in sand. Each "pile" of generations is sifted until the jewel is found, and then the rest is discarded. The story of the sifting for the "jewel" begins in this way:

Midr. Tanḥ. Genesis (Vayeshev) 1

> The child reading the Bible gulps the ten generations from Adam to Noah all at once then afterwards gulps the next ten generations at once. When he gets to the pearls of Abraham, Isaac, and Jacob he begins to explain the story in detail.

Matthew's genealogy begins with the notice: "The book of the generation(s) of Jesus Christ" (1:1), and ends with the report: "[A]nd Jacob was the father of Joseph, the husband of Mary, from whom Jesus, the one called Christ, was born" (1:16). That is, after organizing the generations into equal units of time, Matthew at last has located his jewel and can now explain the life of this jewel — Jesus Christ — in detail.

If one purpose of the genealogy is to show how God's plan is revealed in history, then by beginning with Abraham Matthew indicates not only that God has intervened in history for Abraham's sake, but also that Abraham's appearance has cosmic significance: he represents an ontological shift, visible in the unfolding of God's plan to illuminate the world. Indeed, the Abrahamic covenant, in which God tells Abraham of the coming persecution and eventual redemption of his descendants, marks the beginning of Israel's redemptive history (Gen. 15:13–16).

> *Abraham was the father of Isaac, and Isaac was the father of Jacob, and Jacob was the father of Judah and his brothers, and Judah was the father of Perez and Zerah by Tamar, and Perez was the father of Hezron, and Hezron was the father of Aram, and Aram was the father of Aminadab, and Aminadab was the father of Nachshon, and Nachshon was the father of Salmon, and Salmon was the father of Boaz by Rachab, and Boaz was the father of Obed by Ruth, and Obed was the father of Jesse, and Jesse was the father of David the King. And David was the father of Solomon by the wife of Uriah, and Solomon was the father of Rehoboam, and Rehoboam was the father of Abijah, and Abijah was the father of Asaph, and Asaph was the father of Jehosaphat, and Jehosaphat was the father of Joram, and Joram was*

> *the father of Uzziah, and Uzziah was the father of Joatham, and Joatham was the father of Ahaz, and Ahaz was the father of Hezekiah, and Hezekiah was the father of Manasseh, and Manasseh was the father of Amos, and Amos was the father of Josiah, and Josiah was the father of Jechoniah and his brothers at the time of the Babylonian exile. After the Babylonian exile, Jechoniah was the father of Salathiel, and Salathiel was the father of Zerubbabel, and Zerubbabel was the father of Abioud, and Abioud was the father of Eliakim, and Eliakim was the father of Azor, and Azor was the father of Zadok, and Zadok was the father of Achim, and Achim was the father of Eliud, and Eliud was the father of Eleazar, and Eleazar was the father of Matthan, and Mathan was the father of Jacob, and Jacob was the father of Joseph, the husband of Mary, from whom Jesus, the one called Christ, was born. Thus all the generations from Abraham to David were fourteen generations, and from David to the Babylonian Exile were fourteen generations, and from the Babylonian Exile to the Christ, fourteen generations. (vv. 2–17)*

The opening verses introduced the idea of patterns of sacred history whereby the end-time is calculated by a discerned division of time into three units. The threefold pattern of fourteen generations can also be considered in relation to rabbinic traditions that speak of the cycle of the moon. Just as the lunar cycle has twenty-eight nights (the cycle ends at dusk on the twenty-ninth day), so the night of the fourteenth–fifteenth signals the full moon at midmonth. We can now construe that Matthew's genealogy rises to the height, or fullness, with David in the fourteenth generation, after which, starting with Solomon, the genealogy descends through fourteen more generations to the lowest point, or the darkness of moonless nights, that is the Exile. And fourteen generations after the darkness of the Exile, like the moon in its nightly waxing, the genealogy again rises to the height, or fullness, which is Jesus. According to this scenario, both David and Jesus are at "full moon" positions in a complete fourteen/fifteen generation-repeating cycle.

Jewish literature, which I now discuss, also understands history to be patterned on a generational cycle, but it leaves the end point open, since the Messiah has not come. (Josephus even calls Vespasian the expected savior since, apparently, some Jews were calculating the advent of the Messiah in the first century.)[11] Conversely, the Rabbis use 70 C.E., the date of the destruction of the Temple, as the beginning of the final Messianic period. Unlike Matthew, for them the final count began not with the destruction of the first Temple, but with that of the second (*y. Ber.* 2:4).

Some rabbinic genealogies patterned on the lunar cycle begin with Abraham. In *Pesiq. Rab Kah.* 5.12, Rabbi Berekhiah (late third century) speaks of a genealogy whose pattern follows that of the cycle of the moon (cf. *Exod. Rab.* 15:26).[12] Commenting on Exod. 12, "This month shall be unto you...," and referring also to Ps. 89:38, "David's seed...shall be established for ever as the moon," he states that during the period from Abraham through Solomon Israel was worthy before God, and so those days waxed "like the moon's waxing to the full." However, because from Solomon's son Rehoboam to Zedekiah, the last king of Judah before the Exile, Israel was not worthy before God, those days waned just as "the moon wanes into darkness." This genealogy both begins with Abraham, as does Matthew's, and depicts Abraham in the position of the new moon preceding the first day of the new month, after which the genealogy is said to rise.[13] Yet in contrast to Matthew's genealogy, whose apex or fullness, is reached with David, the apex, or fullness, in the rabbinic text is reached with Solomon. For the Talmudic Rabbis, the wane of Jewish fortunes begins with Rehoboam, Solomon's son, and it continues, as it does in Matthew, into the utter darkness that is the Exile, represented here by Zedekiah. Moreover, in the rabbinic genealogy in the period of waxing David is the fourteenth name (the variant reading from *Exod. Rab.* numerically states that there are "fifteen" generations from Abraham to Solomon). In the (waning) period of decline, Zedekiah — who is not mentioned in the Matthean genealogy — represents the new moon of the following month. We need not worry that the genealogies drop names or miscount because counting conventions varied. Sometimes forty-two means a full forty-two and sometimes it just means forty-one, not including forty-two.[14]

The rabbinic genealogy associates Solomon with the fullness of the moon because the Rabbis regarded him as a positive figure in Jewish history: his glory and that of his Temple outshone all their predecessors.[15] But after Solomon this glory was gradually extinguished until the utter darkness of the Exile.

Some rabbinic genealogies begin the messianic story with Jacob's son Judah. *Gen. Rab.* 98:7 interprets both Gen. 49:9 ("[Judah] stoops, he crouches like a lion") and Num. 24:9 ("He has crouched, he has lain down like a lion") with reference to a messianic genealogy divided into generations, but in two different ways; the interpretations of the verses vary according to the way the genealogy is divided. Like the Matthean genealogy, first is a threefold division, from Perez (son of Judah) to David, then from David to Zedekiah, and then (presumably, for this is not stated) from Zedekiah to the Messiah. With regard to this division, the midrash states that from Perez to David "[Judah] crouched, he has lain down like a lion" (Num. 24:9). That is, during this period Judah was in a position of uncontested strength and so had no need to confront his enemies; he had every reason to think he could lie down in safety. From David to Zedekiah, "[Judah] stooped down, he crouched like a lion" (Gen. 49:9): because Judah no longer occupied a position of uncontested strength, he had to be in a position of readiness to strike. It is probable that the ending of this first tradition relates that from Zedekiah to the Messiah Judah crouched like a lion, in fear of his enemies.[16]

Yet here the midrashic editor abruptly introduces a variant that divides the genealogy from Perez not to David but through to Zedekiah, then from Zedekiah to the Messiah.[17] There is also a different interpretation of the divisions: crouching is now seen as the position of strength; lying is the position of weakness. This midrash states that from Perez to Zedekiah "[Judah] stooped, he crouched" (Gen. 49:9), which means that during this period of unbroken kingship and statehood he occupied a position of strength and was ready to fight his enemies. However, from Zedekiah to the Messiah "[Judah] crouched, he lay down" (Num. 24:9), which means that beginning with the Exile, Judah was utterly weak, incapable even of being prepared to fight. Only the Messiah could bring about the change needed so that again Judah could be "stooped down [and] crouched" (Gen. 49:9), that is, in a position of strength and ready to fight. The midrash goes on to say that during the messianic period Judah's enemies would be defeated so that again he could be "crouched" and he could "[lie] down" (Num. 24:9), but this time in safety. For Judah, the advent of the Messiah, who is the last of the generations, means strength, security, and peace.[18]

According to Matthew, Jesus too (and also David) represents a period of strength and peace (Matt. 11:25–30), only this is to be a lasting and final period of strength and peace. Or perhaps the model for Matthew's genealogy is one of decline after David, as in *Gen. Rab.* 98.7 (see above), where the period from David through to the Messiah is one of Judah's oppression. This interpretation may serve as a model for understanding Matthew's view of the Davidic line as moving from decline to utter decline to redemption.

> *Now, as for Jesus[19] the Messiah his birth was like this: When his mother Mary was promised in marriage to Joseph, but before they had been intimate with each other, she was found to be pregnant by a holy spirit. (v. 18)*

In the time of Jesus (and still symbolically today) there was a twofold process by which a Jewish man and woman came to be married. There was first the betrothal, and then about a year later the marriage, after which the man and the woman lived together (*m. Ketub.* 5.2). Marriages were considered to be literally made in heaven. Indeed, some rabbinic sources understand that providence decreed the woman to the man fit for her: *Lev. Rab.* 29:8 is instructive:

> Rabbi Hiyya Bar Abba said: Rabbi Levi preached on Ps. 62:9: As a matter of course, people say: "Mr. So and So is marrying Miss So and So." [Concerning this, the Psalmist says: 62:9] — People are mindless. Miss So and So is marrying Mr So and So [Ps. 62:9] — Folks deceive themselves.

The clarification of this sermon is found in *b. Soṭah* 2a, God decrees marriages:

> Rabbi Judah said in the name Rav: 40 days before the embryo is formed a heavenly voice goes out and says "the daughter of so and so is destined for so and so, the house of so and so is destined for so and so, the field of so and so is destined for so and so."

There is reason to think that the usual age of the young man at the time of his betrothal was about eighteen to twenty years (*m. 'Abot* 5.21), and that the age of the young woman was about twelve and a half or thirteen (*m. Ned.* 10:5; *Gen. Rab.* 95).[20] It is possible that when the Gospel opens Joseph is about eighteen and Mary about thirteen years old.[21] The actual age of marriage in ancient Palestine seems to have been around puberty for the woman, perhaps thirteen or fifteen, and as late as the mid-twenties or even early thirties for the man. Evidence shows that the ages at which Jewish men and women were being betrothed to each other in first-century Palestine were not much different than the ages of the young men and women who were being betrothed in the contemporaneous Roman world.[22]

While much has been made of Jesus' bachelorhood, it would be a mistake to think that bachelorhood for a man in his early thirties during this period was unusual. When his first child was born (c. 73 C.E.), Josephus was about the age that Jesus was when he died, thirty-five or so.[23] We may assume, therefore, that Joseph was somewhere in his mid- to upper-twenties at the time of his betrothal, while Mary was twelve to fifteen.[24]

At the time of the betrothal the woman legally became the man's wife, though she did not yet live with him (*m. Ketub.* 1.2). Betrothal — in Hebrew, *Qiddushin*, or *erusin* — was the act by which a husband created a legal prohibition for the woman to marry anyone but her intended.[25] The betrothal consisted of the groom giving his betrothed a small sum of money or gift declaring in some fashion, "Be thou betrothed to me by virtue of this money," and she agreed to be consecrated to him (*m. Qidd.* 1.1)[26]. Following the betrothal, the young woman was called the man's "wife," and the man was then called her "husband." This is why in Matt. 1:19, even though Joseph and Mary have not yet married, he is referred to as Mary's "husband" and she in 1:20 is referred to as Joseph's "wife."

Matthew refers to Mary's liminal marital stage by describing her as *mnesteutheses*, usually rendered "promised in marriage." *Mnesteutheses* is to be understood in the passive sense. In fine, "betrothal" is the act by which the woman becomes bound to the husband, who indicates to her that he would have her for a wife. It is passive in the sense of her (tacit) agreement by accepting his betrothal money or gift, signaling that she is committed to him alone. The Syriac translation of 1:18 gives us *makira* (*leih*) and in Prov. 19:14 we discover the word again, "And from the Lord a woman is *betrothed* [perhaps more accurately bound] to a man."[27] This reflects the passage in *b. Soṭah* 2a above: marriages are ordained on high. (There is one more time the word is used for "betrothed" in the Peshitta: 2Sam. 3:14.) It is curious to note that this semitic root — *mkr* — is generally used for the commercial transactions of buying (taking) and selling (giving).[28] The Mishnah (*Qidd.* 1:1) uses the term *nikneit* for this commitment. *Nikneit* in this context means "legally reserved for her husband," while elsewhere in rabbinic literature it is used with trade connotations (e.g., *m. B. Meṣ.* 4:1).

In Judea, sexual union prior to marriage was customarily forbidden (*t. Ketub.* 1:4). Nonetheless, betrothal remained a legal state of matrimony. Once betrothed, the woman was not free to marry another man without first receiving a divorce.

Matthew states that Mary came to be pregnant before she and Joseph had "come together" (1:18). This "coming together" refers to the conclusion of the second part of the marriage process. Most commentators properly see here a reference to the married couple's entering the marital home. This "entrance," which permitted the couple to have sexual relations and allowed them to live privately as husband and wife, is known as *kenissat hakallah lehupah*, or *nisuin*, or *ishut*, and, in Judea, it was often preceded by the ceremony of *yihud* — "being together, uniting," remaining alone for a short period (*t. Ketub.* 1:24). The Syriac of the word *synelthein* in Matt. 1:18 — *nishtutefun* (literally: joined in union) — possibly suggests the "yihud" (literally: being joined) ceremony event. In Palestine, it was the custom before the *nisuin* to investigate the claims of the families as to the sexual conduct of the bride and groom during the betrothal period (*t. Ketub.* 1:4–6). According to this source, in some communities the claims of the marriage agreements concerning the bride, or concerning the willingness of her family to let her go, were also investigated. It had to be determined that everything was in order, which meant especially that adultery had not occurred in the betrothal period. If it was discovered that adultery had occurred, then the marriage arrangements would almost certainly have been changed. Such investigations could involve either one or both parties bringing evidence of guilt and innocence. In Judea, if everything in the betrothal period had been properly carried out, the bride and groom would be encouraged to be alone together just before the wedding so that the bride might become familiar and desirable to the groom (*t. Ketub.* 1:4).

> *But Joseph her husband, being a righteous man, and not wishing to expose her,*[29] *decided to divorce her secretly.* (v. 19)

Because the betrothed woman had legally become the man's "wife" she could, though not yet completely married to him, be divorced by him (*m. Ketub.* 1:2; *m. Yebam.* 2:6). During the period in which the woman was betrothed, and also while she was fully married, adultery was a reason for which a man could and should divorce his wife (*m. Ketub.* 7:6); the school of Shammai held that it was the only reason for which a man could divorce his wife, though this was not the prevailing view, as Matt. 19:8 notes (see also *m. Giṭ.* 9:10; Josephus, *Ant.* 4:253; Philo, *Spec.* 1.30).

M. *Soṭah* 7:6 defines divorce as a proper remedy for "those who transgress Mosaic rules" and "those who transgress Jewish or Judean rules [*dat yehudit*]."[30] Included in the second type are women who go out with their hair uncovered, or women who weave in the marketplace and speak with men. *T. Soṭah* 5:9 (ed. Lieberman) sets out rules in greater detail.[31]

> If he saw his wife going out and her hair uncovered and dressed immodestly and in company of slaves and maidservants, or she wove in public and bathed and sported with any man — one fulfills a commandment by divorcing her, as Scripture states: "When a man marries a woman, having relations with her, then it shall be if she does not find favor in his eyes because he finds in her lewd conduct then he shall write her a document of divorce and give it into her hand and send her from his house" (Deut. 24:1).

This passage refers to a married woman living with her husband, as the citation of Deut. 24:1 makes clear. The same rules apply to a betrothed or an *arusah* ["bound to him"]. In these cases, her *ketubah* settlement is annulled, and there is a supposition that it is meritorious to divorce her, much in line with the passage concerning a married woman. An adulteress of any kind is forbidden to have further sexual relations either with her husband or with her lover.

B. Ketub. 11b/12a explains the procedures to be undertaken were a woman believed to have been a virgin at the time of the betrothal subsequently "found" otherwise. If proof were strong that she had been unfaithful during the betrothal period the penalty, under a number of conditions, could have been death (Deut. 22:24; *b. Ketub.* 51b). On the other hand, were there were no such proof and the woman claimed that she was not a virgin prior to the betrothal, she is believed but her *ketubah* (prenuptial, financial terms governing divorce) marriage settlement amount would have been reduced to zero for misleading her husband at the time of the betrothal. Had the woman lost her virginity during the betrothal period as a result of a fall while climbing a fence, say, then her settlement amount would be reduced to 100 zuzim, the amount a nonvirgin normally received. With regard to Mary, the case was not that of suspected but rather of certain adultery, for Mary was pregnant. Since Matthew makes clear that Joseph was contemplating divorce, as readers we assume it must have been apparent to him that Mary was pregnant from another man.

Although it was the case in Judea that the betrothed man could be alone with his "wife," in Galilee this was not the case, and so no one would question that Joseph was the father of the child (*m. Ketub.* 1:5).[32] In terms of the Law, then, and as a "righteous" man, Joseph, knowing he was not the father, had no choice but to divorce her (Deut. 22:23–27; *m. Soṭah* 5:1).[33]

When witnesses see that a man has delivered to his wife a divorce document, which states that she is now free of any legal ties binding her to him and so free to marry again, the divorce procedure is concluded. This process could be done privately. Betrothals were likely, then as now, public knowledge; for if not, how could a man be made forbidden to a betrothed woman he seduced (*m. Soṭah* 5:1), not to mention more severe punishments.[34] No witnesses would know to warn him and he could always claim he had no idea of her status. The whole force of legislation for betrothed women assumes betrothals were public knowledge. After all, as I said, Joseph knew for a fact that the child was not his and by Law he was forbidden to her and her to him at the very least.

In the end Joseph decided to do two things. First, he decided to divorce Mary — indeed rabbinic Law would have encouraged this since he could no longer live with her. He believed her to have been a virgin at the time of betrothal, she was now pregnant from another man's union with her. This is classic adultery in the Law. There is no difference in the laws of adultery between the rules governing a betrothed woman and a married woman Second, he decided to do this privately so as not to embarrass either Mary or her family, about which Matthew is silent. With reference to this private manner of divorcing Mary, Matthew commends Joseph's righteousness. Likely for Matthew "privately" here means "in a secret way,"[35] that is, Joseph would hide the reason for the divorce. Perhaps we should understand that Gospel account is based on a likely scenario: since people in Joseph's community would know that he was righteous and that if he was getting divorced it was likely on account of adultery, he had to divorce her without fanfare. In Jewish Law known to us from the Mishnah (*m. Qidd.* 1:1) only death and divorce can break a marital union. The term *Qiddushin* refers to the first stage of marriage but the same manners of dissolving the union holds true of the later stage as well. There is no way for us as readers to determine Joseph's thoughts as the Gospel writer hides them. At any rate, it is not difficult for us to imagine that Mary's pregnancy would soon be known in any case and so Joseph must have been in a quandary.

Although, as readers we know, Joseph was the wronged — and even humiliated — party,[36] whose betrothed, he might well imagine, has betrayed him, still he did not wish to humiliate Mary publicly but rather, as the Gospel pictures him, planned "to divorce her in secret."[37] For the informed reader, Joseph made a wise decision. Instead of bringing Mary before a tribunal to discuss settlements, he would arrange a brief ceremony before several witnesses, handing her a written bill of divorce stating that she was now free to marry another (*m. Giṭ.* 9:3).[38]

> *But when he had thought about these things, look, an angel of the Lord appeared to him in a dream, saying, "Joseph, son of David, do not fear to accept Mary as your wife, for that which is born in her is from the Holy Spirit." (v. 20)*

However, before he had an opportunity to act on his divorce plan, an angel explained to Joseph the circumstances by which Mary had come to be pregnant, circumstances he accepted; he then "took his wife." That is, he married her and brought her into his home. Mary thus came to be a member of Joseph's family, the family of David, as does her child.

To "accept Mary as his wife" indicates that the angel commanded Joseph to complete the second stage of the marriage: the living together of the man and woman under one roof. According to Matthew, God knew Joseph's thoughts of divorce and so sent an angel to convince him to turn away from such thought. It is clear from the angel's words that Joseph was afraid to proceed with the marriage: he thought that Mary had proved herself both untrustworthy and sinful.

The angel refers to Joseph as "son of David" so that he might understand the messianic nature of the situation. While there are examples in Jewish literature of other pregnancies said to have been caused by God, none stresses conception apart from sexual intercourse. Matthew's passage, which is unique, seems to be a development of the term "Son of God" known to other early Christian writers such as Mark (3:11) as well as Paul (Rom. 1:4) though perhaps not with of the involvement of the Holy Spirit.

According to Josephus, God appeared to Amram in a dream while Amram's wife was pregnant with Moses. In this dream God told Amram that Moses "shall escape those who are watching to destroy him, and…he shall deliver the Hebrew race from their bondage in Egypt" (*Ant.* 2: 210–17).[39] According to Matthew, the angel told Joseph not to worry about proceeding to stage two of the marriage rite. Nothing was amiss, and Joseph needed to have no qualms about the propriety of entering into union with Mary. She had not been unfaithful.

It is not uncommon in the Hebrew Bible for either God or an angel[40] to inform someone "not to fear" to set upon a course of action that seems initially to be contrary to the divine will. For instance, God told Abraham in a dream not to fear going to Egypt (for "I will protect you") (Gen. 15:1). He told Jacob not to fear doing the same (46:2–3). And an angel of the Lord tells Hagar not to be afraid of an arduous journey (for God has heard the voice of the boy) (Gen. 21:17).

Matthew states parenthetically (since no one in the story knows this as yet) that Mary became pregnant from the Holy Spirit. The pious gloss concerning the activity of the Holy Spirit prevents readers from thinking that an impropriety has occurred. The phrase (*ek*) *pneumatos hagiou* is a Greek rendering of the Hebrew (*al yedei*) *ruah haqodesh*, which signifies divine agency, through prophecy or some other means. *Ecclesiastes Rab.* (2:8) to Eccles. 2:7 [literally: and sons of the house *was* to me][41] notes that Solomon's "Household staff" refers to "the Holy Spirit" — *Ruah haQodesh* — a personification of a supernatural process that accomplishes the divine will. Here the Holy Spirit is seen as the collective staff of servants serving Solomon's (which name the Rabbis often see as an allusion to God's royal being) needs.

*She will bear a son, and you will call his name "Jesus" [God saves],
for he will save his people from their sins. (v. 21)*

The angel informed Joseph that Mary would have a son and that he was to name him Jesus.[42] This verse is probably based on Gen. 16:11: "And the angel of Lord said to her, 'Look, you are pregnant, and you will bear a son and you shall call his name Yishma-el, because God heeded your pain.'" Strengthening the form of prophetic naming is Gen. 10:25: "To Eber were born two sons. The name of one was Peleg; for in his days the people of the earth were divided; and the name of his brother was Yaktan." Peleg's name is prophetic of events that were to occur in his time (namely, "people of the earth" were divided). According to *Pirqe R. El.,* chap. 31, which dates from the eighth century but which preserves much earlier traditions, the following were named before their births: Isaac, Yishmael (in whose name, as with Peleg, the Rabbis saw prophecy: God will heed the pleas of the Jews whom the Yishmaelites persecute), Moses, Solomon, Josiah, and the Messiah.

This list brings together people who were born to fulfill programmatic destinies. For example, commenting on Num. 13:16, "Moses called Hoshea, Yehoshua Bin Nun," *Num. Rab.* 16 states that Moses saw that the spies he sent to Canaan were impious; the name reflects the prediction for that generation — "God will save us!" *B. Soṭah* 34b interprets the names of the other spies in a similar fashion. Thus when Matthew, or his source, relates that the angel says the child is to be called "Jesus" because he will save his people from their sins, his point is not that Jesus but rather God will save Israel from its sins. In the Hebrew Bible "his people" always refers to the nation of Israel (Sam. 1:12; Ps. 29:10; Ps. 105:24; Ruth 1:6; 2Chron. 2:10, 25:11, and 32:10). The parallel is Ps. 130:8: "He will redeem Israel from all his sins." The two terms — "his people" and "nation" — appear together in Judg. 11:23, 2Sam. 5:12, 1Kings 8:59, 1Chron. 14:2, and 2Chron. 31:8 and 35:3. So indeed the reference is to Israel. Since Matthew sees Jesus as Israel's savior only in the first stages of his gospel, it may be that Matthew simply follows his early Jewish-Christian Gospel source, thinking that the reference is to the salvation of the Gentiles, and not Israel alone. Perhaps, he sees some irony in that Jesus was supposed to save Jews and in the end saves the Gentiles. The term "save his people," in the end, will refer to save his Gentiles nations."

All this happened to fulfill what was said by the Lord through the prophet . . . (v. 22)

The Isaiah text is Matthew's first of several fulfillment quotation meant to show that the divine plan foretold by the prophets was now being fulfilled in Jesus.

"Behold, the virgin shall conceive and bear a son, and they shall call his name 'Emmanuel' (Isa. 7:14), which is translated 'God is with us.'" (v. 23)

Parthenos, the word used by LXX in Isa. 7:14, can mean either a young woman or a virgin, just as can the English term "maid." (After her rape,

Dinah is referred to as a *parthenos*: LXX Gen. 34:3 and 34:4.) Matthew uses the meaning "virgin" as he tells us that Jesus is sired by the Holy Spirit and not by a man. For Matthew, the LXX rendition of the verse has found its fulfillment in a surprising reading that would not have been its general understanding prior to Matthew's use of it.

It is of note that here Matthew, or his source, finds two clauses in Isa. 7:14: a virgin conceives a son and he will be named "Emmanuel" but only the first demands fulfillment while the second is descriptive and not prescriptive.[43] Indeed, the given name, Jesus, will reflect that "God is with us."

> *When Joseph woke from sleep he did as the angel of the Lord commanded him, and he accepted his wife. (v. 24)*

The final verses indicate that Joseph was commanded rather than urged to accept the procedures to bring Mary into his marital home. No room is left for lingering doubts (what will the neighbors think?). Verse 24 states that immediately upon waking, Joseph acted.

> *And he did not have sex with her until she bore a son, and he called his name "Jesus." (v. 25)*

It would have been usual after this final stage of the marriage process for the couple to engage in the conjugal act, but Matthew further notes that the couple did not have sexual relations until after Jesus was born; apparently this command to refrain from sexual activity with Mary was also part of the angel's instructions to Joseph. The story of Tamar (whose son Perez is considered the father of the messianic line): "When Adam sinned [creation's] fullness became defective and will not be completely restored until the Son of Perez comes" [see *Gen. Rab.* 12:6]) resonates here: "And [Judah] did not lie with her again" (Gen. 28:26). However, although the two stories are connected by the motif of suspected adultery, the conception of Mary's child, unlike the children of Tamar, was not as a result of the sexual act.

Finally Matthew recounts the birth of the child and that Joseph "named the child Jesus." This act of naming resonates in tension with the genealogy at the head of the chapter: son of David. A savior, yes; genetically descended from David, no. We have left the genealogy and its sequel behind and now enter the narrative. The door from the past has swung open onto the life of Jesus.

NOTES

1   F. Brown, S. R. Driver, and C. A. Briggs, *A Hebrew and English Lexicon of the Old Testament* (Oxford, 1907), *s.v. ivri* (p. 720), agrees with Rabbi Judah's etymology: one from beyond, from the other side.

2   The Talmudic Rabbis (*t. Ber.* 1:15) relate that Abraham's historic mission was to bring God's presence down to dwell in the Temple. In obeying God, Abraham divided himself from others whom he left at the foot of the mountain to offer his child to God. The place of that offering, in turn, was chosen as the site *par excellence* for God's lower residence. However, the place was laid waste to its foundations by those on the other side of the divide — the enemies of Abraham's children. At this point, the mountain (read: Israel) began a process of shaking up its foundations until, throughout the course of many years of desolation, it continually reforms. Finally the rabbinic passage concludes: In the future *eschaton*, when it will be formed into a perfect mountain, then God's Presence will alight at the site for all time.

3   It might be noted that such reckonings of *Qetz* times are not always precise or consistent. Jubilees uses a forty-nine-year jubilee count in general but sometimes it is fifty. Rabbinic counting of generations may count a *Qetz* time twice, once as the end of a period and again as the first of the next period. Matthew's count is also not precise but that need not detain us here.

4   For a source critical view of the role and structure of these verses see Brown, *Birth of the Messiah,* 97–105.

5   The full text of *Kallah Rab.* 4:11 is as follows:

> *"When good is done to you [you must offer praise]"* (*Kallah* 1:29).
> How do we know this? Scripture states, "and you shall eat and you shall be satisfied and you shall bless [the Lord…] (Deut. 8:17). But how we know [we must offer praise] even if we eat and are not satisfied? Scripture writes [and tradition records praise was offered] — *Give the people and they will eat [for thus says the Lord — eat and leave over]"* (2Kings 4:44). And then it says *"and he gave it to them and they ate and they left over — "According to the word of the Lord"* [which oral tradition assumes to be the text of their praise and that we should emulate them]. A series of objections [from three verses in the Book of Kings] was raised [to the assertion that the people who got the food but did not fill themselves, offered thanksgiving praises]: "According to the word of the Lord the God of Israel who spoke through his servant" (2Kings 14:25). In this case also [assuming all cases of promises happening are of the same nature], a praise [formula] is customarily offered [when they read it]. Come hear another objection: "According to the word of the Lord that He spoke to Elijah (2Kings 2:17)…" In this case also the readers say [a liturgical formula]: *"Blessed is the One who fulfills his word."* Come hear another objection: "According to the word of the Lord that he spoke through his servant, Ahiyah the Shilonite" (1Kings 15:29). [And likewise the

formula is said when it is read, so we can raise a string of objections to the notion that the people in the stories gave praise for their food.] Now if you think that the case of 2Kings 4:44 ("and they left over according to the word of the Lord") means praise is offered only when one reads the fulfillment of this promise (but the people on the spot did not offer praise) — [consider a crucial difference]. In the case where we offer praise during the reading of the passage, those verses refer explicitly to the narrative in which the divine word had been delivered through a prophet (and offering the praise is just custom, not generated by any text). In the case of 2Kings 4:44 there is no such qualification [to prevent us from understanding "*according to the word of the Lord*" refers to the very text of the praise offered on the spot.]

6   The Hebrew reads: *kikar zahav tahor ya'aseh otah, et kal hakelim ha-eleh.*

7   The culmination of generations, the apex of all. A Jewish work mocking the story of the Gospels, a kind of countergospel, which dates from a time after Matthew became known as *Sefer Toldot Yeshu* (The Book of the Generations of Jesus). See *Newman*, "The Death of Jesus in the Toledot *Yeshu* Literature."

8   The next highest point in the messianic lineage.

9   See also Josephus, *War* 6:312–13.

10   This spelling (final "ayin") is that of the Syriac Peshitta. Shamma Friedman wrote me that the very reliable Yad Harav Herzog ms (Sanhedrin) has "Yeshua" with "ayin." It has also been suggested that the name Joshua was likely pronounced in the Galilee as "Yeshu" as a truncated form of "Yeshua." Galilean names can often drop the letters "ayn," "heh," and "aleph." See further, D. Flusser, *Jesus in Selbstzeugnissen und Bilddokumenten* (Reinbeck bei Hamburg, 1968), 13–14.

11   "Now this prophecy certainly referred to the government of Vespasian, who was appointed emperor in Judea" (see Josephus, *War* 6.312–313). "This mysterious prophecy really referred to Vespasian and Titus" (Tacitus, *Hist.* 5.13). "This prediction, referring to the emperor of Rome — as afterwards appeared from the event — the people of Judea took to themselves" (Suetonius, *Vesp.* 4.5).

12   In *Exod. Rab.* the count of fifteen generations until Solomon is duly noted, but the further count of another fifteen generations is not, since the number of generations is sixteen and the number fifteen may have been removed by an astute copyist. Likewise, in the Matthean genealogy, besides the fact that some names are missing and others are botched (Asaf instead of Asa), a generation has been left out of the final section. The Matthean genealogy follows Ruth 4:18–22 precisely but whereas 1Chron. 3:1–19 shows that Uzziah is given as the son of Joram, Matthew's list jumps four generations. Errors occur, whether by intention or otherwise, when trying to conflate traditions or to solve textual problems or create patterns.

13   *Pesiq. Rab Kah.* 5:12 reads in its entirety as follows:

        Rabbi Berekhiah said: "This new moon shall be to you ... (Exod. 12:2)

It shall be a symbol to you — [Once for all, I have sworn by my holiness, and I will not lie to David, that his line will continue forever and his throne endure before me like the sun.] It will be established forever *like the moon*, [the faithful witness in the sky]." (Ps. 89:35–37). Just as the moon waxes and wanes so when you are pure you will count up to its fullness and when not, you will count down to its obscurity. Abraham, Isaac, Jacob, Judah Perez, Hazron, Ram, Aminadav, Nahshon, Salmon, Boaz, Oved, Jesse, David, Solomon, "And Solomon sat on the throne of Lord to rule" (1Chron. 29:23). Look, he is the [count of the] "moon in its fullness." Then you count to its dimness, Rechaboam, Abijah, Asa, Jehosaphat, Jehoram, Ahaziah, Joash, Amaziah, Uziah, Jotham, Ahaz, Hezekiah, Menassa, Amon, Josiah, Zedekiah, "And he blinded the eyes of Zedekiah" (2Kings 25:7). Look, he is the moon in its obscurity.

14   So forty lashes (Deut. 25:3) can mean thirty-nine lashes: 2Cor. 11:24 refers to thirty-nine. The number thirty-nine is confirmed by Josephus, "but for him that acts contrary to this Law, let him be beaten with forty lashes save one" (*Ant.* 4:253) and the Talmud. (*b. Mak.* 22a)

15   The *dayyenu* hymn sung at the Passover seder is thought to have ancient roots as a song of pilgrims bringing first-fruits as they came to the Temple: its fifteen stanzas match the fifteen steps that ascended to the Temple. That hymn portrays the blessings of God culminating in the Temple, the chosen place.

16   See *Gen. Rab.*, trans. Freedman (London: Soncino Publishers, 1983). There is a sharp break from the one tradition to the other. Whether it is the case that from Zedekiah to the Messiah Judah again was crouched in fear we can only surmise. At any rate, clearly in the Matthean genealogy Jesus, the Messiah, represents a peak, to say the least.

17   *Gen. Rab.* 98:7 printed editions read as follows — with a double ending, suggesting an addition has carelessly fallen into the text from some other source (which I present in italics below).

"You are a lion's cub, O Judah" (Gen. 49:9). The verse teaches us that God gave him the power of a lion and the boldness of its cubs.
"You go up from the prey, my son" (Gen. 49:9) — from the prey of Joseph you rise in glory, from the prey of Tamar, you rise in glory.
"[Judah] stoops, he crouches like a lion" (Gen. 49:9) — from Perez until David.
"He has crouched, he has lain down like a lion" (Num. 24:9) — from David until Zedekiah.
Others interpret: "[Judah] stoops, he crouches like a lion" (Gen. 49:9) — from Perez until Zedekiah.
"He has crouched, he has lain down like a lion" (Num. 25:9) — from Zedekiah until King Messiah.
"Judah stoops, he crouches like a lion" (Gen. 49:9) — in this world. "He has crouched, he has lain down like a lion" (Num. 24:9) — in the future to come.

> *"Judah stoops, he crouches like a lion" (Gen. 49:9) — when he is not threatened by enemies.*
> *"He has crouched, he has lain down like a lion" (Num. 24:9) — when he is threatened by enemies he rises to face them.*

[18] I present here the manuscript reading and the conjectured ending [in parentheses] preferred by Theodor-Albeck, *Bereshit Rabba* (p. 1258):

> "You are a lion's cub, O Judah" (Gen. 49:9). The verse teaches us that God gave him the power of a lion and the boldness of its cubs.
> You go up from the prey, my son (Gen. 49:9) — from the prey of Joseph you rise in glory, from the prey of Tamar, you rise in glory.
> From Perez until David — "He has crouched, he has lain down like a lion" (Nu 24:9) —
> From David until Zedekiah. — "[Judah] stoops, he crouches like a lion" (Gen. 49:9) — .
> Others interpret: From Perez until Zedekiah — "[Judah] stoops, he crouches like a lion" (Gen. 49:9) — from Zedekiah until King Messiah. "He has crouched, he has lain down like a lion" (Num. 25:9).
> In this world — "He has crouched, he has lain down like a lion" (Num. 24:9)
> In the future to come — "[Judah] stoops, he crouches like a lion" (Gen. 49:9). When he is "not threatened" [a euphemism meaning when he is threatened] by enemies. — "Judah stoops, he crouches like a lion." (Gen. 49:9).
> "When all his enemies are destroyed ["He has crouched, he has lain down like a lion" (Num. 24:9)]

[19] The word "Jesus" might be a scribal addition as it is absent in some citations and at least one manuscript. It is not Matthew's style to have the article "the" before the name Jesus but it is usual to have it before "Messiah (Christ)."

[20] See Buechler, "The Induction of the Bride and Bridegroom into Chupa in the First and Second Centuries in Palestine," 82.

[21] The view is based on ages found said by the Rabbis to be the ideal for rabbinic society. Nevertheless, the funerary evidence shows that epitaphs of people who died in their teens were unmarried and the epitaphs were dedicated by parents (S. Klein, *Sefer haYeshuv* [1974], 39, 63; Schremer, *Male and Female He Created Them*, 85–91). The Jewish ossuaries in Palestine generally do not supply the age at death.

[22] Professor Dale Allison was kind enough to comment thoroughly on my work and drew to my attention the work by P. W. van der Horst's *Ancient Jewish Epitaphs*, 73–84. The author claims the average life span in antiquity was 28.4 years old. However, ancient Jewish writers speak of that age as the age of marriage. *T. Levi* (11:1) speaks of 28 for Levi's marriage; *T. Iss.* (3:5) also gives 30 for his marriage and the *T. Jud.* (7:9, 8:1) allows that he was post 20. In *Tarbits* 40 (1970), Itamar Gruenwald gives us records for marriages also at 29 and 30. Our evidence from the *Manual of Discipline* Qumran scroll 1QSa 1: 9,10 allows for marriage not earlier than "the completion of his 20th year."

23   At least according to what he writes about himself in *Life* 1:4, though in *War* 5:419 he seems to indicate that he was married somewhat earlier.

24   See chap. 5 in *Satlow, Jewish Marriage in Antiquity*.

25   See Moore, *Judaism in the First Centuries of the Christian Era*, 122.

26   Safrai, *Literature of the sages*, 755.

27   Which is the same word used in *b. Mo'ed* Qaṭ. 18b to refer to a "betrothal."

28   See Gropp, "The Samaria Papyri from Wadi Daliyeh II (Cave 4)," 3–32. See p. 24 n. 42.

29   And so disgrace her.

30   See also *t. Ketub.* 7:6.

31   The issues are most recently discussed by Rosen-Zvi, "Tractate Kinui."

32   See also Safrai, *Literature of the sages*, 756–57, and . Brown, *Birth of the Messiah*, 97–105.

33   See also Safrai, *Literature of the sages*, 762.

34   See *b. Sanh.* 41a.

35   Amy-Jill Levine, in a private communication, pointed out that the same word in connection with Herod's meeting with the Magi where secrecy was necessary.

36   Keener, *A Commentary on the Gospel of Matthew*, 92.

37   Jewish sources have much to say about how the term "righteous" is applied to people who refuse to shame others. Gen. 38:6–30 tells the story of Judah's daughter-in-law Tamar, who is said by Matthew to be one of Jesus' ancestors (1:3). For pious reasons, Tamar disguises herself as a prostitute and deliberately allows herself to become pregnant by Judah who, when he comes to hear of her pregnancy, is convinced that his daughter-in-law has committed adultery, and so orders her to be burned. But when Judah discovers that it was he with whom she conceived, and when he also discovers the reason she brought this to pass, he exclaims, "She is more righteous than I." Tamar did not shame Judah; she was willing to die in order to protect his honor (Gen. 38:25–26). *B. B. Meṣ.* 59a states: "It is better that a person throw himself into a fiery furnace than shame his neighbor in public." *Gen. Rab.* 24:7 relates that God feels shame when someone embarrasses another human being.

38   See also Tosato, "Joseph Being Just Man (Matt 1:19)," 551, and Keener, *Commentary*, 94.

39   This is not unlike the dream of Miriam in L.A.B. (Pseudo-Philo 9:2–10): "I will work a miracle through him and save my people." See further Crossan, "Virgin Mother or Bastard Child?" 45. Crossan considers the tradition history behind these stories.

40   The word "angel" is a transliteration of the Latin *angelus*, which in turn is a transliteration of the Greek *angelos* (messenger). In the LXX *angelos* is the word most commonly used to translate the Hebrew *mal'ak* (i.e., messenger). In the Hebrew Bible the *Angel of the Lord* appears, for example, to Abraham (Gen. 22:11), or to Moses (Exod. 3:2ff), or to Hagar (Gen. 16:7ff), or to Manoah's wife (Judg. 13:3ff). In the case of the latter two, the angel announces not only the birth of but also the destiny of the children of Hagar and Manoah. The angel is a "messenger," bearing the word of God to each of them. It is noteworthy that the examples from the Bible above and in the Joseph story nothing is said about the messenger except that he appears. This is so because what matters is not the messenger but the message he bears. Because it comes from God, the angel proclaims His will.

41   While the verb "were" would be appropriate for the plural subject (sons), the Rabbis understood something singular was being alluded to. That "Holy Spirit" in Hebrew is feminine should not disturb us. The use of the masculine singular occurs with feminine subjects as well. For example, 1Sam. 25:27: "which your maidservant brought" (third p. ms.).

42   Note the similarity in "angel-speak" by comparing the angel's message in Matt. 1:20–21 to Luke 1:13, which states that the angel said to the father of John the Baptist, "Do not be afraid, Zechariah, for your prayer has been heard, and your wife Elizabeth will bear you a son, and you shall call his name John."

43   For Matthew, the event and the Scripture are now united. For the sense of "fulfillment text" see the introduction to this chapter. Matthew states that Jesus' birth fulfills ancient prophecy: "Behold, the virgin shall conceive and bear a son" (Isa. 7:14). Modern translators render this verse from the Hebrew as "Look, the young woman is with child and about to give birth to a son. Let her name him Immanuel" (JPS). The LXX of Isa. 7:14 is: "Behold, this *parthenos* is about to conceive, and she will bear a son, and you shall call his name 'Emmanuel.'" Both "you shall call" and "she shall call" are proper translations of the Hebrew *veqarat*. This verb form appears in both Deut. 31:29 and Jer. 44:23; in both cases it means not "to call" but "to happen," and in both *veqarat* here is normally translated in the third feminine singular. Yet Gen. 16:11 is an almost exact parallel to Isa. 7:14, and this verse can only mean "you [fem.] shall call his name…" Isaiah was speaking to Ahaz about the young woman; thus for Isaiah the better translation is "she shall call." Matthew writes that "they"—rather than "she" or "you"—"shall call his name Emmanuel." That is, Matthew makes an emendation to suit his context.

CHAPTER TWO

INTRODUCTION

From this chapter forward the author of Matthew tells us a story in which Jesus is placed entirely within the social and religious milieu of the Jewish society that was current in Jewish Palestine during the first century. At the same time the story gradually moves away from the literary and social structures that were current in this society to meet the needs of the members of Matthew's own community, who were both socially and theologically removed from this milieu.

The members of the Matthean community understood that they had broken away from the community of Israel (they may even have thought of themselves as *minim*). This separate identity would have been produced by two factors: partly a gradual process of differentiation, confrontation, and rejection (of which more later), but partly also the distinction made by the Romans between Jews and the followers of Jesus. The religion of the Jews was considered a *religio licita*, which meant that it was officially tolerated by the Romans even though in their homeland the Jews remained under martial law. The religion of the Christians, on the other hand, was designated *religio illicita*, which meant that it was not to be tolerated by the Romans.

As a result, they were among those of the non-Jewish communities who were periodically persecuted by the Romans as a cult. Tacitus (*Ann.* 15:44) records that Nero turned on the Christians in Rome after the fire there in 64 C.E. But there is no record of a sustained persecution of the Christians in the first century. There was no systematic persecution of the Christians before the second half of the second century. Pliny, governor of Bithynia

— 43 —

(Turkey) in 111/112, exchanged letters with Trajan and informs us that it was illegal to be a Christian but that Christians should not be sought out; as for the most part, they were not until the time of Decius (although there were exceptions).

Christians were by Matthew's time quite separate from Jews. Allusions in Matthew to specifically Christian (as distinct from Jewish) Scribes (Matt. 13:52), to Jesus having "disciples of all the nations" (Matt. 28:19),[1] and to Jesus warning that "the Kingdom of God will be taken from the Jews and given to another nation" (Matt. 21:43); all these are evidence to show the break was somewhat earlier.[2] However, we cannot say exactly when and how for certain. Jewish evidence suggests that Jews of this community may have attended synagogues at which they were not welcome, assuming a first-century date for the institution of the *birkat haminim* imprecation in Jewish prayer.[3] At any rate, according to the New Testament, the members of this community did not follow Temple practices; nor, after the Temple's destruction, did they mourn for it. Their connection to Jewish oral law must have been negligible, to judge from Matthew's own assessment of it. I write here in general terms but in the commentary proper we shall see how Matthew believed that God had turned away from the Jews and towards the believers in Christ; we shall also see how he inveighed against the unwritten traditions of the Jews.[4] So by the time Matthew was writing his account of Jesus in about the year 70, both Roman and Christian sources strongly suggest that the followers of Jesus were thought to be distinct from the Jews. Moreover, Jewish sources that focus on this period indicate that those Jews who were part of the Jesus movement were thought by other Jews to be even worse than pagans.[5]

The author of Matthew deliberately chose to construct his narrative with a Jewish vocabulary that has the feel of prechurch tradition (contrived or real). His story begins with the birth of Jesus in Bethlehem, the traditional site for the birth of the Messiah, in the latter years of Herod's rule. Herod was thought by the Jews to be a descendant of Esau, the elder twin brother and sometime rival of their patriarch Jacob, whose life Esau once sought. Herod was in fact an Edomite (of Idumean lineage), and Edom was understood to be the national embodiment of Esau. The Romans appointed him king of the Jews in 40 B.C.E. and he gained control of Judea in 37 B.C.E. Although he was a ruthless tyrant he kept Judea politically independent during his reign, which ended with his death in 4 B.C.E.[6]

The author of Matthew fills out the circumstances of Jesus' birth by turning to Jewish traditions concerning Moses[7] and Abraham.[8] His purpose in doing this was not to show that Jesus was a new Moses through whom would come a new law, nor to suggest that Jewish history was turning in on itself to draw the curtains to a close (in Matthew's day Christians hoped to see the Jews punished for their having rebelled against the will of God by having Jesus crucified). His purpose was to use Jewish materials in the way the Jews themselves used them — pouring new wine into old skins, as it were.[9]

For the ancient Rabbis the words of a biblical verse produce sounds and images, in and of themselves devoid of universal meaning, which suggest other sounds and images. Information, but not systematic thought, might be derived from the new sounds and images but at the end of the day this information expresses things already known from elsewhere in the tradition. The play of sound and image all but ignores concept. This is because the Rabbis assume that the tradition, right down to the letters of a biblical verse, is a closed system in which there is no worthless information: no filler, nothing extra. To the Greek and western mind, however, a text, even a sacred text, consists of two parts: vehicle and concept. And the concept is the point of the text, the meaning of a literary image. A word, let alone a single syllable, only has importance for the western reader insofar as it is needed to convey the concept, the point. If, then, a particular word is only present in a text because grammar or sense require it, that word — and any image it might have evoked in some other context — is of no importance to the reader.

It is generally assumed by New Testament scholars that, for the most part, the Gospel writers read their Greek versions of the Hebrew Bible from the Greek view that word images yield universal concepts. Jewish readers of the Hebrew Bible in the early Christian centuries, on the other hand, tended to connect the words with associated images that had well-defined specific contours but they, for the most part, resisted finding any universal concept. So the question becomes — what is the nature of the Greek gospels, which interpret the Hebrew Scriptures? Do they use the Greek interpretive mode of conceptual thought, or the Hebrew visual/auditory mode of providing stark images to describe specific evil characters, good characters, and God? I take the position that while Matthew's rhetoric slides along the surface of the Moses stories in Scripture and Jewish traditions, the intent is not to cut a deep slice out of these Exodus Scriptures. Matthew, likely following an older source,[10] uses the images and the words as no more than evocative of biblical vocabulary but devoid of the conceptual paradigm of a Moses or a Pharaoh. Jesus is simply Jesus and Herod is Herod. They play themselves.[11]

Most of the Jewish literature from the Second Temple period is known to us from the Greek writings of the Jews preserved by the Church. However, Hebrew and Aramaic versions of some of these texts have recently been discovered near the Dead Sea. The authors of these texts show us how familiar phrases from the Bible could even then be used as literary devices, to describe events not mentioned in it.[12]

Moreover, the typological vocabulary used by the Jews to denote a deliverer or a persecutor was governed by biblical descriptions. Deliverers were invariably Moseses or Davids, while persecutors were either Pharaohs or Hamans. To be sure, Jewish typologies of the Messiah also found in Matthew, such as comparing him to Moses riding on an ass (Exod. 4:20) or calling him the King of the Jews, could suggest more than just a casual description by utilizing phrases borrowed from the Mosaic or Davidic narratives, but the Jesus stories do not. The narrative of Matthew makes it clear that Jesus was to lead the nations out of the promised land and to establish himself as an eternal Temple far removed from temporal time and space.

To sum up so far: chapter 2 of the Gospel of Matthew introduces us to the features that are typical of its Jewish aspect and may contain fragments of Jesus tradition from earlier writings when Jews and Christians were still of one community. Acts 10 indicates that if initially the Jesus movement had been open to Jews only, that situation came to an end in the days of Paul.

Some issues require specific investigation in this chapter: parallel birth narratives, the origin of these parallels, and what these parallels can (and cannot) mean. A significant amount of literature on the Matthean birth narrative focuses on what are believed to be parallels between Jewish stories concerning the birth of Moses and the Gospel account of the birth of Jesus. Many have argued that a number of verses in Matthew are parallel to those in the stories of the birth of Moses,[13] while others have claimed that Matthew's purpose was not to compare the births of Moses and Jesus or to model one story after the other.[14] If these parallels are intentional, Matthew's likely purpose in drawing on extrabiblical birth narratives of Moses to flesh out the story of the birth of Jesus was to show that the early biographical histories of Jewish saviors share certain features, among which, for example, is the typically violent reaction of the king to the news, which has often been acquired in a supernatural way, of the savior's birth. That is, the king in whose homeland the savior was born, and whose position was threatened by the birth, often sought to have the putative newborn savior killed, even if it meant that a number of innocents were killed along with him.

These Jewish biblical and extrabiblical traditions incorporated many of the "birth motifs" of the hero that were commonly found in the birth stories of heroes in the various cultures of the ancient Near East. Otto Rank makes much of the common features found in the birth stories of the hero.

> The hero is the child of most distinguished parents, usually the son of a king. His origin is preceded by difficulties, such as sexual abstinence, prolonged infertility, or secret intercourse of the parents due to external prohibition or obstacles. During or before the pregnancy, a prophecy, in the form of a dream or oracle, warns against the birth. As a rule, he is surrendered to the water, in a box.[15]

As Rank points out, the very earliest histories of such figures as Buddha, Sargon, Oedipus, Gilgamesh, Cyrus the Great, Romulus, and Hercules loosely fit into this pattern.[16] But the birth of Moses as it is recorded in Exodus is greatly expanded in Jewish interpretive sources to follow more closely the formulaic Near Eastern pattern even if Rank, drawing from the biblical account alone, includes Moses among those whom he sees as fitting into this pattern.

It is, however, instructive to look at the language of the Jewish stories in the midrash/Targum tradition about a dream that preceded Pharaoh's decree to kill every Israelite infant male (preserved among other places in Yalkut Shimoni, Exod. 154). Here we find that both in language and in structure that there are allusions in them to an earlier Pharaoh's dreams in the story of Joseph (Gen. 41:1–7). The text is cited in full in my comments to 2:2 below. In other words, the authors of these stories reworked the language of an earlier biblical story to convey a particular image, but this does not mean that conceptual narratives of their stories are congruent.

In the same way, texts from the Bible are frequently referred to in the great works of Western literature to simply convey ideas; the stories from which the texts are taken are for the most part not borrowed at the same time. For example, Hamlet sings a version of a popular contemporary ballad, which refers to Judg. 12:7 (*Hamlet* II ii).

> *O Jephthah, judge of Israel, what a treasure hadst thou!*
> (— What treasure had he, my lord?),
> (— Why) '*One fair daughter and no more,*
> *The which he loved passing well.*'

A copy of the ballad, as Shakespeare knew it, was reprinted in Evan's *Old Ballads* (1810). The first stanza reads as follows (in part):[17]

> I have read that many years agoe,
> *When Jephtha, judge of Israel,*
> *Had one fair daughter and no moe,*
> *Whom he loved passing well...*

The point is that the author of the original ballad knew of the story of Jephthah in Judges but that Shakespeare's use of it in the mouth of Hamlet was simply his way of describing Ophelia as the "fair daughter" of Polonius.

We are not supposed to think, because of this literary allusion, that the character of Polonius is modeled on the biblical Jephthah, or even that there is a shared motif here. Shakespeare might even be intimating that Ophelia's demise can be traced back to Polonius, but that does not make Polonius the New Jephthah.

> *In the days of Herod the king, when Jesus was born in Bethlehem of Judea, behold, magoi from the East came to Jerusalem. (v. 1)*

This verse serves as the topic of the unit. The word *magos* (pl. *magoi*) is the Greek word for "astrologer." An astrologer was anyone who, using enchantments, was able to divine the future.[18] A *magos*, then, was someone who could discern hidden events or predict what had not yet occurred. Philo refers to Balaam, the biblical enchanter, as *magos*,[19] and in Dan. 2:2 one reads of Nebuchadnezzar calling, among others, "the enchanters" (in Hebrew *vela'ashafim* and in Greek *kai tous magous*) to interpret one of his dreams.

> *saying, "Where is the king of the Jews who has been born? For we saw his star in the east and we came to worship him." (v. 2)*

There are many Jewish stories which tell of astrologers and/or dream interpreters who reveal the meanings of the miraculous portents associated with the births of Israel's saviors. In Eisenstein's *Otsar Midrashim* (356–57), there is a late version (Lewow/Lemberg, 1865) of the Hebrew text of the *Chronicles of Our Master Moses*,[20] which Eisenstein identifies as being likely the work known as the *Midrash of Our Master Moses,* cited by medieval commentators of the twelfth century. In style it appears to be a Hebrew retranslation of a lost pseudepigraphic Greek work likely written originally in Hebrew or Aramaic. Another Hebrew text of the same story is found in *Yalkut Shimoni* Exod. 164 (YS) (mentioned above), while an Aramaic text of it is found in *Tg. Ps.-J.* to Exod. 1:15 (TJ). This story relates a dream concerning the birth of Moses, which angered the Pharaoh so much he was determined to kill all the children of a certain age to make sure he had gotten rid of the redeemer of the Jews.

In the sixtieth year after Joseph's death [In the 130th year after Israel came to Egypt (YS)] Pharaoh dreamt a dream. Behold in the dream [he was sitting on his throne] an old man stood before him who held in his hands a pair of [merchant (YS)] scales. He [the old man took the scales and suspended them before Pharaoh (YS)] placed all the inhabitants of Egypt, men women and children, [the sages of Egypt, her ministers and nobles and bound them together (YS)] on one hand of the scales. And he put a [afterwards he took a suckling (YS)] lamb on the other

hand of the scale. And the lamb outweighed all the Egyptians [everyone (YS)].
He [Pharaoh (YS)] was startled and thoughts raced through his mind. He was
truly amazed at this great [terrifying (YS)] vision [why had the lamb outweighed
them all? (YS)]. When he awoke, it was but a dream so he [got up early and (YS)]
he gathered all the wise-men of Egypt and all the magicians. ...And he (one of
his advisors — a eunuch [YS]) said to him [this is certainly a bad omen of terrible
evil which will come upon Egypt in the final days for] a son would be born to the
Israelites who would destroy all [the Land of (YS)] Egypt. And now, my lord king,
I will counsel you wisely that [*if the matter is good with the king the proclamation
of the kingdom should go out before him and be written in the laws of Egypt* that
every male child of the Hebrews shall be killed (YS)] you should command that
every son born to the Israelites shall be killed. Perhaps then the message of the
dream will not be fulfilled. *And the matter was good in the eyes of Pharaoh and in
the eyes of his servants* [*And the king did so* (YS)].

According to the Aramaic portion of text in TJ, Pharaoh relates that
he had seen in a dream all the land of Egypt placed in one hand of a scale
and a lamb in the other hand and the hand on which the lamb was placed
outweighed the hand on which all of Egypt was placed. Then at once he sent
for all the magicians in Egypt, and Jannes and Jambres, the chief magicians,
were able to interpret his dream for him. They said to Pharaoh that a male
child was soon to be born into the assembly of Israel through whom all the
land of Egypt would be destroyed: "Whenever a [Jewish] son is born you
shall kill him."

The Aramaic portion in the TJ is more closely tied to the biblical text and
so does not contain the fuller story of the Hebrew portions of these texts.
It is probable that the Hebrew portions are later additions and so postdate
the Aramaic text in the TJ. This hypothesis is supported by the fact that the
italicized passages in the Hebrew text I translated above are paraphrases of
several passages from the Book of Esther (1:19, 1:21). It was not common
for Hebrew writers in the Second Temple period to borrow passages from
the Book of Esther to use in narratives that speak of Pharaoh.[21] Of course,
anyone who approaches these texts first and foremost as a reader of Matthew
perceives that the closest link is to the (later inserted) Hebrew texts, since in
Esther the Persian king and his prime minister issue a decree to kill all the
Jews in Persia, and in Matthew Herod issues a decree to slaughter the Jewish
male infants in and around Bethlehem.

Another source tells us that it was one of Pharaoh's astrologers who
informed him of the birth of Israel's redeemer (*Exod. Rab.* 1:18–22). This source
is thought to be from the medieval period but it does seem to derive from
sources known to Josephus and also from *Yalkut Shimoni* source materials.
The basic facts of this story are common to all four texts: "Astrologers" tell

Pharaoh here; "magicians" tell him in the TJ and an "advisor" tells him in the *Yalkut Shimoni* version, while Josephus writes that the announcement is made by "one of the sacred Scribes." Following this, Pharaoh issues the decree to kill "every male child born to the Israelites" (*Ant.* 2:205).

The Gospel narrative, by beginning with the predicted birth of the deliverer and the terrible consequences of that prediction for the deliverer's peers, aims to draw an *inclusio* around history — bound at one end by Moses the deliverer and at the other end by the ultimate deliverer, the Messiah. The idea is expressed in a statement attributed to Rabbi Berekhiah (around 340 C.E.) speaking in the name of Rabbi Isaac (around 300 C.E.) and we see the same *inclusio*. The source of this midrash is *Pirqe R. El.*, chap. 30, of late composition (eighth, ninth century) but containing much older traditions, much the same way *Targum Pseudo-Jonathan* does.[22]

> *Just as the first Deliverer was, so will the last Deliverer be.* As Scripture says about the first Deliverer: "Moses took his wife and his sons, setting them upon on an ass" (Exod. 4:20), so also the last Deliverer: "Lowly and riding on an ass" (Zech. 9:9).

In these extrabiblical stories,[23] the members of the families of these saviors have already received prophecies and so they are alert to what lies ahead that fulfills these prophecies. And so we find stories not mentioned in the Bible where the lives of heroes are foretold before their births. This is so not only of Moses[24] but of Abraham as well as I have already indicated in the introduction to this chapter. The reader, aware of these prophecies, understands the pattern better than the actors themselves.

When King Herod heard this, he was greatly distressed (v. 3)

Herod came to power through conquest and deceit. He was not a native Jew and he was not recognized as a legitimate king by the Jews. He poisoned, or otherwise did away with, anyone who even remotely aspired to the throne, including his first wife, Mariamne, and the children Alexander and Aristobulus he had through her. Hearing that another had been born about whom it was foretold that he would be king of the Jews would certainly have distressed him.

and Jerusalem was distressed with him (v. 3 continued)

This part of the verse has often troubled commentators, who wonder if the reference to Jerusalem here is a reference to the Jews of the city only, or to the Romans, or to both. The key to understanding this part of the verse lies in Esther 3:15, in which it is said that the city of Susa was "in distress" after the Persian king Ahasuerus issued the decree that all the Jews throughout all of Persia were to be killed.

In his retelling of the story of Esther, Josephus (*Ant.* 11:220) has given us his understanding of what it meant for the city of Susa to be "in distress." He seems to have been following the text from the LXX. He relates that haste was made (about ordering the death of the Jews in Persia) in Susa as well. Then he tells is that the king and Haman were busy feasting and drinking, "*while the city was in commotion.*"

As well, according to *b. Meg.* 11a, Rava, a Babylonian teacher of the fourth century, once gave a sermon based on a tradition that related Esther 3:15 to Prov. 29:2:

> *When the righteous are in authority the people rejoice (Prov. 29:2) — the "righteous" refers to Mordecai and Esther, as it is said, and the city of Susa was delighted and happy (Esther 8:15). But when the wicked beareth rule, the people groan (Prov. 29:2) — the "wicked" refers to Haman, as it is said, and the city of Susa was distressed (Esther 3:15).*

The Jews of Jerusalem were in distress because the times were indecisive. The Jews knew something ominous was afoot but they did not know what. A king in distress meant trouble. Herod was in distress because he did not know if his plan to find Jesus would succeed. The Jews were made nervous because of Herod's obvious displeasure; though they could not account for it, they nevertheless intuited that something terrible was about to come of it. This is the very sense of Esther 3:15. Matthew foreshadows Herod's wicked decree about to erupt in verse 7 with this allusion to the Persian decree to kill the Jews. Ahasuerus and Haman were up to no good, but just what they were up to was not known as yet. Did Herod issue orange alerts, or close off entry into Jerusalem, or show his anger in ruthless ways as was his habit? The narrator tells us only that he was distressed because he had just been informed that a rival to his throne has just been born and because the Jews of Jerusalem sensed his distress, they were distressed too.

The language of distress may have been borrowed from Esther, but the contemporary reader realized that Herod was not Ahasuerus who threatened to annihilate Mordecai and all the other Jews of Persia, nor could he be cast easily as Pharaoh who threatened to do away with Moses for killing an Egyptian. Indeed, our narrator shows us Joseph and his family fleeing, not to the oppressive Egypt of Moses' day and the oppressive

Pharaoh but to first-century Egypt with its metropolis of Alexandria. Everyone knew Alexandria of that time to be a cultural haven and it boasted Jewish philosophers, merchants, and well-established, hospitable Jewish communities.[25]

> *and gathering all the principal priests and Scribes of the people,*
> *he inquired of them where the Messiah was to be born. (v. 4)*

Priests and Scribes were Jewish religious leaders who were most familiar with the oral Jewish traditions that Herod could not access himself. Priests administered the Temple rites, while Scribes were experts in the oral laws and traditions surrounding all aspects of Jewish life. Surely these teachers would know where the birth of the Messiah was to take place. Herod is portrayed here, not wholly unrealistically, as a believer in Jewish traditions, though a little further on (v. 7ff.) he is also shown to be a believer in Chaldean astrological wisdom.

Jewish understanding of *the Messiah* is partly based on a passage from the oracle of Balaam (who came to curse the Israelites and blessed them instead) in the Book of Numbers 24.[26]

> How goodly are thy habitations, Jacob, and thy tents, Israel! as shady groves, and as gardens by a river, and as tents which God pitched, and as cedars by the waters. There shall come a man out of his seed, and he shall rule over many nations; and the Kingdom of God shall be exalted, and his kingdom shall be increased. God led him out of Egypt; he has as it were the glory of a unicorn: he shall consume the nations of his enemies, and he shall drain their marrow, and with his darts he shall shoot through the enemy. He lay down, he rested as a lion, and as a young lion; who shall stir him up? They that bless thee are blessed, and they that curse thee are cursed. (24:5–9)

It would seem that Jewish tradition also stressed the military role of the Messiah. Philo of Alexandria (15 C.E.–70?) writes about the messianic figure spoken of in the oracle of Balaam for his gentile readers.

> *For "there shall come forth a man," says the oracle, and leading his host*
> *to war he will subdue great and populous nations, because God has*
> *sent to his aid the reinforcement which befits the godly. (On rewards*
> *and punishments 95, Loeb)*

Many commentators identify *the star* that guides the magi with the star that is referred to in Num. 24:17:

I see him, but not now; I behold him, but not near; A star ʃ
forth from Jacob, A scepter shall rise from Israel, And s
through the forehead of Moab, And tear down all the sons

Others suggest that the star resembles more the pillar of light which leα ιιιͺ Israelites in the desert. There is no need to think that star here is a reference to the one or the other. Rather, the point is that a supernatural light in the form of a star is guiding the magi and there need be nothing more to it than that. There is no promised land here and no conquering hero; the image stands on its own.

They said to him, "In Bethlehem of Judea; for thus it has been written
by the prophet [Micah 5:1]" (v. 5)

A rather strange story in *y. Ber.* 2:4[27] speaks of some local Arab peasant telling a Jew to lock away his oxen and utensils for the Messiah has been born and he should go and visit him. From the bellowing of certain animals the Arab can discern that the Messiah's name is Menahem, son of Hezekiah, and that he has been born in the royal city of Bethlehem of Judah. Now it would appear that that the author of the story knows something of Matthew's narrative. For bizarre though the story is, the author finds it plausible that a non-Jew can come to know through extraordinary means not only that the Messiah has been born but that he has been born in Bethlehem of Judah. The figure of Menahem in this story has been plausibly identified by some as Menahem ben Judah, one of the leaders of the *zealots*, or as they were known, *sicarii*.[28] And perhaps this Menahem was also the Menahem ben Hezekiah who is referred to Sanhedrin 98b as the Messiah. It seems that the real Menahem also saw himself as a Messiah.

About this Menahem, Josephus (*War* 2:433–34,) tells us that Menahem was the son of Judah, the Galilean who under Quinarius had scolded the Jews for recognizing the Romans as their masters in place of God. Menahem had taken some friends and broke into Herod's armory at Masada. He distributed the arms to some brigands and with this force entered Jerusalem as if he were king.

"And you Bethlehem, land of Judah, are not at all least among the
leaders of Judah. For out of you shall come a leader, who will shepherd
my people Israel." (v. 6)

"Bethlehem Efratha" is the reading in the MT. Matthew writes "Bethlehem, land of Judah" because he likely understood that "Bethlehem land of Judah" is the meaning of "Bethlehem, house of Efrath. (LXX)." In any event, what

Micah means is rendered here correctly as "Bethlehem, of Judah." For Bethlehem was the son of Efrath, from the tribe of Judah.[29]

We note here what Ramban had to say about those areas spoken of in the Bible — areas that he traveled through — that were connected to Rachel's burial site. He states that the reason Bethlehem is called "of Judah" in the Hebrew Bible is because the city is the beginning point of Judah's territory. The territory of Benjamin (the son of Rachel and in whose territory it would be natural for her to be buried) ends less than a kilometer away. But Bethlehem is mentioned in Jeremiah as her burial site. The solution to the apparent conflict is easily resolved since Bethlehem is the closest city to the site of Rachel's weeping for her children. So it was mentioned as a marker although she was not buried in that city. The confusion about the precise location of Rachel's tomb is settled in this way in his commentary to Gen. 35:16.

> And I witnessed that she [Rachel] was not buried in Rama or in its environs since Rama of Benjamin's territory is four *parsaot* distant [from her grave] and the one in Mt Ephraim (mentioned in 1Sam. 1:1) is over 2 days journey from it. Therefore I conclude that the verse "a voice in Rama is heard" (Jer. 31:14) is poetic license [*mashal*]. It means that Rachel cried so loud and bitterly [as if] her voice would be heard upon that [distant] Rama which was atop the mountain that came to be in the territory of her son Benjamin ... And it seems most likely that Jacob buried her by a road rather than bring her into Bethlehem of Judah which is near by it. He understood through the Holy Prophetic Spirit that Bethlehem of Efrath would be given to Judah and he wanted to bury her in the territory of Benjamin her son ... And accordingly [Rabbi Meir] says in *Sipre Deut.* (piska 352 to Deut. 33:11) that she died in the territory that would be apportioned to Benjamin ... I noticed that the [Aramaic translation] of Jonathan ben Uziel was sensitive to this understanding of the verse.

Then Herod, having summoned the magi secretly, learned from them the exact time the star had appeared. (v. 7)

The secrecy of the meeting shows that Herod sought to move quickly against the child. Except for Joseph and Mary, and also Herod and the magi, no one as yet knew of the birth of the Deliverer.

and in sending them to Bethlehem, he said, "Go, search carefully for the child, and as soon as you have found him report to me, so that I might go and worship him." (v. 8)

The magi, who did not know as yet where the child was born, were sent to Bethlehem. Note that "worship" here means to prostrate oneself before someone who is recognized as one's superior; akin to "falling" (v. 11) which connotes specifically religious worship perhaps with a conscious echo of Num. 24: 4, 16. Herod showed them his intelligence gathering was not to be trifled with. He also put them at ease (which will later be called "tricking" them) as to his intentions since Jerusalem itself was uneasy about something lurking in the air.

> *When they heard the king, they went, and look, the star which they saw in the east led them, until they came to the place where the star stood still, over the place where the child was. Seeing the star, they rejoiced, filled with exceedingly great joy. (vv. 9–10)*

The star led the magi directly to Bethlehem. Herod had not had them followed, an oversight that the historical Herod would never have committed.

> *When they came to the house they saw the child with Mary his mother, and falling, they worshiped him, and opening their treasure chests they brought him gifts, gold, incense, and myrrh. (v. 11)*

Falling upon one's face was the final position of worship (for the High Priest and the people in the Temple) (*m. Yoma* 6:2). In this position the Priest declared the ultimate glory of God's Kingdom.

Gifts that are to be brought to the Messiah are mentioned in the late source *Exod. Rab.* 35.5 that all peoples will bring gifts to the king, the Messiah; Egypt brings first, then afterwards Ethiopia, but no gifts will be accepted from Edom (Rome).[30] The midrash is primarily based on Ps. 68:30–34 and 80:14. It is not unlikely that the Rabbis knew a tradition that was also known, in some shape or form by Matthew.

> *And having been warned in a dream not to return to Herod, they departed to their own country by another way. (v. 12)*

Whereas in the midrashim concerning Pharaoh's fear of Moses, the wisemen of Egypt advised Pharaoh to take steps against Moses, here the wisemen from the east, upon hearing of the deceit of Herod toward them, simply escape. They had no interest in cooperating with the dangerous king. Matthew is careful to avoid telling us if anyone other than Herod and his councilors, and also the magi, were aware that a child had been born whose sovereign status had been foretold.[31]

Following verse 12, three problems with the text confront the reader. First, why do verses 13–15 occur where they do, seeing that, from the point of view of sense and sequence, verse 16 clearly follows verse 12.

> 12 And having been warned in a dream not to return to Herod, they departed to their own country by another way. … 16 When Herod saw that he had been deceived by the magi he was greatly aroused, and he sent out the order to kill every child two years old and younger in Bethlehem and in all of its surrounding villages, according to the time when he learned from the magi.

Second, how is it that Matthew tells a whole story (of the flight into Egypt) in verses 13–15, and then tells most of it again (vv. 19–21)? Third, what would account for Matthew's departure from his usual sequential style? Almost everything in his narratives proceeds in clear, step-by-step order, with little or no backtracking. Yet in these verses the narrative jumps about in a way that is far from typical; the structure is awkward, and shows signs of having been edited.

What follows verse 12 until verse 13 can be viewed as an interpolation based on the following hypothesis: Having taken the text of verses 13–15 from an older source, Matthew has inserted it into the Gospel here as a kind of summary of events to come and also so that he can include another passage with a fulfillment verse into the text. The first part of verse 13 — "When they had departed, look…" — is a bridge that leads back to Matthew's older source (vv. 13–15). Then follows the text that comes from that older source, which contained the fulfillment prophecy: "An angel of the Lord appeared in a dream… 'From Egypt I have called my son.'"[32] Then the narrative picks up again in verse 16, in which we are told of Herod's anger and of his plot to kill the male children under two years of age in and around Bethlehem. Matthew then may have once more turned to his older source at 2:18 until the end of the chapter but this is too speculative to consider seriously. I wonder about this because the fulfillment exegesis in 2:18 is not as convincing as that in 2:15, since the text from Jeremiah, unlike the text from Hosea, lacks a clear reference to anything in Matthew's narrative.[33] At any rate, the structure of the narrative as it now stands is awkward and shows signs of having been edited by Matthew. The upshot of this is that there are signs of the narrative jumping about which is very atypical of Matthew's usual sequential style, first this and then that and then later something else. Everything in his narratives proceeds along a clear narrative with little or no repetitions or backtracking. I have tried to account for this by positing Matthew has joined an older source into his story — perhaps intending it to be something like a footnote.

When they had departed, look, an angel of the Lord appeared in a dream to Joseph, saying, "Get up, take the child and his mother, and flee to Egypt, and be there until I tell you. For Herod is about to seek the child, to kill him." (v. 13)

Matthew (or perhaps one of his sources) begins this section that ends with the fulfillment verse from Hosea. As I say, the purpose of the fulfillment verses in the Gospel is to show that a certain action described in the Gospel conforms literally to what has been said in a number of texts from the Prophets. The fulfillment prophecy always follows immediately upon the description of the act that fulfills the prophecy (in 2:18 the wailing follows the decree of Herod to slaughter children, and that decree would of course have been the occasion for wailing). In this case, it is Joseph's going down to Egypt with his family and his staying there until he is called to return. It must be understood here that the angel/God will himself go down to Egypt to call Joseph from there in order for the prophecy to be literally fulfilled.[34] Literal readings of fulfillment verses are typical in Jewish sources.

The angel uses three verbs of command in quick succession to indicate the urgency of the situation in which Joseph and his family find themselves: "*Get up, take…* and *flee.*" The use of such verbs of command in quick succession is commonplace in biblical narrative. We can compare Matthew's language here to that of Gen. 19:14–15, in which Lot first urges his sons-in-law, and then the angels urge Lot, to flee Sodom: "Lot went out and spoke to his sons-in-law, who were to marry his daughters, and said, '*Get up, get out* of this place, for the Lord will destroy the city,' the angel urged Lot, saying, '*Get up, take* your wife and your two daughters…'" and also to that of Gen. 31:13, in which Jacob tells Rachel and Leah of his dream in which the angel of God instructed him to return home, "'I am the God of Bethel, where you anointed a pillar, where you made a vow to Me; now *get up, leave* this land, and *return* to the land of your birth,'" and also to that of Gen. 35:1, in which God appeared to Jacob telling him to return home: "And God said to Jacob, '*Get up* now to Beth-el and *make* your living-place there: and *put up* an altar there to the God who came to you when you were in flight from your brother Esau.'" Either Matthew or his source imitates the Hebrew biblical style.

He got up, took the child and his mother by night, and departed for Egypt. (v. 14)

Without hesitation, Joseph obeyed the threefold command of the angel and left his land for Egypt.

> *He was there until Herod's death, in order to fulfill what was spoken*
> *by the Lord through the prophet, "From Egypt I called my son"*
> *(Hosea 11:1). (v. 15)*

The phrase "*In order to fulfill…*" reproduces the Hebrew "*k'dei leqayem.*" The phrase is found in a tradition preserved in the *Midrash Tanhuma* (*pikudei* 2) which discusses the proper procedure for stoning a criminal.

> [The witnesses] shall place it [the stone] upon his heart—in order to fulfill [Heb. *k'dei leqayem*] what was written [in the Torah Deut. 17:7]: the hand of the witnesses shall be upon him first.

We note the steps that, according to this tradition, are involved in the process of fulfillment. 1) There is an act—the stone is placed upon the heart; 2) then there is a statement of purpose—"in order to fulfill"; 3) then a reference to the biblical text as a source for the command; and 4) then the verse itself (Deut. 17:7).

The text, "my son," from Hosea in Matthew closely matches the source quoted by the Rabbis in Hebrew, and by Aquila in Greek: *kai apo aiguptou ekalesa ton hion mou*, and not in the plural as in the LXX, which says "his sons" (*ta tekna autou*). However, the Aramaic Targum "sons [*banin*]" agrees with the plural reading of the LXX. We do not have any Greek text that could serve as the model for Matthew's version. Matthew and the standard Hebrew text do not say "and" (*kai* in Greek) as both LXX and Aquila do. Aquila uses *apo* and Matthew *ek* for the preposition "from," or "out of." The terms in New Testament Greek are virtually interchangeable.

As in the tradition from the *Midrash Tanhuma*, so here in this verse we see a four-step process of fulfillment. 1) There is an act—"And he was there until Herod's death"; 2) then a statement of purpose—"in order to fulfill"; 3) then a reference to the text as a source for the act—"which was spoken by the Lord through the prophet"; 4) then the verse itself—"*From* Egypt I called my son."

Fulfillment verses can at times depend upon the literal interpretation of the prepositions within them in order for them to be fulfilled. We have seen that this was the case in the midrash on Deut. 17:7 above, which spoke of the necessity of the placing of the hands of the witnesses *upon* the criminal who is to be stoned in order for the verse to be fulfilled. Another account of a verse being fulfilled by means of a literal interpretation of a preposition in it is found in the Passover Seder service.

> Thus did Hillel during the time the Holy Temple stood: 1 [act] he used to wrap together *matzah* and bitter herbs (and the Passover lamb) and eat them together 2 [fulfillment clause] *to fulfill* [*leqayem*] 3 [scriptural source] that which Scripture

says, 4 [scriptural citation] "*upon* matzah and bitter herbs they shall eat it [the Passover lamb].

The phrase "in order to fulfill" indicates that a verse is being read and carried out according to the letter.[35] I have already written extensively on this matter in my comments to chapter 1:23.

Despite the great volume of commentary claiming otherwise, there is no reference being made here to a specific theology of divine sonship or to the context of Hosea, or to Israel or Moses, or to anything other than the very words of the verse alone.[36] Matthew wants us to focus on "from [Egypt]" for that is precisely the word upon which the fulfillment of the text depends. The citation of this fulfillment verse in no way relates to anything more than the words of the verse that are cited. Matthew is not thinking of Moses, or Israelites in Egypt or anything else besides the literal words "From Egypt — my son." The verse (Hos. 11:1–2) and its context reads:

> When Israel was a child I loved him, from Egypt I called my son. The more I called them, the farther they went from me, Sacrificing to the Baals and burning incense to idols.

Hosea condemns "my son" who was called "out of Egypt." Matthew isolated those words to have us think Hosea predicted God's bringing back his son, Jesus, in a way that is complementary to "my son." We are not to think of the Hosean context: Jesus worshipping idols would be absurd for a Matthean fulfillment text. This kind of selective referencing, "atomization," surgically removes a phrase from a biblical verse for the Jewish preacher's purposes. For instance, Num. 27:11: "If his father had no brothers, give his inheritance to the nearest relative in his clan, that he may *yarash otah*."[37] The actual meaning here in context is "that he will inherit it." But the word for "it" (i.e., the inheritance), *otah,* refers to the inheritance property, a feminine noun, and if atomized (removed from context) could mean "that he will inherit her." So Rava (*b. B. Bat.* 111b) remarks the verse tells us that a man will inherit his wife (= her) and the gendering of the sentence implies a wife will not inherit her husband. Atomized interpretations, which are usually far from contextual meanings, give the authority of Scripture to rules and events that appear extraordinary.

In the following example a verse from Ezekiel (who lived in the time of the Exile after 586 B.C.E.) is said to have been *fulfilled* at the time of the Exodus (some six or seven hundred years earlier). Ezekiel is speaking about the destruction of Edom on Mount Seir as an event yet to come. The preacher atomizes the verse to have it apply to the battle against Amalek (*Mekhilta of Rabbi Yishmael Beshalah* [*Amalek,* end of *parasha* 1]):

Exod. 17:13
So Joshua overwhelmed Amalek and his people with the edge of the sword.
Others say (Exod. 17:13 — the slaughter of Amalek by the sword) is a fulfillment of Ezekiel 35:6:
"Therefore as I live," declares the Lord God, "I will give you over to bloodshed, and bloodshed will pursue you; since you have not hated bloodshed, therefore bloodshed will pursue you."

The bloody execution of the Amalakites is given scriptural explanation — those who live by the sword shall die by the sword.

When Herod saw that he had been deceived by the magi he was greatly aroused, and he sent out the order to kill every child two years old and younger in Bethlehem and in all of its surrounding villages, according to the time when he learned from the magi. (v. 16)

I have already spoken at length of Jewish literary models concerning this verse in my introduction to this chapter. The verse needs very little in way of explanation.

Then was fulfilled what was spoken by Jeremiah the prophet (v. 17)

The verse is awkward. One might think this is not, strictly speaking, a fulfillment-exegesis in form, because it anticipates something that will happen: the slaughter of the innocents. Nonetheless, it is likely that once Herod's decree was known (and bad news travels quickly) the response of those parents anticipating the slaughter was continuous wailing. What makes it awkward is the use of this verse in a passage into which Matthew has interpolated material suggesting slaughter and then the death of Herod. He then backtracks, and it makes one wonder if the verse relates to what has happened offstage (vv. 12–16), or confirms something that is yet to happen. The prophetic text in the Gospel suggests that "as far away as Rama will be heard the wailing and weeping of the parents whose children in and around Bethlehem are to be killed." The fulfillment text is given in accord with what we noted earlier in 1:23.

"A voice was heard in Ramah, crying and loud wailing; Rachel is crying for her children, and she does not wish to be comforted, because they are not" (Jer. 31:15). (v. 18)

The manuscript evidence suggests that *threnos kai*, "lamentation, and," which is missing from a number of early witnesses to the text, was added to some of the later manuscripts so that it would conform to the passage in the LXX, which is not unlike what is found in the Masoretic Text. If Matthew's text originally lacked these words it would perhaps indicate that he departed from the Theodotian Greek model he used in 2:15 to cite Hosea, thus substantiating my earlier suggestion that the author of verse 18 is not the same as the author of verse 15. However, copyists lose words, especially redundant ones, and so no firm source criticism can be based on this evidence alone.

When Herod died, look, an angel of the Lord appeared in a dream to Joseph in Egypt (v. 19)

Here Matthew informs the reader that what the angel said to Joseph in 2:13 about how long he was to remain in Egypt with his family and when he would know that it was time for them all to return — "and be there until I tell you" — has come to pass. Matthew is careful to mention that this communication actually occurs in Egypt, fulfilling the words of Hosea 11:1: "*From* Egypt…"

saying "Get up, take the child and his mother and go to the Land of Israel, for the ones who were seeking the life of the child have died." (v. 20)

The threefold command in this verse mirrors the threefold command in verse 13: "'Get up, take … and go'"; the reason for the command here also mirrors the reason for the command in verse 13. The reason Joseph took his family to Egypt was because "Herod [was] about to seek the child, to kill him," and the reason Joseph and his family could now return from Egypt was because "the ones who were seeking the life of the child have died." Commentators such as Brown[38] find in this mirroring reason enough to compare the Matthean story of the flight to, and return from, Egypt to Moses' flight to, and return from, Midian, about which we read in Exod. 4:19 — "And the Lord said unto Moses in Midian, 'Go, return into Egypt: for all the men who were seeking your life have died.'" But a cautious reading, though it certainly will allow that Matthew has borrowed the language from the text in Exodus, stops far short of the inference that Jesus was a new Moses. The flight to, and return from, Egypt, of Joseph and his family have only been included in the Gospel text to fulfill to the letter the prophecy from Hosea.[39]

He got up and took the child and his mother, and entered into the land of Israel. (v. 21)

We recap here for clarity although there is not too much to add to what we have already said concerning the family's flight from, and return to, the Land of Israel. We have noted how Matthew shows by using parallel structures that the return from Egypt is the mirror image of the earlier flight to Egypt The overall scheme of this section is this:

> v. 13 — the angel instructs Joseph to leave for Egypt;
>
> v. 14 — Joseph complies.
>
> v. 15 — mentions how long Joseph stayed in Egypt and gives us the fulfillment prophecy.
>
> vv. 19 and 20 — the angel instructs Joseph to return to the Land of Israel;
>
> v. 21 — Joseph complies.

The language of verses 13 and 14, which seems to be taken from some presynoptic version and interpolated into Matthew's narrative, is artfully and purposefully mirrored in verses 19–21. I accept that these verses could have been written by Matthew, whose structural sense of narrative completed his source's story using its terms. Thus a sense of structural unity compensates for the awkward interpolation from verse 12 to verse 16. The net effect is of a tightly structured narrative with an awkward summary of events in mid-story but nicely smoothed over at the end. The history of the text is murky and difficult to unravel. We can only wonder why Matthew, who is so careful in his storytelling to build his plots along straight lines, allowed his narrative to veer off course in midstream before steering it back.

But having heard that Archilaos ruled Judea in the place of his father Herod, he was afraid to go there; being warned in a dream he departed to the district of Galilee (v. 22)

When Herod died in 4 B.C.E. his kingdom was divided among three of his sons. Herod Archelaus, the principal heir, was given Judea along with Jerusalem to rule (as well as other territories), but he was not given the title "king" but rather "ethnarch" — ruler of the people. He governed poorly and came to be hated by all in Judea, so that the Romans were forced to replace him with a procurator in 6 C.E.

It is not clear to me what the verse intends. Did Joseph hear from someone that Herod Archelaus ruled in Judea in place of his father, as the first part of the verse suggests; or did he hear of this in a dream, as perhaps the second part of the verse suggests? At any rate the text says that it was because of the dream that Joseph did not return to Judea with his family but instead went to Galilee and the city of Nazareth.

It seems likely that the phrase "being warned in a dream" was clumsily added by Matthew (or an editor). Had this phrase been part of the original narrative we would almost certainly have been told that it was the *angel* who directed Joseph to Nazareth so that the prophecy spoken of in verse 23 might be fulfilled, as was the case in 2:13–15. As it is now, the narrator provides the prophecy in hindsight. He does not claim that Joseph consciously moved to Nazareth to fulfill a verse — but once they had moved there it was apparent to a clever exegete that the name Nazorean could now be explained as a prophetic honor (see v. 23 below). Perhaps he meant to tell his readers that the names used of Jesus in Jewish (or non-Christian circles) "Jesus Ha-Nozri"[40] fulfills a prophecy. It is impossible to know the date or significance of this title.

And so the text concerning the dream is secondary. Perhaps Matthew inserted it as an afterthought at some time, so that he could include the fulfillment text in verse 23 and imitate the usage of his presynoptic source. The intention might have been to smooth over the rough edges in the interpolation. I agree that except for this brief text concerning the dream, all the rest of verses 22–23 can be taken to be Matthew at his best. The language in these verses mirrors the language of Matt. 4:12–16, as Brown points out.[41] While the insertion of the fulfillment text is part of the Matthean narrative, I cannot help thinking that he might have had a testimony list of such verses at his disposal that he spent liberally.

> *And when he arrived he settled in a city called Nazareth, in order that*
> *what was spoken by the prophets might be fulfilled, "He will be called*
> *a Nazorean." (v. 23)*

There are two texts to look at in relation to this concluding verse of the chapter. First a text from *b. Ber.* 55b, which reads

> And everything that happened to me fulfils the verse that says, "all dreams
> materialize according to oral interpretations." Do you mean to say there is such
> a verse as "all dreams materialize according to oral interpretations"? Certainly —
> as Rabbi Eleazar said: all dreams materialize according to oral interpretations,
> as it is said in Gen. 41:13: "And it came to pass; just as he interpreted for us, so it
> happened."

The point is that, at least according to the Rabbis here, insofar as fulfillment exegesis goes, an authoritative interpretation of a verse from the Scriptures has itself the status of Scripture.

Next we consider Isa. 60:21. In a tradition preserved in Wertheimer's *Batei Midrashot,* this verse is interpreted in a *pesher*-style midrash, a form which was not uncommon in Tannaitic literature.[42] The exact date of the tradition is unknown. *Midr. Alpha Beta* appears to be from the *gaonic* period but contains many rare (and likely ancient) interpretations concerning the Messiah. The tradition reads:

> "The branch [*nezer*] of My planting" (Isa. 60:21) — *this refers to the Messiah.* HE IS CALLED *nezer,* as it is said, "And a rod hath come out from the stock of Jesse, And a branch (netzer) from his roots is fruitful" (Isa. 11:1).

In this tradition "He is called Nezer" is offered as a designation of the Messiah based on an interpretation of Isa. 11:1. Now we have just seen above that a fulfillment text need not be from Scriptures to be cited as a fulfillment proof-text. It is enough that the fulfillment text be an interpretation of a text from Scripture to be cited as Scripture in a fulfillment exegesis.

Matthew, or perhaps his source, writes: "And when he arrived he settled in a city called Nazareth, in order that what was spoken by the prophets might be fulfilled, 'He will be called a Nazorean.'"

This fits the conscious type of fulfillment discussed above in 1:23. What is cited as a verse is in reality the explanation of Isa. 11:1, at least as the Rabbis, reading the verse from Isaiah literally, understood it. "The Messiah is [to be] called Nezer." This is no different from saying "and everything that happened to me fulfilled the verse that says 'all dreams materialize according to oral interpretations,'" which, as we have seen in the tradition from *b. Ber.* 55b above, was how the Rabbis interpreted Gen. 41:13. Matthew's insertion of this text, while somewhat strange, is within the range of Jewish tradition and must have originated within circles that were adept at interpreting Hebrew Scriptures. I suspect Matthew had a source he relied on and did not bother to consider where in the Scriptures it was when he copied it from his source and so cites it as from "the Prophets."

NOTES

[1] I do not buy the argument that "all the nations includes Jews" for Ps. 117:1–2 draws distinction between "all the nations" and "Israel." "Praise the Lord, *all the nations;* laud Him, all the peoples! For His loving-kindness is great *toward us...*" Paul uses this and other verses to show that all the Gentiles are referred to in Scripture. See Rom. 15:7. While Paul sees Jews as primary and the Gentiles as equals, Matthew's use of "all the Gentiles" would make them alone disciples.

[2] Professor Allison objects to my use of "break" since the process was highly complex and seems to have differed from region to region, time to time. However, Matt. 21:42–45 ("Did you never see in the Writings, 'The stone which the builders put on one side, the same has been made the chief stone of the

building: this was the Lord's doing, and it is a wonder in our eyes.' (Ps. 118:22)? For this reason I say to you, *The Kingdom of God will be taken away from you, and will be given to a nation producing the fruits of it.* Any man falling on this stone will be broken, but he on whom it comes down will be crushed to dust") strongly suggests that Matthew knows Jews and Christians have parted ways for him and his readers. See further 12:15–17.

3   See Basser, *Studies in Exegesis,* 61–71.

4   Matt. 15:1, the tradition of the elders, which is the sense of *paradosis ton presbuteron* in Greek. See Baumgarten, "The Pharisaic Paradosis."

5   *B. Šabb.* 116a Rabbi Tarfon: "For even if one pursued me to slay me, or a snake pursued me to bite me, I would enter a heathen Temple [for refuge], but not the houses of these [people], for the latter know (of God] yet deny [Him], whereas the former are ignorant and deny [Him], and of them the Writ saith, and behind the doors and the posts hast thou set up thy memorial." (Isa. 57:8).

6   The prayer recorded in minor tractate *Sop.* 13:12 — "may a foreigner not sit on his [David's] throne" — must have been composed during Herod's reign.

7   See Luz and Selle, *Studies in Matthew,* and Brown, *Birth of the Messiah.*

8   One early story concerning the birth of Abraham is preserved in a number of late works and was also recorded by Eisenstein in his *Otsar Hamidrashim:* "Avaraham Avinu," s. 15. (Also in *Sepher-ha-Yashar* [Wilna, 1870], 11a, and in A. Jellinek, *Beth-ha-Midrash* 2:118, and in *Maaseh Avraham* by Horowitz, *Collection of Small Midrashim,* 1.48.)
    In this story it is said that when Abraham was born a star appeared and the wise men told Nimrod the king that this star meant that someone had been born who would produce a nation that was going to destroy his kingdom. Nimrod then sought to kill Abraham but Abraham's father hid him in a cave for three years.

9   The same sentiment is eloquently expressed by Luz and Selle, *Studies in Matthew,* 33.

10 See Brown, *Birth of the Messiah,* 99–113, for his view of detecting presynoptic materials.

11 Brown, in ibid., 114–21, suggests, in contrast to my views, a conceptual patterning of Jesus on the life of Moses.

12 See Basser, "Pesher Hadavar."

13 Typical of these is Aus, *Matthew 1–2 and the Virginal Conception.*

14 An excellent overview of the positions can be found in Allison, *The New Moses,* and Bourke, "The Literary Genus of Matthew 1–2."

15 Rank, *The Myth of the Birth of the Hero,* 47.

16 Ibid., 9–46.

[17]   I cite Henry N. Hudson, who edited *The Complete Works of William Shakespeare*, 1462–63: "Hamlet is teasing the old fox, and quibbling between a logical and a literary sequence. The lines he quotes are from an old ballad, entitled, *Jephtha, Judge of Israel*."

[18]   The Syriac version of Matthew calls them *magoshei* and reflects the usage of Palestinian Targumim, such as *Targum Pseudo-Jonathan* in Exod. 7:15. In this source Pharaoh casts spells upon the water "like an *amagosha*" — a magician. (Aramaic and Hebrew often adds a prosthetic *aleph* to the beginning of words that have consonant clusters and also especially to foreign words). See Diest, "Appayim (1Sam. 1:5) * Pym?" 205.

[19]   Young's edition, *Life of Moses I* (264). And he was celebrated and renowned above all men for his experience as a diviner (*magos*) and prophet.

[20]   Identical to Jellinek, ed., *Bet ha-Midrash* 2:111.

[21]   As already noted, the Joseph story is also reflected in the opening passages of this text which speak of Pharaoh having had a dream (Gen. 41:1 and 41:7), and this — one story reflected in another — is a common feature in late Hebrew narratives.

[22]   The *Targum Pseudo-Jonathan* and *Pirqe de Rabbi Eliezer* share some traditions found nowhere else.

[23]   In the midrash Miriam has a dream. She tells her father: "In the end you will beget a son who shall deliver Israel from Egypt" (*Mekhilta of Rabbi Yishmael* to Exod. 15:20). This is not unlike the dream of Miriam in L.A.B. (Pseudo-Philo 9:2–10): "I will work a miracle through him and save my people." See further Crossan, "Virgin Mother or Bastard Child?" 45. Crossan considers the tradition history behind these stories.

[24]   See Brown, *Birth of the Messiah*, 113: Matt. 2:13 = Exod. 2:15, Matt. 2:16 = Exod. 1:22, Matt. 2:19 = Exod. 2:23, Matt. 2:19 = Exod. 4:19, Matt. 2:21 = Exod. 4:20).

[25]   Prof. Dale Allison in private communication tells me the passage is generally understood to mean that the family stayed in the Egyptian desert. However, I remain skeptical that there was much demand for carpenters in the desert and if they lived on miracles surely the text would say something about it.

[26]   Also see the references to Num. 24:9 above, in the commentary to chap. 1.

[27]   A similar story is found in *Midrash Zuta Lamentations* (ed. Buber) 1:2, version 2, animal behavior predicts he has been born and his name there is Menahem ben Amiel.

[28]   He was killed in 66 C.E. (Horbury, Davies, and Sturdy, eds., *Early Roman Period*, 506–7).

[29]   1Chron. 4:1–4: The descendants of Judah … 4) … the firstborn of Ephrathah and father of Bethlehem.

30 The same passage also appears in *b. Pesaḥ.* 11b.

31 Bethlehem is a very short distance from Jerusalem. Matthew supposes the magi must have left Herod's kingdom by a route that both avoids Jerusalem and was also, presumably, free of any of his troops. "The other way" is not specified.

32 See my article, "Sharing in the Divine," where I argue that the term "son" here does not signify a genetic relationship. The term is used of those who adhere to God's plan and obey him and share some of his power.

33 The point should not be pushed too far because obviously the verse obliquely "refers" to an event spoken of in the Gospel, and presumed to have happened off stage, as it were.

34 The idea of God going to Egypt is not unknown. Gen. 46:2–4 says: "And God spoke to Israel in a vision at night and said, 'Jacob! Jacob!' 'Here I am,' he replied. 'I am God, the God of your father,' he said. 'Do not be afraid to go down to Egypt, for I will make you a great nation there. *I will go down to Egypt with you, and I will surely bring you back again.*'"

35 The reading is worthy of an Amelia Bedelia, the loveable, literal-minded housekeeper (a children's character created by Peggy and Herman Parish) who has no concept of idiomatic language.

36 See Howard, "The Use of Hosea 11:1 in Matthew 2:15." Also Moises Silva, "The New Testament Use of the Old Testament." Soares-Prabhu, *The Formula Quotations in the Infancy Narrative of Matthew.* Stendahl, *The School of St. Matthew and Its Use of the Old Testament.* Fitzmeyer, "The Use of Explicit Old Testament Quotations in Qumran Literature and in the New Testament."

37 The preceding verses read: "Say to the Israelites, 'If a man dies and leaves no son, turn his inheritance over to his daughter. If he has no daughter, give his inheritance to his brothers. If he has no brothers, give his inheritance to his father's brothers" (Num. 27:8–10).

38 See Brown, *Birth of the Messiah.*

39 Professor Dale Allison was kind enough to write me at length about this point and to send me his careful work (*The New Moses*) on the subject. He points to the similarities of circumstances of birth, evil king, slaughter of infants, flight and return of the deliverer, water (Red Sea, baptism), wilderness temptations, and even perhaps the teaching on a mountain.) The unpublished dissertation of my friend and colleague, Dr. Basil Robert Bater, "The Church in the Wilderness: A Study in Biblical Theology," Union Theological Seminary, New York, 1962, made the case based on the same creative idea of "parallels" that would be fashionable for the next forty years. I could not help but think that if this were the case, why is Jesus nowhere called "prophet" as a serious title (the word in 13:57 seems to be part of a popular saying independent of Jesus)—the signal feature of the personage of Moses. In truth, I wish it were so. I will try to argue that Matthew sees Jesus as originally intended to save the Jews, he himself a Jew of the highest rank in learning and

piety. But things go wrong at the end and then Jesus speaks of replacing his people with another and making disciples of the Gentiles. How nicely it would serve my argument to allow that Matthew's Jesus was a veritable Moses who then abandoned the rebellious Jews! However, too many, perhaps all, of the alleged parallels strike me as far-fetched. Matthew, on his own, has little to say of Moses and what little is there is neither particularly laudatory nor sympathetic to Jesus' own views. In the end, I see little wrong if one is persuaded by his arguments, which I find creative and imaginative but not compelling. While I am sure Paul is adept at building typologies, Matthew's Jesus is adept at relating parable and a master of metaphor. The latter was the trait of the Jewish teacher in the synagogues of the Galilee and the former in the synagogues of the (hellenized) communities of the Diaspora.

40   It could be debated when this epithet became attached to Jesus. No one really knows what it means. If it existed in the time of Matthew, the prophecy nicely explains it. On the other hand it may be pure coincidence. There is suggestive evidence that Christians were termed *noṣrim* by the end of the first century and that Jews prayed for their downfall. Martyn's *History and Theology in the Fourth Gospel,* 4–41, argues this case. Others have objected and I have simply shown (Basser, *Studies in Exegesis,* 61–72) that we will likely never know the wording or date of this prayer for certain.

41   Brown, *Birth of the Messiah,* 107.

42   Wertheimer, *Batei Midrashot,* 2:457. "Pesher" is the name used in the Dead Sea Scrolls to indicate that nouns in a biblical verse are symbols representing Israel's history (and especially that of the community who wrote the *pesharim*) and they are identified with historical people. The verbs now connect the decoded nouns into statements of past, present and future history. Here "branch" is a code word for the Messiah and so is a title given to him. Matt. 2:23 sees the term as meaning literally a resident of Nazareth rather than "branch."

CHAPTER THREE

INTRODUCTION

Chapter 3 introduces us to John the Baptist.[1] The Greek *baptiso*, like the Aramaic *tsabe'a* (Hebrew *tabal*), refers to dipping items into water to cleanse them or into dyes to color them. According to both Matthew and Josephus, John acquired the title "the Baptist" because he was the administrant at the ritual immersions of people in the Jordan River.[2] Matthew maintains that John's purpose in doing this was to make people ready for the coming of the *eschaton*, the Kingdom of God in which only the righteous — those who have repented and have been purified — could participate. This repentance was dependent, or so it seems, on John's administering ritual baptism in the Jordan River.

Throughout their history the Jews have ascribed numerous purposes to the act of immersion, including being part of the preparation of the scribe before writing the divine name in a Torah scroll. But while immersion as a final stage in a process of repentance is fairly commonplace, immersion *for the sake of* repentance — in other words, as a precondition to repentance — has almost never been one of them. "Almost never" is, however, not the same as never.[3] There are several texts which seem to suggest, at least on some psycho-mystical level, that immersion brought one to a state to effectively engage in acts of repentance. For instance, Lev. 16:30 says that on the Day of Atonement: "from all your sins before the Lord you shall cleanse yourselves;" and *m. Yoma* 8:9 preserves the well-known passage from Rabbi Akiva interpreting this text from Leviticus, which contains two "proofs" that God is the agent through whom one's sins are cleansed. This passage is as follows:

Fortunate are you, O Israel, for before whom [does Scripture require] you shall cleanse yourselves? [That is] Who is it that cleanses you? Your Father who is in heaven [his paraphrase of Lev. 16:30].
1. Scripture says so [explicitly], "I shall cast upon you clean waters and you shall be cleansed [From all your uncleanness, and from all your idols, I do cleanse you]" (Ezek. 36:25).
2. Now Scripture says, "*Mikvah* of Israel is the Lord…the fountain of living life, the Lord" (Jer. 17:13). [So we derive the notion] Just as the *mikvah* [waters of immersion] cleanses the impure so does God purify Israel.[4]

In this midrash, the last in *m. Yoma*, Akiva pulls sharply away from the tractate's laws of repentance, with their emphasis on the voluntary and ritual acts by which people cleanse themselves to merit forgiveness, and implies that all this process is in fact initiated and made possible by God: "Who is it that cleanses you?" To illustrate his point, Akiva cites two verses whose subject is not periodic repentance, but rather the final redemption, and he understands that the final redemption, like the redemption from Egypt, is about God's intervention in what otherwise would have been a hopeless situation. The intent of this complex of verses is to say that even periodic repentance is, like the final redemption, dependent upon God. By the selection of the first verse, he compares sin to Ezekiel's topic, the idolatry of the Jews in exile. There may be the implication in Akiva's selection of Ezek. 36:25 that idols are akin to the dead, and therefore the cleansing procedure from them requires waters of purification (something like the sprinkling procedures in Numbers 19). In short, Akiva then suggests little more in citing Ezekiel than the prophet intends to say: God's agency is necessary in cleansing from sin.

But Akiva's choice of the next verse, Jer. 17:13, is daring. Here, the plain sense of the prophecy is not Akiva's sense. The verse begins "[The] *mikvah* of Israel is the Lord." And *mikvah* here comes from *kvh*, hope. *Mikvah* is that which is hoped for, what is longed for even if distant. The first words of the verse declare that God('s salvation) is what Israel hopes for; the next eight words describe the fate of those who abandon that hope; only the final four words of the verse identify God as a "fount of living waters."

But to the rabbinic reader, the word *mikvah* also means an immersion pool (defined in *m. Mikwa'ot*) which effects ritual purification of people and utensils when they are dipped in it. Among other things, immersion in a *mikvah* is the final stage in the purification of those who have been defiled by a corpse: after being sprinkled twice, the person must immerse.

Akiva, using an associative technique, "Just as…so does," transforms the meaning of the words of the verse from Jeremiah to show that God himself becomes the *mikvah* waters.[5] Making noteworthy the use of a rhetorical form, he slides one usage of a word into a completely other and unexpected usage. This folding of God from being the savior to being the utensil of salvation mirrors the transformation of Israel. Israel is in a state of impurity, holding on to hope of salvation. In Akiva's midrash they then slide, almost unwittingly, to a state of purity.[6]

M. Šabb. 9:1 preserves another midrash from Akiva, in which a similar kind of transformation occurs:

> Rabbi Akiva said, "From which biblical verse can we support the notion that an idol conveys ritual impurity to the one who carries it (even without direct touching)? From that Scripture which states, 'You shall cast them [idols] away like a menstruous thing, you shall say to it, Get thee hence' (Isa. 30:22). Just as the menstruating woman imparts uncleanness to the one who carries her so an idol imparts uncleanness to the one who carries it."

Here we have the fascinating transformation of a law governing an impure state of a woman into a law governing idols. The transformation occurs as a result of the reading of certain words of the verse in a particularly literal way. The law which resulted from this text depends upon a slide of rhetoric: the exaggeration of "like a menstruant thing"[7] is now said to be a "menstruant woman." Now Akiva reads the simile (as if it meant an idol is like a menstruant woman in one respect) as a fact. Similes are comparisons that imaginatively blend similar items into a single image, but not in concrete fact. For Akiva the simile creates a new legal insight. A purity law governing one who carries a menstruant woman is made to apply to one who carries an idol. Thus the fact Akiva takes phrases (metaphors or similes) from the intended scriptural context can signal the transformation of a being from one thing into another. The formulation is highly complex. In this midrash Rabbi Akiva speaks of carrying, the act of moving an object from point A to point B, and so the set form used for midrashic transformations ("Just as...so also") subtly mirrors the act of physically conveying an idol from point A to point B. Akiva's style of midrash is bold and daring. He will derive *halakhah* from it.[8]

It appears that Akiva's midrash in *m. Yoma* also gave rise to a later custom. Jews immerse themselves in ritual waters shortly before the onset of the Day of Atonement.[9] However, this midrash does not in any way suggest that the purpose of immersion is for the forgiveness of sins. In a poetic way it suggests only that God is Israel's *baptismal source*, once penitents have come before Him for forgiveness.

As if he were in dialogue with those who claimed that the immersions John administered in the Jordan effected repentance, Josephus asserts that this was not the case.[10] In *Ant.* 18.116–19, he speaks of John at length. He writes that John was a good man who had exhorted the masses to lead righteous lives, to practice justice, and to act in piety toward God. John asked them to join in baptism but he did *not* have them use the rite to gain pardon for their sins. It was to serve as a consecration of the body, implying that the soul had already been thoroughly cleansed by right behavior prior to their immersion. Josephus (18:118–19) goes on to tell how the Tetrarch, Herod, became alarmed by John's sway over the people which he feared could turn into sedition and uprisings. Deciding to strike first, Herod had him put to death.

Josephus' account suggests that he wanted to correct a common misconception about John. He makes it clear that the purpose of the ritual cleansing, which he administered, was to bring the body of those he immersed to the same state of purity as the soul.[11] Probably Josephus had observed how others understood that the purpose of John's baptism was to effect repentance and he wanted to make clear that what John did was in fact normative.[12] Josephus also reports that the Essenes performed frequent ritual cleansings (*War* 2:159–61).

While Matthew's infancy narrative forms a prologue to his gospel; it is with John that the synoptic tradition begins. It is noteworthy that Matthew draws a parallel between Jesus and John. For as he begins his ministry Jesus' first words are almost the same words that John himself first says in the Gospel: "Repent, for the Kingdom of Heaven is near." John is made to be a forerunner and prototype of Jesus.[13] And this volume of my work takes us to John's death in anticipation to that of Jesus'.

In those days John the Baptist came proclaiming in the desert of Judea
(v. 1)

"In those days" replicates the style of Hebrew biblical recitations that report significant historical happenings. The phrase is found in straight narrative, for example, "In those days, when King Ahasuerus sat on the throne of his kingdom, which was in Shushan the capital" (Esther 1:2). It is also found in prophecies concerning the end of time, for example,

> "In those days and at that time," declares the Lord, "search will be made for the iniquity of Israel, but there will be none; and for the sins of Judah, but they will not be found; for I will pardon those whom I leave as a remnant" (Jer. 50:20)

and,

> "I will pour out my Spirit on all people. Your sons and daughters will prophesy, your old men will dream dreams, your young men will see visions. Even on my servants, both men and women, I will pour out my Spirit in those days." (Joel 2:28–29)

Even so, it is not clear what exactly "those days" refers to in Matthew 3. I prefer to read it this way: "In those days when John the Baptist *began to preach*" — so that the time being referred to with the phrase "in those days" is the time of John.

It has been argued that for Matthew John is Jesus' model who had, in fact, baptized him. Jesus, like John, (the argument goes) was an apocalyptic prophet foretelling the overthrow of Rome and the establishment of a new world order under the rule of the righteous.[14] These arguments have strengths and weaknesses. The argument goes that on occasion Matthew does have John and Jesus saying the same, or nearly the same, thing (compare 3:1–3 with 4:17, and 3:7–10 with 23:33). Casting John in the role of Elijah and having him proclaim the end makes him very much like an apocalyptic figure.[15] Moreover, it might be noted that Matthew 3 is patterned after Malachi 4, in which apocalyptic motifs dominate.

> 1 "Surely the day is coming; it will burn like a furnace. All the arrogant and every evildoer [likely Matt. 3:7 sees here Pharisees and Sadducees] will be stubble, and that day that is coming will set them on fire," says the Lord Almighty. "Not a root or a branch will be left to them [comp. Matt. 3:12]. 2 But for you who revere my name, the sun of righteousness will rise with healing in its wings. And you will go out and leap like calves released from the stall. 3 Then you will trample down the wicked; they will be ashes under the soles of your feet on the day when I do these things," says the Lord Almighty. 4 "Remember the law of my servant Moses, the decrees and laws I gave him at Horeb for all Israel. 5 See, I will send you the prophet Elijah before that great and dreadful day of the Lord comes. 6 He will turn the hearts of the fathers to their children, and the hearts of the children to their fathers; or else I will come and strike the land with a curse."

However, the relationship between John and Jesus is ambiguous. In this chapter John recognizes Jesus as his superior (3:11) and would this be likely if Jesus was a devotee of John?16 Perhaps. Second, every faithful Jew believed that the end would surely come and that Elijah would be its herald. The question was when, now or later? Urging repentance, no matter what the motive, is not exceptional. Threatening a change of leadership and authority is exceptional. Concerning this latter point, a text from *y. Ta'an.* 4:5 is instructive. The text reads:

> Rabbi Simeon ben Yohai taught: "Akiva, my teacher, used to interpret *a star,* [Aramaic Kochba] *goes forth from Jacob* (Num. 24:17) as, 'Kozeba [Simeon bar Kozeba was a military leader who fought the Romans 130–135 C.E.] goes forth from Jacob. Rabbi Akiva, when he saw Bar Kozeba, said: 'This is the king Messiah!' Rabbi Yohanan ben Torta said to him: 'Akiva! Grass will grow on your cheeks and still the son of David will not have come!'"[17]

A text from *t. Menah.* 13:23 is also instructive.

> Rabbi Yohanan ben Torta said: "But of the last Temple that in the future is to be rebuilt, *may it be in our lives and in our days,*[18] it is written, 'And it shall come to pass in the last days, that the mountain of the Lord's house shall be established on the top of the mountains, and shall be exalted above the hills; and all nations shall flow to it. And many people shall go and say: Come, and let us go up to the mountain of the Lord, to the house of the God of Jacob; and he will teach us of his ways, and we will etc.'" [Isa. 2:3].

The expectation of the coming of Elijah together with the hope of the advent of the Messiah is reflected in this prayer in minor tractate *Sop.* 9:7:

> May *Elijah the prophet* come speedily to us. May *King Messiah* flourish in our days.

In other Jewish traditions concerning the coming of Elijah it is said that Elijah was to separate the wheat from the chaff, that is, to divide between those who were far or who made themselves far from God, and those who were close or made themselves close to God. But a message of comfort was added at the close of these discussions denying that Elijah would come to divide, and affirming that the opposite was true: Elijah would in fact bring peace and harmony to all.[19]

Some Jewish sources suggest that at least some of those who believed in the imminent arrival of Elijah did not assume that Elijah would be clearly recognizable to all. Someone might claim to be Elijah and merely be a pretender; how was one to tell? The text in *Midrash Zuta* (ed. Buber) to Song of Songs (7:14) asks this question, and Rabbi Yosi suggests tests for any putative Elijah. The tone of the text, though, is difficult to read: does it belittle those who think Elijah is to be tested to make sure that he is in fact Elijah, or is it serious about suggesting that such tests be carried out? I suspect the text is being serious and not sarcastic. According to the text Rabbi Yosi said that when someone comes claiming to be Elijah, he should be asked to revive the dead who are to be specified, because those among whom he has come will be able to recognize these people as having really died. Rabbi Yosi also says that he personally would ask Elijah to enumerate the vows he himself had made. His words suggest that he believed that Elijah's arrival was imminent and he had his own test prepared. That does not mean, however, that there was no one who, having heard about the tests, thought them presumptuous. It will be noted in the next chapter that Matthew has Satan, not some well-meaning innocent, propose tests to see if Jesus is "the Son of God."

On the other hand, some thought that Elijah would come but that his arrival was not imminent. *T. Soṭah* 13:2 cites Ezra 2:63.

> And the Tirshatha [Governor] said to them that they should not eat of the most holy things, *until there will stand up* a priest with *Urim* and with *Thummim*.

According to this text, the expression "until there will stand up" means much the same as "Don't hold your breath," which is what one might hear today.[20] The text also points out that it was common for people to say to one another, "Until the dead rise," or "Until Elijah comes." First Maccabees 4:46 also suggests that the arrival of Elijah or someone in that role was not imminent: "and they stored the stones in a convenient place on the Temple Mount until a prophet should come to tell what to do with them."

In sum, activism and disobedience (not mere critique) characterized the extreme forms of eschatological prophecy. Though it is not at all clear if Matthew wants to cast John in this extremist mold, he will insist that Jesus be cast in this role in chapters 23:43 and 25:13–40.

Saying, "Repent, for the Kingdom of Heaven has come near." (v. 2)

Since John the Baptist is cast as Elijah, whose coming was promised by Malachi (4:5), we note also that Malachi reports that Elijah will turn the hearts of fathers and their children to each other (4:6). "Turning" (Heb. *hashavah*) connotes "bringing to repentance" (Heb. *teshuva*).

The phrase "the Kingdom of Heaven" is uniquely Matthean among the Gospels; the other Gospels say "the Kingdom of God." The following text from *Pesiq. Rab.* (ed. Friedmann), chapter 2, illuminates the phrase. In this text, the Song of Songs is *pesherized.* This means the verse was broken into units in which the nouns were assigned coded values (often with things or people referring to the end-time which is about to come to fruition now). When these things or people are read in place of the nouns that are really in the verse, the substitution code reveals a hidden message. In this case the message is of messianic import. The "Kingdom of Heaven" in this passage refers to that kingdom which is to arrive at the time of the uprooting of all the kingdoms — but especially Rome — which have been persecuting Israel until that time. It is with the arrival of this kingdom that God's sovereignty is to be established.

Pesiq. Rab. (ed. Friedmann), Chap. 15.

Song 2:11 The rains are over and gone.
This symbolizes the [end of Israel's] subjugation to the nations.
Song 2:12 The flowers appear on the earth.
Rabbi Isaac[21] said, "And the Lord showed me four craftsmen" (Zech. 1:20–21). And I said, "What are these coming to do?" He said, "These are the horns that scattered Judah, so that no one raised his head. And these have come to terrify them, to cast down the horns of the nations who lifted up their horns against the land of Judah to scatter it" (Zech. 1:21, in the Hebrew text 2:3–4).
These symbolize the following: Elijah and King Messiah and Melchizedek and the priest Anointed for War.
(2:12 continued) The time of pruning the vines has come.
The time for pruning the not fully formed: the time of [pruning] the wicked when the Lord will break the staff of the wicked [Is. 14:5], the time has come of this wicked kingdom which will be uprooted from the world —
The time of the Kingdom of Heaven *has come, which will make manifest "and the Lord will be King over all the Earth [on that day the Lord will be one and his name one]" (Zechariah 14:9).*

It is obvious, and virtually all commentators note, that Matthew has John and Jesus saying some of the same things as I noted above at the beginning of this chapter. Compare John's words here:

Matt. 3:2: John the Baptist says: *"Repent, for the Kingdom of Heaven has come near."*

Matt. 4:17: From that time Jesus began to proclaim, *"Repent, for the Kingdom of Heaven has come near."*

Again note Matt. 3:7: "When he saw many of the Pharisees and Sadducees come to his immersion, he [John] said to them, '*Offspring of poisonous serpents, who told you to flee from the coming wrath?*'"

In Matt. 23:33: Jesus retorts to the Pharisees "Snakes! *Offspring of poisonous serpents! How will you flee 'the judgment of Gehenna?'*"[22]

We have yet to ascertain to what extent Matthew's Jesus really knew John. Certainly, chapter 3 reports they were connected. On the other hand, chapter 11 is difficult to reconcile with chapter 3. For according to chapter 11, it seems that John never met Jesus and he sent his disciples to observe him.[23] When they told him John wanted to know if Jesus was really the expected Messiah — "Jesus answered and said unto them, 'Go and show John again those things which ye do hear and see'" (11:4).

By saying that the "Kingdom of Heaven has come near" John seems to mean the "the end-time," or the *Qetz*, has come near. Concerning the coming of end-time, we turn again to a text in *Pesiq. Rab.* (ed. Friedmann), chap. 45:

They asked wicked Balaam: "Do they [the children of Israel] have knowledge of the end-time of salvation?" He said, "Certainly!" They asked him, "When is it?" He replied to them, "It is distant 'I see it, but not now; I behold it, but not near[24] [A star shall come forth from Jacob, A scepter shall rise from Israel'" (Num. 24:17)]. So he pushed the end to a distant time with his words. ... Malachi came and said, "For behold, the day is coming, burning like an oven [when all the arrogant and all evildoers will be stubble. The day that is coming shall set them ablaze,' says the Lord of hosts, 'so that it will leave them neither root nor branch'" (Mal. 3:19; some texts: 4:1)].

In Malachi, salvation for the saved means destruction for the wicked, who will be reduced to "stubble" and "set ablaze." This corresponds with Matthew's rhetoric, which portrays the Pharisees and Sadducees as "arrogant" and as "evildoers." The double reference of "arrogant" and "evildoers" in Malachi necessitates a double referent, "Pharisees and Sadducees," for Matthew (v. 7). It is not common for Matthew to group together the "Pharisees and Sadducees"; normally he writes "Scribes and Pharisees."

This is the one spoken about by Isaiah the prophet, "A voice of one crying out in the desert: Prepare the way of the Lord, make his paths straight" [Isa. 40:3].[25] (v. 3)

The text of Isaiah in Matthew here is not that of the MT, which reads, "A voice reads/calls in the wilderness, 'Prepare the way of the Lord; make straight in the desert a highway for our God,'" and which reflects what is found of this text in the documents from Qumran (1QS 8.12–14; 4Q176). The text from Isaiah in Matthew is almost word for word the same as that which is found in the LXX.

Over and above the issue of textual provenance, I have not found any ancient Jewish sources which suggest that Isa. 40:3 text alludes to either the Messiah or to Elijah. Dunn's claim that Qumran materials are pertinent is an exaggeration.[26] He cites a single text (1QS8:12–14) from this community which states that its members shall study Torah in the desert, for only by doing this can the way of the Lord be prepared. However, it might be said that the style of exegesis in this text is the *pesher*-style for which the Qumran community is well known. "Clearing the way" means clarifying the text of the Torah and has no eschatological sense at all. None of the Qumran texts which cite Isa. 40:3 "reading/calling in the desert…etc." read it as in Matthew: "Crying out: in the desert prepare…" Perhaps the community advised its beginning students to begin their study by considering the biblical text as a massive desert that needs to be clarified and paved with exhausting study. Whatever the case, the full members of the community did not study in the desert, and it may be that even the initiate did not physically go there either.

John himself had his clothing made from camel's hair, and a leather belt around his waist, and his food was locusts and wild honey. (v. 4)

The image is that of Elijah in 2Kings 1:8: "'Wearing a hairy garment,' they replied, 'with a leather girdle about his loins.' 'It is Elijah the Tishbite!' he exclaimed." In a famous passage attributed to Phineas ben Yair, which we have already referred to below in n. 11, it is said that the resurrection of the dead is a prerequisite for the advent of Elijah the prophet.[27] *M. Soṭah* has emended this difficult text to say that the resurrections will come through him.[28] All other traditions only know of Elijah coming to announce the Messianic Era. The antiquity of this idea of the arrival of Elijah to announce the Messianic Era should not be doubted (see further chapter 11, n. 2), for the Gospels themselves bear witness to its antiquity.

Then Jerusalem and all of Judea went out to him, and all the region around the Jordan. (v. 5)

According to the sources John attracted large crowds. Matthew claims that before these crowds John proclaimed the end-time. As we have seen, Josephus suggests that Herod Antipas feared John, which means probably that not only was John proclaiming the end of subjugation to sin but also the end of subjugation to earthly kings and so to this hated new Herod, the son of the Wicked Herod (as Jewish sources call him). See the introduction to this chapter for more extensive discussions concerning this verse.

And they were immersed in the Jordan River by him, confessing their sins. (v. 6)

The "sins" referred to here are likely breaches of the laws of the Torah and of its interpreters. What would the Jews have said in order to confess their sins in the brief time it would have taken for them to prepare and to be immersed in the Jordan River. A text from the Tosefta, in which the major confessions alluded to in the Hebrew Bible are reviewed, is helpful here. *T. Yoma* (ed. Lieberman) 2:1 reads:

> How did [the High Priest] confess his sins?
> Please God — I have done *perverse* things and I have done *transgressive* things before you, both my household and me. Please God forgive the *perverse deeds* and *transgressions* and the *sins* for I have been perverse, transgressive and sinful before you, I and my household. It is written in the Torah of Moses your servant, "For on that day he will forgive you to purify you; from all your *sins* before the Lord you shall cleanse yourselves" (Lev. 16:30). And Scripture further says, "And he shall confess upon it [the sacrificial animal] all the *perversities* of the Children of Israel and all their *transgressions* and *all their sins*" (Lev. 16:21). ...For so we find the way of discussion described of those confessed. David said, "We have sinned with our fathers, we have acted perversely and we have acted wickedly (Ps. 106:6). Solomon said, "We have sinned [and] we have been perverse and we have [scribe badly copied *peh* — (*pashanu*) = (transgressed) been [*resh* — *rashanu*] wicked" (1 Kings 8:47). Daniel said, "We have sinned, we have been perverse and we have been wicked" (Dan. 9:5). So what did Moses declare? "He forgives *perversity*, and *transgression* and *sin* He cleanses" (Exod. 34:7).

Lachs discounts the likelihood that these confessions above were of the kind that John would have expected; he cites the more private examples found in *y. Yoma* 8:9 and *Lev. Rab.* 3:3.[29] On the other hand, it could be argued that given the biblical warrant for such confessions as those found in the text from the Tosefta, I think we can safely say that the confessions from this text might well have served the needs of those being baptized, especially if they were used to hearing it on the Day of Atonement in the Temple. Lachs's examples are much shorter: sin is acknowledged and forgiveness requested.

We have said in the introduction to this chapter that Josephus explains that John's baptism was not for the purpose of cleansing the soul from sin and that he likely says this because others, such as the Gospel writer, believed that this was the case.

> *When he saw many of the Pharisees and Sadducees come to his immersion, he said to them, "Offspring of poisonous serpents, who told you to flee from the coming wrath?" (v. 7)*

According to midrashic tradition the wicked prophet Balaam used confession to flee from God's wrath. *Midrash Aggada* (ed. Buber) to Num. 22:34 says the following:

> *And Balaam said to the angel of the Lord, I have sinned* (Num. 22:34). Balaam the Wicked jumped to confess for he knew nothing protected against God's wrath but confession. "And now if I have done evil in your eyes I do repent" (Num. 22:34).

M. 'Abot 4:11 may be the source of the midrashist, for there it says: "repentance (followed by) good works is like a shield against retribution." So repentance is to be followed by good works. This is why Balaam ultimately failed to win divine favor. His repentance was not followed by good deeds. However John does not refuse the Pharisees and Sadducees the opportunity to repent, although by calling them "snakes" he makes clear that he does not trust what *they outwardly profess*. Lachs suggests that as the result of the translator reading *effe* instead of *af'a* in an original Aramaic text,[30] we have the Pharisees and Sadducees being called "snakes" instead of "spotted cat[s]." For Lachs, a spotted cat — "attractive on the outside but inwardly…vicious" — and not a snake, suggests hypocrisy.[31] I know of no uses where hypocrisy is termed "spotted cat." On the other hand, *snake* is a term that is applied to hypocrisy. Proverbs 23:31–32 tells us that some things look enticing but in the end deceive and injure. "Do not look at wine when it is red, when it sparkles in the cup and goes down smoothly. In the end it bites like a serpent and stings like an adder." And these biters and stingers are what the Sadducees and Pharisees turn out to be under their pious veneer. The point is that confession saves one and that even the Pharisees and Sadducees will be saved if they confess sincerely and then follow that confession with good deeds.

Bear fruit worthy of repentance (v. 8)

That is, do good deeds to go along with your repentance. This phrase here may reflect more the MT version of Isa. 40:3, especially the second part of the verse, "make straight *in the desert* [*arava*] a highway for our God," than that of the LXX (and so also that in Matthew) in which the phrase "in the desert" is not found.

There are many rabbinic passages in which "fruit" is used as a metaphor for "good deeds."[32] It appears that one of these passages became attached to the end of a unit now preserved in *Yalkut Shimoni* (Torah, 855) that interprets Ps. 68:5 (literally: "Pave the way for he who is enthroned on the *aravot*").

> Rabbi Pinchas the Priest, the son of Hama, said: *Aravot* [deserts, but likely it was originally the singular *arava* of Is. 40:3], — the Holy one sows upon it [note the

singular here] the *deeds of the righteous* and *they* (the deeds) *bear* [lit: make, as in Matthew] *fruit.*

Since Ps. 68:5 speaks of the "highest heaven," *aravot* (as the Rabbis took it), it is not likely that this verse is the one Rabbi Pinchas was thinking of. It is more likely that an editor by mistake grouped another discussion discussing the desert (*arava* in Isa. 40:3) with the interpretations of Ps. 68:5 because of the similar wording (*arava* and *aravot*).

The question that began the discussions concerned *aravot, heavens.* The Rabbis are asked to establish its meaning in the Psalm. Inexplicably, one answer, late in the discussion, is that "the Holy One takes note of the deeds of the righteous and their deeds are fragrant (*arev*) to Him." It is possible that this text does discuss *aravot*, although it may not. However, the final unit, that of Pinchas the priest above, clearly refers to a desert where the deeds of the righteous are planted and they bear fruit. The image would be more than strange if his discussion concerned fruit growing in God's throne room in the *Aravot* heavens!

It is reasonable to assume that what Rabbi Pinchas is saying is this. "What use is the pathway in the desert that Isaiah mentioned?" I will tell you. "From the seeds of the good deeds of the righteous that God sows in it, a garden of fruits will be produced in it for the enjoyment of all in the time to come." This reading seems to me the upshot of the idea of Rabbi Pinchas. It also suggests to me that originally the Hebrew version of Isa. 40:3 and not that of the LXX lies behind the text cited by Matthew. The expression "bear fruits" may not be as accidental as appears at first glance in this chapter. For we have at least some indication now that Matthew's images of repentance and good deeds can be connected to the idea of making a way in the desert to bear good fruits. In any event, John is telling the Sadducees and Pharisees to change their ways in order to show that their repentance is sincere.

And do not decide to say among yourselves "We have Abraham for a father" for I say to you that God is able to raise up children for Abraham from these stones here. (v. 9)

Lachs thinks that those commentators who see a pun here on the (putatively) original Aramaic words *avanim* (stones) and *banim* (sons) may be right. However he thinks it even more likely that there was a misreading from the Aramaic original: *ebyonim* — "'the poor,' 'the outcasts of society'" — was read as *abanim* — "stones," and so the original meaning of the verse was that these *ebyonim*, these outcasts, who were coming to be baptized by John, could have descendants as worthy as the descendants of Abraham.[33] That is, the Pharisees and Sadducees had no special claim to the patriarch. But is either suggestion sufficient to overcome the Pharisaic and Sadducean claim to special divine dispensation and justify John's severe castigation of Pharisees and Sadducees? Does John mean to point to these social outcasts and say they are base and worthless but God can have them parent righteous children? Furthermore, I do not know why people of poor character would be called *"ebyonim."* *Ebyonim* are the financially poor. Thus on the festival of Purim one gives gifts to the *ebyonim* (Esther 9:22). To my mind, what is intended here is real, inert, lifeless stones[34] (although is true, that for the Rabbis, stones might sometimes symbolize children).[35]

Most commentators to Matthew believe that the Pharisees and Sadducees feel secure because of their belief in the doctrine of "the merits of the fathers" (in Heb. *zekhut avot*). The doctrine claims one's religious debts are covered because of the credit one has gained from one's forefathers and specifically by having Abraham as one's father. This doctrine is spoken of in Jewish sources from all periods. For instance, in *Gen. Rab.* 60:2, Prov. 17:2 is parsed as follows:

> *A servant that dealeth wisely* — refers to Eliezer who bound himself to Abraham; *was likened with a son that brings shame to others* — refers to Isaac whose submission at the Aqeda shamed the faith of idolators;
> *and [likened] to be among brothers [with whom] he will share a part of the inheritance* — refers to Israel. Just as these [descendents] invoked the merit of the fathers, Eliezer likewise invoked it. "And he said: 'O Lord, the God of my master Abraham [send me, I pray Thee, good speed this day], and show kindness unto my master Abraham'" (Gen. 24:12). This is the absolute beginning point of the process [of such merit].

Apparently the Rabbis did not feel that the claim to such credit was theirs alone. However, I do not think that this doctrine is the reference point for Matt. 3:9. The commentators who say that John is referring to this doctrine must resort to clever wordplay that is neither compelling nor contextually likely in order for the reference to stones to fit it.

Rather behind John's words is the belief that stems from God's promise to "establish" a covenant with Abraham and with Abraham's descendants after him (Gen. 17:7). By virtue of being Jews, Abraham's descendants are promised that redemption (here, in this world) will come to them and through them. Consider a text from *b. Yebam.* 64a, in which the Rabbis discuss what would happen to the promise to keep this covenant with Abraham's descendants if his descendants were somehow to be wiped out.

"To be a God to you and to your children after you" (Gen 17:17). Thus when Abraham has "children after you" God's protection extends to them.

When there are no longer "your children after you," to whom should it extend? To trees and *stones*?[36]

In this text the Rabbis ask rhetorically: "If there are no Jews, who inherits God's protection as promised in the covenant? Would the promise go to "trees and *stones*?" So God will not abandon us. Now let us return to John's words in this verse: "I say to you, yes, exactly — God is able to raise up children for Abraham from these stones here even if there are no Jews left." That is, John states here precisely what the Rabbis state in the text above — *stones*. Now it may be the case that Matthew did not know of this midrash when he put these words into the mouth of John, but he does at least anticipate such a retort from the Pharisees. That is why he says: Do not decide to say "We are Abraham's children after him." Do not think that God assures your existence so the promise to Abraham can be kept. He adds with a rhetorical flourish, stones will do just fine to bear the promise.

The reference to "these stones" parallels a midrashic usage, in which "this" and "these" can mean "any old."[37] Matthew's use of that expression here suggests to me both that the usage is quite ancient and that his source for the whole verse is, as I have just argued, based on a Hebrew tradition and not on a pun. His facetious retort is purely rhetorical and does not deserve serious theological analysis.

> *The axe is already set against the root of the trees; every tree failing to bear good fruit is cut down and thrown into the fire.* (v. 10)

Here the emphasis is on the urgency of the situation. Those not doing good deeds are soon to be destroyed. Of them nothing will remain; they shall be thrown into the fire.[38] The metaphor continues from 3:8 above: "Bear fruit worthy of repentance."

In *Sipre Deut.* 308 this same kind of rhetoric is also found:

> *A perverse and twisted generation* (Deut. 32:5) — Moses said to Israel, "You are crooked, you are twisted and you are going nowhere but into the fire."

> *I immerse you in water for repentance, but the one coming after me is stronger than I, whose shoes I am not worthy to carry. He will immerse you in the holy spirit and in fire.* (v. 11)

When in the time of Moses the Israelites captured the utensils made of various metals from the Midianites in their war against them, they were then, according to the command, instructed by Eleazar to purify them.

Num. 31:23 makes clear that fire was considered the superior cleansing agent over water; water was to be used only for the utensils that could not bear the heat of fire.

> Then Eleazar the priest said to the men of war who had gone to battle, "This is the statute of the law which the Lord has commanded Moses: only the gold and the silver, the bronze, the iron, the tin and the lead, *everything that can stand the fire, you shall pass through the fire, and it shall be clean, providing it be purified with the "waters that eradicate pollution." But whatever cannot stand the fire you shall (just) pass through the waters.* (vv. 21–23)

A midrashic text from *b. Sanh.* 39a understands that "pass through" means "immersion" (Aramaic: *tabil*). The text reads:

> A *min* (Jewish-Christian perhaps) taunted Rabbi Abahu:
> When God buried Moses, into what was he immersed? For should you think, in water, does not Scripture write, "Who has measured the waters in the hollow of his hand" (Isa. 40:12)?" So he told him — he was immersed in fire, like it is written, "for behold the Lord comes in fire" (Isa. 66:15). [The *min*] replied, "Is immersion effective in fire?" He said, "Certainly, the preferred immersion is in fire, as it is written, *But whatever cannot stand the fire you shall (just) pass through the waters* (Num. 31:23).[39]

A dead body is prepared for burial by immersion or by something equivalent to immersion (pouring specially prepared water over it). The point here is that God purified Moses' body by immersing it in fire. Indeed we hear that God is fire (Deut. 4:24) and so it may be that John's words here are to be understood in this way: "He will immerse you in fire; namely, the Holy Spirit."

On the other hand a text from *y. Sukkah* 5:5 equates the Holy Spirit with water: specifically, with the ritual waters drawn at the time of the Water Celebration in the Temple during the festival of Sukkot.[40] The text reads:

> Rabbi Yehoshua ben Levi asked: Why is its name called "place of drawing water"? For from there they draw the Holy Spirit, as it says "And you shall draw water in happiness from the sources of salvation (*yeshua*)"[41] (Isa. 12:3).

The text states that somehow in the ritual drawing of water the Holy Spirit is drawn down (likely from Heaven, the source of salvation) upon those who are drawing the water. The Holy Spirit, fire, and water are prominent images in both the Jewish mystical and apocalyptic texts. I do not know what the full meaning of these baptismal rites in Matthew are; what is apparent, however, is that in some mysterious way they are the ultimate agents for cleansing and admission into God's salvation.

The same tradition is also found in *Midrash Tannaim* (ed. Hoffman) to Deut. 16:14 and *Midr. Ruth Rab.* 4:9. The rabbinic passages that speak of drawing the Holy Spirit (likely down from heaven, the source of salvation) see a water-drawing ritual from mysterious sources as enabling the mystical descent of the Holy Spirit upon the drawers. Holy Spirit and fire are images of the divine that fill Jewish mystical texts, apocalyptic and Merkavah writings. They are now said to be the agents of purification to be used by Jesus.

"Whose shoes I am not worthy to carry" is understood by many commentators to mean that John is not worthy even to be a slave of Jesus Yet it may be better to think that what John is actually saying here is that he is not fit to be the coming one's *disciple*. The relevant rabbinic passages are cited by the commentators, among which is *Mekhilta of Rabbi Yishmael* to Exod. 21:2. In this text the Rabbis state that a Hebrew slave must not put shoes on his master or carry his things before him when going to the bathhouse, though one's son or disciple may do these things.

Again the effect is purely rhetorical: to show the greatness of the one to come. The verse, and the one following it, is meant to introduce Jesus onto the scene.

> *His winnowing-shovel is in his hand, and he will clean out his threshing-floor and gather his grain into the barn, but the chaff he will burn with an unquenchable fire. (v. 12)*

This verse pretty much restates what is said in 3:10. It seems out of place here or at best parenthetical. It is also a paraphrase of Mal. 3:19 (4:1).

> *Then Jesus came to the Jordan to John from the Galilee to be immersed by him. (v. 13)*

It seems, like others before him, Jesus feels the need to confess his sins and repent and so he comes to John to be baptized. To avoid embarrassing implications, then, Matthew must interrupt his source here. Almost certainly his source had verse 16 follow directly upon verse 13 (both Mark and Luke lack the brief dialogue between Jesus and John in vv. 14 and 15), so that it would have read:

> I immerse you with water for repentance, but the one coming after me is stronger than I, whose shoes I am not worthy to carry. He will immerse you in the Holy Spirit and in fire.

Then Jesus came to the Jordan to John from the Galilee to be immersed by him.

When Jesus was immersed, as soon as he rose from the water, look, the heavens were opened, and he saw the spirit of God descending like **a dove** and coming to him. (vv. 11, 13, 16)

The narrative flows better without the interruption because when Jesus first comes to John, John does not know who he is. When he has finished administering the baptism, at which point the heavens open and the voice from the heavens calls out to identify him, we still do not know if John realizes who Jesus is. The irony here is that although John has spoken of Jesus and of what he will come to do once he comes (3:11), he may have no understanding that his words are actually prophetic for the immediate moment.

Verse 14 suggests that John is fully aware of whom Jesus is but it seems that the verse breaks the flow and is likely an interpolation into the scene.[42] Matthew is forced to insert his own dialogue here to avoid what he sees as a problem; the very same John who has just spoken of his unworthiness before Jesus is now the administrant at the baptism by which he, Jesus, apparently shall be saved.

> *John stopped him saying, "I should be immersed by you, and you come to me?" (v. 14)*

This verse seems to intimate that John knows full well that Jesus is the one he awaits. This verse does not sit that well with 11:4 when John sends the question to Jesus asking if he is the Messiah.

> *Jesus answered him, "Permit it now, for so it is fitting that we fulfill all righteousness." Then he permitted it. (v. 15)*

It has to be this way, explains Matthew through Jesus' answer, to fulfill what God has ordained for all who would be saved — even if for Jesus, baptism is unnecessary.

> *When Jesus was immersed, as soon as he rose from the water, look, the heavens were opened, and he saw the Spirit of God descending like a dove and coming to him. (v. 16)*

See my commentary to 3:17 below for the connection between John's immersion of Jesus and the descent of the Holy Spirit. I also discuss the Targum to Isa. 42:1 — "This is my servant the Messiah, I draw him close, my chosen with whom my *memra* is very pleased — I set my Holy Spirit upon him" — and other pertinent materials bearing on the synoptic tradition there.

With this verse we enter the world of the earliest Jewish mystical tradition. The baptism of Jesus brings about a mysterious change in the universe as, upon its completion, the heavens open. Ezekiel's visions of the Merkabah throne lie behind Matt. 3:15:

> Now it came to pass in the thirtieth year, in the fourth month, in the fifth day of the month, as I was among the captives by the river of Chebar, that the heavens were opened, and I saw visions of God. (Ezek. 1:1)

However, despite the fact that a whole tradition of Jewish mysticism derives from Ezekiel's vision, the sources say explicitly that this vision was not the most complete in Jewish history. A tradition preserved in the *Mekhilta of Rabbi Shimon bar Yohai* to Exod. 15:2 states that the Israelites saw God, and not just a vision of Him as Ezekiel did, at the parting of the waters of the Sea of Reeds. The tradition reads:

> [The Israelites sang,] "This is my God, and I will worship him" (Exod. 15:2). Rabbi Eleazar said, "How do we know that the lowest maidservant saw upon the splitting seas more than [Hosea] and Ezekiel saw? Hosea reported, 'And through the hand of the prophets I can be imagined' (Hos. 12:11), and Ezekiel reported that, 'The heavens opened and I saw visions of God' (Ezek. 1:1). Everyone recognized Him and they all said, 'This is my God!'" (Exod. 15:2)

"*This is my God*" (Exod. 15:2) implies the heavens parted and they could actually point to him. In the text from Matthew, the reverse happens; here the voice of the Spirit says "*This is my son!*" For this text the presynoptic document conflates traditions from Ezek. 1:1, Exod. 15:2, and Isa. 42:1 to arrive at the present scenario.

In *b. Ḥag.* 15a a text interprets what it meant for the Spirit of God to "hover" over the waters.

> And the *Spirit of God* hovered over the face of the waters. (Gen 1:2)
> Like a dove hovering over her offspring, barely touching them.

Here we have the term "Spirit of God" barely touching the water. Jesus has the vision of the descent of the Holy Spirit as a direct result of his immersion. There seems to be an echo of the creation moment here; if so, it is the moment before the dark and formless world is transformed by the creation of light (Gen. 1:3). A second allusion to creation — this time to the creation of light — will come much later, in the Transfiguzration episode (Matt. 17:1–9), when the heavenly voice repeats what it has said here: "My son…"

> *And look, a voice from the heavens, saying "This is my beloved son, in whom I am well-pleased." (v. 17)*

Virtually all the modern commentators see this "voice from the heavens" as the Hebrew "*bat kol* from the heavens" (*b. Soṭah* 48:2).[43] But perhaps Dan. 4:28 is more relevant:

> The words were still on his lips when *a voice came from heaven*.[44] "This is what is decreed for you, King Nebuchadnezzar: Your royal authority has been taken from you."

Not only is the form of Daniel's phrase closer to Matthew's, but the similarity in content would also suggest a deliberate echo. In Daniel, an immediate regime change is prophesied by the "voice from heaven." and Matthew, as I have shown above, casts Jesus in the role of one who announces not only a time for repentance, but a present change of leadership and authority.

"This is my beloved son, in whom I am well-pleased." The synoptic tradition here borrows from Isa. 42:1: "Here is my servant, whom I uphold, my chosen one in whom I delight; I will put my Spirit on him and he will bring justice to the nations." The Targumic tradition of the same text identifies the servant as "messiah": "This is my servant[45] the Messiah, I draw him close, my chosen with whom my *memra* is very pleased. I set my Holy Spirit upon him; he shall reveal laws to the nations." The term *memra*, which in Aramaic almost always translates as "Word," that is, "the word of God," is a euphemism, used so that God may not be described in any way that is too anthropomorphic. In Hebrew "my chosen" — *bahir* — can be translated as "my beloved," and so *memra* is used here so that it may not be said that God feels emotional love. To be "chosen" can mean to be "loved."

Jesus, in this straightforward scene, is described as the Son of God. "*Ben*," literally "son" in Hebrew ("*bar*" in Aramaic), is the term used to indicate that the one being called this both shares some attributes of a greater entity and also embodies its essence. It is probable that Matthew intends his readers to understand that God's declaration that Jesus is "my son" here is to mean that Jesus shared in God's attributes, but what exactly does that declaration mean? Has Jesus received a mark of special, but not necessarily, unprecedented, divine favor? Or is the reader to understand that this announcement means that Jesus is uniquely fitted for a particular preordained role?

In the synoptic Gospels God calls Jesus "my son"[46] twice: at his baptism (Matt. 3:17, Mark 11:1, and Luke 3:22) and again at the Transfiguration (Matt. 17:1–3, 5, 9; Mark 9:7; Luke 9:35), at which Jesus is seen talking with Moses and Elijah. Now there is a source that talks about what it means to share in the divine glory, and that source mentions Moses and Elijah as examples of those who did so. According to *Tanh. Exod.* (*parashat Va'era*) 8, sharing in God's divine glory means sharing either in one or all three of God's name,[47] God's power,[48] or God's garments.[49] The midrash claims that

> Moses shared God's name, Elijah shared God's power, and the Messiah shared God's glory (crown of gold).

It is apparent, then, that Matthew's received source for the Transfiguration episode assumed that its readers were familiar with this midrashic image. Jesus is portrayed as talking with Moses and Elijah to indicate that he is the third of the three who share the divine glory, namely, the Messiah.

At the Transfiguration Jesus' clothes became dazzlingly white, an indication that he was sharing God's garment of glory as the midrash to Ps. 43:3 points out. The hidden light of Creation is about to dawn at the Transfiguration. We have already drawn attention to the fact that the voice that called "my son" at the Baptism confirms the title at the Transfiguration. It is of note that Moses, Elijah, and the Messiah find their way into *Midrash Shohar Tov* to Ps. 43:3 "Send me your light and your truth; they will lead me."[50] This midrash refers to Isa. 42:1 (discussed above), but also to Mal. 3:23 — "I will send you Elijah the prophet" — and Ps. 105:26: "He sent Moses his servant, and Aaron whom he had chosen. ..." The synoptics, then, by juxtaposing John the Baptist (Elijah) and the heavenly voice which identifies Jesus (Messiah) through the use of Isa. 42:1, seem to have woven their text from the numerous threads of the midrash to Ps. 43:3.[51]

NOTES

[1] John was called *matsba'ana*, "dyer" or "baptist," in a medieval Jesus story that has ancient roots,. See Boyarin, "A Revised Version of the Translation of a Toledot Yeshu Fragment," 250.

[2] Daube, *The New Testament and Rabbinic Judaism,* 111–12, would have us believe that the ritual of baptism was derived from the ritual immersion required by the Rabbis for proselyte conversion.

3 The Pharisees also immersed themselves frequently. In *t. Yad.* 2:20 there is a fascinating debate between the Pharisees and the *Tovlei Shacharit* (Morning Bathers). "The *tovlei shacharit* protest against you, O Pharisees, for you mention the divine name in the morning without immersion." The Pharisees said, "We protest against you, O Morning Bathers, for you mention the divine name from an impure body." Eusebius (*Hist. eccl.* 22:7) cites the memoir of Hegesippus (end of first century) concerning Jewish sects. According to him two groups that were noted for immersion were the Hemerobaptists and Masbothaeans. The former sounds like our *Tovlei Shacharit*.

4 A *mikvah* is a special immersion pool. Many ancient *mikva'ot* have been located in the Land of Israel.

5 In sum, as I said, "*mikvah*" can mean two separate things for a rabbinic reader. An immersion pool subject to many qualifications (laid out in *m Mikwa'ot*) to effect purifications of people and utensils when dipped in it. Also it is simply the word for what is hoped for, what is longed for even if distant — it refers to salvation. The sense is God is the savior of Israel.

6 Or in Matthean language (3:11), "he will immerse you in the Holy Spirit."

7 This is an expression to refer to items that are "untouchable."

8 Ovadiah from Bartenura, in his commentary to *m. Šabb.* 9:1 does not consider this midrash as a serious exegesis. Rather it is designed as *asmakhta* in poetic support of a law designed to distance Jews from idolatry. *Asmakhta* is a very widespread mechanism in Talmudic Law whereby the Rabbis enact laws to safeguard the purity of the people by winking at a biblical verse. Jesus' use of Scripture in his rebuff of Satan in chapter 4 fits this category. Undoubtedly, this idea of God cleansing Israel is equally poetic and not to be seen as unassailable exegesis.

9 The High Priest would also immerse himself on the Day of Atonement. *M. Yoma* 3:3 states: "Five immersions and ten washings of hands and feet were performed by the High Priest on the very day of Atonement." His *mikva'ot* are mentioned in *m. Mid.* 1:4 and 5:3.

10 But the texts that suggest a mystical aspect to immersion nonetheless cannot be used to infer that immersion *for the sake of repentance* was normative in Jewish tradition. See further Swartz, "Like the Ministering Angels."

11 Some teachers saw godliness as something one acquired by stages. Individuals moved through these stages in which the body and soul became more and more refined. The purified state of the soul required a more purified body to hold it. Preserved in several places in rabbinic literature are references to the teaching of Phineas ben Yair. In Talmud *y. Šabb* 1:3, in a legal passage discussing purity issues, we are told that this discussion inspired the rabbi to say that "carefulness is a requisite for cleanliness, which is requisite for body purity, which is requisite for humility, which is requisite for fear of sin, which is requisite for the *holy spirit*,

which is requisite for piety, which is requisite for the resurrection of the dead which is requisite for Elijah (the version at the end of *m. Soṭah* revises the text here slightly so that it says: "which is brought about by Elijah" [adding a single letter in the Hebrew text from *"meviah l'ydai"* to *"meviah al y'dei"*])." Those seeking to be more godly advanced from the lower stages of disciplined repentance for sins against God and fellow person, to the rigorous piety required for eternal life.

12   Josephus himself became a follower of a "Baptist type" named Bannus for three years. This teacher lived in the wilderness and frequently immersed himself in cold water to maintain a high level of purity (*Life* 10–12, in Loeb).

13   Matt. 4:17: "From that time Jesus began to preach, saying, 'Repent, for the Kingdom of Heaven is at hand'" is not an exact parallel to Matt. 3:1–3. While John speaks of the "end" Jesus speaks of the Kingdom of Heaven. In Matthew, the phrase "Kingdom of Heaven" is primarily used by Jesus.

14   Josephus, *Ant.* 18:116–18, could be read that way when he talks about why John was executed (see the introduction to this chapter). Also see Dale Allison's essay in Allison, Borg, Crossan, and Patterson, *The Apocalyptic Jesus,* 18, 24.

15   Matt. 11:14: "If you are willing to accept it, this is Elijah who was to come."

16   In chap. 11, it seems the two were not closely acquainted as John, having heard of Jesus, wonders if he is indeed the Messiah.

17   Identifying the protagonists in current history who will fulfill ancient prophecy has ancient roots. Even God engages in the identifications. Consider Ezek. 38:17–19:

> Thus says the Lord God, "Are you the one of whom I spoke in former days through my servants the prophets of Israel, who prophesied in those days for many years that I would bring you against them? It will come about on that day, when Gog comes against the land of Israel, declares the Lord God, that my fury will mount up in my anger. In my zeal and in my blazing wrath I declare that on that day there will surely be a great earthquake in the land of Israel."

18   I suspect that the words I have put in italics were added by a copyist or teacher, for they stand in tension both with the rest of the text, and with the perspective of the alleged speaker — Rabbi Yohanan ben Torta — in the unit just cited. If I am right, the fact that the bolded phrase is here at all is a clear indication of how strong the belief in the imminent arrival of the Messiah and the reconstruction of the Temple was in the anonymous copyist's day.

19   See *t. 'Ed.* 3:4 and *m. 'Ed.* 8:7. Dale Allison pointed out to me that Matt. 17:11 has adopted the same position and the next verse notes this expectation remains unfulfilled.

20   Dale Allison astutely points out Matt. 5:18 as echoing this idea. But I remain unconvinced Matt. 5:18 is really thinking about a new heaven–new earth

Messianic Age theology (originating from a new interpretation of Matt. 5:17 (heaven and earth passing away).

21   In *Song Rab.* 2:29 the fuller citation is given: Rabbi Berekhiah in the name of Rabbi Isaac. And in *b. Sukkah* 52b this was said by Rabbi Hana bar Bizna in the name of Rabbi Simeon Hasida.

22   *Gehenna* is equivalent to divine wrath in some Jewish texts. *B. 'Abod. Zar.* 18b claims that one who scoffs will fall into *Gehenna* — the proof-text is Prov. 21:24. An arrogant and haughty man — "Scoffer" is his name; he will go off into the *Wrath of the Arrogant.*

23   Dale Allison suggests John in chapter 11 was simply wondering if Jesus was "in the running" for the office of Messiah and so removes the tension between the two chapters. However, in 3:14 John acknowledges that he is unfit to baptize Jesus for Jesus is the superior one. Whatever one might say, there remains a degree of tension between the two chapters.

24   When Balaam says in this midrash that the end is "distant," he makes it distant; but when Malachi says the end is near, he makes it near.

25   LXX Isa. 40:3, cf. Mark 1:3 and Luke 3:4, "A voice of one crying out in the desert, 'Prepare the ways of the Lord; make straight the paths of our God.'"

26   See Dunn, "John the Baptist's Use of Scripture," 45.

27   See *Midrash Tannaim* (ed. Hoffman) to Deut. 23:15; also *y. Šabb* 1:3 and *y. Šeqal.* 3:3; also *Midrash Prov.* (ed. Buber) 15:31; also *Song Rab.* 1:9; also *m. Soṭah* 9:15.

28   See my text critical comments to *m. Soṭah* 9:17 in the introduction to this chapter, n. 12.

29   Lachs, *Rabbinic Commentary on the New Testament,* 37–38.

30   The technique of suggesting a Semitic original for Matthew's sources is known as retroversion and is used to solve difficulties by positing mistranslations in the Gospel text.

31   Lachs, *Rabbinic Commentary on the New Testament,* 42. See also his "Studies in the Semitic Background to the Gospel of Matthew."

32   *Gen. Rab.* 30:6; *Lev. Rab. Emor.* 27.1; *Tanḥ. Emor* 7 and 5; *Midrash Aggada* (ed. Buber) (*Vayikra*) 25.27.

33   Lachs, *Rabbinic Commentary on the New Testament,* 42. See also his "John the Baptist and His Audience."

34   "Raise up from these stones." The term "raise up" has the sense "to establish, set up (replace)." *Tanḥ.* (ed. Buber), Num. (Naso) 18: God will raise up from you children who will be scholars, priests and prophets. *B. B. Qam.* 20b: one who loses a boat, he sets up (replaces) for him another boat.

35   For the Rabbis the stones that Jacob selected as his pillow represented the future progeny of the children of Israel that would be raised up (*he'emidan*) (*Gen. Rab.* 68:11). But these stones are not the physical source material of children, they are only symbolic of the future.

36   A common expression in rabbinic literature for things of little or no value (e.g., b. *Tem.* 17a).

37   Midrashic usage indeed suggests John means: "from any old stones." See my review of D. Rottzoll's, *Rabbinischer Kommentar zum Buch Genesis,* where I fault him for not knowing this feature of midrashic usage.

38   Malachi, who, as we have pointed out, is the source for the promise of the return of Elijah before the day of the coming of the Lord, tells us in 3:19 (4:1).

> Behold, the day is coming, blazing like an oven, when all the arrogant and all evildoers will be stubble, And the day that is coming will set them on fire, leaving them neither root nor branch, says the Lord of hosts.

39   Lachs, *Rabbinic Commentary on the New Testament,* 45 n. 4, supplies some pertinent bibliography for the analysis of this passage.

40   The same tradition is also found in *Midrash Tannaim* (ed. Hoffman) to Deut. 16:14, and *Ruth Rab.* 4:9.

41   Also the very name of "Jesus" in Hebrew.

42   Dale Allison, in his reading of my work, phrases the solution as follows: The Baptist's words are from Q, the baptism itself from Mark, and the seam between them is Matthean redaction (Q plus Matthew's bridge plus Mark).

43   For example see Lachs, *Rabbinic Commentary on the New Testament,* 47 n. 6.

44   *Bat kol* (an audible voice from heaven to comment on an earthly situation) refers to a voice that replaces "prophecy" and is somewhat removed from the godhead. *Kol min ha- shamayim* (voice from the heavens) seems to be a divine voice of a higher order of authority.

45   See *b. B. Bat.* 127b to the effect that "my son" and "my servant" could be interchanged in Hebrew and Aramaic popular usages.

46   At the Transfiguration Matthew and Mark have "my beloved son," while Luke has "my son, my chosen one." At the Baptism all agree on the wording, "my beloved son."

47   See Exod. 7:1, in which God says to Moses, "I have made you as Elohim to Pharaoh [a divine name and even the generic word for God]."

48   See 1Kings 17:17ff., in which Elijah revives the son of the widow of Zaraphath.

49   According to the midrash from *Tanḥ. Exod. Vaʾera* 8, Ps. 21:4 means that David has realized that God will clothe the Messiah with his own garments of glory. The midrash quotes Ps. 21:4: "You have set on his head a crown of fine gold."

50   The midrash refers to Ps. 105:26 and remarks that just as Moses and Aaron brought redemption from Egypt, now another pair — light (Elijah) and truth (the Messiah) — will bring the final redemption.

51   For an analysis of the passages in the Gospels in relationship to the midrashim see my two articles in *Bible Review*: "Sharing in the Divine," and "The Jewish Roots of the Transfiguration." Dale Allison wonders why I do not mention Ps. 2:7, the enthronement scene: "You are my son; today I am your father." The answer is that where we have a clear reference in the Gospels to a verse in Isaiah, what is to be gained by adducing more verses? I have already said in my introduction to chapter 1 that I do not see much purpose in piling up verses or more rabbinic references than are necessary to make the point. That others do so for the sake of "thoroughness" I find wearying but that is a matter of personal preference. .

CHAPTER FOUR

INTRODUCTION

To believe that 4:1 begins a new unit, separate from what came before, would be unwise. For 3:16 through to 4:11 forms a distinct unit and should be read as such. We might call this unit "The Initiation of the Messiah."

From 3:7 to 3:12 the Gospel text through John gives warning to those who, whatever they might think of themselves, are unworthy in God's sight. John says that their destruction is imminent. The text slowly turns its focus away from John and from those who have come to him for baptism toward the one who is to come after John, whose arrival is the reason John gives such warning. For the one coming after him — and who is obviously Jesus — is the one who, according to John, will bring about their destruction (3:12).

Once John begins to speak of the coming of Jesus, the reader's expectation is that he will soon appear, and promptly he does. He, too, comes to John to be baptized by him. Then, once he has been baptized, the Spirit of God descends upon him, and by the heavenly voice Jesus is proclaimed Son of God. But as I say, this scene of the proclamation must be joined to the later scene of the Transfiguration, in which, by resisting the Accuser, Jesus is confirmed as the savior. It is a mistake to separate these two scenes for they are both based on the same midrashic understanding: that Moses, Elijah, and the Messiah are said to be participants in the divine realm.

And so Jesus is led away from the Jordan and into the further wilderness, where he is to face the Accuser alone.[1] The Accuser tries to tempt Jesus with three different tests; these tests have been ordered for him by the Holy Spirit, who is the one who leads Jesus to the Accuser in the first place.[2]

Most theologians and biblical scholars have understood this scene to be one of combat or confrontation with evil,[3] in which in the end Jesus defeats the very embodiment of evil, Satan. But this understanding is difficult to maintain, for Jesus does not enter into any real contest with Satan. In fact he refuses to engage with him and in the end simply sends him away. Dismissing Satan's arguments and avoiding contact with him are stock themes in Jewish lore. Perhaps the worst that can be said of Satan in these tests is that he tries to challenge Jesus' title as "the Son of God." But yet it is precisely the Satan's job to test resolve (for more on these themes, see my commentary to Matt. 4:1 and 4:2).

The details of the tests are as follows. After Jesus has completed his forty-day fast,[4] Satan comes to him to demonstrate what it means to be truly the Son of God by proposing, first, that he turn stones into bread. Doing this would be of immediate practical use to Jesus, in that he would then be able to eat; it would also be verification of his power. In Jewish tradition, as I say, the one who is called Son of God is that one who shares God's powers. The aggadic examples of such figures are Moses and Elijah.[5] The story which best illuminates the Gospel passages here is that preserved in *Midrash Prov.* (ed. Buber) 1:1. The test seems practical. We noted an *aggada* in the last chapter which shows that he who is worthy of the title "Son of God," is the one who has demonstrated that he shares in God's divine glory. Moses has God's name, Elijah can resurrect the dead (*Tanḥ. Exod.* [*Va'era*] 8).[6] However, both had to prove their qualifications publicly to their adversaries — Moses and Aaron to Pharaoh (Exod. 7:10) and Elijah to the priests of Baal (1 Kings 18:1–4).[7] And Elijah at the end of time will have to prove himself by resurrecting the dead or by doing other supernatural feats.

After Jesus refuses to turn the stones into bread, the Satan then proposes that he throw himself down from the highest point of the Temple in order to confirm what Satan understands is said about him in Ps. 91:11–12, that were he to do this he would be caught by holy angels and lifted up before he struck the ground. Most commentaries speculate, and some even discuss aggadic traditions, concerning why Satan removes Jesus to the pinnacle of the Temple before proposing this test. To my mind, the pinnacle of the Temple was the obvious place to bring Jesus for this test since it was believed that it was here that God's holiest angels congregated. The biblical tradition tells us that in a dream Jacob saw angels ascending and descending on a kind of stairway or ladder (Gen. 28:12). In commenting on this text the Rabbis claimed that Jacob dreamt this at the very place where the Temple was eventually built (*Gen. Rab.* to Gen. 28:12).[8] Given this fact, what better place for a Son of God, falling toward the earth, to be caught by angels than at the place where the angels gathered?

The synoptic tradition includes the temptation scene so that a change of status can be conferred on Jesus from simple teacher to "Son of God." Jesus' credentials have been established for the reader through the infancy narrative and the baptismal scene, at which the Spirit of God descended upon him, and the voice from the heavens declared him to be God's Son. But whether anyone else knew of these credentials of the adult Jesus is an open question. It is probable that no one, not even John, took the dove that descended upon Jesus for the Holy Spirit. It is also not certain if John even heard the voice from the heavens proclaiming that Jesus was God's Son. The text gives no indication of this. Apparently, the divine voice designating Jesus as "My Son" was heard in the heavens and God wanted to have Satan confirm the title. For a hero, the confirmation would be by passing tests of power. Instead Jesus passes the tests by refusing to negotiate with the Devil — he will never let the Devil have any control of what he will do or will not do. At any rate at 4:11 the entire initiation scene concludes as Satan is sent away.

As "the one who is to come after" John, Jesus is now set to begin his career as itinerant preacher and healer, that is, to begin his career as savior of Israel, as the name given to him by the angel before he was born suggests. Even though as savior of Israel he will ultimately fail, nonetheless he does succeed in this role with the Gentiles, though this was not his assigned task.

At 4:12, in which the reader is told that John has been arrested, a new unit begins, which moves us into the body of the story. As required by the plot, John must be removed at this point so that Jesus can occupy center stage. Prior to his arrest, it was John who occupied this central place in the drama of Israel's salvation. It is of interest to note that the Gospels tell us that Jesus only hears of John's arrest through third parties — an indication, perhaps, that he was not one of his constant followers. The synoptic account of the arrest is found in Mark 6:17–29 and Matt. 14:3–12. I quote here from Matthew:

> For Herod himself had sent men who arrested John, bound him, and put him in prison on account of Herodias, his brother Philip's wife, because Herod had married her. For John had been telling Herod, "It is not lawful for you to have your brother's wife." And Herodias had a grudge against him, and wanted to kill him."

According to the Gospel text, John was arrested and subsequently executed because he was not afraid to point out to Herod Antipas that his union with his sister-in-law Herodias was illegal in Torah law, since Herod's brother Philip, to whom she was formerly married, was alive and well and had a daughter.[9] While Herodias' divorce from Philip might have been lawful, her union with her brother-in-law was a grave sin.[10] So Antipas had John killed.

Josephus' account is quite different. In a text from his *Jewish Antiquities*, Josephus' sequence of events has it that Herod ordered John executed before (not after as in the Gospels) his marriage to Herodias because he feared that John's religious doctrines were a challenge to his own authority (*Ant.* 18:118–19). He thought John might try to lead a popular rebellion against him.[11] Whatever the case, the sources agree that John was arrested and executed by Herod.

The removal of John from the scene clears the way for Jesus to step into his shoes and preach his message. Jesus can now gather disciples and begin his own mission. Matthew points out that Jesus attracted large crowds, as John had done, but there is no indication in the synoptic Gospels he ever used baptism as a mechanism for salvation.

Then Jesus was brought to the desert by the Spirit to be tested by the Accuser. (v. 1)

The implication is that God has arranged for Jesus to be tested by the Satan so that the strength of his faith can be measured. This testing of Jesus is also in line with Turner's model concerning the initiation rites of social groups and especially in proving the worth of the hero.[12] Typically Jewish tradition has seen that once God has chosen someone to be his representative that someone is then tested by an agent of God. For instance, a tradition in *b. Šabb.* 89b states that while Moses was up on Mt. Sinai receiving the law, Satan came to test God's people Israel by trying to convince them that Moses' prolonged absence was as a result of his having died on the mountain. In the end the Israelites believed Satan, after which they turned to Aaron and proposed that he create a god for them — the golden calf. In other words, the Israelites failed the test.[13]

Abraham's being called upon to sacrifice his son Isaac (Gen. 22) can also be seen to have been for the sake of measuring the faith both of Abraham and Isaac, and here again Jewish tradition sees that Satan appeared to them both in an effort to prevent the sacrifice from being carried out; that is, to prevent the true faith of Abraham and Isaac from being revealed. The tradition states that both Abraham and Isaac were able to resist Satan. Concerning the appearance of Satan before Isaac, a text from *Yalkut Talmud Torah* (ed. Mann), Gen., section 107, reads:

[From *Midrash Yelamdenu*]: While Abraham and Isaac his son were going to the sacrifice (Isaac not knowing he was to be offered), Satan came and stood to the right of Isaac. He said to him, ill-fated man, son of an ill-fated woman — think of all the fasts your mother endured so you could be born. Now your old man has lost his mind and is going to slaughter you. ... Isaac shuddered since he saw no sacrificial ram and intuited what was about to befall him. His father in response told him: God has "chosen" you. Isaac said — since he has "chosen" me, my soul is His. Still, I worry for my mother "and they walked on together" (Gen. 22:7) — one to slaughter and the other to be slaughtered. And Isaac was thirty-seven years old at the time.

Concerning the appearance of Satan before Abraham several texts — Gen. 22:2 and 22:4 — from *Midrash Aggada* (ed. Buber), read as follows:

Gen. 22:2: While they were walking Satan came to Abraham. He said to him, Have you lost your mind! The son God bestowed upon you at 100 years of age — can you go to slaughter him? It was really me who fooled you and [speaking like God] told you, "take your son, your only one..." (Gen. 22:2). I swear it was God who told me. When Satan saw Abraham was disregarding him he immediately approached Isaac...when he saw he had no effect on Isaac he went to Sarah...when she heard she cried out first and wept and her soul left her from so much agony.
"On the third day" (Gen. 22:4) — why did it take three days when the place was so near? But we learn that Satan came and turned himself into a river to block Abraham. Abraham said: I will go into the river to test its depths and he almost drowned. He prayed that [God] should save him from the water so he would not drown in it. God rebuked Satan (for abusing his power) and Abraham was suddenly once again on solid ground.

M. 'Abot 5:5 relates that Abraham was tried with ten trials and passed them all.

After fasting forty days and forty nights, he was hungry. (v. 2)

Chapter three ends with Jesus being proclaimed as the Son of God. Then in 4:1 Jesus is removed by the Spirit far into the wilderness where he is tested by the Satan, but before he is tested he fasts for forty days. It seems that this liminal period is needed to confer a change of status on Jesus, confirming his status as "Son of God," so that he can properly embark on his career as "the one who is to come after" John.

Both Deut. 9:9 and Exod. 24:18 tell of how Moses fasted for forty days while he received the Torah. This biblical account of Moses' fasting while receiving the law provides the model in the Jewish tradition for one receiving divine revelation. Consider the story of Elijah and how he fasted forty days at Horeb, during which time the Lord revealed himself to him (1 Kings 19:8ff.), and also the story of Shimon bar Yohai, preserved in

Midrash Prov. (ed. Buber) 1:1, who prayed for wisdom and fasted for forty days in order to receive it.

It may also be the case that behind the report of Jesus' fast stands Isa. 42:1b (which also stood behind Matt. 3:16–17, as we noted above). The Targum to Isa. 42:1b reads, "I set my Holy Spirit upon him, he shall reveal laws to the nations." Along with several others, this text from Isaiah appears in *Midrash Shohar Tov* to Ps. 43:3. As we have seen above (end of chapter 3),[14] this midrash talking about God's sending light and truth interprets all the verses it cites messianically. In the midrash Moses, Elijah, and "[God's] Servant" are all said to be the redeemers of Israel. In sharing divine powers all three fit the category of Matthew's "Son of God": one who shares in the divine.

As I say, in Jewish tradition the model of the lawgiver who fasts for forty days is Moses, and so it is no surprise that Matthew should describe Jesus as having fasted for this length of time. Matthew understood, as did the storyteller in *Midrash Prov.* (1:1), that a forty-day fast was requisite for the one who is to receive divine wisdom. Matthew also knew the Isa. 42:1b tradition, which concerns the Messiah's role as revealer of the law to the nations, and he combined that tradition with the tradition of the fasting of the lawgiver. The point of beginning this chapter with Jesus' fast is to allow the narrator to begin his account of the first test, acquiring bread.

> *The Tester came and said to him, "If you are the Son of God, speak, so that these very stones may become bread." (v. 3)*

Here begins the testing of Jesus by the Satan. The purpose of the first test is apparently to test Jesus' faith in his own calling: does he share divine power or not? Stones are inert; only someone in possession of divine power could turn them into bread. Presumably it is because Jesus has been fasting for forty days that Satan devises this test; the bread would remove Jesus' hunger, the forty days are over, he has the power, why shouldn't he use it? Nevertheless, Jesus refuses. Precisely because the prompting comes from Satan, Jesus recognizes this seemingly reasonable suggestion for what it is: a test. He refuses to use his divine power because to do so would be to give in, even a bit, to what Satan suggests.

> *He answered, "It is written, 'A person shall not live by bread alone but by every word which comes out of the mouth of God'" (Deut. 8:3).[15] (v. 4)*

Jesus rebuffs Satan's test, which after all would not have involved any act of rebellion. He will later provide food miraculously for large crowds. It is difficult to understand Jesus' response here, since God has not said anything to him about not performing miracles for his own welfare. It seems that for Jesus what is wrong with Satan's request is that it is "Satan's request." As I say, it is Satan's job to tempt God's chosen in order to prove their worthiness as the chosen ones. One has to be careful, as Jesus is here, not to be lead astray by one's adversaries.[16]

Jesus' use of the text from Deuteronomy in his response to Satan is poetic for "get lost," the sentiment he will express at the end. That is, whatever the verse Jesus cites might otherwise mean, in the context of the discussion with Satan it means, "We are not going to go there."[17]

> *Then the Accuser took him to the holy city and stood him upon the summit of the Temple. (v. 5)*

The Temple is the place in which God's glory is found (Ezek. 43:5) and, as I have pointed out, the summit of the Temple is the place where God's angels congregate.

> *He said to him, "If you are the Son of God, throw yourself down. For it is written, 'He will command his angels concerning you, and they will bear you up on their hands, lest you strike your foot against a stone'" (Ps. 91:11–12).[18] (v. 6)*

As before, Satan's request seems a reasonable test of the divine powers of the initiate — which is what initiation tests in the wilderness are supposed to do.[19] That is: Is the Son of God to doubt what has been written by David? (In the LXX the text is from Psalm 90, and the heading says that it was composed by David.)

> *Jesus said to him, "Again it is written, 'You shall not test the Lord your God'" (Deut. 6:16).[20] (v. 7)*

While the proof-text here from Deut. 6:16 appears to be a reasonable counter to the Accuser's request, again it is really a polite "get lost!" The verse is not really applicable to the circumstances at hand. The complete text from Deuteronomy reads, "You shall not test the Lord your God as you tested him at Massa." The reference here is to the time when at Rephidim in the wilderness the Israelites complained to Moses about God's seeming lack of concern for them and their well-being. The Israelites at Rephidim did not test God in the sense that they challenged Him to do something extraordinary; it was more that they tested his patience.

Again, the Accuser took him to an exceptionally high mountain and showed him all the kingdoms of the world and their glory. (v. 8)

This is not a test of sonship. It is a test of faith.

And said to him, "I shall give you all these things, if you fall down and worship me." Then Jesus said to him, "Go away, Satan. For it is written, 'You shall worship the Lord your God, and serve him alone.'"[21]
(vv. 9–10)

Jesus states that it is forbidden to worship anything or anyone other than God.[22] It seems clear that the inclusion of this text from Deuteronomy is a valid answer. It is where Satan was going all along and now he is sent away, so to speak, with his tail between his legs.

Then the Accuser left him, and look, angels came and waited on him.
(v. 11)

The angels now bring Jesus sustenance so that he can break his fast, since he would not, as Satan encouraged him to do, produce bread for himself. It is with this act that Jesus is indeed confirmed as the Son of God.

Having heard that John had been handed over, he departed for Galilee.
(v. 12)

With this verse a new unit begins. John is no longer in the picture and Jesus now departs for the place in which he will carry out his ministry. He is concerned to fulfill the Scripture (Isa. 8:23–9:1) literally and moreover, this is his hometown area.

And leaving Nazareth, he settled in Kfar Nahum by the sea, in the territory of Zebulun and Naphtali, in order to fulfill what was spoken by Isaiah the prophet, "Land of Zebulun and land of Naphtali, the sea road, across the Jordan, Galilee of the Gentiles. The people which sits in darkness saw a great light, and light has dawned for those who sit in the region and shadow of death" (Isa. 8:23–9:1).[23] (vv. 13–16)

Capernaum (in Hebrew, Kfar Nahum), mentioned in *Midrash Prov.* 13:22, compares the inheritance of the good person with that of the sinful person. The Midrash identifies the good with certain Rabbis and the sinful with certain Christians. The inhabitants (or more likely, an inhabitant) of Kfar Nahum is identified as one of these sinners (*Eccles. Rab.* 7:3).

Isaiah 9:1–6 has long been seen as a messianic text in Christian circles — "unto us a child is born" (9:5) — in which a successor worthy to sit on David's throne is promised. The text from this chapter of Isaiah quoted here speaks of those living in a kind of spiritual death who will welcome the great light as it rises first for them. This verse resonates well with the "light" and the "truth" of Ps. 43:3, which in the Midrash signifies "Elijah" and "Moses" respectively, the redeemers of Israel (*Midrash Shohar Tov* to Ps. 43:3).

> *From that time Jesus began to proclaim, "Repent, for the Kingdom of Heaven has drawn near." (v. 17)*

This is the same message preached by John the Baptist (Matt. 3:2). Jesus picks up where John left off, a clear indication that he is the one whom John said was to come after him (Matt. 3:11). There is very little in Matthew's Gospel to suggest that repentance was central to Jesus' mission. Nevertheless, the simplicity and directness of his message may well mark it as an authentic tradition about Jesus believed by early Christians, if it is not from Jesus himself.

> *Walking by the sea of Galilee he saw two brothers, Simon called Peter and Andrew his brother, casting nets into the sea, for they were fishermen. (v. 18)*

"Simon called Peter" is a way of saying that Peter was most often referred to by his Greek name, and not by his Hebrew name, Simon.

> *He said to them, "Follow me, and I will make you fishers of human beings." (v. 19)*

In Matt. 8:22 Jesus also says to a potential follower, as he does here, "Follow me!"

> *Immediately leaving behind their nets, they followed him. Going on from there he saw another pair of brothers, Jacob the son of Zebedaiah and John his brother in the boat with Zebedaiah their father, mending their nets, and he called them. Immediately leaving their boat and their father behind, they followed him. (vv. 20–22)*

In verses 18–20, we are told that the brothers Peter and Andrew abandon their livelihoods to become disciples of Jesus.[24] But in verses 21–22 we are shown something more troubling: Jacob and John abandon not only their livelihoods, but also their father, to become disciples of Jesus.[25] In *'Abot R. Nat.* (version A, 6:13) there is a story about Rabbi Eliezer ben Hyrcanos who, against the wishes of his father, left his home to study Torah with Yohanan ben Zakkai. Rabbi Eliezer's father was wealthy, and so, unlike in the Gospel story, economics there would not have been an issue.

Jesus' lack of concern for the integrity of the family is almost shocking. It is difficult to understand how Jesus can ask poor fishermen whose families depend on them to leave these families. The economic consequences would have been severe. But the Gospel stories show us a Jesus who is intent on having disciples to spread his teachings whatever the human cost.

He went around the whole Galilee teaching in their assemblies and proclaiming the good news of the Kingdom and healing every illness and every sickness among the people. (v. 23)

Jesus is now an itinerant preacher and wonderworker. That is, he is now doing the work of the "anointed one." Isaiah 61:1 explains what the work of the "anointed one" is to be: "The Spirit of the Lord God is upon me; because the Lord has *anointed me* to preach *good news to the meek*." Jesus probably began his sermons with this text (in the commentary to chapter 5 we shall see how Jesus worked this text into the introductory poem of his Sermon on the Mount). Jesus' work takes him into the schools and synagogues of the towns he enters, teaching Torah. There is nothing remarkable in this, although we do not know how he himself became a teacher.

From time immemorial it has been common for Jewish teachers to end their sermons on a note assuring the audience of final consolation and redemption. *Midrash Psalms* (ed. Buber), Ps. 4:12, points out that all the biblical prophets begin by condemning but end with words of comfort. And *Midrash Aggada* (ed. Buber) 30:11 informs us that at the end-time it will be Elijah who will announce the "good news" to Israel. Jesus' preaching should then be consistent with the view that the harbinger of the Messianic Era will bring the message of "good news." But we note that John before him and Jesus in his sermon in chapters 5 through 7 issues stern warnings (even concluding the whole of the sermon on such a note) of judgment and even in chapter 8 mentions gnashing of teeth and punishment.

The report about him went out to the whole of Syria, and they brought him everyone who was ill, with various diseases and pains, those who were tormented by demonic possession, and those who were moonstruck and paralyzed, and he cured them.[26] (v. 24)

Josephus reports that there were a large number of Jews in Syria (*War* 2.461–68); he also speaks of being witness to the exorcism of a demon (*Ant.* 8.42–49).[27] Faith healers are always popular. In *b. Ber.* 34b a number of stories are told of Hanina ben Dosa effecting miracles through prayer.

Great crowds followed him from Galilee, the Ten Cities, Jerusalem, Judea, and from across the Jordan. (v. 25)

The Ten Cities, or Decapolis, refers to a group of ten cities that were mostly located east of the Jordan and south of the Sea of Galilee (though Damascus, well to the north of the Sea, was one of the ten), and which shared the same predominantly Hellenistic culture. The cities belonged to the province of Syria. In these cities people enjoyed a high degree of personal rights but in them the Jews would not have received the formal Jewish education given in the schools and synagogues of Jewish Palestine. The Talmud knows these cities by the designation "Land of the Gentiles" (*b. Git̠.* 7b).

NOTES

[1]   In the first tests he appears not as the fallen angel Devil with horns bearing a trident, but a kind of bureaucrat in the angelic courts whose job is to determine the strength of the faith of those who claim loyalty to God. He is the one who knows how to persuade the "evil urge" to rebel.

[2]   We might speculate on the implications of these tests. Two of these tests are designed to prove that he shares God's power and deserves the title "the Son of God"; the third is designed to test his loyalty to God. In point of fact the narrative suggests that the Accuser needed only one test in order to determine whether God was right to call Jesus "My son." The last test is really the first and last temptation. Now Satan appears as the Lord of this World with riches and kingdoms at his disposal. Writers in this period and even afterwards had no problems combining these dual Satans (the prosecutor of Job and the demonic soul grabber of Faust). These dual images of Satan appear later in Jesus' parables in chapter 13: one who obstructs those who are weak and

one who plants his agents among the righteous. Can Jesus put aside the glory and wealth of this world or will he sell his soul to the Devil? But because Jesus refuses to respond to the first test to show his divine powers, the Accuser then tries to test him with the second test to prove his super powers (which Satan considers worthy of a Son of God and Jesus will be asked again to prove himself throughout — chapter 13 to the people of Nazareth and again on the cross). Jesus will point to his powers at times as proof of who he is (his message to John in chap. 12). Only after Jesus refuses to respond to this second test, too, does Satan refrain from testing him concerning Satan's understanding of what it means to be the Son of God and instead tests his loyalty to God, and this test Jesus passes. He will not worship Satan. In the other cases, the reader knows Jesus could do them but he will not negotiate with Satan — to give in to the Devil for one thing, even if reasonable is to open the door for other things. But this final test does not prove that Jesus is worthy to bear the title "Son of God," at least in so far as this title means that he shares in God's glory. It does prove beyond doubt that he is "righteously loyal."

3   The model of battling is a constant theme in the hagiography of the lives of the Christian saints.

4   Shimon bar Yohai, desiring wisdom, sat in fast for forty days (see *Midrash Prov.* [ed. Buber] 1:1). In this the rabbi emulated Moses and Elijah, who both fasted for forty days.

5   For interesting stories about God sharing his keys with Elijah see *b. Sanh.* 113a.

6   See above Matt. 3:17.

7   *Midrash Zuta* to Song (ed. Buber) 7:14, as mentioned in my comments to chapter 3.

8   Also Isa. 6:1–4 show us the angels around or above the Temple.

9   If a brother dies without any children then his wife will marry a surviving brother through a ceremony of levirate marriage. See Deut. 25:5–10.

10   See further chap. 14.

11   *Ant.* 18:118–19 suggests he was killed for fear of rebellion. "Now when [many] others came in crowds about him, for they were very greatly moved [or pleased] by hearing his words, Herod, who feared lest the great influence John had over the people might put it into his power and inclination to raise a rebellion (for they seemed ready to do any thing he should advise) thought it best, by putting him to death, to prevent any mischief he might cause, and not bring himself into difficulties, by sparing a man who might make him repent of it when it would be too late. Accordingly he was sent a prisoner, out of Herod's suspicious temper, to Macherus, the castle I before mentioned, and was there put to death." (trans. from Whiston edition (18:5:2).

12   The following was excerpted from S. Beyer's study, "Myths and Symbols on the Quest for Vision," Wilderness Drum, 2002, http://www.wildernessdrum.com/html/myths.html.

Probably the central informing myth of the wilderness vision quest is that it is a rite of passage, as classically defined by Arnold Van Gennep [*The Rites of Passage*, trans. M. Vizedom and G. Caffee (1908; Chicago: University of Chicago Press, 1960)]. According to Van Gennep, the function of the rite is to effect the passage from one life stage or social status to another — at birth, puberty, initiation, marriage, old age, and death. Such rituals are performed at special times or places, away from the centers of community life, at night, in the wilderness, naked or in special clothing, in order to remove the participants from normal or profane space and time. They interpose a sacred interval in the flux of profane experience, in order to facilitate the transition from one condition to a totally different one [G. Kirk, *The Nature of the Greek Myths* (Middlesex: Penguin, 1974), 89]. ... Most influential on the contemporary wilderness vision quest was Van Gennep's subdivision of all the rites of passage into three stages — *separation, transition,* and *incorporation* (1908/1960, p. 11). The stage of transition is often called the *liminal* or *threshold* stage; this is the stage of "betweenness," when the participant is at neither one stage nor the other, in neither one condition nor the other. The liminal stage is a sacred state — as anthropologist Victor Turner puts it, "one of ambiguity and paradox, a confusion of all the customary categories" [V. Turner, "Betwixt and Between: The Liminal Period in Rites of Passage," in *Betwixt and Between: Patterns of Masculine and Feminine Initiation,* ed. L. Mahdi, L. S. Foster, and M. Little (LaSalle, Ill.: Open Court, 1987), 7] — and thus is filled with power and the potential for power. ... Thus, the myth of the rite of passage has two functions. First, it provides a structure for the quest process, dividing it into stages, and allowing the apportionment of tasks and rituals appropriate to each phase. Second, it empowers the quester to seek change, to expect a transition, to accept transformation in the wilderness...The quest of the hero is claimed to be the central myth of narrative literature; so basic is the quest pattern to narrative that Joseph Campbell labels it with the Joycean term *monomyth* [J. Campbell, *The Hero with a Thousand Faces* (1949; Princeton, N.J.: Princeton University Press, 1968), 30; J. Joyce, *Finnegans Wake* (1939; New York: Penguin Books, 1999), 581)] Here, in Campbell's words, is the monomyth, the myth of the hero's quest. ... A hero ventures forth from the world of common day into a region of supernatural wonder: fabulous forces are there encountered and a decisive victory is won: the hero comes back from this mysterious adventure with the power to bestow boons on his fellow man (1949/1968, 30). As Campbell points out, the mythological adventure of the hero is in fact a magnification of the formula represented in the rite of passage, which Campbell gives as *separation — initiation — return,* and which he calls "the nuclear unit of the monomyth" (1949/1968, p. 30). ... Another potent myth for the quester is that the vision quest is not simply a rite of passage, or a heroic quest, but something more specific — an *initiation*. Initiation ceremonies are universal among indigenous cultures. It is difficult to draw a bright line between rites of passage and initiations, but perhaps we can best capture the difference by saying that indigenous initiations typically involve some sort of test or ordeal — fasting, darkness, fearful seclusion, endurance of pain, and often scarring or other changes to the body. ...Fasting is a traditional means of self-empowerment and a means of attaining clarity [S. Foster and M. Little, "The Vision Quest: Passing from Childhood to Adulthood," in *Betwixt and Between*, ed. Mahdi, Foster, and Little, 97]. To deliberately abstain from food is to mark the liminal state, the state of paradox and openness, and to negate one's prior human and social existence. Without meals to organize the day, having only constantly recurring circadian rhythms, time quickly becomes timelessness; linear time — that is, history — becomes circular time, the time of beginnings. Thus fasting is a particularly potent way to mark a new transition, a willingness to change."

13   This story also appears in *Exod. Rab.* 43:1 and *Tanḥ. Exod.* (ed. Buber) (Ki Tissa), 13, but in the version in these texts Moses confronts Satan and casts him aside.

14   While only the very first few words of 42:1*a* appear in the midrash — "Behold My Servant whom I uphold" it is midrashic and scribal method to indicate with these few words that the whole verse or more is meant

15   LXX Deut. 8:3: "a person does not live by bread alone, but by every word which comes through the mouth of God will a person live."

16   *B. ʿAbod. Zar.* 16b–17 and *t. Hull.* 2:24 make the same point, but in place of any temptation put forward by Satan the temptation is found to be in the attractive insights of Jesus. However these must not be listened to by the Jews since they can lead them away from the will of God. The text ends with citations from Scripture which speak of the necessity of keeping one's distance from heretics.

17   See chap. 3, n. 3, above.

18   LXX Ps. 90:11–12: "For he commands his angels concerning you, to guard you in all your ways, and they will bear you up on their hands, lest you strike your foot against a stone."

19   See above n. 1.

20   LXX Deut. 6:16: "You will not test the Lord your God."

21   LXX Deut. 6:13: "You shall be made to fear the Lord your God, and serve him."

22   It may be possible to read into Jesus' response to this third test, a rebuke to early Christians who worshipped Jesus. If this were true, it would indicate that at least in Matthew's church it was held that neither angels nor Jesus were to be worshipped. However, I find here no reason to infer any such polemic intent. It may even be that Matthew did worship Jesus.

23 LXX Isa. 8:23–9:1: Country of Zebulun, land of Naphtali, the sea road, and the rest of those dwelling along the coast and across the Jordan, Galilee of the Gentiles, heritage of the Judeans. The people who go in darkness see a great light. You who dwell in the region and shadow of death, light will shine upon you.

24 "Raise up many disciples" was the advice of early teachers (*m. 'Avot* 1:1).

25 This is in contrast to Elijah and Elisha in 1 Kings 19:20–21

> Elisha left the oxen, ran after Elijah, and said, "Please, let me kiss my father and mother good-bye, and I will follow you." "Go back!" Elijah answered. "Have I done anything to you?" Elisha left him and, taking the yoke of oxen, slaughtered them; he used the plowing equipment for fuel to boil their flesh, and gave it to his people to eat. Then he left and followed Elijah as his attendant.

26 Christian faith healers in the manner of Jesus were attractive to Jews. *T. Hull.* 2:22 mentions a certain Yaacov (circa 140) who healed by calling on the name of Jesus ben Pantera, a reference to Jesus. The Rabbis forbade the Jews to avail themselves of the services of healers who healed in this way.

27 Duling, "The Eleazar Miracle and Solomon's Magical Wisdom in Flavius Josephus's *Antiquities Judaicae* 8:42–49."

CHAPTER FIVE

INTRODUCTION

Chapters 5 and the next two chapters contain teachings for those who need to hear the moral fiber of the *Hassid* — the pious and humble servant of God. The trichapter sermon presents a list of exhortations in a form that seems to be that of a manifesto in which, along with the teachings, Jesus encourages his disciples to keep their spirits up while remaining both humble and willing to accept whatever persecutions might afflict them. Jesus assures his disciples that those who suffer persecution either for his sake or for the sake of righteousness shall share in the ultimate reward: The Kingdom of Heaven. I do not read these three chapters as a message directed at Matthew's own church. Rather Jesus' words, making no personal claim, are aimed at strengthening his disciples and the Jewish people of his time. Much later in the Gospel the Kingdom of Heaven will be promised to a different group, the nations of the world who are the enemies of Israel (24:24, 28:19).[1]

Jesus uses the Galilean preacher's style to teach to his disciples. As attendants of the elders, the Scribes had no authority to offer decrees on their own. They could only give exhortations of faith and elucidate Scriptures. In his chapter Jesus will overstep the boundary that defines the scribe in the manner in which he teaches but not in the content of his teaching. That is, while Jesus does not say anything in this chapter that would contravene any of the laws of the sages and Pharisees, nonetheless in six places in it (5:21–42) he teaches in the form of a teacher of law, not citing prior teachers. The Scribes had no authority on their own to offer opinions on the law. There is no scriptural exegesis in his sermon beyond what was the common understanding of the verses. His teaching on divorce and oaths will require some attention as here it is not clear at all what he wants to do. His use of exaggeration is not surprising. What may be surprising are some cases where it seems he wants to be taken literally.

The sermon opens with a hymn of consolation and praise for the humble and the afflicted. Tightly structured, the hymn seems repetitive (there are eight beatitudes in it),[2] but it is not boring as each phrase is developed from a biblical verse that has the word *anav* (meek). It is written in a proto-*piyyut* style (a kind of liturgical poetry that blends Scripture, midrash, and the poet's values).[3] The hymn locates scriptural constellations concerning the phrases alluding to "next world" and "face of God," together with "humble" and "afflicted" (in Heb. *anav* and *ani*). In it there are allusions to biblical texts but none of these are directly cited.[4]

The ninth and final beatitude (5:11) begins a new unit. The *piyyut* style is abandoned and instead Jesus begins to address his hearers directly. Be worthy examples and shining lights, he says to them (5:13–16). Thereafter Jesus speaks of the importance of keeping every law, however minor (5:17–20); for as he says he has not come to abolish the law but rather to see to it that its every part is fulfilled, is practiced.

Many have thought that once Jesus has declared that he has not come to abolish the law but rather to fulfill its every part, he then refers to six age-old laws of the Jews and states what, according to him, it really means to fulfill them. For him a desultory compliance of the law is not enough.[5] I do not agree. The sermon uses these verses to introduce sermonic exhortations on related matters but does not imply literal compliance is anything less than mandatory. The word *murder* introduces a sermon on anger, adultery a sermon on lust. The material of these sermons is standard fare for Jewish teaching.

For the preacher, divine laws are designed to transform human behavior. Sermons tease out of scriptural passages old messages in new ways. The messages are based on a desire to transform one's character and ultimately the society in which one lives. That was the job of the preacher. As in the works of Philo, Josephus, Ben Sirah, and many others, the Jews are not only to refrain from bad behavior; they are also to refrain from any social activity and/or emotional involvement that might in some way lead one toward bad behavior. That is the goal of the rabbinic laws of Mishnah and Talmud. In laying out these moral laws in this way, what Jesus is doing here in form is very roughly akin to what the Rabbis called "making a fence around the Torah" (*m. 'Avot* 1.1).[6] To "make a fence around the Torah" is to extend the law beyond what it minimally requires one to do. The Rabbis extended the reach of certain laws in order either to prescribe or else prohibit matters which, if not prescribed or prohibited, might lead to the transgression of the laws around which the fence was built. Jesus appears to be doing more than Scribes did but in effect he is artistically rephrasing age old messages. Matt. 23:23 tells us that the Scribes and Pharisees added tithes on mint and other spices that are never eaten alone; by doing this they erected a fence, so to speak, around the ritual law concerning the tithing of staple vegetables. That is, if such things as mint and dill are tithed, then obviously the staple vegetables, as the law enjoins, are to be tithed too. Yet, as Jesus points out, the Pharisees would not lift a finger to safeguard the moral law: "Woe to you, Scribes and Pharisees, stage-actors! You tithe mint, dill, and cumin, and you leave aside the more serious things of the Torah, *judgment, mercy, and faith.*" Yet, we must be wary of reading the later portrayals of Jesus into the pastoral sermonic setting.

To say that rabbinic authority was somewhat lenient in demanding higher standards of conscience is to make a valid critique. The Rabbis did not often legislate on matters that were thought to be unenforceable. However they did at least encourage people concerning right behavior in these unenforceable matters. So for instance while prurient behavior was understood by all to be prohibited, still there were few legal safeguards against it. There were rules for keeping males and females from being alone together — but little beyond that was practical. However a text in *'Abot R. Nat.,* version A (chap. 2), shows the extent to which this matter was of concern. In the text the biblical verse, the foundation upon which the fence was built, is interpreted in a most creative way (the careful manipulation of a scriptural text to make a point was considered an art).

> "Keep your way far from her" (Prov. 5:8): ["Her"] refers to a prostitute. A person tells you, "Do not go near a certain market or do not go in a certain lane-way because there is a certain prostitute of dazzling beauty who frequents these places" — Do not then think to yourself, "That warning is of little concern to me. I know my will power will withstand the temptations. Even if I do happen to meet her in these places, I trust in myself that nothing will happen." Even so, do not go there for perhaps you will stumble.

A rabbinic text from *Midrash Tannaim* (ed. Hoffman), Deut. 22:4, shows similar intent. The matter here is mercy toward an injured animal, and again the Rabbis do not legislate. However they do make known that, in this case, it is their preference to show mercy, even if doing this is not strictly required by law. The text reads:

> *You shall not* [stand by] *and watch the donkey of your brother or his ox* [suffer]. This is a negative commandment. How do I know it is also a positive commandment? — Scripture says, "When you see the donkey of your enemy or ox going astray, etc." (Exod. 23:5).

And Scripture says "And can you [can] *ignore it."*—[Indecisive syntax] For some, this is meant to be read as an exclamatory question. Can you ignore the suffering? [Surely not!]. But for others it is meant to be read as a declaration. You can ignore it. [Surely so!]. ... This latter reading applies to an elderly and dignified sage. [For it would be considered dishonourable for such a one to be seen to be coming to the aid of an animal]. Nevertheless, if he is a *Hassid* he will always do more than what is permitted, or less than what is proscribed, by the minimalist reading of the law. And this is the preferred way for all.

A text in *b. B. Meṣ.* 30b comments on supererogatory mechanisms and suggests that the Hebrew Scriptures have already advised that they are normative. In this text Exod. 18:20 is read so that no part of it is seen to be free of meaning.

"And thou shalt teach them the statutes and the laws, and shalt show them the way wherein they must walk, and the work that they must do" (Exod. 18:20).
Rabbi Yosef interpreted the verse...
"and the work," this word refers to the actual law,
"which should be done" means: "go beyond the minimum requirements of the law."

Having said all this, I do not find Jesus legislated in the sermon at all. The two exceptions are his teachings on divorce and oaths which I take as Matthean additions since they are absent in Luke. The teaching on divorce has been put into the sermon form here but it is taken from a later statement (chap. 19) where Jesus has already turned away from teaching and encouraging but instead argues and debates.

I had initially thought to take the approach that Matthew's scheme in the sermon was to add what later Rabbis termed "duties of the heart." I do not think so now. In form it might seem to imply duties but in actuality it really does not demand much more than plucking out eyes and cutting of hands, hardly serious legislation. What we do have is a series of mini-sermons introduced by some Scripture or allusion to Scripture. The Scripture then is really left alone. Jesus goes on to speak about other matters suggested by the Scripture. It is not exegesis at all. There is a hint of wanting to extend prohibitions but the sheer shock of the rhetoric argues strongly against that. In sum, he did not say more than Scribes did, but his form is that of the religious authority promulgating law. In the language of the Rabbis we could say he teaches *midrash aggada* but he sounds like he is teaching *midrash halakhah.*

What can we as historians of religion learn from the sermon? There are very few fully preserved synagogue sermons, designated as such, in Jewish literature. Matthew has taken some sources and shaped them into a sermon. Even so, he shows us that much of what we find in Talmudic literature is closely related in style, structure, and content to much earlier preaching. In general, the value of the Gospels for understanding the continuity of Jewish customs and word usage cannot be overemphasized. Time and again in his important work David Flusser makes this point. For instance. he points out that the custom of the father naming the male child at circumcision, about which we are told in Luke (1:59–64), is not attested in the Talmudic texts;[7] nor is the practice of passing around the "kiddush cup of wine" for which those at the table are to drink, about which again Luke tells us (22:17), attested in these texts either.[8] Only because both of these customs are referred to in the Gospels can it be said that they date from the Second Temple period.

Aside from confirming that certain practices mentioned in late Jewish sources (and also certain types of exegesis)[9] were current in the days of the Second Temple period, the New Testament also shows us that certain phrases or words that appear in the late Jewish sources were also being used in this earlier period. For instance, in Acts 21:21 the phrase "the Jews who are *among the Gentiles*," used by the author to refer to the Diaspora Jews whom Paul is said to be turning away from the Mosaic law, remains unattested in Jewish sources until its appearance in *b. Šabb.* 88b–89a.[10] There Moses is said to have replied to the angels who wanted to possess the Torah:

> Of what use is the Torah for you? I ask you moreover, what is written in it? "Thou shalt have no other gods..." Do you live *among the Gentiles* who worship idols?

And in *Exod. Rab.* (*Vaʾera*) 3:7 and *b. Ber.* 9b there is a parallel to the phrase found in Matt. 6:34: "Each day has enough trouble of its own," which reads: "There is sufficient trouble for its time frame alone" (i.e., "Each time frame has enough trouble of its own").

Also, the word *Hosanna* is found in Matt. 21:9, Mark 11:9, John 12:13, and in each case it means "praised be you." The word is found with other meanings in *b. Sukkah* (a "palm branch" in 31a, 33b, 37a, 46b) and in a midrash (The Great *Hoshanna* — the title of the last day of the Festival of Sukkot) (*Lev. Rab.* 37:2). Only in Medieval *piyyut* do we find that it means "praise to God." In the current liturgy there is a pertinent alphabetical "*hoshanna.*" *Midrash Psalms,* chap. 17:5, relates that after the Destruction of the Temple a synagogue official stood in the center of the synagogue on a platform while the congregants encircled him. This practice continues to this very day. Praises called "Hoshanna" are now sung and the phrases of the poems are generally begun by the word "Hoshanna."

Finally, I need to say something about my methods in this work as a whole and in chapters 5, 6, and 7 in particular. I have read a large chunk of the various books and articles dealing with the interpretation of the Gospel of Matthew. Moreover colleagues who have looked at my work, and in particular Prof. Dale Allison who also sent me articles and unpublished papers, have wondered about my methods. I seem to use Jewish exegetical materials indiscriminately without care for date or provenance and reject the "blatantly" obvious suggestions offered by scholars that have been current for forty years or longer.

Any scholar faces the following question (since we do not have a tradition handed down from Bultmann from Matthew from Jesus from the Mount of Sermons): Is it better to a) *invent* an exegesis that nowhere exists by using sources that might have been available to Matthew's sources or to Jesus using extant Jewish hellenistic writings; or, is it better to b) find an exegesis that *does exist* but comes from any time and any place within the interpretive culture of Judaism? To my mind the latter presents, at the very least, a real possibility of what a Jewish interpreter in the first century might have thought since someone did cite such a tradition at some point. It was not fabricated by a scholar with Matthew in mind. When the very language and images of Matthew's story are so visible in these "later" statements that come from deep within the conservative culture of Rabbis who breathed the same civilization (to use Mordecai Kaplan's apt term) as did Jesus and the early Christians it seems to me to be the better option. However, there is latitude for speculation as well using Hebrew Bible where the genre of writing indicates one was meant to do that. This is the case in the beatitudes that begin chapter 5. Hebrew poetic forms are riddles that require the listener or reader to scan Scripture for the language the poet uses and the traditions attached to those Scriptures. Of course, all rules of thumb have their exceptions and I have used my own judgments on where to draw lines. The question of method and viable approaches were discussed 85 years ago by Strack-Billebeck in their "After-Word to the Sermon on the Mount" (*Evangelium nach Mattaus,* 470–74). Around the same time Joseph Klausner noted, "So extraordinary is the similarity that it might almost seem as though the Gospels were composed simply and solely out of matter contained in the *Talmud* and *Midrash.*"[11] If modern scholars need convincing and the battle is to be uphill, what better place to begin than with the "sermon on the mountain"?

> *Seeing the crowds, he went up to the mountain, and when he was seated, his students came to him. (v. 1)*

When teachers taught before large crowds they taught outdoors, either on mountaintops or in fields. The teachers sat and those whom they taught also sat. A text from *b. Šabb.* 127a tells us of teachers having whole fields of grain cleared so that space could be made to accommodate audiences too large to be indoors. And a text from *'Abot R. Nat.* (version A, chap. 38), tells us that Rabbi Shimon ben Gamaliel sat when he taught on the Temple Mount, and that those whom he taught also sat. A teacher's students apparently sat at his feet in those days.[12]

But Matthew tells us something more here. Apparently people had heard that Jesus was going to speak but when they gathered at the building where he was to speak it proved to be too small, and so, realizing this, Jesus went up the hill to speak. As teachers did not sit on the ground when they taught, a seat would have been prepared for him.

He opened his mouth and taught them (v. 2)

It may be that in antiquity sermons began with some kind of poem or midrash fashioned from the Book of Psalms or the Book of Proverbs.[13] As documents recently discovered in the Cairo Geniza show, the Targum reciter began with a poem and our midrashim often begin with a citation from Psalms or Proverbs.

Let us consider what the phrases "opened and taught," "opened the mouth," and "open" by itself might mean.

In *'Abot R. Nat.* (version A, addition to chap. 3), the story is told of a man whose death by drowning Rabbi Akiva was sure he had witnessed, only to have the man appear before him alive and well as he stood in court testifying to his death. When Rabbi Akiva asked the man how it was that he had not drowned, the man said that it was his habitual charity that saved him. Then:

> Rabbi Akiva immediately opened and taught (*patah ve'darash* — in chap. 3 itself the text is "opened and said" — *patah ve'amar*), "Blessed is the Lord God of Israel who has chosen the words of the Torah and the words of the sages [for] they shall be true for all eternity." As it said, "Cast your bread upon the face of waters for after many days you will find it" (Eccles. 11:1).

"Opened and taught," the phrase found in this text, is not necessarily the same as "opened his mouth (and taught)," which is what we read in the Gospel. "Opened and taught"[14] seems to be either a technical phrase that indicates that a public lecture is about to begin, or it may mean "opened [i.e., interpreted] the Scriptures and taught," which is what seems to be happening in this rabbinic text. I have found well over 100 instances of this phrase being used in the rabbinic literature. It is of interest that Rabbi Akiva pronounces a blessing upon the midrashic lesson he is about to deliver.

Conversely, the phrase "opened his mouth" does not mean that something is about to be taught but rather that a blessing (or a curse) is about to be recited. The rabbinic literature has not a few examples of this phrase, and never is it followed by teaching. A text from *Song Rab.* 2:4 is instructive here:

> Usually when ten men come to a house of mourning not a single one of them is able to "open his mouth" to recite the mourner's blessing. Then someone else may come and open his mouth and bless the mourner's blessing.

Concerning the word "open" used alone, scholars have suggested that the word might mean "to explain," or "to open the mouth," or "to begin a lecture" or "to talk about the lead verse of a discrete unit in the Torah."[15]

In the text from Matthew the phrase "opened his mouth and taught" may mean the same as did the later, rabbinic usages of the phrase "opened and taught," or it may reflect the fuller version of "opened and taught," referring to the "opening up and analysis of texts," that is, "to give a sermon."[16] It is also possible that Matthew's source here emended the words "opened and taught" in a Hebrew original by adding the object "mouth" to the verb "opened." That is, perhaps "opened" did mean "interpreted" in the original but was not clearly understood by the transmitters who changed it to "opened his mouth." The point is that we might not be wrong to suggest that the original opening of the sermon followed a typical Hebrew/Aramaic format.

"Blessed are the poor of Spirit, for theirs is the Kingdom of Heaven."
(v. 3)

Matthew begins his sermon by having Jesus offer praise to those he sees as being especially virtuous, and also by having Jesus declare what rewards are to be theirs for being so virtuous. From last to first the list of the virtuous is as follows: the afflicted, the peacemakers, the pure of heart, the merciful, the seekers of righteousness, the meek, the grieving, the poor in spirit (the *anvei ruah*, attested in Dead Sea Scrolls 1QM 14:7). Despite the variety, these virtuous types are all, in essence, "the meek" (Heb. *anavim*).

To play with a word whose meaning is associated with a virtue or with the virtuous by ever-extending its range of meanings is at the heart of rabbinic preaching. Then, once its range of meanings has been extended so that the word comes to be associated with other virtues, the preacher finds suitable proof-texts to confirm that the word can indeed be associated with these other virtues. And so a word in a biblical text is much like a door that opens onto many rooms, all of which can be called by this same word, although the meaning of the word can also shift in accordance with other biblical texts in which this word, though in a different context, is found. Words can operate like magnets and attract similar words in biblical verses into a symphony where the words shuttle the meaning of one verse to another — absorbing the sense in one place and spreading that sense to another, which enhances the meaning of both verses.[17] Then, in the latest stage of a prayer's development, a poet reworks the whole, eliminating the awkward citations of verses (that generated the whole) and filling in catch phrases with specific details. The final product will still grow at the hand of others but always with the creative elegance and charm set in motion at first.[18]

The way of turning biblical texts into beatitude form is shown in *Midrash Psalms* (ed. Buber) 25:3. Here the preacher affixes the term "blessed" to a text from Proverbs that enjoins one to act in a certain noble way. It is noteworthy that this text from Proverbs associates "the meek" with "the poor of spirit," for "the meek" are "the poor of spirit."[19] The text reads:

> It is better to be low of spirit with the meek than to divide the spoil with the proud (Prov. 16:19) — Blessed is he who takes his portion with the meek.

The Greek *makarioi* ("Blessed are") translates the Hebrew *ashrei,* which means "fortunate" or "blessed."[20] Matthew's poem is composed of a series of beatitudes, each of which singles out a type of virtuous person and/or activity worthy of being "blessed."[21] Rabbinic teachings also utilize this form. For example, "Rabbi Hanina said to him [Rabbi Eleazar ben Perata] '*Blessed* are you that you have been arrested over five charges and you are to be spared. Woe to me who has been arrested over one charge and I am not to be spared. *For* you occupied yourself with both Torah-study and deeds of loving-kindness, but I only occupied myself with Torah-study' (b. 'Abod. Zar. 17b)." Another striking example is found at the close of mishnaic tractate *Kelim:* "Rabbi Yosi says, '*Blessed* are you Kelim, *for* you entered in defilement [the subject matter of five defilements in Kelim 1:1] and you departed in purity'" (the last word of the tractate). This form is almost that of Matthew's "Blessed are the poor in spirit: for theirs is the Kingdom of Heaven" (5:3). The rabbinic forms mention current or imminent reasons "to be blessed" and Matthew refers to a future consequence. In fact, there is no real discrepancy because Jesus' assurance is that the consequence is guaranteed to the extent it is as if it had already happened. The beatitudes are therefore prophetic in their tones with a sense of immediacy.[22]

Isa. 61:1 has not been directly cited in the poem, because it is the artful style of liturgical poetry to work the biblical text into the poem allusively, leaving it to the reader to recognize the text.[23] As I have pointed out in my comments to 4:23, the phrase "The Lord has anointed me" in this context means that Jesus has been designated Son of God "to preach good news to the meek" and "the brokenhearted" (see Matt. 11:29 for the juxtaposition of "meek" and "lowly of heart").

"The meek" are also spoken of in Ps. 37:11, which is the source — again uncited — for this first beatitude (as well as the beatitudes in 5:5, 5:6, 5:9, and 5:10): "But the meek shall inherit the land and enjoy great peace." But there is a problem here. If Jesus is using Ps. 37:11 as his source for this beatitude, then why does he say here "Blessed are the poor in spirit" rather than "Blessed are the meek"? The answer is because the two — "the poor in spirit" and "the meek" — are synonymous, as I have said above, citing Proverbs, and later Jewish commentary. Matt. 5:5 actually supplies the wording we would expect, though surprisingly here "the land" has not been replaced by the "Kingdom of Heaven," as was the case in Matt. 5:3. Some scholars think "poor in spirit" in this case means "contrite" in the spirit of Isa. 57:15.[24]

There is a tradition in the *Mekhilta of Rabbi Yishmael* (*Bahodesh*) *Yitro* 9 that, drawing on some of the same texts that are the source for the poem, states that especially on the humble does the divine spirit rest. The text reads:

> *The people stood far off, while Moses drew near to the thick darkness where God was* (Exod. 20:21). What enabled him to achieve this great feat [to face God]? — His humility, as stated, "And the man Moses was very humble" (Num. 12:3). So this verse informs us that for anyone who is humble, in the end the divine spirit will rest upon him on earth. And it says, "For thus says the One who is high and lifted up, who inhabits eternity, whose name is Holy: I dwell in the high and holy place, and also with him who is of a contrite and lowly spirit, to revive the spirit of the lowly, and to revive the heart of the contrite" (Isa. 57:15). And it also says: "The Spirit of the Lord God is upon me; because the Lord has *anointed me* to preach *good news to the meek*" (Isa. 61:1). And it also says: "The offering of the Lord is a broken spirit" (Ps. 51:19).

In 5:3 Jesus substitutes "Kingdom of Heaven" for "Land," which is what is found in his source, Ps. 37:11. For the Rabbis, "Inherit the land" is nearly identical in meaning to "inherit the Kingdom of Heaven," and this would almost certainly have been known to the audience of Matthew's source (reporting Jesus' words). *Mishnah Sanhedrin* 10:1 paraphrases, "They shall inherit the land forever" (Isa. 60:21) in this way: "All Israel have a share in the World to Come." In the Matthean tradition, the phrase "inheriting the land" also means "to have a share in the World to Come." While the concept of Kingdom of Heaven is somewhat amorphous in Matthew, here we know exactly what it means. It is the World to Come where life is eternal and the dead will rise.

In a text from *Pesiq. Rab.* (ed. Friedmann), 36, it is said that the "meek ones" are Israel, who have suffered persecution and worse at the hands of the Romans and others.

> Our Rabbis taught that when King Messiah will be revealed, he will come and stand on the roof of the Temple. He will inform Israel and say to them, "Meek ones, the time of your redemption has come."

It is also the case that God's people are said to be "the meek" in Isa. 49:13:

> Shout for joy, O Heavens! And rejoice, O Earth! Break forth into joyful shouting, O mountains! For the Lord has comforted his people and will have compassion on his meek.[25]

His people and the meek are parallel in this verse and so are one and the same. This text also speaks of comfort and compassion and joy, which are the themes of verses 4, 7, 12.

"Blessed are those who are grieving, for they shall be consoled." (v. 4)

Jesus continues his poem with a poetic rendering of Isa. 61:2b — "to comfort all who mourn." Though he speaks of mourners, the underlying subject remains "the meek," for it is "the meek" who are spoken of in the texts from Isaiah and the Psalms which shape the flow and content of the beatitudes.

A rabbinic text that associates mourning with joy in the World to Come is found in *t. Bava Batra* (ed. Lieberman), 2:17. The text reads:

> All who mourn over it (Jerusalem) in this world, their heart will be gladdened in the World to Come, as it is said, *"Rejoice with Jerusalem and be glad for her, all you who love her; rejoice greatly with her, all you who mourn over her"* (Isa. 66:10).

Some have tried to argue that there is a correlation between the structure of the beatitudes and that of the following section in which Jesus speaks of the laws (vv. 21–48). To my mind the beatitudes are a poetic introduction to the sermon, which stand alone, and with which Jesus exhorts and encourages his hearers in the face of persecution and the suffering this brings. It need not be Matthew's church (did he even have one?) that is being addressed here but rather Jesus' audience, who are the Jews. However, by the end of the gospel, as Matthew tells, the Jews will have turned their backs on Jesus and his message and will be shown to have been responsible for his death. Without this eloquent sermon, the "Jewish rejection" of Jesus, as Matthew tells it, would not appear unreasonable, but because he has put it into his gospel, the Jews can be portrayed as evil and haughty. That is, by the end of the Gospel the Jews will have ceased to be "the meek" people of God, and their gentile enemies, according to Matthew, will have come to bear this designation. For this reason I seriously doubt whether Matthew was Jewish-Christian. If he was Jewish-Christian, he can only have been a self-loathing one.[26]

"Blessed are the meek, for they shall inherit the Land." (v. 5)

Here we have sermon material in its pre-Matthean form. That is, except for the addition of the words "Blessed are," the text is a straight rendering of the phrase concerning the meek inheriting the land in Ps. 37:11. I have the impression that at this point Matthew follows a source to the letter, making no substitutions.

"Blessed are those who hunger and thirst for righteousness, for they
will shall be given enough to eat." (v. 6)

At first glance it appears that in this beatitude there is no reference to the meek, and so here Jesus moves away from its main theme; but in point of fact the beatitude is here precisely because it refers to the meek.

A text from *Batei Midrashot* (ed. Wertheimer), vol. 2, *Midrash Alpha Betot*, p. 454, asks about food and drink, and finds the answer in Ps. 22:7:

> How do we know about food and drink? As it says, *The meek shall eat and be satisfied; those who seek him shall praise the Lord! May your hearts live forever!* (Ps. 22:27). The word "forever" refers to the World to Come.

In *Gen. Rab.* 25:3 there is an interesting text concerning the visitation of ten famines on the world. Nine of these famines are famines of physical want, which have occurred at various times from Adam through to Elisha; the tenth is said to be a famine of the spirit. Moreover, according to the text, which cites Amos 8:11 as proof, the famine of the spirit is to occur in the World to Come: *Not a hunger for bread and not a thirst for water but only to hear the Word of the Lord.*

"Blessed are the merciful, for mercy shall be shown to them." (v. 7)

A similar understanding of how God repays mercy for mercy is found throughout the rabbinic literature. For instance, a text from *Gen. Rab.* 33, on the verse "The Lord is good to all and his mercy is over all his works (Ps. 145:9)" takes note of a drought in the days of Rabbi Tanhuma. The rabbi decreed three fast days and still not a drop fell. Then he came in and told them:

> "Shower mercy for each other and the Holy One will shower mercy upon you." … When charity is being distributed to the poor people it is a welcome sight that a man [although not ordered to do it] gives money freely to his divorced wife.

And a text from b. Šabb. 151b reads:

> Rabban Gamaliel, the son of Rabbi [Judah the patriarch], says: *And He will show you mercy and will be compassionate to you and cause you to increase…* (Deut. 13:17–18) — whoever is merciful to others mercy is shown to him from heaven.

"Blessed are the pure in heart, for they shall see God." (v. 8)

It is a commonplace in both the rabbinic literature and the Hebrew Bible that those with pure hearts will see God. A text from *Lev. Rab.* 23:13 reads:

> Rabbi Menassia son of Rabbi Yehoshua ben Levi said: We find that whoever chances to see lewdness and does not "fill his eyes with it" will merit to see the face of God [*Shekhina*]. What is the proof-text? And closes his eyes from seeing evil (Isa. 33:15). And what follows? Your eyes shall see the king in his beauty: they shall behold the land that is very far off (Isa. 33:17).

Ps. 24:4–6 contains a very similar sentiment.

> He that hath clean hands, and a pure heart; who hath not lifted up his soul unto vanity, nor sworn deceitfully. He shall receive the blessing from the Lord, and righteousness from the God of his salvation. This is the generation of them that seek him, that seek thy face, O Jacob.

"Blessed are the peacemakers, for they will be called God's children."
(v. 9)

Again though at first glance it doesn't appear to be the case, this beatitude also refers to the meek, for it too is drawn from Ps. 37:11; for Ps. 37:11 not only promises that "the meek shall inherit the earth," but also that "they will be gladdened for the increase of peace."

In a tradition found in *Pesiq. Rab Kah.* 18:6, it is said that in the time of the Messiah people will only ever seek peace. Then follow four texts that confirm the point:

> Ps. 72:7: "In [the Messiah's] days may the righteous flourish, and abundance of peace till the moon is no more!";
> Ps. 119:165: "Those who love Your law have great peace, and nothing causes them to stumble";
> Ps. 37:11: "And the meek…"; and
> Isa. 54:13: "And all your children shall be learned of the Lord, and your children [shall have] *abundant* (Heb. *rav*) peace."

As an aside, we note that *b. Ber.* 64a suggests that even now there can be peace by interpreting "your children [shall have] abundant peace" from Isa. 54:13 to mean: "the disciples of the wise *increase peace* (i.e., not simply have peace) in the world." The point is that those disciples of the wise who increase peace between their neighbors are called by Scriptures "your children."[27]

> *"Blessed are those who are persecuted for the sake of righteousness, for theirs is the heavenly kingdom." (v. 10)*

Anavim not only means "the meek"; it can also mean "those who are persecuted." Ps. 9:11–12 makes clear: "Sing praises to the Lord, who dwells in Zion; declare among the peoples His deeds. For He who requites blood remembers them; He does not forget the cry of the *anavim*." And so Ps. 37:11 also proves to be the source for this beatitude which brings the liturgical poem to an end.

> *"Blessed are you when they reproach you and persecute you and speak every evil against you falsely for my sake. Rejoice and be glad, for your reward is great in the heavens, for so they persecuted the prophets who were before you." (vv. 11–12)*

Now that the poem has ended, Jesus turns to address his disciples directly; no longer does he address all the Jews. His direct address is in the form of an exhortation, a common Matthean device (see 19:6). The device is also known to the Rabbis:[28]

> *Sipre Deut.*, piska 306 to Deut. 32:1:
> And is it not reasonable that if these [natural phenomena] when they obey their laws have no ability of getting reward or loss such that obedience gets them reward or disobedience punishment, and they do not worry for their offspring

they do not rebel against their limitations, you who if obedient do get reward and for disobedience do get punishment and you do worry for your offspring, how much more so you should not rebel against your limitations!

Jesus says to his disciples that the prophets who came before them were persecuted and because of this, he implies, their heavenly rewards have been great; and so because they too are to be persecuted, they too can expect their heavenly rewards to be great. But in order for Jesus to make this claim, a dramatic shift must occur in the poem. Whereas before when Jesus was speaking of the persecuted ones (v. 10), it is almost certain that he meant the children of Israel, here it is Matthew's followers who are said to be the persecuted ones, and their persecutors are the Jews. Whether one thinks that this poem came directly from Jesus, or from a later hand, still verses 11–12 should be seen as a very late edition to the poem.

> *"You are the salt of the earth. But if the salt has lost its flavor, how can it be made salty again? It is not capable of anything except to be thrown outside and stepped on by people."* (v. 13)

Jesus' point here is that if his disciples are to fail they should then be as worthless as refuse. It is a harsh statement.

> *"You are the light of the world. No city built lying on a hill can be hidden. No one lights a lamp and places it under the basket, but on the lamp-stand, and it gives light to everyone in the house. So let your light shine before people, so that they may see your good works, and they might glorify your heavenly father."* (vv. 14–16)

That doing good works leads to *kiddush hashem* — the sanctification of God's name — is a commonplace in Jewish literature. The following passage from *b. Yoma* 86a, in which Isa. 49:3 is cited as a proof-text — "And he said to me, 'You are my servant, O Israel, you through whom I will be glorified'" — is illustrative of this. It is noteworthy that the passage contains several beatitudes (as well as several "woes"), which resemble those found in 5:3–12. The text reads:

> Yizhak the disciple of Rabbi Yanai said: When a man's companions are ashamed of his reputation, it profanes God's name. Said R. Nahman b. Itzhak: (What is meant by reputation?) When people have to say of a man: "May his Lord pardon him for his deeds." And Abaye says, this is what we have learned in the following teaching: It is written, "And you shall love the Lord your God" (Deut. 6:5). The verse should be read to mean, "heaven's name should become loved through

you"; that is to say, a man must study the written Torah, the oral Mishnah and serve scholars. His interactions with other human beings should be pleasant. What will people then say of him? *Blessed* is his father, who taught him Torah; *blessed* is his teacher, who has instructed him in Torah, and *woe* to those people who have not studied Torah! Behold, the one who has learned Torah, how beautiful are his ways, how perfect his deeds! Of him the verse says the "And he said unto me, 'You are my servant, O Israel, you through whom I will be glorified.'" (Isa. 49:3) But if one has learned written Torah and oral Mishnah and served scholars, but is not honest and in his manner of speech with others is unpleasant, then what do people say about him? Behold, the one who has learned Torah, *woe* to his father who taught him Torah; *woe* to his teacher who instructed him in Torah! See the one who has learned Torah, how evil are his ways, how evil his deeds! Of him the verse says, "They profane my holy name, because they said of them, 'These are the people of the Lord, and out of his land are they gone forth'" (Ezek. 36:20).

For the Pharisaic sages respect for the divine name was of crucial importance. A text from the *Scholian* commentary to *Megillat Taanit* (ed. Lichtenstein [Jerusalem, 1986], 81) speaks regretfully of the period when under Antiochus IV the Jews were forbidden even to mention the name of God; and also of the period when the Hasmoneans, who overthrew Antiochus, introduced a policy which led to the repeated desecration of His name.

> *On the 3rd of Tishrei they [sages] annulled the [Hasmonean] edict requiring the divine name to be written in all business documents* — When the evil kingdom of Hellenists (under Antiochus Epiphanes) had issued anti-Jewish decrees against Israel, it was announced, "Deny the Kingdom of Heaven by showing, 'We have no portion with the God of Israel.'" And so they could not even mention the name of Heaven with their mouths. After their victory against Hellenism, the Hasmonean authorities declared that the name of Heaven must be written in every business document by stating [the name of the high priest] "who is the priest of Almighty God." [The passage continues to tell how the sages, on the 3rd of Tishrei, convinced the rulers to annul the decree governing the writing of such documents "with the name of Heaven on them," knowing these would eventually be thrown into garbage dumps. The date of the annulment of the decree came to be the date of a yearly celebration after that.]

The value of a public sanctification of God's name over a private one is stressed repeatedly in the rabbinic literature. A text from *b. Sotah* 36b is illustrative of this:

> Rabbi Hanna, son of Bizna, said in the name of Rabbi Shimon the Hassid, "Joseph sanctified God's name in private [by refusing the advances of

Potiphar's wife (Gen. 39:9)], and so the letter *heh* was given from the divine name to his name [i.e., "Jehoseph" (Ps. 81:6), so that he had three letters of the tetragrammaton in his name], Judah, who sanctified the name of Heaven in public [confessing his misdeeds with Tamar (Gen 38)], has all four letters of the divine name in his."

The image of light signifying correct teaching is apt, as the following traditions show. From *Derekh Eretz* chapter Ha-Minin 18 we read:

Those who confess righteously, and those who repent righteously, and those who receive penitents and teach them so that they do not slide back to their old ways, concerning them Scripture says, "Then shall your light shine forth like the dawn" (Isa. 58:8).

And from *Midrash Tanh.* (ed. Buber) (*Lev. Beha'alotecha*) 2, we read:

It was as if God had said to Moses, Tell Israel it is not because I need your light that I told you to light [Temple] lights but to give you merit. And so Scripture says, "The Lord desires for the sake of his righteous one's merit that he make the Torah praiseworthy and he make it esteemed" (Isa. 42:21)...and if you are scrupulous about lighting lights for my name also I will shine for you a great light in the future world to come. ...For Scripture says, "Arise, shine, for your light has come, and the glory of the Lord has risen upon you. For behold, darkness shall cover the earth, and thick darkness the peoples; but the Lord will arise upon you, and his glory will be seen upon you. And nations shall come to your light, and kings to the brightness of your rising" (Isa. 60:1–3).

Commentators and theologians repeatedly find that Jesus' teaching in Matthew (chapters 5–7) is ambiguous. That is, should his teaching be taken as normative for Christians or should it be taken simply as part of Matthew's technique of storytelling? If it is the latter, Jesus' teaching is meant to show him in the role of a traditional teacher whose teaching in the end, however, was rejected by the Jews but embraced by the Gentiles. The ambiguous nature of Jesus' teaching not only troubles modern scholars but it also troubled the early Christians (and apparently some Jews) in antiquity. For they understood that Matthew 5 could be read either as an eternal teaching or else as something that had come to an end when (as the Church Fathers taught) God rejected the Jews, this rejection having been confirmed by the destruction of the Temple. In *b. Šabb.* 115a there is a charming and well-crafted satire which, playing with texts from Matt. 5:16–17, pokes fun at the ambiguity inherent in the wider text, and shows how this ambiguity allowed certain Christians to profit from it. The text reads:

Ima Shalom was the wife of Rabbi Eliezer and the sister of Rabban Gamaliel. There was a "philosopher" [a euphemism for Christian theologian] in their neighborhood who had encouraged the reputation that he did not accept bribes. So the brother and sister wanted to expose him. [She said,] "I will bring him a lamp of gold," and they went to see him. She said to him, "I wish you to allow me my portion of an inheritance from the estate of my deceased father." He said to them "divide it!" [The brother said, In short,] the law is written for us, "Where there is a son then a daughter cannot inherit." He replied, "From the day you were exiled from your land, the law of Moses has been removed and been replaced by the Gospel. And that says, 'A son and daughter shall divide an inheritance equally.'" On the following day [when they came back] he [the brother] brought him a Libyan ass. He [the Christian] then declared to them: "I have looked further into the Gospel and it is written there. 'I have not come to subtract and I have not come to add to the law of Moses.' And it is written in this law that where a son exists then a daughter cannot inherit." Thereupon she exclaimed, "May your light shine like a lamp." Rabban Gamaliel retorted, "The ass came and kicked the lamp."

"Do not suppose that I have come to annul the Torah or the Prophets.
I did not come to annul but to fulfill." (v. 17)

The point here is in no way related to Matthew's use of fulfillment texts to illustrate that Jesus' path has been foretold in Scripture. Rather here Jesus is telling his audience that he is not some kind of unfettered apocalyptic preacher who sees that the law is about to be annulled because the final days have come. That is, Matthew wants to stress that Jesus was not antinomian (as Paul and John were post-Easter), but an erstwhile student of Torah teaching and a faithful Jewish preacher. When later Matthew's Jesus enters Jerusalem he will speak differently than he does here. Jesus' words show that he is not among the sinners who are reflected in Dan. 9:10–11: "For we did not obey the voice of the Lord our God to go in his teachings [Torahs] which he gave us through his servants the prophets. And all of Israel transgressed your Torah and turned without heeding your voice. And you placed upon us the curse and the oath which are written in the Torah of Moses, the servant of God, for we have sinned against Him."

"Amen, I say to you, until the heaven and the earth pass away, not
one iota or one flourish will disappear from the Torah, until all things
occur." (v. 18)

"Amen" is the answer to an implied oath; "I say to you" has the sense of "I swear to you." The force of this "amen" continues throughout this unit of the sermon (5:21–48), appearing again at 5:26 (Jesus says "I say to you" six more times in this unit — 5:22, 28, 32, 34, 39, 44). The use of these expressions heightens the importance of the words that follow. Such a device is a commonplace in the rabbinic literature.

The phrase "until heaven and earth pass away" should be understood as *reductio ad absurbum* rhetoric — heaven and earth can "pass away" but not even the smallest jot of a letter of the law can disappear, at least not *until all things occur,* that is, until the world is utterly gone. Compare Job 27:5: "Far be it from me that I should say you are right; *until* I die I will not put away my integrity from me." There is no allusion in this text to Paul's claim that Jesus' death and resurrection has rendered the law of Moses superfluous, as many used to say. What is meant by a letter of the law passing away is that no part of the law, however seemingly minor, should be transgressed.

Let us examine several passages from several different periods that can help us to understand what Jesus means to say in this text.

A close parallel to what Jesus says here is found in a text from *y. Sanh.* 2:6 (also *Exod. Rab.* 6.1, *Lev. Rab.* 19:2) as others have pointed out.[29] I include it here because it is instructive to compare this passage with the ones that follow it. The text reads:

> Our Rabbis said, When [Solomon disregarded] the Torah the miniscule letter *Iodh* (in [*the king*] *shall not increase wives,* (Deut. 17:17)) came up to God and prostrated herself and said to him, "Master of the Universe, did you not say not a single letter would ever be annulled from the Torah? Solomon arose and has annulled me! And if today he annuls one letter, tomorrow he will do another until the whole Torah will be annulled!"
> God replied to her, "Solomon and a thousand like him will disappear but the smallest speck of a tail of you will never be annulled."

A text from *b. Ber.* 32a refers to the passing away of heaven and earth in order to contrast their temporality with the eternal nature of God's name and word. The eternal nature of God's covenant with Israel is a common feature of the rabbinic literature. The text reads:

> *Remember Abraham, Isaac and Israel your servants, to whom you swore by yourself* (Exod. 32:13). What is the meaning of "by yourself"? Rabbi Eleazar said: Moses said to the Holy One, "Master of the Universe, if you had sworn to them by the heaven and the earth, I would have said, 'Just as the heaven and earth can pass away, so can your oath pass also away.' Now, however, you swore to them by your Great Name. Just as your Great Name endures for ever and ever, so your oath endures for ever and ever."

That the covenant has cosmic import is sometimes confirmed with a text from Jeremiah (33:25). In *Batei Midrashot* (ed. Wertheimer), vol. 2, *Otiot de Rabbi Akiba,* version A, p. 386, we read:

[The Torah saves Israel from the fires of *gehinom*], for with it the upper and lower beings endure, as it is said, "So says the Lord, 'If not for my covenant, the day and the night, the laws of heaven and the laws of the earth I would not have set' (Jer. 33:25). And through it [the Torah] heaven and earth will be renewed in the next world, as the verse says, "For behold I create a new heaven and a new earth" (Isa. 65:17). On whose merit? On the merit of Israel who fulfills the Torah.

To fulfill the Torah does not mean to preserve it but rather to keep its commands. This, too, is what Jesus means to say here.

In the following text from *b. Yebam.* 79a, the rather shocking point is made that even the integrity of the law can be set aside, if this is done for the sake of the sanctification of God's name. Jesus places great value on both the law and the Divine name but he does not weigh them against each other. The text reads:

> Rabbi Yohanan said in the name of Rabbi Shimon ben Yehozadak: It is preferable that a letter be let loose from the Torah if then the name of Heaven would be publicly sanctified.

"Whoever breaks one of the least of these commandments and so teaches people will be called least in the Kingdom of Heaven, and whoever does them and teaches them, that person shall be called great in the Kingdom of Heaven." (v. 19)

This provides the interpretation of 5:18. The way in which one performs the commandments determines one's portion in the World to Come.

"For I say to you that unless your righteousness greatly exceeds that of the Scribes and Pharisees, you will never enter the Kingdom of Heaven." (v. 20)

Again the force of the expression "I say to you" stresses something which, though it could never come to be in fact, should nonetheless be striven for. Hyperbole is an important didactic device. The brief text from *b. Ber.* 4b, which states that "all who transgress the word of the sages are liable to the death penalty," is not meant to be taken literally; its purpose is to underscore the importance of the behavior the sages claim the law requires.

Traditionally there have been three different ways of understanding this unit (5:21–48). The first and oldest way is to see that what Jesus is doing here is revising certain legal texts from the Bible in accordance with his own "Law of Righteousness." That is, in this unit Jesus boldly contradicts the Mosaic law to reveal a law of the heart. Hence the name with which the unit is often called — "The Antitheses." The second way of understanding this unit is to see that in it Jesus is citing certain laws verbatim from Scripture and then interpreting them according to a specialized reading of the Scripture.[30] That is, what he repeatedly says in this unit is something like this: "You might think that this law means what it literally says but I tell you that it does not."

However, the problem with understanding this unit in either of these ways is that in both the assumption is made that Jesus is setting aside the literal meaning of the laws about which he speaks. This is obviously the case in the first way of understanding this unit; for here even anger, for example, is said to be forbidden, so that there is no longer a need to forbid murder. If there is no anger, then there can be no murder. But there can be anger and yet no murder. Would Jesus have overlooked the murder and complained only about the anger? It is absurd to think so. In the second way of understanding the unit, in which it is believed that Jesus interprets the laws according to a specialized reading of the Scriptures — which is said to be based on a rabbinic form — what is meant by this is that although it might be thought that a scriptural text says x, because of the presence of a certain word in the text it actually means y.[31] And so here too the obvious meaning is abandoned. But if it is the case that in this section Jesus puts aside the traditional meaning of the laws about which he speaks, then what he has said in 5:17 would be false: he has not come to fulfill the Law and the Prophets but rather to annul them. Besides that the importance of physical murder and adultery would be pushed aside. No one could seriously think that Jesus meant to teach this.

The third way of understanding this unit is to see that what Jesus is doing here is erecting "fences," so to speak, around the laws about which he speaks, in order to prevent these laws from being transgressed. That is, if the law enjoins one not to murder, the best way to see to it that one does not transgress this law is to enjoin one not even to become angry at all. It is worthwhile to quote Jacob Neusner here.

> We have to distinguish the substance of what Jesus is saying from the form that he gives to his statements. Specifically, Jesus sets forth as his demonstration of how not to abolish the Torah and the prophets but to fulfill them, a set of teachings that, all together, point to a more profound demand — on the Torah's part — than people have realized. Not I must not kill, I must not even approach that threshold of anger that in the end leads to murder. ... "Make a fence around the Torah." That is to say, conduct yourself in such a way that you will avoid even the things that cause you to sin, not only sin itself.

Neusner goes on to show that many of these very teachings are found in the Hebrew Bible, especially the Book of Proverbs.[32]

I am not sure one can say that what Jesus is doing here is erecting "a fence around the Torah." (The erecting of a "fence around the Torah" was done in two ways, either through legislation or voluntarily.) Rather I think something else is going on here.

As did certain Rabbis, Jesus also practiced what is known as *Mishnat Hassidim*; that is, he lived his life according to especially strict purity rules (for more on this, see my commentary to 5:22 below). At some point Jesus, and also these Rabbis, endeavored to find a scriptural basis for the way they were living and for what they were preaching but this was simple homiletics, not serious exegesis. And so I do not think that in pronouncing on these laws in the way that he did Jesus was doing exegesis at all; he was simply making pronouncements on them under familiar scriptural headings. I see no warrant for the claim that Jesus is attempting to supersede the Scriptures here. As a preacher, he is telling us what he thinks is the proper way to observe God's will, both written and unwritten. The *Sipra* (*Kedoshim*) to Lev. 19:2 expresses well the intention behind Jesus' manner of preaching:

> *And the Lord spoke to Moses, saying, Speak to the children of Israel and you shall say to them, You shall be holy* (Lev. 19:2). This verse teaches us that the present section was taught to the congregation as a whole since most of the laws of the Torah are dependent on it. "You shall be holy" means, "You shall be *perushim* (*abstemious*)."

Concerning this text Ramban (Moses Nachmanides) claims, in his notes to it that are included in Maimonides' *Book of Commandments* 4, that when it says "You shall be holy" it means that "You shall be *perushim*." It is saying that one must endeavor to eliminate all one's unholy characteristics, for this is what God wants. In these same notes Ramban also points to other biblical texts whose purpose is to encourage self-discipline, such as: "And you shall guard every commandment I command you this day" (Deut. 11:8), and others (Deut. 8:1, 27:1). "You shall be Holy," though not strictly a command and so not open to legislation, encourages one to ever-refine one's character so that one acts more and more piously. It is this injunction to "be holy, for I the Lord your God am holy" that underlies all that Jesus says in this unit of the sermon. That is, to be holy it is not enough simply to act in a holy way, but one must also try to be holy within. Again Ramban, commenting on this matter in his *Commentary to the Torah* to Lev. 19:2, says that it is perfectly possible to act piously, and so not be liable to enforceable punishments, but to remain impious in mind.

The texts from Leviticus and Deuteronomy above are found throughout the Talmud to justify extrajudicial safeguards, but also to foster *imitatio dei* rules that the Rabbis followed, such as visiting the sick and showing mercy to the poor. We shall have more to say about this at the close of this chapter. When later in the Gospel we see Jesus debating with the Pharisees over their Sabbath safeguards we discover that his position, set out in a very sophisticated way, is in fact the one that is normative in the Talmud. It is only because of the venomous nature of Matthew's rhetoric that Jesus' (or the pre-Matthean gospel's) proper adherence to Pharisaic understanding of Jewish teaching is kept hidden.

"You have heard that it was said to the ancients, 'You shall not murder' (Exod. 20:13), and 'whoever murders will be liable to judgment.'"
(v. 21)

The first quotation here is verbatim from Exod. 20:13; the second is a paraphrase of Gen. 9:6. According to the Rabbis, one could not be punished for any act,[33] unless it had been made clear in the Torah that this act was forbidden.[34] This is why in their discussions concerning the meting out of punishments, both the text that states what is prohibited, and the text that makes clear what the punishment is for having transgressed the prohibited act are included. It is also why before any punishments were meted out the Rabbis required witnesses to ascertain whether or not the one who was accused of transgressing a law knew both of the law he had transgressed and the punishment that went with having transgressed it (*b. Mak.* 6a; *b. Sanh.* 8b). The following text from *b. Sanh.* 60b is typical of these discussions. Note here how the Rabbis point out that the text indicating the punishment for the transgression is far removed from the place where the text stating the crime is found. The text reads:

How do we know that prostrating oneself before an idol is punishable by death? The Torah says "and he went and he worshipped other gods and bow down to them." And this is followed by, "and you shall take out that man or woman … and stone them with stones that they die" (Deut. 17:3–5). So now we know a punishment, but where is the actual command found that forbids it? Scripture states, "For you shall not bow down to another god" (Exod. 34:14).

Jesus is correct to say that Jewish tradition maintains that this prohibition concerning murder (and the following prohibitions concerning adultery and divorce, and so on) was taught by Moses on divine authority, and then by teachers from Moses down to Jesus. Jesus, and I need to emphasize it time and again, does not teach here that the traditional understanding concerning those who commit murder is wrong in any way, or that this injunction against murder is to be removed from its age-old understanding.[35]

Jesus opens this unit of the sermon by emphasizing the necessity of abiding by the laws of the Torah, whether great or small, to do which, in effect means, to exercise total self-control (5:21, 28, 34, 39, 44). In 4 Macc. 5:16–24 the soon-to-be-martyred Eleazar gives an impassioned speech in which he says much the same thing. In both Jesus' sermon and Eleazar's speech, the importance of the law in molding the model Jew is made clear. This model Jew is not seen to be any different in Philo or in Josephus or in the rabbinic literature as he or she is in Jesus' sermon or the speech of Eleazar. This speech reads as follows:

> "We, O Antiochus, who have been persuaded to govern our lives by the divine law, think that there is no compulsion more powerful than our obedience to the law. Therefore we consider that we should not transgress it in any respect. … To transgress the law in matters either small or great is of equal seriousness, for in either case the law is equally despised. … [The law] teaches self-control, so that we master all pleasures and desires, and it also trains us in courage, so that we endure any suffering willingly; it instructs us in justice, so that in all our dealings we act impartially, and it teaches us piety, so that with proper reverence we worship the only living God" (4 Macc. 5:16–17, 18–19, 23–24).

"But I say to you that everyone who is angry with his brother (without a cause) shall be in danger of judgment, and everyone who says "Raka!" to his brother shall be in danger of the Sanhedrin, and whoever says, "Moron!" shall be in danger of fiery Gehenna. (v. 22)

Again here the expression "I say to you" highlights the importance of the words that follow. The courts heard cases involving insults (*m. B. Qam.* 8:1 and *m. Ketub.* 3:7). Name-calling was considered a grave sin, but to be on the receiving end was not necessarily thought to be an "embarrassment," although this would have been up to the courts to decide (*m. B. Qam.* 8:1, and *b. B. Qam.* 86b). *Mekhaneh shem ra le-havero* (*b. B. Meṣ.* 58b) is how the name-caller was called and, whatever the courts may have decided (if they bothered with the case at all) the Rabbis claimed that such people had permanent places in *gehinnom* (*b. B. Meṣ.* 58b).

The word *raka* means "idiot" or "someone who is devoid of good sense." In a text from *'Abot R. Nat.*, version A, chap. 16 (addition 2), it is the word by which the Rabbis said one's good conscience addressed one's evil urge while warning it against committing serious offenses. The evil urge was addressed in this way to show that it was indeed "idiotic" and/or "devoid of good sense." The text reads:

> How does the evil urge work? They said, the evil urge is 13 years older than the good conscience and is with him from the womb. For 13 years if he starts on the path to desecrate the Sabbath there is nothing to stay his hand, to commit murder, there is nothing to stay his hand, to do a lewd act—nothing to stay his hand. After the age of 13 he develops a good conscience and now if he sets out to desecrate the Sabbath, it says to him, "*Raka*, Scripture states: 'Whoever desecrates it shall surely die'" (Exod. 31:14). If he sets out to murder, it says to him "*Raka*, Scripture states: 'Whosoever sheds the blood of a person by a person his blood shall be shed'" (Gen. 9:6), if he goes to do a lewd act, it says to him, "*Raka*, Scripture states: 'They shall surely die, the adulterer and the adulteress'" (Lev. 20:10).

The phrase "without cause," which occurs in some late readings, reminds one of the expression *sinat hinam*—"hatred without cause."[36] The Rabbis considered that hatred without cause was as grave a sin as the sin of idolatry, adultery, and murder combined (*y. Yoma* 1:1, *b. Yoma* 9b). Senseless anger they saw as being tantamount to idolatry;[37] insulting someone as being tantamount to murder.[38]

Jesus says here that to be angry is sinful enough, but that it is more sinful to call someone "*Raka*," and even more sinful still to call someone "*moros*." The ever harsher punishments he spells out for each of these sins make this clear. He also implies that it is anger that leads to name-calling and, taking into account verse 21, that it can, perhaps, lead to murder, and so it can be said that anger is as grave a sin as murder. Now again it might seem that in warning against anger Jesus is erecting a "fence" around the law enjoining one not to kill. But I think rather that what Jesus is saying here is something more like this: "Everyone knows that murder is a grave sin deserving of harsh punishment, but you should also know that to be angry and to insult someone in anger are equally grave sins deserving of equally harsh punishments."

As I say, because of the ever-harsher punishment he declares one deserves for each, Jesus makes plain that the gravity of the sin from being angry through to calling someone "*moros*" only increases; and that cases involving insults were heard in the local courts. Now the supreme Sanhedrin would never have heard such cases, which is something Jesus' audience would have known, as very likely his audience would have thought that the fires of hell were reserved for far greater sinners than those who simply called others names. But all this is beside the point. Jesus' use of hyperbole here was the accepted homiletic way to point out how serious was the effect of a certain kind of immoral behavior. We do not have here the case of a *Hassid* going beyond the measure of the law or of a legal midrashist finding that biblical texts dealing with murder are really speaking of anger and insult. That is, Jesus is not saying here that the law prohibiting murder should be interpreted more stringently than it has traditionally been interpreted. Rather he is saying, as I point out above, that just as murder is a grave sin, so are anger and name-calling. Indeed, the Rabbis did find scriptural warrant both to prohibit name-calling and to punish those who did. Indeed Rabbis also compared name calling to be "like murder." Just as punishable murder required intent to kill, so punishable name-calling required intent to insult (*b. B. Qam.* 86a).

The early medieval sage and ethicist Rabbenu Yonah, in his classic work *Sha'arei Teshuva* (3:140), states that committing an act of public ridicule is so serious an offense that one is obligated to sacrifice one's life rather than transgress it. What lies behind this kind of thinking also lies behind what I consider to be the most radical teaching found in all of the rabbinic literature.

A tradition in *t. Ter.* 7.20 states that it is forbidden for the Jews in a city to hand over to their enemies — that is, the Romans — another Jew for execution, even if it has been made known to these Jews that every last one of them in the city shall be killed if this is not done. What is so radical about this teaching is that the lesser matter was the fact that hundreds of Jews (if not more) should end up being slaughtered for the sake of a single Jew whom they would not turn over and who, in any event, would be slaughtered along with all the others Jews in the city. The fact that the moral character of the Jews was thought to be compromised by the handing over of one of their own to the Romans was the greater matter. This was more important than life itself.

Now this teaching was clearly from *Mishnat Hassidim*, or the "Mishnah of the Pious." For in this tradition from the Tosefta it says further that the Jews of a city *could* hand over to the Romans one of their own for execution, but only if this Jew who was to be handed over was already deserving of execution according to Jewish law as well. This, of course, seems the more practical approach in that it allows the saving of Jewish lives while forfeiting a life that in any event deserved to be forfeited. In *y. Ter.* 8:4 (var. *Gen. Rab.* 94:9) there is also a text concerning the matter of the Jews handing over one of their own to the Romans, and in which also the tradition from *t. Ter.* 7.20 is referred to. It is of interest to note that in this text Elijah upbraids Rabbi Yehoshua ben Levi for handing over to the Romans the Jew they had been seeking, that is, for not acting according to the *Mishnat Hassidim*. It should be said, however, that no court would ever have imposed penalties for not adhering to *Mishnat Hassidim*. The text reads:

> Ulla bar Koshev was wanted by the Roman authorities and he fled to Lod, to the house of Rabbi Yehoshua ben Levi and they came after him in force to the city. They said, "If you don't give him to us we will slaughter the city." Rabbi Yehoshua ben Levi went to him and convinced him and he surrendered himself to them. Elijah used to regularly appear to the rabbi but then he failed to appear. He fasted numerous fasts and finally he appeared to him. [Elijah] said to him — "Am I to appear to *traitors* [who hand Jews over to the Romans]?" He said to him "Did I not do the *teaching* [i.e., from *t. Ter.* 7:20, which states one is permitted to hand over to the enemy a criminal if the enemy asks for him by name so that everyone else might be saved]. Elijah replied "Is this *the Mishnah of the Hassidim* [*Gen. Rab.* adds, "which is sufficient for others but not for you]?"

The normal way of *Hassidic* teaching is to be seen in the tradition from *Pesiq. Rab.* 23 (also *y. Šabb.* 15.3) that follows. A biblical text from the Decalogue concerning the Sabbath (Exod. 20:9) is first stated, which is then followed by the teaching from Rabbi Aivo. This teaching from Rabbi Aivo, which also concerns the Sabbath, but whose scrupulousness far exceeds the traditional understanding of the biblical text, nonetheless does not derive from the biblical text although it does not override it either. The point of including the biblical text is simply to show what Scripture demands. What follows is a sermon, which is not suggested either by the verse or by any other law.

No version of the *Pesiq. Rab.* midrash includes the phrase from *y. Shabbat*—"Just as God ceased from thinking…" It is almost certain that this is a gloss that has been inserted into the text of *y. Shabbat* to explain the connection between Rabbi Abahu's dictum—"Cease from non-Sabbath thoughts!"—and Exod. 20:9, which is present in all versions of the tradition, and that this gloss has been taken from another tradition based on Exod. 31:17 (about which I will say more below). In all probability the original tradition included the biblical text from Exodus as a way of indicating the topic of the sermon to follow and nothing more. And so the biblical text was used as a kind of peg upon which Rabbi Aivo set his teaching in order that it might seem to carry with it divine sanction, for what Rabbi Aivo teaches has no scriptural basis; hence the impulse to create a seeming connection between it and Exod. 20. All versions of the tradition make plain that what Rabbi Berekhiah says in it is based on the teaching of the *Hassid*: "Do not do labor on the Sabbath; do not even think about it." (To me this Hassidic way of teaching is the basis for understanding the teachings of Jesus in this unit concerning anger and lust etc., which he introduces first by quoting the appropriate biblical texts from the Decalogue.) The text from *Pesiq. Rab.* 23 (*y. Šabb.* 15:3) reads:

> "And the seventh day is a Sabbath for the Lord your God (you shall not do any work)" [Exod. 20:9]. Rabbi Aivo [*y. Šabb.* 15:3 reads Abahu] said, "Cease from [non-Sabbath] thoughts!" [*y.* reads: "Just as God ceased from thinking of his work — (of creation), so you cease from your thinking about work."] Rabbi Berekhiah said [to illustrate the teaching], It happened that a *Hassid* took a walk in his vineyard on the Sabbath to see its condition and he saw a breech in the fence. He thought he would repair it after the Sabbath but then he said, "Since I thought about the repair on the Sabbath I will never ever repair it."

By telling himself that he will never mend his fence, the Hassid is censuring himself for having transgressed a teaching not of the law but of the exceptionally pious concerning certain activities on the Sabbath.

As I say, the above mentioned gloss in *y. Šabb.* 15.3 — "Just as God ceased from thinking" — comes from a tradition based on Exod. 3:17 that is found in *'Abot R. Nat.,* version B, chap. 21. Here the prohibition against thinking about non-Sabbath activities on the Sabbath is derived from Exod. 31:17. Again it sounds like something from *Mishnat Hassidim* — the law of the extra-pious.

> This story was told about the seemingly bizarre custom of Rabbi Josiah. He used to empty out his house to another of all the utensils at the onset of the Sabbath, or even from one corner to another corner. People asked him, Rabbi, why do you do this? He answered, "So that the Sabbath can have full precedence for us." Scripture states, "It is a sign forever between me and the people of Israel that in six days the Lord made heaven and earth, and on the seventh day he ceased and stopped" (Exod. 31:17). [There is no redundancy.] "He ceased" means "from physical work," and "stopped" means "from thinking about work"[39]

Let us now return to the Hassid who left his fence in disrepair for the rest of his life. According to rabbinic law it was not necessary for him to do this. For according to the law, in times of emergency or when it was necessary to expedite the fulfillment of the Torah some measure of nonlaborious activity was permitted on the Sabbath for the sake of something that was to be done once the Sabbath had passed. However, the product of any *physical* work done on the Sabbath, even if this work were to have been done by a Gentile, was forbidden to be used by a Jew. This exegesis is based on the idea that whatever constituted rest for God on the Sabbath must also be what constituted rest for the Jews on the Sabbath. A text from *m. Šabb.* 23.4 confirms the above:

One can spend Sabbath waiting for nightfall at the Sabbath boundary {beyond which the Rabbis forbade leaving) to later supervise the needs of a bride, the needs of a funeral — to bring one a casket or shrouds. If a (well meaning) non-Jew brought mourning pipes into the boundary on the Sabbath they cannot [ever] be used by a Jew, unless of course they came from close by. If the non-Jews constructed [on the Sabbath] a casket for someone or dug out a grave for some [gentile], a Jew may be buried in it [after the Sabbath]. Yet if such things were done for the sake of a Jew, no [Jew] can ever be buried in it.

The Rabbis, of course, could not make rules governing gentile behavior, so the measure forbidding the Jews from using the product of gentile labor done on the Sabbath was designed to prevent the Jews from bypassing the Sabbath laws. Hence the products of gentile labor made on the Sabbath, even if this was for the purpose of helping a Jew to fulfill a sacred duty, were not to be used at all.

If Matthew had been concerned to have Jesus discuss the Sabbath in the sermon, he might well have had Jesus say something like this: "You have heard what was told to the ancients, 'And the seventh day is a Sabbath for the Lord your God. You shall not do any work on this day.' But I say unto you: Do not even think about doing work on this day." In his discussion under the rubric "You shall not murder," Jesus goes on to say (vv. 23–25) why it is necessary to refrain from being angry and from causing others to be angry. It is true that hatred leads to murder (Lev. 19:11). But what is more important is that one's sacrifice to God is of no account if, while offering this sacrifice one is either angry with another, or if the one making the sacrifice knows that another is angry with him. That is, if one wants to be forgiven by God, one must first forgive one's fellow man and/or see to it that one is forgiven by one's fellow man (compare Prov. 16:7, *m. 'Abot* 3:10). I take this to be the salient point of the discussion on anger, rather than to see that in it Jesus directs one to "behave beyond the measure of the law." As I say, Jesus is not doing exegesis here, nor is he erecting "fences around the Torah." Rather he is speaking of pious rules that have only a very loose connection to the biblical texts he uses to introduce his brief sermons in this unit of the larger sermon.

"If you are offering your sacrifice upon the altar, and remember that your brother has something against you, leave your gift there before the altar and first go, be reconciled to your brother, and then go and bring your sacrifice." (vv. 23–24)

These verses make clear what is implicit in 5:22.

"Be quickly on good terms with your accuser [debtor], while you are still with him on the road [to trial], lest your accuser hand you over to the judge and the judge to the attendant and you will be thrown into prison." (v. 25)

The model here is Prov. 6:1–5:

My son, if you have put up security for your neighbor, have given your pledge for a stranger, if you are snared in the words of your mouth, caught in the words of your mouth, then do this, my son, and save yourself, for you have come into the hand of your neighbor: Go, hasten, and plead urgently with your neighbor. Give your eyes no sleep and your eyelids no slumber; save yourself like a gazelle from the hand of the hunter, like a bird from the hand of the fowler.

Using this text from Proverbs as the proof-text, a tradition in *Gen. Rab.* 93.1 states that among other things one should "cleave" to peacemaking. This tradition also suggests that if in debt one should cast oneself down before one's debtor and acknowledge his superior position, as Judah did before Joseph (Gen. 44:18–34).

"Amen, I say to you, you will never get out of there until you have repaid the last quadrans." (v. 26)

Jesus states here that to be reconciled with one's accuser is in the end far less costly than to refuse to be so. The legal process described here sounds like the one in which the Roman military tribunals in Palestine judged the Jews according to laws that would never have been applied to Roman citizens. And so Jesus also seems to be saying here that one should avoid being judged by the Romans. Better to be at the mercy of your fellow man than to be at the mercy of the Romans.

"You have hear that is was said, 'Do not commit adultery' (Exod. 20:4, Deut. 5:17), But I say to you that everyone who looks at a woman to covet her has already committed adultery with her in his heart." (vv. 27–28)

The language Jesus uses here, although rhetorical, borders on the language of the decree. Jesus says that one can commit adultery with the eyes, that is, with one's imagination. He also points out that in sinning with the eyes, one is also sinning in one's heart.[40] Much the same thing is said in a tradition attributed to Shimon ben Lakish, in which he is commenting on Job 24:15. The tradition, from *Lev. Rab.* 23.12, reads:

"The eye of the adulterer also waits for the twilight, saying, 'No eye will see me'; and he veils his face" (Job 24:15). Shimon ben Lakish says no one should think that only one who engages in physical adultery is termed an adulterer. One who commits "adultery in his eyes" is also termed an adulterer.

Neither Jesus nor Shimon ben Lakish recommends corporal punishment for having committed adultery in this way.[41] But Jesus does say that for those who sin in this way the gates of hell are opened.

This prohibition against sinning with the eyes is different from the prohibition against some of the moral and ritual sins instituted by the Rabbis because these sins were in terms of deed too much like biblical prohibitions. I speak of rabbinic prohibitions against mild forms of usury, rabbinic laws against Sabbath work, rabbinic laws against theft, rabbinic amounts for tithes, rabbinic defilements and others. Certain acts the Torah law permitted the Rabbis forbade because these acts seemed physically similar to the divine prohibition.

> *"And if your right eye offends you, remove it and throw it from you. For it is to your advantage to destroy one of the parts of your body than for your whole body be thrown into Gehenna. And if your right hand offends you, cut it off and throw it from you, for it is to your advantage to destroy one of the parts of your body than for your whole body to be thrown into Gehenna." (vv. 29–30)*

In relation to either the eye or the hand, the full meaning of "offends" here is "offends in a sexual way."[42] When Jesus speaks of either removing the eye, or cutting off the hand, that offends, he is of course speaking rhetorically. Minor tractate *Kallah Rab.* 2.5 mentions three types of hands it would be better to cut off: the hand that sins through the penis; the hand that (habitually has dangerous material on it that) causes blindness; and the hand that commits murder.

> *"It was said, 'Whoever divorces his wife, let him give her a bill of divorcement." (v. 31)*

It is almost certain that this brief section on divorce (vv. 31–32), and the one following on the swearing of oaths (vv. 33–37), were originally absent from the sermon. They are Matthean insertions. There is no Lukan parallel to either of these sections in the form Matthew has them.

What Jesus says here is a loose paraphrase of Deut. 24:1. It might have made more sense to include what follows in 24:2: "And when she is departed out of his house, she may go and be another man's wife." This paraphrase of Deut. 24:1 cuts through much legal detail on divorce to present the normative Jewish practice: a man gives his wife a bill of divorce and the marriage is dissolved. Jesus does not engage in biblical hermeneutics here, as he does in 19:7–9.

> *"But I say to you that anyone who divorces his wife, except for the reason of her sexually immoral behavior, causes her to commit adultery, and whoever marries a divorced woman commits adultery himself." (v. 32)*

No rabbi ever suggested that anyone who gave to his wife a properly executed bill of divorce would then be guilty of adultery upon remarriage. This was so even if the grounds for the divorce were not sanctioned by their laws; in this case still the divorce was final and the parties were free to remarry.

In 19:7–9 there is this dialogue between Jesus and his Pharisaic interlocutors.

> "Why then did Moses command one to give a certificate of divorce and to send her away?" He said to them, "Because of your hardness of heart Moses allowed you to divorce your wives, but from the beginning it was not so. And I say to you: whoever divorces his wife, except for sexual immorality, and marries another, commits adultery."

What Jesus says to his disciples in 19:11, who have questioned him about his saying on divorce — "Not everyone can receive this saying, but only those to whom it is given" — might suggest that that this saying is *mida Hassidut* (see *b. Šabb.* 120a, *b. B. Meṣ.* 52b, *b. Hul.* 130b).[43]

At any rate here is what emerges as Jesus' teaching on divorce in chapter 19 from this dialogue. For practical reasons, Jesus says, Moses allowed divorce on whatever grounds. But Jesus says that divorce should be permitted only in the event that one's wife has been sexually immoral. That is, Jesus is essentially setting aside (for those who can hear it) the Mosaic laws on divorce in favor of God's original law. For as he says God's original law on divorce was different from, and preferable to, that of Moses. The Pharisees made no distinction between the Divine and the Mosaic legislation (*y. Ber.* 1.4)[44] In the Mosaic law, as understood by the Rabbis and Jesus, sexual immorality on the part of the wife was only one of the reasons a man might give for divorcing his wife, whereas Jesus sees that it is the only reason. The Rabbis agreed that sexual immorality on the part of the wife should lead to divorce (apparently, there is no option here).[45] But it seems in Matthew 19 Jesus forbids polygamy — quoting from

Gen. 2:24, he says that "the two become one flesh" — and so remarriage by a man is adultery, except in the one case in which the man has come to be divorced as a result of the sexual immorality of his wife. In this case alone is he free to remarry. Jesus says nothing in this dialogue about the remarriage of a woman who was divorced for having engaged in unfaithful behavior.

Matthew 5:32 seems to have been added by Matthew to his received list of *Mishnat Hassidim*. His source for 5:32 was the synoptic version of Matt. 19:7–9, which he reworked, but this seems to have been somewhat different from the text we have.

The differences between 5:32 and 19:7–9 are interesting. In chapter 19 Jesus' teachings on divorce focus on the man. In 5:32 the focus of Jesus' teaching on divorce is still on the man but here he also speaks of the woman, stating that a man who divorces his wife for any reason that the Mosaic law allows, can cause her to stumble into an adulterous relationship. Also in 5:32 there is no suggestion that polygamy is not allowed. All that is said is that a woman who has been divorced for any reason but unfaithfulness remains married to her husband. Thus if she has had relations with another after her divorce, Jesus says she is still legally married to her husband. Then, she is an adulteress and the man with whom she has been is also an adulterer. This would be case under Mosaic law as well (as the Rabbis understood it): a woman who has not been divorced with a proper bill of divorce is forbidden to all but her husband (and to him too if she has been unfaithful but it is not adultery for her to be with him even so). She and the man with whom she has been unfaithful (even if living as man and wife) are both guilty of adultery. What is at issue then is what constitutes a proper divorce. We do not know if Jesus means that both the woman and the man are subject to the death penalty (not necessarily administered) or rather that what Jesus says is adultery is so only in the eyes of God but not in the eyes of humans.

There is another issue to consider here, namely, the somewhat haphazard way in which in this text Jesus makes reference to Deut. 24:1 and 2; but we shall leave this until our discussion of chapter 19, in which Jesus also refers to these verses from Deuteronomy, but more directly, even if they are dismissed as concessions.[46]

> *"Again, you have heard that it was said to the ancients, 'You shall not swear oaths deceitfully,' (Lev. 19:12) [And you might think it means] 'But you shall perform to the Lord your oaths.'" (v. 33)*

LXX renders Lev. 19:12: *kai ouk homeisthe tw onomati mou en' adikw*, which literally translates as: "And you shall not declare an oath by my name unjustly."

The Hebrew reads: *ve-lo tishave'u vi-shemi lashaqer*, which translates as: "and you shall not declare an oath by my name dishonestly." Matthew condenses this to *ouk epiorkeseis* — "You shall not swear an oath deceitfully." As a result of this injunction from Lev. 19 it was common for people to swear by something other than God's name, though this something else was usually something of value. What these other things were varied.

Jesus introduces the text from Leviticus, and then by way of a paraphrase of Num. 30:2 states what one might deduce from this text — that it is fine to swear an oath so long as it is fulfilled. But this is not Jesus' position at all. In fact, his position is precisely the opposite. Avoid swearing oaths at all, he says (v. 34). In like fashion (v. 43) Jesus will state that from the ancients saying, "Love your neighbor as yourself [Lev. 19:18]" one might conclude that one can then hate those who are not one's neighbors. But this, Jesus says, is not what should be deduced from this at all, but again just the opposite. In neither of these cases does Jesus transcend the written law, but he does reject the facile assumptions that one might reasonably make based on these laws.

Consider the following text from *Midrash Aggada* (ed. Buber), Lev. 5:1, in which, like Jesus, the Rabbis make clear that it is best not to swear at all:

> *And when a person sins, [and having heard the voice of an oath, and he was witness, or saw, or knew — if he does not declare it, he shall bear his iniquity]* (Lev 5:1). Our Rabbis said, even if done honestly it is not good for a person to take an oath. One should not become reckless in respect to taking oaths (and then suffer horrid consequences).[47] It once happened there was a royal mountain on which two thousand cities were situated. These were all destroyed on account of a truthful oath [perhaps sworn, "on the life of the king."]. How did it happen? Each person swore an oath [of an unnecessary nature] with his friend, "I will go and eat!" "I will go and drink!" and they went and did so. But if for this [seemingly harmless taking of an oath] for the sake of eating and drinking which oath they swore and performed [the royal cities] were destroyed, then consider how much more so, on account of people who swear to no purpose whatsoever, [will havoc ensue].

> *"But I tell you not to swear any oath, neither by heaven, because it is the throne of God [Isa. 66:1]." (v. 34)*

The form here is familiar from the rabbinic literature. A general rule with a broad sweep is stated, which covers all the lesser cases; and even though one might think that the rule allows for a lesser case because this lesser case has become common practice, this is not so. Therefore the Rabbis state the rule and then, although they say that it is not necessary to speak of any of the lesser cases that would contravene the rule, still they do speak of the lesser cases that would contravene it, to make clear that the rule remains wholly operative. The Rabbis used the form: "This is the case...and I need not have mentioned that one also [but I did]."[48]

With regard to the swearing of oaths, Jesus says here that one should not assume that Lev. 19:12 means that, because it says one should not swear falsely, it is acceptable to swear honestly. That is, even though this might seem to be an acceptable exegesis for this verse, Jesus says rather that one should not swear at all.[49] Now because Lev. 19:12 states that one should not swear falsely by God's name — and it was the custom not to swear by his name[50] — one might think there were at least several other reasons contained within the verse that would allow one to swear an oath. First, Lev. 19:12 only forbids the swearing of an oath that is not meant to be kept; and, second, the prohibition against swearing an oath applies only to those sworn in God's name but not to those sworn by any of the other conventional things that people swore by in first century Palestine and later, such as heaven and earth, as Jesus indicates here.[51] But again Jesus denies both of these things.

Concerning what one was able to swear by, the Rabbis finally formulated a rule: if something by which one swore could at times be understood to be a reference to God, but at other times could be understood to be a reference to something else, then unless both parties agreed to accept that by which the oath was sworn, the oath could be retracted (b. Šebu. 35a–b). But Jesus claims that, either because these conventional things — such as heaven and earth — were not circumlocutions but in fact did refer to God, or that because it was not clear if the oath taker intended to refer to God by these circumlocutions, they should not be used at all.

Much of the parallel material from the rabbinic literature that discusses the things Jesus mentions that people commonly swore by and the rationales for their popularity has now been collected and any scholarly commentary provides these sources from this literature.[52] The benefit of our knowing these sources is that now we can see that what Jesus says here concerning the swearing of oaths was in no way revolutionary.

> *"Nor by the earth, because it is his footrest (Isa. 66:1), nor by Jerusalem,[53] because it is the great King's city (Ps. 48:3). Nor should you swear by your head, because you are not able to make a single hair white or black." (vv. 35–36)*

Mishnah Sanhedrin 3:2 speaks of swearing by the head. *Lev. Rab.* (*Metzora*) 19:2 states that if everyone in the world were to gather together in an effort to find a way to make a (the tone of the text suggests that one should add here — a single feather of the) raven's wing turn from black to white they would not be able do it.

"Let your speech be 'Yes, yes,' and 'No, no.' More than this comes from the evil one." (v. 37)

Here too the commentators mention all the relevant parallels, such as *b. B. Meṣ.* 49a and *Ruth Rab.* 7.6. For the righteous yes is yes and no is no. According to *Derech Eretz* 5:1, oaths should always be avoided by saying instead "Yes, yes" and "No, no." Rava derived this same teaching from Gen. 9:11, where God swears that never again shall he bring a flood to destroy the earth: "I establish my covenant with you, that never again..." A covenant is an oath and the Aramaic Targums regularly translate "covenant" (Hebrew: *brit*) as "oath" (Hebrew: *shevuah*). For example, *Targum Onqelos* renders both the oath in Gen. 26:3 and the covenant in Deut. 8:3 as *qeyama*. So Rava finds that in Gen. 9:11 God swears an oath because not once but twice in Gen. 9:11 he says "no." "[And I will establish my covenant with you], No — cutting off of all flesh any more by the waters of a flood. No — more waters to be a flood to destroy the earth" (*b. Šebu.* 36a). For Jesus, the law of piety demands that one should not swear oaths and this was also the teaching of scrupulous Jews of his time and such is the practice of pious Jews to this day.

"You have heard that it was said, 'Eye for eye and tooth for tooth' [Exod. 21:24]." (v. 38)

We must understand that Matthew's source materials were not simply various unedited texts. To the contrary, Matthew used established materials that are found in the Jewish oral traditions. For instance, most of the ordered list found in 5:38–41 — i.e., 1) eye, 2) cheek, and 3) coat — can be found in the rabbinic literature though not in Hebrew Scriptures. Laws concerning the penalty to be paid for the damaging or destroying of someone's eye and/or for the slapping of someone's cheek are found in Hammurabi's Code (c. 1750 B.C.E.).[54] That is, at least part of this list had a very long history in the Ancient Near East before it came to appear in Matthew and in the rabbinic literature.

"But I say to you, do not oppose the evil one, for whoever slaps you on the right cheek, turn to him the other also." (v. 39)

It is best to deal with verses 38–41 as a whole, since altogether these four verses proclaim one message, which is that one should forego one's claim to justice. A tradition found in *t. B. Qam.* 9:29 contains a similar sentiment:

> Concerning injury to one's fellow: Even if the one who perpetrated the attack did not ask forgiveness from his victim, the injured party must pray for the other's welfare. Scripture so states, "And Abraham prayed to God, and God healed Abimelech [who had wronged him" (Gen. 20:17)].

The Rabbis also discussed waiving payments that one could claim in court. A text from minor tractate *Derekh Eretz* 6:3 reads:

> Whoever forgives payments due him, he is forgiven retribution against all his sins. Scripture states, "*Who is a God like you, forgiving iniquity and forgoing trespass?*" (Micah 7:18) [Read the verse to mean] Whose iniquities does He forgive? The one who foregoes payment due him [from others' trespasses against his body or property.]

Yet the rabbinic literature also contains much detail about what sort of restitution, if any, one needed to make for having either injured and/or humiliated another. The literature also speaks of the many ways in which one can injure and/or humiliate another, but the main examples are injuring the eye (which for the Rabbis meant both damage as well as physical pain); slapping (which meant pained embarrassment); and garment-taking (which meant embarrassment). For our purposes it is sufficient to look at *m. B. Qam.* 8:

> (1) When one injures another he becomes liable to pay for five categories of damage. How so? If he blinded his eye, etc... (6) If he slapped his face he gives him a flat rate of 200 *zuz*, if backhanded [on the right cheek] — 400 *zuz*;...if he removes his garment from him he gives him 400 *zuz*. [55]

We now turn to the ordered list in Matt. 5:38–41:

> [38] "You have heard that it was said, 'An eye for an *eye* and a tooth for a *tooth*.'
> [39] But I say to you, Do not oppose evil. But if any one strikes you on the right *cheek*, turn to him the other also;
> [40] and if any one wins a lawsuit against you (so Syriac) to take your *coat*, let him have your cloak as well;
> [41] and if any one forces you to *walk* one mile, walk with him two miles."

In this list, the examples of injury suffered and/or humiliation received appear in diminishing severity. The further down the list the injury and/or the humiliation appears, the less severe the one or the other is. This is also the case in the list from *m. B. Qam.* above.[56] While the list from *m. B. Qam.* and the list from Matthew are similar in structure, what is meant by the garment being removed in the list from the Mishnah has nothing to do with its having been taken away as a result of a judgment, as in Matthew (v. 40), but rather it concerns one who shames another either by lifting up, or else tearing, another's garment. In other words, Matthew deviates from the pattern here.

Matthew 5:40 in the Greek reads: "And to the one who desires to go to law with (or to stand trial with) you and to take your shirt, grant him your coat as well." The Syriac version is clear that the one who is being accused is told not to resist the plaintiff: "And if any one wins a lawsuit against you to take your *coat*, let him have your cloak as well." As I say, this example seems out of place in Matthew. Losing a court case (or being sued) is hardly the same thing as suffering violence and the point of this clause is not entirely clear. To be consistent with the supererogatory ethic of the entire list, we should expect to read here something like: "And if one should grab your coat, give him your cloak too."

The final example on the list, which concerns the one who forces another to walk with him, is not seen to be either an injury or a humiliation in any of the Jewish legal codes and seems to have been added to Matthew's list to complete a series of three instances in which one is to forego any claim to justice. Verse 38, which introduces the list, seems to carry with it the rabbinic notion that either injury suffered and/or embarrassment received requires monetary, not corporal, redress because Jesus says nothing about "if someone pluck out your eye."[57] The assumption then remains that whoever forces another to walk with him is also liable for damages.

It is instructive to note that Matthew's language in 5:30 approximates the expression found in Lam. 3:30 whereby one is to "give one's cheek to the smiter; one is to be filled with insults." The parallel of cheek/insults drives home the point that Matthew's "striking the cheek" is an expression of insult rather than physical damage.

> *"And to the one who wishes to take your shirt in a judgment, give him your coat as well. And whoever forces you to go a mile, go with him two. Give to the one who asks from you, and do not turn away anyone who wishes to borrow from you. You have heard that it was said, 'Love your neighbor' (Lev. 19:18) and [you might infer from this that it also means to] hate your enemy. But I say, Love your enemies and pray for those who persecute you." (vv. 40–44)*

We would do well to approach this unit (vv. 43–45) carefully, for it is of a different order than the other units in this section of the Sermon on the

Mount.[58] For unlike in the other units, here Jesus gives a full sermon on the biblical text that introduces the unit (Lev. 19:18) — the commandment to love one's neighbor. In this sermon it is not the written law to love one's neighbor that Jesus objects to; rather it is the inference that one might draw from the verse, that loving one's neighbor means that one should hate one's enemy.

We begin our discussion with an explanation of how the Rabbis went about transforming the meaning of certain laws that seemed to them no longer acceptable to their cultural sensitivities and world view. The method used to transform the meaning of these laws might be characterized in this way: "literal unacceptable; stretch apt." For with this method the literal meaning of a biblical text was rejected for whatever reason, after which the text was then reinterpreted in such a way that a new meaning was found for it that was more in keeping with the current world view of the Rabbis. In the rabbinic literature this three-step exegetical method appears like this: 1) the text is given; then 2) the plain meaning of the text is stated, followed by objections to this meaning; then, 3) the new meaning is established. To show how this method worked, and also to show how it was that both the Rabbis and Matthew's Jesus used this same method to interpret both biblical and oral law, we shall first present several examples of it from the rabbinic literature, before turning again to the Gospel text. Our first example is from *b. Zebaḥ.* 22b.

The prophet Ezekiel proclaimed: "Thus says the Lord: *Any stranger,* uncircumcised in heart, and uncircumcised in flesh, shall not enter into my sanctuary" (Ezek. 44:9); And also: *In that you have brought strangers, uncircumcised in heart, and uncircumcised in flesh, to be in my sanctuary, to profane it, my house* (44:7)... The Rabbis taught: 2. *Any stranger* — might I think Ezekiel literally means a stranger [a non-Israelite, who could under no circumstances officiate in the Temple]? The Scripture state his disqualification, "uncircumcised in heart." [So it was not a non-Israelite Ezekiel was speaking of here, but a Jewish priest who was "uncircumcised in heart," that is, whose intentions were impure.] 3. So why call him "stranger"? It means "one whose characteristic behaviors have estranged him to his Father Who Is in Heaven."

For the Rabbis the "stranger" in this text from Ezekiel, who was not to enter the Temple, did not mean a non-Israelite, which is what it originally meant. Rather for them it meant an Israelite, who because of his being "uncircumcised in heart" was "estranged" from God. The Rabbis used this text from Ezekiel to make known that a Jewish priest with an impure heart was as unfit for divine service as any non-Israelite would have been. Both circumcised flesh and a circumcised heart were required for a priest to officiate in the Temple.

As can be seen from this example, in reinterpreting the legal texts from the Scriptures and the oral documents to fit the needs of their current worldview, the Rabbis stretched the meaning of the words in the texts far beyond what the context would seem to allow. It was never the texts alone they were interpreting but rather the value system of their current worldview that provided the context for their interpretations. But this "stretching" of the meaning of the words in these texts was in no way seen to be a violation of the texts, since it was done using the standard hermeneutical methods universally accepted by the Rabbis. That is, for reasons that were wholly intelligible to the community, the Rabbis set aside the literal meaning of these biblical texts and replaced them with a new meaning that was, if not opposite to, at least far removed from the original meaning of it.[59] Let us take a look at another example of this three-step interpretive method from the rabbinic literature (there are hundreds to choose from), this one from *b. Menah.* 99b. The three steps — statement of the verse; objection to its literal meaning; then reinterpretation — are clearly apparent in it.

1. And thou shall set upon the table show bread before me *continually* (Exod. 25:30).
It was taught: 2. Rabbi Yosi said [the literal is impractical], If the old show bread was removed after a part of the morning and the new set down during a part of the evening there would be no problem. 3. So what meaning do I establish for the words of Ex. 25:30, "before me *continually*"? — That the table not rest [for a whole night or day] without bread on it.
Said Rabbi Ammi, From the words of Rabbi Yosi we can derive that even if one reads a mere chapter of Torah in the morning and a chapter at night he can fulfill Joshua 1:8: "This book of the Torah shall not depart out of thy mouth; [but you shall meditate in it *day and night*]."

In interpreting Exod. 25:30, Rabbi Yosi determined that the show bread did not need to be on the table at all times, as the biblical text says literally that is should be. That is, new loaves did not have to be set on the table before the old ones were removed to fulfill the requirement that the bread be "before [God] continually." It is not made clear what Rabbi Yosi's objection to the word "continually" was. Nevertheless what he understood by "continually" is far removed from what is normally meant by the word. As a result of this interpretation, Rabbis such as Rabbi Ammi, as the text points out, found reason to shorten the times required for daily Torah study. It should be noted that Rabbi Yosi's interpretation of Exod. 25:30 was dismissed long ago but his intention, as usual, was to alleviate unnecessary strain and hardship in the community.[60] This was always the reason for uncovering a new meaning for these legal texts.

Let us now turn back to the Gospel text in which, as I say, by applying the same exegetical method to Lev. 19:18, Jesus determines that the word "neighbor" also means "enemy." Here is the text with the steps (differing in a minor way from the examples we have seen from the rabbinic literature above in that in it they appear 1-3-2) marked in it.

> 1. (Matt. 5:43) "You have heard that it was said, 'Love your *neighbor*' and [by implication] hate your enemy (5:44). But I tell you: 3. Love your enemies and pray for those who persecute you...2. (5:46) If you love those who love you, what reward will you get? Are not even the tax collectors doing that? And if you greet only your brothers, what are you doing more than others? Do not even pagans do that?

Since Scripture has no need to talk about loving one's friend and/or one's neighbor, Jesus suggests that the real point here concerns hating one's enemy. The text from Leviticus does not say explicitly that loving one's neighbor means that one should then hate one's enemy, but this is accepted as if it were written. Since Scripture commands one to love one's neighbor, which means God will reward one for fulfilling the commandment, why should He bother to reward what comes naturally between friends anyway? A friend is by definition someone one loves. That is, it is unnecessary for the Scriptures to command one to love one's friend or neighbor, for people do this anyway. Thus Jesus must establish a different meaning for the text, namely, "love your enemies."[61]

> *"So that in this way you will be children of your heavenly father, because he causes his sun to shine upon the evil and upon the good, and it he sends rain upon the righteous and the unrighteous both." (v. 45)*

The homiletic mechanisms Matthew uses (and further on we will look at them in some detail) to produce the argument Jesus makes in this unit — which is that you must love one's enemies because that is exactly what God does and you are to be just like him — are fairly complex. What Matthew wants to develop here is the sermonic materials that will confirm the argument Jesus makes and so we must now take a wider look at what Jesus says in his argument — that one must be like God.

I begin with what most would consider a very late written text from *Exod. Rab.* 46:4, which comments on Deut. 14:1: *"You are children of the Lord your God."* This text teaches that the Children of Israel must be like God because they are also his children. In its present form the *midrash* is somewhat corrupt but for our purposes we need look only at a short parable from it. The text reads:

> A parable. There was a *synkletos*-officer [i.e., a senator] who had children who associated with riffraff and turned to evil ways. ...[T]he father claimed they were not really his children. ...[B]ut he was told: Everyone knows they are your children for they are similar to you.
> The key to the parable: The "synkletos" symbolizes God; "his children" symbolize the Children of Israel, as it is said, You *are children of the Lord your God* (Deut. 14:1).

The point of this parable seems to be that in the end Israel shall be redeemed because as God's Children they innately share in his goodness. Though living among the nations has corrupted them, they will be welcomed back by God because he is their father and they are "similar" to him. The parable does not let us know in what way Israel is "similar" to him.[62] We are only told that the key to its meaning lies in Deut. 14:1. Israel is set apart from the nations because they are God's own children and therefore deserving of salvation.

Another midrash, from *Tanh. Deut. Ekev* 5 which also refers to Deut. 14:1, states that the Israelites are God's children only when they are obedient to his commands.

> "You are children of the Lord your God" (Deut. 14:1). When are you my children? When you are of the Lord your God by obeying my commandments.

In still another midrash, from the *Mekhilta of Rabbi Yishmael* to Exod. 15:2 (see also *y. Pe'ah* 1:1 and *b. Šabb.* 33b), it is said that to be like God means to be generous in spirit as he is.

> *This is my God, and I will glorify Him; [my father's God, and I will exalt Him]* (Exod. 15:2). Abba Shaul says, "Be similar to him (*hidameh lo*). As he is kind and merciful so you also be kind and merciful."

Note here the joining of "kind" and "merciful."

Finally, in a text from *Tanh. Gen. (Vayishlah)* 10 (abbreviated in what follows), which serves as a midrash on Deut. 13:5 and Deut. 8:6, the command to imitate God is confirmed by several citations from the Scriptures.[63]

> When Moses told Israel "after the Lord your God you shall go" (Deut. 13:5) and "to go in his ways" (Deut. 8:6)? (They said: who can go in his ways...?) Moses said to Israel: That is not what I said to you — rather [follow] his ways which are kindness and truth and charity as it is written, "All the paths of the Lord are mercy and truth" (Ps. 25:10), and charity. ...So you also, go after these traits of the Holy One.

In Luke 6:35 Jesus gives us a reworking of Deut. 14:1: "And you shall be a) *children of* b) *the Highest,* c) for he is kind to the thankless and the wicked" (blanket universal statement); which is followed by: "Be therefore *merciful,* as your *Father* also is *merciful*" (6:36).

For Luke, that God is kind to the thankless is visible and obvious. Although biblical texts were available as proof, Luke's Jesus does not make use of them. Using empirical data is sometimes preferred by midrashists even when biblical texts are readily available to them.[64] The midrashic themes concerning *imitatio dei* which we saw in the examples from the rabbinic literature above are simply stated by Jesus in Luke 6:35 as the conclusion of a somewhat intricate exegesis of Deut. 14:1. Matthew's approach is different and we will dwell on that shortly.

Finally, we should also consider *Targum Pseudo-Jonathan* to Lev. 22:28. This biblical text reads: "And whether it be cow or ewe, you shall not kill it and its young both in one day," concerning which the Targum comments: *My people, the children of Israel, just as our* [var. *your*] *father is merciful in heaven* [var. *in heaven is merciful*], *so shall you be merciful on earth.*[65]

The substance of Luke 6:35 was likely available as a midrash, not unlike the one attached to Lev. 22:28 in the *Targum Pseudo-Jonathan.* As I say, in Luke 6:35 Jesus does not cite any verse for his assertion that God is kind to the thankless and the wicked but instead relies on the well-known fact that God is kind, which he appends to his paraphrase of Deut. 14:1: "You shall be children of the Lord your God."

Likewise in our text from Matt. 5:45 Jesus does not cite any verse as a proof-text for his assertion that God too loves those who do not love him, but uses the well-known fact of God's beneficence toward all, including the wicked, as proof that he is indeed kind to his enemies. However, in the next sections of chapter 5 (46–48) Matthew goes beyond Luke to find Scriptures and traditions that bolster the claim that God is perfect and kind and so are we to be. I cited Luke at length here because the sections that follow will show Matthew's stunning ability to simplify complex exegesis in going beyond Luke's version.

> *"For if you love those who love you, what reward do you have? Do not the tax collectors do the same? And if you greet only your siblings, what especially are you doing? Do not the Gentiles do the same?"* (vv. 46–47)

Jesus has made the case that the command to love to one's neighbor does not also mean that one should hate one's enemy, but rather just the reverse. And now to confirm this claim Jesus gives us several examples of what loving one's neighbor normally meant — loving those who love you in return, and greeting those whom you already know — and he explains why there is nothing special about doing either of these things. How can there be reward, he asks, if both the Gentiles and the despised Jewish tax collectors do the same? If "neighbors" cannot refer to friends, then it must refer to enemies. This interpretive method is called *im eyno inyan — tehei inyan* (e.g. b. Pes. 24a).

It is of interest that Jesus groups together the Gentiles with the tax collectors here. Initially in Matthew's Gospel Jesus shows an antigentile bias; but after a time he begins to show an anti-Jewish bias, which then remains. But here Matthew presents Jesus as a completely loyal Jew who has no sympathy for pagans. As we proceed into chapter 8 we will find the Gentiles are destined to dine with Abraham, Isaac, and Jacob at the great feast in the next world while the Jews will be kept out, gnashing their teeth. Progressively, Jesus turns away from the Jews until he orders that Scribes be made of all the nations, all the Gentiles.

"So you shall be perfect, as your Father in heaven is perfect." (v. 48)

Here Jesus tells the members of his audience that it is in loving their enemies that they will become perfect, as their Father in heaven is perfect. They are not to be like the Gentiles and the tax collectors whose imperfection means that they love only those who love them (vv. 46–47).

Jesus' argument here is essentially that of Luke's Jesus (6:35–36): be like God; God loves his enemies (those who are "ungrateful and the selfish"); therefore to be like God means to love one's enemies. But unlike in Luke, here in Matthew Jesus also states that the proof of God's love for those who do not love him is found in the fact that he does not withhold the sun and rain from them, when certainly he could.[66] Moreover in Matthew Jesus ends his sermon not with a syllogism, as he does in Luke, but with a close paraphrase of Deut. 18:13.

Matthew's literary achievement in this brief unit is masterful, but especially here in this final verse in which he brings into play the various rabbinic midrashim which had come to be associated with Deut. 18:13. In Matthew's version of Deut. 18:13 — "So you shall be perfect as your Father in heaven is perfect" — the text demands *imitatio dei*. Let us take a closer look at what lies behind Matthew's rendering of Deut. 18:13.

First, to see the way Deut. 18:13 was written in the various biblical texts from antiquity will be helpful here. The Masoretic version of the text reads: "You shall be perfect with the Lord your God." Now the Hebrew for perfect, *"tamim,"* is used in the Scriptures to mean either "without blemish," which gives the word a passive sense (e.g., "If his offering is a burnt offering from the herd, he shall offer a male without blemish ['*tamim*']" [Lev. 1:3]); or to act kindly or justly, which gives the word a more active sense (e.g., "The Rock, his work is perfect ['*tamim*'] for all his ways are justice" [Deut. 32:4]). The Septuagint and Peshitta (the Syriac version) give us: "You shall be perfect before the Lord your God." That is, before God be both without blemish and also act kindly and/or justly toward others. The *Targum Onqelos* gives us "You shall be perfect in the fear of the Lord your God," which gives us an essentially submissive sense to the word; whereas *Targum Neofiti* has "You shall be perfect in good deed with the Lord your God," which gives the word a somewhat more active sense.[67] The Vulgate brings together both the completely active and passive senses of "*tamim*" in its version of the text: "You shall be perfect and without defect with the Lord your God." As can be seen, none of these versions of Deut. 18:13 above is very close to Matthew's version of it.

Now let us return to the Masoretic version of Deut. 18:13: "You shall be perfect with the Lord your God." The word "with" in Hebrew is "*im*," but "*im*" can also mean "even as," in the sense of being "similar to." For example, a tradition found in *Tanḥ. Gen.* (*Vayera*) 23 states that before Abraham went up the mountain with Isaac he said to his servants, who had just before responded to a question of his in such a way as to make their obtuseness obvious: "Stay here with (*im*) the donkey (Gen. 22:5), for you are *even as* he is."[68] That "*im*" can mean "even as" explains why in *Midr. Ps.* 119:10 Deut. 18:13 is rendered in this way: "You shall be perfect with [im] the Lord your God — even as he is perfect."

In another tradition from *Midrash Psalms,* but from 119:3 (some texts 119:10), it is said that the word "*im*" from Deut. 18:13 means "similar to," and not "before," as in the version of the text in either the LXX or Peshitta. The midrashist then reminds that one should be perfect, and states that it is in being perfect that one is "similar to" God, for God too is perfect (however the proof-text he uses here to confirm his claim that God is perfect is not entirely apposite, for in it the word "perfect" — (*tamim*) — does not in its biblical context refer to God but to his work. The midrashist has purposely read the verse only partially to make his point). The tradition reads:

> Blessed are the perfect ones of the way who go in the instruction (Torah) of the Lord (Ps. 119:1).
> King Solomon said: "The righteous one who walks in his perfection, his children are blessed on account of him" (Prov. 20:7). Now if his children are blessed [only] on his account, he himself all the more so [is blessed.]. ... And likewise Moses said to Israel, "You shall be perfect with the Lord your God" (Deut. 18:13): "*Before*" the Lord your God is not written here but rather "*with/similar to*" the Lord your God. *If you would be perfect then you would be with/similar to the Lord your God. — Why is this? — Because he is also perfect. — This is as it is said: the Rock, his working is perfect* (Deut. 32:4).

The following variant from *Midr. Ps.* 119:10 goes out its way to try to harmonize the meanings for "*im*" that we have seen in several of the versions of Deut. 18:13 above — "before" (in the LXX and Peshitta), and "even as" (in Matthew and in *Midr. Ps.* 119:3). The text reads:

> For perfection is congenial [*yafeh*] before God, as it is said: *You shall be perfect with the Lord your God — even as he is perfect.* This is as it is said: the Rock, his working is perfect (Deut. 32:4).

As is obvious, Matthew's rendering of Deut. 18:13 is similar to that which appears in *Midrash Psalms* above: *So you shall be perfect even as* [Greek *hos*] *your Father in heaven is perfect.*

Both Matthew and the Rabbis in *Midrash Psalms* produced such a similar rendering of Deut. 18:13 because they both had in mind Lev. 19:2, whose opening injunction, "*You shall be* holy," is a close parallel to "*You shall be* perfect" of Deut. 18:13. Moreover the latter part of Lev. 19:2 reads: "for [*ki*] I the Lord your God am holy." Now the Rabbis understood that like "*im*," "*ki*" could also mean "even as," which is why in a tradition found in both *Tanḥ. Lev. (Kedoshim)*, 2 and *Yalkut Shimoni Lev.* 604 we read:

> [God said,] "Tell Israel, "And you shall be for me a kingdom of priests and a holy nation (Exod. 19:6). — Why? Even as (*ki*) I the Lord [your God] am holy so you shall be holy. ... As it is said, 'You shall be holy, for ("*ki*," even as) I the Lord your God am holy'" (Lev. 19:2).

The clearest proof that both Matthew and the Rabbis understood that Deut. 18:13 was a close parallel to Lev. 19:2 is found in an antique source, *Sipra* (to *Lev. Kedoshim*), *parashah* 1. In discussing Lev. 19:2 in this text, Abba Shaul says: "*[Israel is the family] of the King — and so how must she act? She imitates the King.*" This midrash is also very much like the *midrashim* we have seen in the rabbinic traditions above concerning Deut. 14:1, in which we are told that the children of Israel are to imitate God because they are also his children.

It now remains to show, finally, that Lev 19:18 — "And you shall love your neighbor as yourself [I am the Lord]" — which was the starting point for this sermon, has also been made part of the network of traditions concerning Israel's call to imitate God. Lev. 19:18 concludes with the declaration from God that "I am the Lord," and this declaration connects with the phrase "the Lord your God" found in all the other biblical texts that lie behind this sermon on love of one's neighbor in Matthew — Deut. 14:1, 18:13; and Lev. 19:2. The traditional exegesis of these latter texts connects with the commandment to love one's neighbor by way of the declaration from God that "I am the Lord." (Lev. 19:18). In his sermon here Jesus has found the connection between these two latter parts of Lev. 19:18. "I am the Lord" is the pointer that explains that "your neighbor" refers to both the righteous and the wicked; for which reason Jesus can intimate that because God loves both then everyone else should love both too.[69]

For Luke it was enough to incorporate the substance of Deut. 14:1 — "You are children of the Lord your God" — to establish the principal that one should act as God does (Luke 6:35). By including in his version of the sermon a paraphrase of Deut. 18:13 — "You shall be perfect *with/as* the Lord your God" — Matthew not only goes beyond Luke; he also greatly enhances the sermon.

In essence, then, Matthew does give us here (v. 48) a midrash that incorporates the rabbinic understanding of Deut. 18:13, which he then combines with a paraphrase of Deut. 14:1 — "You are sons of God" — to drive home the point that because God is Israel's father, it is necessary for Israel to imitate him.[70] Thus Deut. 18:13 is to be rendered precisely as Matthew has it.

The appreciation of Matthew's literary skill here suffers when we avail ourselves only of the English translations of the verses. The richness of the midrashic traditions associated with these various texts allows us to see that Matt. 5:45–48 was part of a complex and ongoing homiletic performance. Indeed his text here is nothing short of sheer poetry constructed from various biblical texts and the midrashim associated with them, whose overall purpose is to show that the word "neighbor" must be stretched so that it can also mean "enemy."

NOTES

[1] See the introduction to chapter 2, n. 1; also see chapter 12, verses 15–17.

[2] In his collection *Ha-Esh Ve-Ha-Etzim* (The Fire and the Wood), S. Y. Agnon has devoted his first story, "According to the Suffering Is the Reward," to this theme. A *paytan* (modeled after the geonic descriptions given of Yehudai Gaon, ca. 800 and the "neila" prayer of *Besht*) writes such poetry until one day he meets an afflicted soul, a suffering servant figure. At the end the *paytan* learns in a revelation that the poet whose art is the expression of a meek life which is immersed in human suffering makes a mark in heaven. So much for Agnon's story. Jesus' sermon begins with a series of beatitudes celebrating the purity of the meek. In alternating usages of blessed we sometimes find the phrase, "Blessed are the nouns who are X," and other times, "Blessed are those who do X." In order to

make contact with his hearers he ends by adding a blessing — "Blessed are those who are persecuted," "Blessed are you, the persecuted." This blessing sums up Jesus' liturgical "Ode to the Harassed."

3   Mirsky, *Yesodot Tzurot Hapiyyut*. See also by the same author, "From Midrash to Piyyut to Jewish Poetry."

4   Scholars have studied these beatitude forms in Qumran Scrolls and other literature of the Second Temple period. While the form and genre are fixed, the meaning of any piece is open to the listener or reader to decide. See Viviano, "Beatitudes Found Among Dead Sea Scrolls"; Meier, *A Marginal Jew*, 323; Fitzmyer, *The Dead Sea Scrolls and Christian Origins*, 116–18; and perhaps most important, Puech, *Qumrân grotte 4, XVIII*.

5   See Sanders, *The Historical Figure of Jesus*, 210–12.

6   Chapter 6 continues his encouragement to go beyond the externals of religious observance and reach through to the inner core. We shall address these issues as we meet them in the commentary.

7   *Machzor Vitry*, dating from the twelfth and thirteenth centuries, knows the custom, and Tirna (1380, *Sefer Ha-Minhagim*, "Laws of Milah circumcision," 94) claims to have seen a *baraita* which gives the source of the practice. Abraham received his full name after his circumcision. Thus, that day is the earliest opportunity for bestowing a name.

8   See Flusser, *Jewish Sources in Early Christianity*, 10. In chapter 10 of the same work he demonstrates that midrashim that surfaced in very late collections are attested as early as New Testament times.

9   L. Ginzberg and S. Kraus have noted that midrashic themes appear in the works of the Church Fathers some 700 times. All of these appearances are attributed to Jewish informants and they all appear in the works of the fathers before they appeared in written Jewish texts. See L. Ginzberg's notes to vols. 5 and 6 of *Legends of the Jews*, and in particular "Die Haggada bei den Kirchenvätern und in der Apokryphischen Litteratur," in *Monatsschrift*, xlii. *et seq.* See also Kraus, "Church Fathers." See also his "The Jews in the Works of the Church Fathers."

10   There are other places in the Babylonian Talmud where the phrase occurs with this meaning, e.g., *b. Ber.* 59a.

11   Klausner *Jesus of Nazareth*, 388–89.

12   For examples of sitting at the feet of the master see *m. 'Abot* 1:4, Luke 10:39, Acts 22:3.

13   The introductory *piyyut* to the daily morning Jewish prayer service begins with beatitudes and is quoted in full in *Tanna Dvei Eliyahu*, 4. Accordingly it may have been composed at the close of the Talmudic period. It appears to be spun out of statements of Mishnah and formulated as a messianic ode.

14 Kris Linbeck tells me she does not think the phrase occurs anywhere else in the Gospels to introduce Jesus' teaching nor does even the Greek word *anoigo* in any phrase introducing speech (although it appears other places to refer to opening things which were sealed, e.g., Matt. 2:11). As a result, I suspect the passage derives from a source used by Matthew alone.

15 See my article, "A Distinctive Usage of PTH in Rabbinic Literature," 60–61; and also *In the Margins of the Midrash* (Atlanta: Scholars Press, 1990), 17.

16 See n. 14 above, and note Rev. 13:6, "an he opened his mouth in blasphemies."

17 Humility and a willingness to suffer are the virtues that Jesus stresses above all in the poem. Matthew's beginning text for this section, which begun at the end of chapter 4, is Isa. 61:1–9, which introduces the preacher who proclaims "the good new to the poor…to comfort all who mourn…to call them 'planting of the Lord'…who will reward them…they are blessed." These words will serve as the subject matter of those he praises. The "poor" resonates with Ps. 37:11 "But the meek will inherit the land and enjoy great peace." "Poor (in spirit)," "meek," parallel each other, dance together. And the process of words resonating from verse to verse will continue.

18 I have tried to illustrate the phenomenon in my "Approaching the Text."

19 Ps. 119:1–3 shows us the beatitude form of the Book of Psalms. It is undoubtedly the source for the genre used in the Dead Sea Scrolls, rabbinic literature, and Matthew chapter 5. "Blessed are those whose way is perfect, who walk in the law of the Lord! Blessed are those who keep his testimonies, who seek him with their whole heart, who also do no wrong, but walk in his ways!"

One of the more interesting *piyyut* blessings is found in the morning service introducing the standing prayer of eighteen blessings (which is the Rabbinic Prayer *par excellence*) that contains sentences introduced by "truly" a synonym of "amen" and deriving from the same root. "Truly—blessed is the man who obeys your commandments. And your Torah and your Word he places on his heart." The construction of such hymns seems to have been ongoing from biblical times through to Geonic times, a span of some 1500 years. Matthew's hymn is about midway in the process.

20 E.g., Ps. 1:1: "Blessed is the man [*makarios aner*]." E. Puech, "4Q525 et la Péricope des Béatitudes en Ben Sira et Matthieu," *Revue biblique* 98 (1991): 80–106, and "The Collection of Beatitudes in Hebrew and Greek (1Q525 1–4 and Mt 5,3–12)," in *Early Christianity in Context,* ed. Manns, Alliata, and Testa, 359–62, argues that Matthew's form is original to him, preserves accurate word counts and rhythm and that the eight beatitudes do not rework any previous collection. Further, he points out the existence of the form *anvei ruah* "poor of spirit" in the Qumran Scrolls, 1QM 14:7, 4Q491, 8–10, 9:5, 1QH 6:14.

21 The introduction to chapter 5 has further discussion of these forms. See especially nn. 2 and 3 there.

22 I call this feature of hymn, the "prophetic now." It might be noted in this regard that a Qumran text, the Thanksgiving scroll, promises rewards to the meek, contrite, and mourners (13:14–15).

23 Dale Allison suggests it would be useful to mention here Matt. 11:4–6 where Isaiah 61 is used. I note here his practical advice.

24 Compare Flusser, *Jewish Sources in Early Christianity*, 62.

25 Similarly, *Deut. Rab.* (ed. Lieberman), 19, identifies the meek with Israel: Rabbi Meir said, "In the future world Israel is destined to be meek as it is said, 'The meek will inherit the land and enjoy great peace (Ps. 37:11).'"

26 Dale Allison sees the whole thrust of my commentary is to look at Matthew through Jewish tradition. He wonders what I am doing by doubting that Matthew was a Jewish Christian. Any number of Gentiles from the time of Gaius (Philo was amazed at his command of the Torah and even his knowledge of the secret of the pronunciation of the tetragrammaton) to Peter Schafer (a real friend of the Jews today) have been knowledgeable about Jewish tradition. As well, Matthew has good sources and likely learned Jewish informants (as did some of the Church Fathers). Yet I reject that Matthew himself adds any of his own exegesis or knowledge of Jewish law to his writings. Matthew is an artist and as such succeeds in making his Jesus a Jew among Jews, in order to dramatize the perfidy of the Jews in rejecting his exclusive "sonship."

27 The text explains that *banayikh* (your children) should be read (*bonayikh*, builders, or more likely *bunayikh*, wise) and through their preaching and study they increase peace.

28 Hillel's famous speech, *b. Šabb* 31a, to a convert concerning the Golden Rule ends with "Go! Learn!" *M. Ta'an.* 2:1 contains an exhortation to be sincere in repentance and not rely on the outer trappings of fasting and sackcloth.

29 Strack/Billerbeck, 244.

30 The list of scholars adhering to this view is extensive: Schechter, Abrahams, Smith, Daube, Urbach, Boxel, Sanders, Keener, and others.

31 Compare Daube, *The New Testament and Rabbinic Judaism*, 55–61.

32 Neusner, *Talmud Torah*, 28.

33 In the case of Matt. 5:21, "Whoever sheds human blood, by humans his blood shall be shed, because in the image of God, God made humans" (Gen. 9:6); and "You shall take no ransom for the life of a murderer,…he shall surely be put to death" (Num. 35:31).

34 Again in the case of Matt. 5:21, "You shall not murder" (Exod. 20:13; Deut. 5:17).

35 *T. Sanh.* 8:3, *b. Sanh.* 37b, and *y. Sanh.* 4:3 all point out that God punishes where the courts are prevented from doing because of a technicality. Further, the text

from *b. Sanhedrin* claims that the method of the divine punishment is similar to what the human punishment would have been had it been carried out.

36   The date of a manuscript reading and the frequency of the reading are not guarantees of whether or not a phrase is original to a text or is not. Unless we know why something might have been added or subtracted we cannot form any judgment.

37   *Otzar ha-Midrashim* (ed. Eisenstein), chap. 15, p. 270, preserves:

> Said Rabbi Yonatan in the name of Rabbi Shimon bar Nachmeni, "Whoever gets angry, all the fury of *gehinom* will flare up upon him. Scripture states, "Remove anger from your heart and remove evil from your flesh (Eccles. 11:10). Evil refers to "*gehinom*," as it says, "Yea the wicked are destined for the day of evil" (Prov. 16:4). Indeed one should strive to separate oneself from fury and anger, for all who get angry are as if they worship idols.

Also in this anthology of midrash, we find (p. 84) the Talmudic account (*b. B. Meṣ.* 58b) that three people can never get out of gehinom and the one who insults another publically is prominent on the list.

38   So we find in *b. B. Meṣ.* 58b:

> A memorizer of tradition stated to Rabbi Nachman bar Yizthak, "Whoever embarrasses his fellow publicly is as if he spilled blood."

39   A paraphrase to what Rabbi Josiah said is found in *Midrash Aggada* (ed. Buber) to Exod. 3:17, "The Sabbath must not be absent at all."

40   *Num. Rab.* 9:11: *There are six things which the Lord hateth, yea seven which are an abomination unto Him* (Prov. 6:16). …*A heart that devises wicked plans* (Prov. 6:18a): The adulterer and the adulteress always have thoughts about when they will sin and tell each other which place and which time… [*and*] *feet that make haste to run to evil* (Prov. 6:18b): For a certainty they will now rush to accomplish the sinful act.

41   As far as punishments are concerned, the courts had the authority to punish beyond the measure of the law, and also "to repair a breech." The Aramaic term for repairing "a breech" is "*migdar milta.*" *B. Yebam.* 90b has a number of cases in which the courts administered punishment in order to "repair a breech" (e.g., "There was another incident when a man had relations with his wife under a date tree. They brought him to court and flogged him. No — in point of law, he did not deserve that punishment but the times required it.") *Migdar milta* provisions were exceptional. They tended to be performed in times of religious slackness.

42   Allison, *Jesus of Nazareth,* 175–81, lists references and parallels to the cutting off of limbs in order to save one from sexual lusts to show that this type of hyperbole was widespread. See also my "The Meaning of 'Shtuth,' Gen. Rab. 11 in reference to Matt. 5:29,30."

43   *Midah Hassidut* is a rabbinic concept of what pious rabbinic scholars should engage in. *Mishnat Hassidim* refers to group who followed teachings for those only who are capable of living an extra-pious life.

44   *Y. Ber.* 1:4: Rabbi Matnah and Rabbi Shmuel bar Nachman both said it was proper to continue to read the ten commandments daily. So why do we not read them? Because of the anxiety over Christians — that they not say (you people also agree) "these alone were given to Moses on Sinai."

45   See the discussion in Sigal, *Halakah of Jesus of Nazareth According to the Gospel of Matthew,* 97ff.

46   For background to the scholarly discussions on this passage see Geller, "Early Christianity and the Dead Sea Scrolls," 82–86. The claim is that *11QTemple Scroll LVII 17–19, CD IV 20–21* forbids divorce and polygamy. I still think it is doubtful that divorce is at issue in these texts, as I wrote in "Response to Marcus Bockmuehl."

47   Josephus, *Ant.* 3:91 warns against frivolous oaths in paraphrasing the third commandment from the Decalogue.

48   *B. Hor.* 2a–b shows the two forms used in Mishnah where there is no point in mentioning the obvious. The Talmud points out that rabbinic masters taught in certain rhetorical styles.

49   That one should always be very cautious about swearing oaths is stated in Sir. 23:9–11, Philo, *On the Decalogue 84–86,* Josephus, *Ant.* 3.91, *Num. Rab.* 22:1 (and *Tanh. Num.* [ed. Buber], Mattot 30:2), and in *b. Šebu.* 35a.

50   *Mekhilta of Rabbi Yishmael* to Exod. 21:17 refers to substitutes for the divine name in oaths and their admissibility (p. 268 n. 4 in the edition of H-R discusses the issues of the names). *B. Ned.* 22a and *Pesiq. Rab.,* chap. 22, speak of the seriousness of, and the danger in, making vows. In *Pesiq. Rab., Piska* 22.6, it is said that even an oath affirming a certain olive tree is an olive tree is taking God's name in vain.

51   In his *On the Special Laws,* Philo also mentions that people swore by the sun, the stars and the universe. In *b. Šebu* 35a it is said that people also swore by Adonai, the Almighty, The Lord of Hosts, etc.

52   See Lachs, *A Rabbinic Commentary on the New Testament,* 100–103.

53   *T. Ned.* 1:2–3 discusses oaths and vows in which one vows by Jerusalem and/or the Temple. See also *b. Ned.* 11a and *y. Ned.* 1:3.

54   Thomas, *Documents from Old Testament Times,* 27–37, but esp. 34.

55   See also *b. B. Qam.* 92a.

56   At first glance one might think this is not the case. The one who is slapped is to receive 200 zuz and is mentioned earlier than the one who loses his garment but receives 400 zuz. However, the order of descending stringency is in the

categories while in each category the order moves from the more frequent to the less frequent without regard for the size of the fines or liabilities.

57 See here the discussion in Daube, *The New Testament and Rabbinic Judaism*, 259–63.

58 While my approach rests essentially on my own constructions, there are a number of older works that should be mentioned: Guedemann, *Naechstenliebe, ein Beitrag zur Erlkaerung des Mathaeus-Evangeliums*, and Taylor, *The Teaching of the Twelve Apostles, esp.* 8–10.

59 Sometimes a similar principle is said to be "If it does not suit its immediate scriptural context find another where it will fit." *B. Šabb.* 70a, *b. Pesaḥ.* 23b–24a, *b. Yoma* 32b, and a hundred more places in the Talmud and halachic midrashim.

60 Basser, "Uncovering the Plots."

61 A text from *'Abot R. Nat.*, version A, chap. 16, wonders then who is excluded from the love commandment.

> What constitutes [the grave sin of] misanthropy? We have been taught that one [who is a scholar] cannot (infer from "And you shall love your neighbor") that it means "love scholars" and [by extension] "hate disciples." [Or for one who is a disciple] "love disciples" and "hate the untutored." [This is misanthropy.] But "love everyone" and [by exclusion] "hate the apostates, renegades, and those who hand Jews over to the Romans."

62 The sermon of which this parable is but a small part is so inscrutable that Rabbi Ze'ev Einhorn, one of the greatest commentators on *Midrash Rab.*, declared it to be far beyond his grasp.

63 *B. Soṭah* 14a tells us that Rabbi Hama son of Rabbi Hanina knew another version of this idea: Why is it written "to go in his ways" (Deut. 13:5) — can anyone really go after the Shekhina? Does Scripture not say, "For the Lord your God is a consuming fire (Deut. 4:24)? — But Deut. 15:5 means to follow after the attributes of the Holy One.

64 See, e.g., *b. Pesaḥ.* 21b.

65 "As I am merciful," is also reflected in *y. Ber.* 5:3. In this text R. Yosi, from the fourth century, complains about the midrashic addition to Lev. 22:28 in the Targum: "Rabbi Yosi son of [Rabbi] Bun, said: 'They do not do well who make the injunctions of the Holy One, Blessed be He, into traits of mercy and render (Lev. 22:28): "*My people, children of Israel, just as I am merciful in heaven, so shall you be merciful on earth.*" Yet Matthew's sermon's reference to "your father" has a sound basis. In the Maher edition of *Targum Pseudo-Jonathan*, he points out that the text in the London library reads: "Children of Israel, just as our father is merciful in heaven."

66 *B. Ta'an.* 7a records in the name of Rabbi Abbahu: The day of rain is greater than the resurrection of the dead. The resurrection of the dead is reserved only for the righteous *but rain falls both on the righteous and on the wicked.*

67 *M. 'Avot* 3:9 puts fear of God and good works on the same level.

68 Gen. 30:8 seems to know this meaning for *im*; at least Onqelos and Rashi assume so: "Then Rachel said, 'God has heeded my requests in my pleadings, in my dearest prayers, that I might have a child EVEN AS [*im*] my sister, yea it was given to me'; so she called his name Naphtali." Numerous other examples of texts in which "*im*" means "even as" or "similar to" are found in *Bereshit Rabba*, ed. J. Theodor and Ch. Albeck (Jerusalem, 1965), 893 (at the bottom).

69 I am grateful to the panel of the Society of Biblical Literature (annual meeting, Washington, D.C., November 2006) for mentioning the importance of this point while discussing my paper, "Imitatio Dei: A Note on the History of Exegesis Based on Luke, Matthew and the Rabbis."

70 David Flusser (*Jewish Sources in Early Christianity*, 63) confirms my approach: "In these midrashim, various biblical verses which some similarities between them, were combined. Once a conclusion was drawn from one of them, it was possible to pass on to another verse for additional proof of what had been said in the first, and thus some long midrashim were created in the New Testament, This shows that this method was already employed by the sages and the biblical exegesis of that period."

CHAPTER SIX

INTRODUCTION

Over the course of chapter 5 the Matthean Jesus speaks of numerous different types of virtuous people — the humble, the meek, the merciful, the persecuted, the forgiving — and of how one can come to be as virtuous as these are. Then at the close of the chapter he focuses on love of neighbor that, as he later states, is the second of the two great commandments (Matt. 22:34–40).[1] Now here in chapter 6 he focuses on what he calls the first great commandment, the love of God. To say that these two commandments are "great" is to say that all the other commandments are there for the sake of these two commandments. That is, it is in fulfilling all the other commandments that one thereby comes to fulfill either of these two "great" commandments. In chapter 6 the Matthean Jesus speaks of the ways in which one must fulfill several of these other commandments in order to fulfill the great commandment that one must love God.

The command to love God is from Deut. 6:5: "And you shall love the Lord your God with all your heart, with all your being and with all your substance."[2] Now for the Matthean Jesus this love of God is shown through acts of charity, prayer, and fasting, each of which is underlain by faith: charity, which by giving to another affects one's substance or wealth; prayer, which comes from the heart; and fasting, which refines one's being. Moreover Jesus says that each of these acts of love is to be done modestly and in secret.

It is noteworthy that Jesus speaks of three acts of love here rather than, say, four or five, for the triad has been a favored stylistic feature of Jewish (and also non-Jewish) rhetoric from very ancient times to the present. For example, in *y. Sanh.* 10:2 the Rabbis state that in order to prevent a catastrophe from occurring about which one has been warned in a dream one should "seek three things": prayer, charity, and repentance (which, once one comes to realize that repentance involves fasting, are the same three "things" that Jesus speaks of here in chapter 6). The proof-text for this tradition is 2Chron. 7:14: "If my people, which are called by my name, shall humble themselves, and *pray,* and *seek my face* (by giving charity), and *turn from their wicked ways;* then will I hear from heaven, and will forgive their sin, and will heal their land." Another well-known triad is found in *m. 'Abot* 1:2: "On three things the world stands: on Torah, on Sacrifice (prayer), on Charity."

In the rabbinic literature it is said that Torah study is the supreme virtue. "If you have studied much Torah, your reward will be abundant" (*m. 'Abot* 2:21). But in his discussion here of these acts of love upon which one should base one's religious life, Jesus makes no mention of Torah study. And so here we encounter that which divides Matthew's world from the Jewish world. In Matthew's world faith is the ultimate value, whereas for the Rabbis faith is of course necessary, but Torah study is the virtue *par excellence* (both Philo and Josephus also see Torah study as a prime virtue). But Jesus' audience here is almost certainly the Galilean *am-ha'aretz,* that is, the hard-working people of the peasant class who were loyal to what they knew but ignorant of the finer legal matters associated with pious observance. They were people of faith but they were also distant from, and perhaps even antagonistic toward, the scholarly class.

It is also in this chapter, of course, that what has come to be known as the "Lord's Prayer" is found. In discussing the Lord's Prayer we must keep in mind that until at least the eighth century the Jews did not use prayer books for public prayer. Rather the custom was that a trained reader would recite the prayers aloud and his audience would repeat after him or else right along with him. As a result, we can only speculate as to the form, genre, and content of prayers in the Second Temple period. We do know that there were fixed prayers and fixed times of the day at which people said prayers, and that for those living outside Jerusalem it was necessary to face that city when praying. The Book of Daniel tells us all this: "he went into his house; and his windows being open in his chamber toward Jerusalem, he kneeled upon his knees three times a day, and prayed, and gave thanks before his God, as he had done in the past" (6:11).

Jesus' prayer shows us that many of the conventions found in rabbinic prayers go back to the period before the destruction of the Temple in 70 C.E. One of the texts upon which the glorification of God (in prayer texts) was based was the prayer of the *seraphim* from Isa. 6:3 (another being the song of Israel sung at the parting of the sea in Exod. 15). Structurally the prayer of Jesus in Matthew (and in Luke, too) also appears to be based on this angelic prayer from Isaiah, known as the *Kedushah* or *Trisagion*: "And they called out to each other, and said: 'Holy, holy, holy is the Lord God of hosts, all the earth is full of his glory.'"

The early liturgical history of the *Trisagion* is unclear but at some point with the addition of poetic glosses it was turned into a prayer of consolation and messianic hope as we shall cite the text below. The threefold use of the word "holy" in praise of God[3] gave rise to a threefold sanctification of 1) God's name, 2) the heavens and the earth, and 3) messianic hope. From the designation of God as "Lord of Hosts" more elaborate praises for Him were developed. And the final phrase of the *Trisagion* — "all the earth is full of his glory" — was expanded to become a doxology that referred to heavenly peace and the time when this peace would finally prevail on earth. This threefold Universe of the Upper Realm, the Lower Realm, and the Next World, read through Isa. 6:3, Ezek. 3:12, and Exod. 15:18,[4] was to become the backbone of prayer-structures in Judaism that echo the angels. The *Kaddish,* dealing with hallowing the Name, God's power in creating heaven and earth according to his will, and anticipating the messianic era, was recited at the close of sermons and midrashic lectures in the study halls. The *Kaddish* fulfills the requirement that sessions devoted to Scriptural interpretation and oral law were to conclude with an emphasis on final redemption. All such prayers came to be known as *nechemta* prayers — prayers of comfort. Verses from the prophets — called "consoling verses" — were recited before the consoling prayer that was built around them (e.g., Isa. 59:20, "And a redeemer will come to Zion, and to them that repent from transgression in Jacob, says the Lord"). At a later date the daily prayer services incorporated these prayers and others which were said in private, which were known as "*Kedushah de Sidra,*" or the "*Trisagion* praise of the study session."[5]

The previously mentioned liturgical proto-*piyyut,* expanding each of the three utterances of Holy, was incorporated into the Targum, or Aramaic translation, of Isa. 6:3. Here the Targum and *Kedushah de Sidra* read (the italicized words represent the actual verse, with the poetic expansions of each "holy" in regular type):

- *Holy* — in the highest heavens above — the Dwelling [House] of his Shekhina (Logos — Divine will).[6]
- *Holy* — on earth — the work of his Power (Geuvrah/Dynamis).[7]
- *Holy* — forever — and ever and ever is the Lord of Hosts.[8]

The whole world is full of the splendor of his Glory (Isa. 6:3) (Kavod/Doxa).

What I have put into brackets includes the Greek terms—*Dynamis, Doxa* (Glory and Power)—that were part of the Judeo-Hellenistic world's theological system, as explained by Philo of Alexandria (*Abraham* 97–103; see *Theological Dictionary of the New Testament,* 2:233). But Jewish midrash also utilized the royal imagery associated with God and his cohorts. And so *Mekhilta of Rabbi Yishmael* (*Beshalah*) to Exod. 14:21, states that: "when the Holy One was revealed with his *Glory* and with his *Power,* the Sea began to flee, as it is said, 'The sea saw [Him] and fled'" (Ps. 114:3). But we have strayed from the texts of our *Kedushah de Sidra* liturgy.

As we can see, in this *piyyut* in the Targum the threefold repetition of "Holy" has been transformed into three manifestations of the Divine. The *Kedushah de Sidra* as real proto-*piyyut* is still a midrash and shows us how this poem in the Targum came to be. In midrashic custom the proof-text reference is sometimes hidden. In the poem parts of two other texts in their Targumic form, which are explicit sources for this poem, were inserted after each "Holy" of the *Trisagion.* These texts are Ezek. 3:12: "Then the Spirit lifted me up, and I heard a great rumbling sound behind me, 'Blessed be the glory of the Lord from His place,'" which the *piyyut* cites verbatim, and then renders "*Blessed is the Glory of the Lord from the Place* of the Dwelling [House] of his Shekhina";[9] and Exod. 15:18: "The Lord will rule for ever and ever,"[10] which *the piyyut* cites verbatim and then renders: "*The Lord,* his Kingdom is for ever and ever and ever." The poet expands the *Trisagion* so that the three realms he specifies—the heavenly, the earthly, and the final kingdom—are not only seen as the sacred locations of divine history, but also as the very holy name of God, the Lord of hosts, and then cites other biblical praises in order to elaborate upon the heavenly Shekhina and the coming kingdom. We shall leave for the commentary our detailed discussion of the *kaddish* recitation that is another form of liturgy inspired by the *Trisagion.*

Now looking again at Jesus' prayer in Matthew we can see that it contains the themes of the *Kedusha de Sidra* in a reworked order: Holy (hallowed) be thy name — 3) thy kingdom come; thy will be done; 2) on earth, as it is 1) in heaven. Even Jesus' mention of repentance in the prayer is also part of one of the consoling verses (Isa. 59:20, as we have seen) that introduces the *Trisagion* hymn in the *Kedusha de Sidra.* The concluding doxology, which appears in some of the later texts of Matthew — "For thine is the kingdom and the power and the glory, for ever. Amen" (or something like this) — shows us that the content of religious poetry varied and that different communities possessed different versions of the same prayer. The *Didache,* in which Jesus' prayer concludes with the phrase "for thine is the power and the glory forever" (8:2), also shows us this.[11] The "coin of prayer" (as the Rabbis called a prayer's fixed format) still allowed for the addition of poetic glosses and also for the rephrasing of the too obvious into something more subtle.

It is noteworthy that the conclusion of the eschatological prayer found in the *Rosh HaShanah* liturgy makes numerous references to God's kingdom and also includes the Targumic rendering of Exod. 15:18, which speaks of God's rule, as we have seen: "The Lord, his kingdom will be forever and ever." In the prayer this text is used as the proof-text for its assertion that "Yours is the kingdom." The text reads:[12]

> For *to you every knee will bend, every tongue will swear,*[13] before you O Lord our God they will kneel and fall and they will *give praise to the glory of your name.* And all of them will accept the yoke of your kingdom and may You soon rule over them forever. For *Yours is the kingdom* and forever you will rule in glory, as it says in your Torah, "The Lord will rule forever and ever" (Exod. 15:18).[14]

Now one suspects that a first-century Christian eschatological hymn might well have ended in more or less the same way. That is, there is no reason to doubt that Jesus' prayer in Matthew might once have appeared in a form (not recorded in the Gospel) that ended with something like this same assertion. That certain Scribes added this assertion to Jesus' prayer in certain later texts of Matthew indicates that they were aware of an earlier version that had such an ending (as we have seen from the *Didache*).

On these grounds then we might argue for an early date for the existence of a proto-version (lacking later expansions with sophisticated themes) of Jesus' prayer which preserves a subtle reference to the *Trisagion Kedushah* poem in the Isa. 6:3 Targum. In its most primitive form the prayer might have looked something like this: "Hallowed be thy name, for thine is the kingdom, the power and the glory." It may be of interest to note that when God's name was mentioned in the Temple, everyone responded by saying: "Blessed be the Name of—the Glory of—his Kingdom forever and ever" (*y. Ber.* 9:5). The vocabulary of these adorations is drawn from Ps. 145:11–13:

> They will speak of the Glory of your Kingdom, and talk of your Power, to make known to the sons of men his deeds of Power, and the Glory of the majesty of his Kingdom. Your Kingdom is an everlasting Kingdom, and your Dominion is for all generations.

We now have to consider the requests or petitions that follow the *Trisagion* section of the *Kedushah de Sidra*. They are drawn from a rather long list of scriptural citations that are anchored in two initial requests — avoiding temptation and, when one is unable to do this, obtaining forgiveness. They are: 1) Guard against the (evil) inclinations in the heart of your people and direct their heart to you; 2) forgive sins without anger; 3) deliver us, He will answer us; 4) He gave us the Torah of truth and planted everlasting life in our midst; 5) to do his will and serve with whole heart; 6) to do your law in this world, inherit good in the days of the Messiah, and life in the next world; 7) trust in God, he will not desert those who seek him.

Jesus' prayer in Matthew also asks for protection against temptation and for forgiveness. We shall consider his poetic elaborations in the commentary proper. What we lack in *Kedushah de Sidra* is a request for food but instead we get an emphasis on learning and doing the laws of the Torah. We must remember that Jesus' prayer was for the Galilean peasant and not the rabbinic scholar of the study house. Jesus continues his sermon with the message of trust and faith in the beneficence of God, which is a theme found in the final section of the *Kedushah de Sidra*.

> *"Take care not to perform your righteousness before people, in order to be seen by them. Otherwise, you will not have a reward from your heavenly father."*[15] (v. 1)

The verse that underlies this chapter is Micah 6:8: "[He has shown you, O man, what is good.] And what does the Lord require of you? To act justly and to love mercy and to walk *hatsneah* with your God." The word *hatsneah* (literally "hidden") means "to do something modestly and in private." The Rabbis understood that this text from Micah referred to those people who performed their acts of righteousness in public when they should have been doing them in private. They also understood this text to mean that, if possible, they should do even more privately still what acts of righteousness they were already doing in private (*b. Sukkah* 49b). Finally the Rabbis understood that because the Hebrew for "with" in the phrase "privately with your God" from this text is "*im*," this phrase actually meant, "even as God is privately with you" (*Elihau Rab.* [ed. Friedmann], end of chap. 26).[16] So Jesus introduces this entire section of the sermon by saying that the proper way to fulfill the commandments is to do them as privately as one can. We might call this section of the sermon the "Laws of *Tseniut* [modesty and privacy]."

In Jewish tradition it is understood that only once does one get punished for having committed a single sin, and only once does one get rewarded for having done a single good deed. The rationale for performing the commandments as privately as one can is based on the idea that, whether for punishment or reward, it is always better to be dealt with by God than by man.[17] To be praised by man for performing a commandment is to receive the only reward one can receive for performing it; that is, it is to forego receiving any reward from God.

Jewish tradition also suggests that the one who gives charity in view of others is liable to judgment (*Midrash Sechel Tov* [ed. Buber], Gen. [*vayigash*], chap. 47), but this is obviously hyperbole. Conversely, in commenting on Exod. 12:33 (*Midrash Sechel Tov*, Exod. [*bo*], chap. 12), the Rabbis assure us that the one who gives charity in secret will, like the one who does other righteous acts in secret, be rewarded openly. The proof-text for this assertion is Prov. 21:14: "A gift in secret subdues anger." From the same chapter in Proverbs we also read that: "The proudly arrogant man — 'Mocker' is his name; he behaves with wrathful pride" (21:24).

What happens when Micah's advice is ignored and people do not walk in secret with God is what Jesus explains next.

> *"When you give alms, do not blow a trumpet to announce your presence as the 'impersonators' do in the synagogues and in the streets, in order to receive people's praise. 'Amen,' I say to you, they have received their reward." (v. 2)*

Throughout the following brief sermons on charity, prayer, fasting, and gaining rewards, Jesus first begins, as he does here, with the countermodel — "Do not do X" — followed by the exhortation — "but do Y." This form of persuasion can be traced back to Antigonos of Soho (third century B.C.E.), who said, "Do not be like slaves who serve the master on condition that they receive a daily allotment. But be like slaves who serve the master not on condition of receiving any daily allotment" (*m. 'Abot* 1:3).

The word for "impersonators" in the Greek is *hupocritai* — "hypocrites" — and for Matthew the "hypocrites" are those who make a very public display of their alms-giving. That is, the type of hypocrite to which Matthew refers here is not the one who seeks monetary gain by way of a pretense, and which the Rabbis knew as *hanafim*;[18] nor is it the one who harshly condemns others but who is also a sinner himself, about whom both Marcus Aurelius in his *Meditations* 1:11, and the author of the Psalms of Solomon 4:1–12[19] write. Rather, the type of hypocrite to which Matthew refers, and which the Scriptures (Hab. 2:5, Prov. 21:24) know as the *yahir* ("haughty" and/or "arrogant"), is captured by the rabbinic *gassei ruah* (presumptious, haughty).[20] This type of hypocrite is the exact opposite of the humble and/or the poor in spirit whom Jesus praises in the Beatitudes. It is of interest that what Matthew says here of this type of hypocrite is what, though much more harshly, the Rabbis say of the Gentiles in *b. B. Bat.* 10b (though the text does imply that all people, including Jews, who perform acts of righteousness only so that they can be seen to be doing them are doomed to perdition):

All the charity and kindness that the *Gentiles* do are sins for they do them only to show off (*lehityaher*). All who show off fall into *Gehenna,* as is said, "The proud showoff (literally 'haughty' in biblical Hebrew) — 'Mocker' is his name; he behaves with wrathful pride" (Prov. 21:24). "Wrathful" is always used [by Scripture] to refer to *Gehenna,* as it says, "That day is a day of *wrath,* [a day of trouble and distress, a day of wasteness and desolation, a day of darkness and gloominess, a day of clouds and thick darkness"] (Zeph. 1:15).

In fact the problem Jesus addresses here is not so much the sin of hypocrisy but rather the need for praise that motivates the hypocrite's public displays of piety. This type of hypocrite may be sincere in his wish to act righteously but what mars his acts of righteousness is his need to call attention to the fact that he is doing it. That is, Jesus does not suggest here that this type of hypocrite pretends to give charity; he does give it. But Jesus does say that for having given charity in this way he will not be rewarded by God, since he is being rewarded by men. For the Rabbis, as we have seen, it is not just that this type of hypocrite does not receive any reward for his act of righteousness; it is also that he will be severely punished because of the ostentatious way he has done them. The use of hyperbole here makes plain that the Rabbis considered such ostentatious displays of piety to be completely unacceptable. For them, the Jews must not behave this way.

This text also speaks of the sounding of trumpets and, thinking that this refers to some ancient Jewish practice, most commentators exhibit much ingenuity in attempting to explain the occasions during which the sounding of trumpets might have accompanied the giving of alms, or else they speak of the trumpet as being some kind of horn-shaped vessel that the Jews in antiquity used to collect coins.[21] But what the sounding of trumpets refers to here is the way in which what Jesus calls the "impersonators" draw attention to themselves as they perform their acts of righteousness, so that they might be seen and praised by others for having done them. That is, the sounding of the trumpets here is a metaphor for the attention-getting devices the "impersonators" use to draw attention to themselves and to what it is that they are doing.

Finally, the synagogue was a place in which before he said his prayers the one seeking forgiveness from God could give alms in order to gain credit with Him.[22] It is also the case that in some locales both streets and market-places were used as places in which prayers were said (*y. Ber.* 4:6,[23] *y. Meg.* 3:1). However, by referring to synagogues and streets, Matthew might mean here those places where the poor would come to be near the crowds who were being exhorted by preachers to give alms.

"And when you do give alms, do not let your left hand know what your right hand is doing" (v. 3)

In a very memorable way Jesus says here that one should give alms in utter secrecy. That is, one should give alms in such secrecy that not even one's left hand should know that one's right hand is giving it. The Rabbis understood that the one who gives alms with the one hand in this world can expect to receive his reward with the other hand in the next world.[24]

"So that your alms will be in secret, and your father who sees in secret will repay you." (v. 4)

This verse brings the first brief sermon of this section to a close. What Jesus says in verse 1 about performing acts of righteousness — that they should be done in private or in secret — he now says here concerning a particular kind of righteousness. This conclusion of the *inclusio* draws out the finer implications of the text from Micah which, as we say, underlies this whole section of the sermon. What acts of righteousness you do in secret, though they are not seen by men, are seen by God, since he is with you in secret, and it is from him that you receive your reward for doing them in this way.

"And when you pray, do not be like the impersonators, for they love to pray standing in the synagogues, and in the corners of the wide streets, so that people will see them. 'Amen,' I say to you, they have received their reward. But when you pray, go into your back room, and, closing the door, pray to your father in secret, and your father who sees in secret will repay you." (vv. 5–6)

In verses 5–6 we have another brief sermon, concerning how one should pray. And as in verse 4, so again in verse 6, which marks the conclusion of a second *inclusio*, there is an echo of what Jesus says concerning acts of righteousness in verse 1, only this time concerning the act of prayer. The idea of praying in private is not as exceptional at it might at first appear. For as well as taking part in public prayer, which had fixed times and a more or less fixed liturgy, most Rabbis also prayed in private. When praying in public the Rabbis kept their prayers short and their emotions in check, but when praying in private they often prayed with real fervor. A tradition from *t. Berakhot* (ed. Lieberman) 3:1 tells us that when Rabbi Akiva prayed with the assembly he was brief and restrained but when he prayed in private he prayed with utter passion.

When Jesus speaks of those who love to stand in the synagogues and the streets to pray, he has in mind those who stand apart from all others — that is, the "impersonators" — and pray in a conspicuous way. The phrase "stand in prayer" echoes the phrase "*omed ba-tefillah*," which is a reference to what the Rabbis referred to as "The Eighteen Blessings" (see *y. Ber.* 3:5). This was considered the central prayer *par excellence* and had to be recited, under normal circumstances, while standing erect. Its order and wordings were arranged at the academy of Yavneh after the Temple's destruction in 70 c.e. but its roots are more ancient.[25] At any rate the idea of standing in prayer is clearly ancient as 1Sam. 1:26 testifies. The Rabbis find in Hannah's behavior in this verse the perfect model for effective prayer.

Since, as we say, Matt. 6:6 marks the conclusion to the second *inclusio* in this section, we must see that what immediately follows concerning how not to pray (vv. 7–8), and then the Lord's Prayer itself (vv. 9–15), were initially separate from the sermon. In verses 7–8 the matter concerns not the ostentatious way one prays but rather something else. Moreover here it is the Gentiles who are held up as the countermodel, whereas in verses 2 and 5, and again in verse 16, it is the "impersonators," who are Jewish, who are the countermodel (the positive model being, obviously, the way in which Jesus says that one should pray and also Jesus' prayer itself). Nevertheless the form here is identical to what we have seen in verses 2 and 5 — "Do not do or be like X, do or be like Y."

"When you are praying, do not blather like the Gentiles, for they think they will be listened to because of their many words." (v. 7)

Mishnah Menahot concludes with a very fine exegesis in which it is said that the burnt offering of a large animal, the burnt-offering of a small bird, and the meal offering, in spite of the difference in cost and quality of each, nonetheless have in equal measure a "savour pleasing to God" (Lev. 1:9, 1:17, 2:9); for which reason the exegesis concludes with this exhortation: "It is all the same whether one does much or little, only let a person direct his mind to heaven" (*m. Menah.* 13:11). Prayer came to be known as "service of the heart."[26] *B. Ta'anit* 2a finds the biblical injunction "You shall serve God with your whole heart (Deut. 11:13)" to refer to prayer.

Jesus does not say that to pray using many words is a sin. Rather he says that it is not necessary to pray in this way, for God sees into the hearts of men and knows the needs of the one who prays even before he opens his mouth to pray. The Rabbis also felt that there was no reason to pray at length. A text from *b. Ber.* 55a states:

All who are verbose in their prayers and protract it — at the end they will come to heart-ache, as it says, "Stretched out appeals makes the heart sick" (Prov. 13:12).

The Rabbis also did not see that there was any good reason to pray aloud, as though God needed to hear the voice: "Whoever lets his words be audible in prayer is of those of little faith and those who raise their voice in prayer are of the false prophets" (*b. Ber.* 24b). The Talmud also has other things to say about how one should pray. For instance, if in private one needs to pray aloud to keep one's concentration that is fine; however, in public prayer one should only ever pray in a whisper. The Talmud also tells us why one should pray in this way in public — it causes others to lose their concentration as they pray.

The priests of the pagan god Baal stood a long time shouting aloud to be answered. Whereas Elijah prayer was soft and direct (see 1Kings 18:28).

"Do not imitate them, for your Father knows what you need before you ask him." (v. 8)

In his *Mos.* 2.217 Philo says something similar to what Jesus says here about the foreknowledge of God. He says that God is "the Judge Who Knows all before He hears it." The common source is very probably Isa. 65:24: "And it shall come to pass, that before they call, I will answer; and while they are yet speaking, I will hear."

"Pray, therefore, like this: 'Our Father who is in Heaven: Hallowed be your name." (v. 9)

I have dealt with the structure of Jesus' prayer in the introduction to this chapter. The Jesus-prayer is sometimes compared to the *Kaddish* liturgy of the Rabbis, a prayer of hope for the end-time when God's name will be blessed forever, which itself has various forms and uses. In the introduction of a form of the *Kaddish* in Aramaic, which is perhaps an addition from an earlier and shorter supplication, the words are given: "May our prayers and requests be acceptable before our Father who is in Heaven." So there is perhaps reason to think that Jesus was suggesting here that one say this prayer in Aramaic, the language he spoke. On the other hand, this introduction is also known in Hebrew from another very brief supplication. "May be it be willed before our Father who is in Heaven that Joseph's eyes be restored to their place" (*Midrash Psalms* [ed. Buber] 25:13). The *Kaddish* in all its forms has the words "hallowed be His great name."

"May your kingdom come, may your will be done, on earth as it is in heaven." (v. 10)

Matthew's words are reflected in the *Kaddish's* hope that God's "kingdom may endure" (literally, "come to rule…speedily and in short time"). A sentiment reflecting Matthew's desire that God's will be manifested on earth is sometimes placed as the final line of the *Kaddish*. It may be an addition as it is phrased in Hebrew while the *Kaddish* itself is in Aramaic. This line shows a similar sentiment to the Jesus prayer. "He who creates harmony in the heavens, may he create harmony over us and over all of Israel."

"Give us today the bread that we need today." (v. 11)

There is nothing in the *Kaddish* or in any other Jewish prayer of this genre, in which the wish for the establishment of God's kingdom on earth is expressed, which also contains a request for a personal need.[27] Eschatological song serves to project the emotions into a sense of wholeness, a mood envisioning the complete mending of the rift between God's harmonious social world and that of the tyrant. There can be no sense of lack or need in this mood. In a sense the prayer to establish this kingdom obviates the need to ask for physical and spiritual gifts since in this world nothing is lacking. The human condition is other than it is now. There can be no awareness to ask for things now when we cast ourselves into the future realm of peace. Other genres of prayer certainly mandate the petitioning of food, forgiveness, redemption, and even the speedy advent of the Messianic Era for the mood is that of the here-and-now requirements. This petition, unlike the messianic odes, comes from an empty stomach as it were. The Jesus prayer seems to blend the two as if the petitioner stands in the space between two moods, two worlds.

In the introduction to this chapter I suggested that the core of Jesus' prayer was contained in the phrases in the form most are accustomed to, "hallowed be thy name, for thine is the kingdom, etc." Why then were additions made to this prayer in the form of requests, such as this request for bread, or for the forgiveness of sins? The answer is given in the declaration Jesus makes later in the sermon concerning what human beings must do above all: "But seek first his *kingdom* and his *righteousness*, and all of these things shall be given to you also" (6:33).

Verse 6:33 also contains the rationale for the inclusion of the supplications "thy kingdom come" and "thy will be done" in Jesus' prayer. That is, Jesus says here that one must seek God's kingdom and God's righteousness. But to seek his righteousness means first to seek repentance and one first seeks repentance by asking God for pardon from sins. But why ask God for bread, then, if it is to be freely given to the one who seeks his kingdom? In 6:34 we hear that what Jesus says about the benefits one is to receive by seeking first God's kingdom is somewhat exaggerated; what he says here is that one should not ask today for what one may need tomorrow. This helps to clarify that the bread about which Jesus speaks in 6:11 is the bread one needs for today.[28]

In writing about 6:11 in his commentary to Matthew (*On Matthew* 1, de Santos 21), Jerome tells us that in the "Gospel According to the Hebrews" (which he regarded as the original Hebrew, or Aramaic, Gospel of Matthew) the bread about which Jesus speaks here was said to be bread "for tomorrow":

> In the Gospel which is named According to the Hebrews (secundum Hebraeos), instead of "supersubstantial" (spiritual) bread I found "ma[h]ar," which means "of tomorrow," so that the sense would be: "Our bread for tomorrow," that is, "[for] the future give us this day."

In this text the word that modifies bread in the Greek is "*epiousios*," which means, as we have seen, something like "for today." Apparently the reading of this word in 6:11 in the "Gospel According to the Hebrews" was copied from a Greek variant that read *epiousa* (next day) as opposed to *epiousios*.

Two possibilities can be suggested to get behind the rather odd usages of the Greek term. First, we can suggest that *epiousios* may point back to a particular Aramaicism which is related to a form of the word *almin*, which can mean "supernal" in reference to the miraculous, as in *Targum Habakkuk* 3:3, though it usually means "eternal."[29] A form of *almin* may even have meant "ordinary," and I suggest that a form of *almin* may have had as a source what later came to be part of the phrase *lehem be'alma* (*Tosafot to Menahot* 78b) or *lehem de'alma*.[30] The term *be'alma*, meaning "common," is frequent in the Babylonian Talmud, for example, *b. Pesaḥ.* 16b ("common" dust), and is also present, though more rarely, in the Jerusalem Talmud, for example, *y. Yebam.* 12:3 ("common" air). As for the particular expression *di'alma* (as opposed to *be'alma*), it seems to be absent (as far as I can tell) from the Yerushalmi Talmud, but it is very common in the Babylonian Talmud, for example, *b. Ker.* 21a ("common" food). This expression also occurs in a Hebrew form in some Tannaitic sources, for example, *shoteh sheba'olam* ("common" fool), and also in the *Mekhilta of Rabbi Yishmael* to Exod. 16:1 and in *t. Šeb.* 3:6 ("common" rebel). Accordingly, the translation of Matt. 6:11 in the King James Bible — "Give us this day our daily bread" — is perfectly acceptable provided we understand that "daily" means "ordinary and work-a-day."[31] This suggestion assumes a specialized understanding of the word *epiousios*, which as we posit points back to a particular Aramaicism, *de'alma*.

Our second suggestion to explain the Greek usage of *epiousios* seems to me somewhat better founded. The expression *kedei hayyav* in *b. Giṭ.* 59a, *b. Beṣah.* 21b appears to render *mipnei hayyehen* (their lives) in the Yerushalmi Gittin parallel 5:8. The term is reported in the name of scholars who cite Rabbi Yohanan, the teacher who taught in the Land of Israel in the third century. The upshot of all pertinent discussion is that the expression refers to food provisions sufficient for one day (this day or the next).[32] The *Rosh,* Rabbi Asher ben Yehiel (c. 1300, Germany and Spain), in his comments to *b. B. Meṣ.* 1:41 relates the understanding of *kedei hayyav* as "sufficient for his needs this day" to Rabbi Hai Gaon. Others (commentary of Ramban to *b. B. Meṣ.* 16a) disagree with this view but the context of many of the Talmudic passages lends weight to the argument. Elsewhere, Rabbi Yohanan seems to use another expression, *mipnei hayyei nefesh* (*y. Demai* 4:5) to mean something similar. I suggest that *mipnei* and *kedei* are synonymous since they interchange from Talmud Yerushalmi to Talmud Bavli in the Gittin parallels. *Ke-dei* is literally "as much as to suffice for" and so then *mi-pnei* must likewise expresses a limited amount of food consumption. The word *hayyei, nefesh,* and *hayyav* (*hay* literally refers to "life") in these passages refer to one's livelihood, one's needs. Yet *nefesh* has a wider range of meanings including "one's physical substance or essence," and also "one's spiritual being, the life of the soul." Thus *mipnei hayyei nefesh* might mean limited provisions to ensure the welfare either "of one's body" or "of one's soul." The former is clearly the better sense of the expression as used by the Rabbis but this does not preclude a spiritual understanding by others in different contexts. *Mipnei* or *kedei* limits the amount to a daily or two-day amount of food according to long tradition extending down to the geonic commentaries on the Talmud. Thus Greek *epi-ousios* literally translates *mi-pnei hayyei nefesh*. If so, all ancient renditions of the Greek term are intelligible when traced back to this expression. Unfortunately, the usage of the expression is not common knowledge among New Testament scholars. One can see how the versions have traditions rendering the Greek (which literally reproduces "sufficient need for the soul/person") as "for today," "for the [next] day," or "for the soul."

A tradition from *b. Sanh.* 108b tells us that, upon taking the olive branch in his mouth, the dove which Noah sent out from the ark prayed to God: "Master of the Universe, I prefer a morsel of poor bread served from your hand rather than delicacies served from human hands." This tradition also refers to Prov. 30:8, "[F]eed me with the food I need," which is a close parallel to the translation of Matt. 6:11 in the Syriac: "Give us bread for our need this day."

The Rabbis understood that it was meritorious to pray for bread every day (*b. Yoma* 76a); for in the wilderness God provided only enough manna to meet the needs of the Israelites each day so that his people might realize how dependent they were on him and so how necessary it was to pray to him daily.

> *"And forgive for us our sins, as we ourselves have forgiven those who*
> *have sinned against us."* (v. 12)

Although the matter of forgiveness as it is expressed here seems to belong to a kind of "theology of reciprocity" — that is, as we have forgiven others, so may God forgive us — in fact it does not. The idea that one receives good for having done good, or conversely receives ill for having done that, might seem sufficient to understand what is being said here in the prayer. Indeed there are numerous passages in the ancient literature in which the concept of "measure for measure" is spoken of (e.g., Matt. 7:2, *m. Soṭah* 1:7, and others).[33] But Matthew's point here (and many Talmudic passages concur with this) is that the showing of mercy represents an exceptional case, for the one who shows mercy to others receives mercy not from others but from God. That is, the act of showing mercy to others overrides the theology of reciprocity, which states that because I have injured another, I now deserve to be injured by another in turn. But if I have forgiven either what another owes me, or else what another has done to me, then it is God who shows mercy on me.

If we were to choose a Semitic term for what Matthew's Jesus means here by "forgive," it would likely be *"mehilah,"* which is also the word used in expressions concerning the forgiving or foregoing of collection of loans. Later Jewish prayer did not ask for forgiveness in the way it is asked for in Jesus' prayer. Rather the "Eighteen Blessing" prayer simply requests, "Forgive us, for we have sinned." Matthew says more about this theme of forgiveness in verses 14–15.

> *"And do not lead us into trial, but rescue us from the evil one."*
> (v. 13)

The form of the Greek *poneru* is ambiguous. It can be either the genitive of the neuter word *"poneros,"* meaning "wicked" or "evil," or else it can be the genitive of the masculine of the same word, meaning "evil one," which is what we have here.

The use of the word "but" in this verse is similar to the way it is used in the antitheses in chapter 5: "You have hear that it was said that you must do X, *but* I say do Y." Yet perhaps what Jesus really means to say here is something like this: "O Lord, do not ensnare me to test me; *yea*, save me also from Satan's snares."

In the Jewish prayers from antiquity it was common for one to ask to be delivered from "evil," which can have meant either "evil" events, or "evil" people, or the "evil" urge, or the "evil" of Satan. In *b. Ber.* 60b several prayers are found in which there are close parallels to this request in Jesus' prayer for the deliverance from evil. One of them is a private prayer that is said as one retires for the night:

> May it be thy will, O Lord, my God, that you guide me to lie down in peace and place my portion within thy Torah. *And lead me to the hands of good deeds and do not lead me to the hands of sin. And do not bring me —* [not] *to the hands of iniquity and not to the hands of transgression; And not to the hands of Trial and not to the hands of disgrace.* And may my good urge rule over me and may my evil urge not rule over me, and *deliver me from Evil mishap and from terrible diseases.*

Another prayer from this same source is said at the daily morning service in the synagogue:

> "May it be thy will that you habituate me into thy Torah and help me cleave to your commandments. *Do not bring me to the snare of sin or to the snare of transgression — nor to the snare of Trial or disgrace.* Encourage my Evil Urge to be subservient to You. Keep me far from *Evil* people and *Evil* neighbors. *And (on the contrary) induce me to cleave to my good urge and good neighbors who are in your world.* And give me this day and every day, grace, mercy and kindness in your eyes and in the eyes of all who see me.

Also in *y. Ber.* 4:2 a very moving prayer contains something like the request that is being made in Jesus' prayer here. Though the text says that Rabbi Tanhum alone recites it, his use of the plural throughout indicates that he is speaking on behalf of his community.

> Rabbi Tanhum bar Iskolastika would pray, "May it be Thy will, O God, and God of my fathers, *that you break the hold of the evil urge from our hearts.* For you created us to do your will and we are obligated to do your will. You want this and we want this. What hold us back? The leaven in the dough. It is well known to you that

we have not the power within us to withstand it. But may it be Thy will, O Lord, my God, and God of my fathers, that you silence it from [provoking] us and force its submission, so your will be may be done as our will with a perfect heart."

Another example of a Jewish prayer from antiquity includes the request that God deliver the community from Satan. This prayer is said in the evening service just before the recitation of the "Eighteen Blessings." It is likely a very early prayer, a form of which is found in *b. Ber.* 4b. The form of the prayer we include here is from Seder Amram Gaon:

> Save us for your name's sake and remove from us *plague, war and suffering.* Break the power of *Satan* from before us and from behind us and guard our comings in and goings out from now and forever more. For you are our protector and deliverer.

Finally, in Jesus' prayer there is the suggestion that because one has performed certain acts of righteousness one is in the position thereby to ask God to be protected against temptation from sin and against being delivered over to evil. A tradition in *b. Ned.* 40a, in which Ps. 41:1 is cited — "Blessed is he who has regard for the weak; the Lord delivers him in times of trouble" — contains a similar sentiment. Then in this same tradition it is asked what rewards are to be given to the one who performs such goodness in this world, the answer to which is drawn from the following verse in the same Psalm: "The Lord will protect him and preserve his life; give him well-being in the Land and will not deliver him to the desire of his enemies" (41:2).

> *The Lord will protect him* — against the [temptations of] *evil urge. And preserve his life* — from unbearable suffering. *Give him well-being in the Land* — that all will respect him. *And will not deliver him to the desires of his enemies* — such as the likes of Rehoboam (son of Solomon) who created the [tragic] rift in Israel's united kingdom.

This broad sampling of Jewish prayers from antiquity in which are found parallels to certain phrases in the "Lord's Prayer" makes plain that certain themes in the Lord's Prayer had a long history and were already well known by the first century C.E.

As we have said, in some manuscripts of the Gospel of Matthew Jesus' prayer concludes with an eschatological glorification: "For yours is the kingdom and the power and the glory forever. Amen." We have already seen that the *Didache* ends with a similar glorification, the difference being that the phrase "for yours is the kingdom" is absent (8:2). It is likely that this phrase was removed from communal prayers because it was too obviously a challenge to Rome's power, and the entire doxology was very probably removed from some of the Gospel sources for this same reason.

> *"For if you forgive people their transgressions, your heavenly father will forgive you yours. And if you do not forgive people, neither will your father forgive your transgressions." (vv. 14–15)*

Something very similar to what Jesus says here is found in *Midrash Tannaim* (ed. Hoffman) to Deut. 13:18.[34]

> "And he will give you 'Mercy' [a gift meant for you to apply] — and he will be merciful to you" (Deut. 13:18). [The meaning is —] If you are merciful, mercy will be extended to you. And if you are not merciful, mercy will not be extended to you.

> *"Whenever you fast do not be sad-faced like the impersonators are, for they ruin their faces in order to show people that they are fasting. 'Amen,' I say to you, they have received their reward." (v. 16)*

With this verse we return to the form of the brief sermon we encountered earlier in the chapter (vv. 2–4, 5–6), namely, "Do not do or be like X, do or be like Y." What Jesus says about fasting is that one should not make it obvious that one is fasting by either refraining from washing one's face or else anointing oneself with oil, which forms of neglect were a clear indication to all that one was indeed fasting.

> *"But when you fast, anoint your head and wash your face." (v. 17)*

Here Jesus states that, in contrast to the usual practice, those who fast *should* wash and anoint themselves, the reason for which he makes clear in the next verse — so that only God may know that you are fasting.

In Judaism there are two types of twenty-four-hour fasts: Those that are public and are required by Jewish law, such as those carried out on the ninth of Av and on the Day of Atonement; and those that are strictly voluntary and are undertaken for personal reasons (which means usually for reasons of repentence). About Jewish fasts, a tradition in *t. Ta'anit* (ed. Lieberman) 2:4 explains:

> What are the differences between private fasts and public fasts? On public fasts one may eat and drink as long as it is still daylight — which is not the case on

an individual's fast. On a public fast day it is forbidden to work, *to wash oneself, to anoint oneself,* to wear leather sandals, to have sexual intercourse — which is not the case on an individual's fast day.

This text tells us that while on a private fast one might do whatever one wishes, beyond taking food, of course, but in the case of the public fast one must do more than simply abstain from food. The reason that one must also prohibit oneself from doing these other things listed in this text on the public fast days is so that one can experience a significant discomfort on these days, for these days are either days of repentance or days for mourning the loss of the Temple (of course not working or not wearing leather sandals was not uncommon for many in antiquity, and so there would have been many who, although not fasting, would have been, as a matter of course, barefoot and/or idle). Private fast days are not governed by rules requiring prohibitions beyond fasting itself, since these fasts are voluntary. Jesus must be speaking here only about these private fasts; on public fast days it would have been well known that all were fasting and so there would have been no point for anyone to hide it.

> *"So that you are not showing that you are fasting to people, but to your father who is in secret, and your father who sees in secret will repay you." (v. 18)*

Here ends this section of the sermon that is made up of the three brief sermons Jesus gives to explain fully what he says in 6:1. In what follows Jesus continues to use the form he has repeatedly used in this section — do not do X but do Y — with the difference that he no longer provides either models or countermodels. For the most part the advice he now gives is straightforward and does not require much analysis. Perhaps it is worth pointing out that with this verse this brief sermon on fasting concludes in the way the other brief sermons in this chapter have concluded, by forming an *inclusio* with 6:1.

> *"Do not store up treasure for yourselves upon the earth, where moth and tarnish destroy and where thieves break in and steal. But store up treasure for yourselves in heaven, where neither moth nor tarnish destroy and where thieves neither break in nor steal." (vv. 19–20)*

A tradition from *y. Pe'ah* 1:1,[35] in which certain activities of King Monbaz (Monobazus II of Adiabene, Josephus praises him, *Ant.* 20.95–96), who ruled about the year 60 C.E., are written of, contains a number of parallels to Jesus' saying here in these several verses. The tradition in *y. Pe'ah* 1:1 reads:

King Monbaz abandoned all his properties to the poor. His relatives summoned him and complained: your ancestors added to their inheritance and to that of their ancestors and you have abandoned your own and that of your ancestors. He replied: My ancestors stored on earth and 1) *I stored in heaven.* ...My ancestors stored treasures that do not bear fruit and I stored treasures that bear fruit. ...My ancestors stored away in a place where others could reach it but 2) *I stored away in a place where no other could reach it.* ...My ancestors stored material wealth and I stored people. ...My ancestors stored to enrich others and 3) *I stored to enrich myself.* ...My ancestors stored in this world and I stored for the World to Come.

In fact the parallels are so similar here that one suspects that both Matthew and the Rabbis drew from an earlier common source that later came to be this more developed Talmudic tradition. The equivalent passage in Luke is much more rudimentary:

"[Y]ou have so many good things stored up for many years, rest, eat, drink, be merry!" But God said to him, "You fool, this night your life will be demanded of you; and the things you have prepared, to whom will they belong?" Thus will it be for the one who stores up treasure for himself but is not rich in what matters to God. (12:19–21)

The texts of both Matthew and the Rabbis share much more with each other than either do with the text from Luke.

The theme of temporal, material wealth being contrasted unfavorably with eternal, spiritual wealth has a long history and is a well-known theme in biblical wisdom literature. A tradition from *b. B. Bat.* 10a includes a discussion of two texts from this literature that are almost identical. These texts are Prov. 11:4, "Stores of wealth will be of no avail on the day of wrath, but righteousness saves from death," and Prov. 10:2, "Treasure chests of evil gain will be of no avail, but righteousness saves from death." In this tradition it is explained that performing a certain type of righteous act protects one against a torturous death while another type saves one from the judgment of Hell.

"For where your treasure is, there will be your heart as well." (v. 21)

One's heart is on what one value's most. Hence the injunction in Numbers not to stray after one's heart and/or one's eye (in the next several verses Jesus speaks of the eye): "And it shall be a tassel for you to look at and remember all the commandments of the Lord, to do them, not to follow after your own heart and your own eyes, which you are inclined to whore after. So you shall remember and do all my commandments, and be holy to your God" (Num. 15:39–40).

A tradition from minor tractate *'Abot R. Nat.*, version A, chap. 20, which comments on a text from Psalm 19, is relevant here:

> It is written in the Book of Psalms by David, King of Israel: "The precepts of the Lord are upright, illuminating the heart; the commandment of the Lord is pure, enlightening the eyes" (Ps. 19:9). Hence, anyone who does not put words of Torah on his heart will have many fantasies — hungering fantasies, nonsensical fantasies, lewd fantasies, fantasies provoked by the evil urge, and fantasies provoked by wanton women.

> *"The eye is the body's lamp. If, then, your eye is sound, your whole body will be illuminated. But if your eye is wicked, your whole body will be dark. So if the light in you is darkness, how great is the darkness!"*
> (vv. 22–23)

"The eye is the body's lamp." This statement stands alone and means simply that the body needs the eye to see its way forward. That is, the light of the eye lights the way of the body (in Hebrew "eyesight" is "*meor eynayim*," literally "the shining of the eyes").

That "the eye is the body's lamp" is an obvious statement. Proverbs 4:25 assumes it as obvious, "Keep your eyes on what is in front of you, looking straight before you."[36] But in what he says following, Jesus interprets the statement to mean that the eye, rather than lighting the way for the body, actually lights up the body itself. That is, Jesus says here that the eye is something like one's inner character or spirit, and if one's inner spirit is alight, then the *whole* person is filled with light. Conversely, if one's inner spirit is dark, then the *whole* person is filled with darkness. For Jesus, then, a good eye means a spirit alight, and the one whose spirit is alight is the one whose character is marked by generosity (this is also the meaning of the one whose spirit is alight in the rabbinic literature as well), whereas the character of the one whose spirit is dark is marked by the reverse. A tradition from *m. 'Abot* 5:19 (ed. Albeck, var. 5:22 or 23 some editions) says much the same:

> Whoever possesses these three traits is of the students of our father Abraham, and [whoever possesses] three other traits is of the students of the wicked Balaam. [Those who have] *a good eye*, a humble spirit and a lowly spirit [are] of the students of our father Abraham. [Those who have] *a wicked eye*, an arrogant spirit and a haughty spirit [are] of the students of the wicked Balaam. What is the difference between the students of our father Abraham and those of wicked Balaam? The students of our father Abraham enjoy this world and inherit the World to Come,

as it is said, "There is for those who love Me to inherit (i.e., in the World to Come), and their storehouses (i.e. in this world) I will fill" (Prov. 8:21). But the students of the wicked Balaam inherit Hell and descend into the pit of destruction, as it is said, "And You, Lord, will bring them down to the pit of destruction, men of blood and deceit; they will not live half their lives. But I will trust in You" (Ps. 55:24).

Jesus would also have understood that the one who has the good eye, by virtue of his having it, is also "humble" and of "a lowly spirit," whereas the one who has the wicked eye, by virtue of his having it, is also "arrogant" and of "a haughty spirit."

*"No one can be a slave to two masters, for either he will hate the one
and love the other, or he will be loyal to the one and despise the other.
You cannot serve both God and Mammon." (v. 24)*

This verse refers back to verses 20–21. The rabbinic phrase is somewhat different: "Not everyone can manage to eat at two tables" (*b. Ber.* 5b). God must be served with one's whole heart (Deut. 6:5), so there is no way one can also serve Mammon — material wealth — which is personified (and demonized) here.

The division between the material and the spiritual in the Gospels is sharp whereas in the rabbinic literature this division is not so clear cut. In 7:18 we shall hear that a corrupt tree cannot bear good fruit. On the other hand *b. Ber.* 5b insists that the goal of living in this world is to seek to suppress the evil inclination by means of the good.[37]

*"Therefore I say to you, do not be anxious about your life, what you
will eat, nor about your body, what clothes you will wear. Is not life
more than nourishment, and the body more than clothes?" (v. 25)*

Exod. 21:10 makes plain that under no circumstances can a man withhold food and clothing from his wife, for these are the necessities of life.

*"Consider that the heaven's birds neither sow nor reap nor gather grain
into barns, and your heavenly father nourishes them. Aren't you worth
more than they?" (v. 26)*

A text attributed to Rabbi Simeon b. Eleazar that is found in *b. Qidd.* 82b[38] makes plain that the point Jesus is making here is both ancient and well known. By way of conclusion Rabbi Simeon explains why most people now need to work.

Rabbi Simeon b. Eleazar said: Did you ever see a wild beast or bird with a trade? I have never in all my life seen a deer drying fruits in the field, a lion carrying heavy burdens, or a fox who kept a shop, and yet none of them die of hunger. Now, if these, who have been created to serve my needs are able to support themselves without trouble, how much more reasonable is it to expect that I, who have been created to serve my Master, should be able to support myself easily, without trouble. However, my deeds were evil and I have therefore ruined my livelihood.

"And which of you by being anxious can add one cubit to his span of life? Concerning clothing, why be anxious about it? Look at the wildflowers in the field, how they thrive. They neither labor nor spin. But I say to you that not even Solomon in all his glory was arrayed like one of these. But if God so clothes the wild-grass in the field, which exist today and are thrown into the oven tomorrow, will he not clothe you much more, you of little faith?" (vv. 27–30)

In *b. Sanh.* 90b Rabbi Meir speaks of how the dead will be resurrected in finest robes:

If a grain of wheat, which is buried naked, sprouts [clothed] in many robes, how much more so will the righteous [be clothed], who are buried in their clothes already.

Traditions in which it is said that certain things are compared to Solomon or to how they would have been done in Solomon's time (such as banquets, in *m B. Meṣ..* 7:1), or in which it is said that the people of a certain generation or time were "of little faith" (such as the people of the generation of the Exodus, in *b. Pesaḥ.* 118b), are standard in the rabbinic literature. Arguing from the complex to the simple is also a standard feature of this literature.

"So do not be anxious, saying, 'What will we have to eat?' or 'What will we have to drink?' or 'What will we have to wear?' For the Gentiles seek after all these things, but your heavenly father knows that you seek all of these." (vv. 31–32)

Some Rabbis thought in the way Jesus does here. For example, what is said by Rabbi Eleazar in a tradition from *Midrash Sechel Tov* (ed. Buber) to Exod. 16:4 is very like what Jesus says here.

Then the Lord said to Moses ["Behold, I will rain bread from heaven for you; and the people shall go out and gather a day's portion on its day, that I may test them, whether or not they will walk in my Torah" (Exod. 16:4)], *"Gather a day's portion on its day."* He who created the day created its sustenance with it. He intended that people never feel they do not need to pray and receive mercy. *"That I may test them."* From here Rabbi Eleazar of ha-Moda'i said, "Whoever has something to eat today and asks — What will I eat tomorrow? — is of those of little faith."

> *"But seek first his kingdom and his righteousness, and all of these things will be given to you also."* (v. 33)

Here Jesus makes absolutely clear that his theology was centered on "kingdom" (by which he meant "doing God's will in this world") and "righteousness" (by which he meant "being free of sin"), in contrast to the Rabbis, for whom the essential thing was Torah study. Indeed, in a tradition from *Eliahu Zuta* (ed. Friedmann), chap. 17, what Jesus says shall be given to those who seek God's kingdom and righteousness Rabbi Eliezer says shall be given to "those who labor in the Torah for its own purpose." But the Rabbis were also aware that righteousness went further than simply mastering the legal traditions. In a tradition from *Esther Rab.* 6.1, in which Ps. 106:3 is discussed — "Blessed are the keepers of justice who do righteousness at every moment" — the Rabbis asked: Who performed righteousness at every moment? They answered that it was not those who taught the written and oral law, since at least some of the time they ate and slept; nor for the same reason was it those who wrote sacred documents. Rather for the Rabbis those who performed righteousness every moment were those who raised orphans in their homes.

While sharing the values and language of the later Rabbis, Jesus passes over this central feature of the Jewish religious life of the Second Temple period and later. Of course Jesus teaches about the Scriptures and later in the Gospel he will also teach oral tradition to defend his actions and those of his students on the Sabbath, but he does not encourage either his audience or his disciples to study Torah.[39] This may be because his audience and disciples come from the Galilean peasant class.[40] Still, the almost complete silence in Matthew on deteriorating social and political life under the boot of Rome sets the Gospel apart from Jewish writings of the period.

The second part of the same tradition from *Midrash Sechel Tov* to Exod. 16:4 above tells us that some should be ahead of others when it comes to studying the Torah.

Whether or not they will walk in my Torah: Rabbi Joshua said: One who learns two laws [of oral law] in the morning and two at night and works a full day in between, Scripture considers him as if he has learned the entire Torah. Yet, from this very verse, Rabbi Shimon bar Yohai argued [against him]: The Torah was only given to the eaters of the manna for them to expound and secondly to those dependent on tithes from foods. How is this? If a man sits and expounds but does not know from where he really receives his food and his drink, from where he receives the garment which covers him [then he will fail in his studies]. Thus you see that the *Torah* was only given to the eaters of manna to expound and second to those dependent on tithes from foods [who see that God provides for them].

It is inconceivable that Jesus would not have identified fully with the covenantal outlook of his times. Nevertheless the teachings of Jesus that Matthew and the other Gospel writers provide are so selective as to confirm that Judaism and Christianity had already moved in separate directions by the time these writers set these teachings down.

"Therefore, do not be anxious for tomorrow, for tomorrow will be anxious for itself. Sufficient for today is today's evil." (v. 34)

Both in *b. Ber.* 9b and *Exod. Rab* (*Shemot*) 3:6 one can read something almost identical to what Jesus says here: "Each trouble is enough for its own time." The meaning is that one should only be concerned with the problems one faces today and not worry about what may arise tomorrow.

NOTES

1   These two commandments nicely balance the main ideologies of ancients and moderns: Embracing the king as the totalitarian ruler of all (the totalitarian state); embracing the self as the measure of all (the supremacy of the individual).

2   *M. Ber.* 9:5 — suggests it applies to one's resources: wealth or one's lot in life. God is to be served through the sum totals of one's wherewithal.

3   The point is nothing said by God or angels is merely aesthetic repetition without some further sense.

4   The verses from Isaiah and Ezekiel relating angelic praises introduce the *Shema* recitation in the morning service, while the verse from Exodus, the redemption praise, follows it and introduces the Eighteen Benedictions.

5   For the text of the *Kedusha de Sidra* in English see the *Complete ArtScroll Siddur*, 157–58: "A redeemer will come to Zion."

6   The Targum to Ezek. 3:12 is reflected in this expansion and this verse is recited after the three "holy"s and their interpretations are given.

7   I assume this reflects the Targum of Isa. 60:21: "And your people are all righteous, they shall inherit the *earth*, planting of my delight, *the work of my Power.*"

8   The Targum to Exod. 15:18 is reflected in this expansion and this verse is recited after the three "holys" and their interpretations are given.

9   Meaning the angels praise God in his heavenly Temple.

10   For the Rabbis of the Targum it was not proper to ascribe actions to God, rather the actions were turned into descriptions — God really does not rule forever — his kingdom endures forever.

11   I. Elbogen (*Ha-tefila Be-yisrael Be-hitp'hutah ha-historit,* 80) thinks that the concluding section of a prayer (following the evening *shema* recitations, which are still recited to this day) preserved in *Siddur Rav Amram Gaon* was originally from an earlier classic messianic hymn. The emphasis of the mini hymn is on "thine is the kingdom." After citing the words of Exod. 15:18, "The Lord will rule for ever and ever," the Targumic form of which, as we have seen, reads, "The Lord, his kingdom is forever and ever," the poet expands the idea of this reign: "For thine is the kingdom and for all ages thou wilt rule in glory for we have no king but thee. Blessed art thou, the king in his glory, always let him rule over us for ever and over all his works."

12   The date and provenance of this hymn are unknown. It certainly dates from the third century as *terminus ad quem*. Nevertheless, its forms and references may be more antiquated. It exhibits features that are common to prayers of hope for the end of time.

13   Isa. 45:23, which is the text from which these opening phrases are taken, reads from the Hebrew: "To me every knee shall bow, every tongue shall swear allegiance." The same text from the LXX reads: "To me every knee shall bow, every tongue shall confess to God," which is the version of the text that has shaped what seems to be an excerpt from a Christian liturgical hymn in Philippians 2:10–11 (of course in the hymn the text has been glossed so that it conforms to a Christian message): "That at the name of Jesus *every knee shall bow* — of beings in heaven, and beings on earth, and beings under the earth; *And that every tongue shall confess* — that Jesus Christ is Lord, to the glory of God the Father."

14   Targum Onkelos renders this: "The Lord, his kingdom endures always, and for all eternity."

15   Compare minor tractate *Derekh Eretz* 6:2 ([ed. Cohen] 7:2–3): A scholar must be modest in his manner of eating, drinking, washing, anointing himself, putting on his shoes, in sexual matters, in his manner of walk, his manner of dress, his speech, his spittle, his good deeds: but he must be public about his pleasant demeanor, seeking truth and eschewing falsehood, dealing uprightly and not deceitfully, modestly and not showing off, peaceful and not divisive, adhering to the counsel of elders and not youngsters, fixing his gaze even after a lion rather than after a woman.

16   This has already been discussed at length in my commentary to 5:48.

17   While 2Sam. 24:14 — "But let us fall into the hands of the Lord, for his mercy is great. Do not let me fall into human hands" — refers to punishment, the principle certainly holds for rewards as well.

[18] This is the word used by the Syriac translator.

[19] The text reads:

> "Wherefore sittest thou, O profane (man), in the council of the pious, Seeing that thy heart is far removed from the Lord, Provoking with transgressions the God of Israel? Extravagant in speech, extravagant in outward seeming beyond all (men), Is he that is severe of speech in condemning sinners in judgement. And his hand is first upon him as (though he acted) in zeal, And (yet) he is himself guilty in respect of manifold sins and of wantonness. His eyes are upon every woman without distinction; His tongue lieth when he maketh contract with an oath. By night and in secret he sinneth as though unseen, With his eyes he talketh to every woman of evil compacts. 6 He is swift to enter every house with cheerfulness as though guileless. Let God remove those that live in hypocrisy in the company of the pious, (Even) the life of such an one with corruption of his flesh and penury. Let God reveal the deeds of the men-pleasers, The deeds of such an one with laughter and derision; That the pious may count righteous the judgement of their God, When sinners are removed from before the righteous, 10 (Even the) man-pleaser who uttereth law guilefully. 11 (9) And their eyes (are fixed) upon any man's house that is (still) secure, That they may, like (the) Serpent, destroy the wisdom of [the wise] with deceptive words, His words are deceitful that (he) may accomplish (his) wicked desire." And Dan. 11:32 also notes the technique of the deceptive flatterer. "He will flatter and win over those who have violated the covenant. But the people who know their God will be strong and will resist him."

[20] Over time the biblical *"yahir"* (arrogant) slowly evolved into the rabbinic *"yohara."* The Rabbis also made a distinction between the types of *"yohara."* The term *"yohara"* alone referred to the former type of hypocrite above; the term "akin to *yohara*" (i.e., *mechze keyohara*. See *b. Ber.* 17b and *b. Pesaḥ.* 55a) referred to the latter type of hypocrite.

The Roman Empire as a whole was termed "arrogant" (*zed*—a word used in Prov. 21:24 together with *yahir*). In *Tanḥ. Deut.* (*ki tetsei*) 8, Rabbi Banaʾah interprets Prov. 11: 1–2: "Deceptive scales are an abomination to the Lord, but accurate weights are his delight." When the Arrogant One (*zadon*) comes, then comes disgraceful behavior, but with the *Tsenuim* comes wisdom." The arrogant one for him is Rome and he notes that when you have a generation who is deceitful it is due to the influence of Roman culture. The *tsenuim* are those who deal modestly and in private fashion as we said at the start of this chapter.

[21] My favorite outrageous comment (with no evidence to substantiate it) to Matt. 6:2 comes from the Internet site http://www.cathtruth.com/catholicbible/matt6.htm: *"Therefore when you do an alms-deed, sound not a trumpet before you. Syr. do not blow a horn.* When the Scribes and Pharisees were about to give away alms in the public streets they either sent a trumpeter before them, or else blew a horn themselves, under the pretext of drawing together by that means

crowds of poor persons, who might run and receive alms, but in reality out of ostentation, and that their liberality might be seen and talked of by those who flocked together."

22   *B. B. Bat.* 10a.

23   *Y. Ber.* 4:7 in the English translations of J. Neusner.

24   *Midrash Prov.* (ed. Buber) 11:21 interprets Prov. 11:21, "Hand to hand, the wicked one shall not be held innocent: but the seed of the righteous shall be delivered" as follows:

> "Hand to hand." [That is to say,] one hand is meant to do good deeds and the other will then receive the reward for them. Now if you have not done good deeds in this world where you live, how can you claim reward [in the next]? What do people really do with these two hands I created? With one they sin and with the other do righteousness and so it is written, "The wicked one shall not be held innocent." So do not think you will escape from the judgement of *Gehenna* [because the good one did well], since the evil one will nevertheless not be held innocent. Rabbi Yohanan commented on this interpretation saying: "Here is a parable. A man went and sinned and paid a prostitute. Even before he got out the door he met a poor man who said to him, "Give me charity!" He gave him and left on his way. That man thought — May it be that God find appeasement here to atone for my sin.

25   See Finkelstein, "The Development of the Amidah," and Elbogen and Scheindlin, *Jewish Liturgy.*

26   See *Mekhilta Rabbi Shimon bar Yohai* to Exod. 23:25. I find 1Cor. 14:19 to be similar. "In the church I would rather speak five words with my mind, so as to instruct others also, than ten thousand words in a tongue."

27   Which is not to deny that prayers containing requests for sustenance and messianic redemption were/are standard fare in Jewish practice. "And satisfy us from [the earth's] bounty" is followed by "Sound the great horn for our freedom and raise the banner to gather in our dispersion" is the center of the "Eighteen Blessings" standing Amidah prayer (the essential of daily services). The rabbinic grace after bread-meals says, "Have mercy, O Lord our God, on Israel your people, and on Jerusalem your city, and on Zion the dwelling place of your Glory, and on the *kingship of the House of David your anointed,* and on the great and holy House upon which your name is called. O Lord our God, *sustain us, feed us, provide for us, and nourish us, and give us relief.*" However, these petition prayers and praises do not utilize numinous vocabulary (e.g., his Great Name) nor address at once the worlds above, below and future but rather speak to the desire for immediate redemption to restore the glory of Israel. In this way, there is a divide between "petition-prayer" and "messianic-prayer." The Jesus prayer combines the two genres.

28 The Syriac version says, "Give us *bread* for our need this day." The Syriac translators apparently took the Greek *epiousios* to mean "extremely essential," a possible understanding of this unusual Greek term.

29 This word also appears in Luke 11:3, which Jerome in the Vulgate has translated as "*quotidian*," i.e., something that is ordinary or that occurs daily; whereas this same word in Matt. 6:11 he translated in the Vulgate as "*supersubstantial*," i.e., supernal and supernatural.

30 See Rabbenu Asher's *Halakhot Ketanot to Menahot*, "Laws of Hallah" 2, and Rabbi Moses Nachmanides' "Laws of Hallah" 26b.

31 It is noteworthy that John 6:34 reads: "give us our bread always." "Always" is the exact translation of *le'olam*, and perhaps such a variant (*le'olam* in place of *be'olam* or *b'alama*) was current in the Hebrew/Aramaic prayers of the first century.

32 A very complex discussion of the passages and sources concerning *kedei hayyav* can be found in Zwi Moshe Dor (*The Teachings of Eretz Israel in Babylonia*), 203–10.

33 One of the most interesting passages in this regard is found in a later midrash, *Deut. Rab.* (ed. Lieberman) (*Devarim*) 23: "'Honest scales and balances are from the Lord; all the weights in the bag are of his making' (Prov. 16:11). The Holy One does not withhold payment from any person but with the measure that a person measures to others is it measured back to him."

34 *B. Šabb.* 151b knows a variant phrasing: "All who have mercy on all other beings, they will receive mercy from heaven. And all those who do not have mercy on all other beings, they will not receive mercy from heaven." Here it is made clear that habitual behavior is being spoken of, not something that is only occasional.

35 This tradition is also found in *t. Pe'ah* 4:18 and *b. B. Bat.* 11a.

36 Num. 15:39–40 makes eyes and heart near parallels: "[A]nd remember all the commandments of the Lord, to do them, not to follow after your own heart and after your own eyes, which you are inclined to whore after. So you shall remember and do all my commandments, and be holy to your God."

37 This is the theme of Odeberg's *Pharisaism and Christianity.*

38 See also *m. Qidd.* 4:14, *t. Qidd.* 5:15, *y. Qidd.* 4:11.

39 Kingdom and righteousness alone without Torah study and national or social institutions would later prove to be a disastrous recipe. For example, those communities that sustained schools of study and fixed days to mourn the fall of Jerusalem and funds for the poor provided a framework for Jews to live (even if persecuted and impoverished) creative, spiritual lives within their own communities aspiring to return to their homeland. Every Jewish movement

which abandoned these Jewish boundary markers ended in calamity and this trend will likely continue to be the case. The Jews are a nation, and the Torah and the aspirations of homeland are the links that hold them together.

40   J. Klausner, in his book *Jesus of Nazareth,* 389–98, has pointed out that Jesus' agenda in his sermons could never have been relevant for his implied audience. Its exaggerated demands are simply not realistic for those living in small peasant communities. Jesus' teaching is devoid of the national aspirations inherent in being a "holy nation before God." His teaching is always polemical and directed against some group or other whose members act as straw men for his teaching, for which reason it often seems driven by anger and the need to utter threats rather than love and/or compassion. But Klausner's main point is that the teachings of Jesus do not address the needs of a nation that must support national institutions, law courts, synagogues, celebrations, and mourning days. The impossibly high expectations of the gospel's ethic never seriously served the political ends of Christian countries and rulers, which eventually turned to cruelty and oppression (feeling little or no guilt for the hardships and persecutions they initiated). The reported teachings of Jesus ignore the social, political, and religious needs of Jews seeking to live fully the rich religious life pictured in Torah and tradition. For Klausner, that was actually the goal of Jesus — to discard the essential nationhood of Israel, and all that celebrated it, in favor of the divine kingdom that posed a challenge to any human kingdom. He thinks that that was why in the end it did not appeal to most Jews, and the Gentiles it attracted had little interest in taking the Jesus' teaching seriously. A new theology had to overlay the original Jesus movement for it to take hold.

CHAPTER SEVEN

INTRODUCTION

The sermon as a whole is essentially an anthology of Jewish teachings organized thematically. In this section of the sermon in particular Jesus teaches lessons based on scriptural texts that are embedded in the Jewish homiletic literature. However he has removed the texts upon which these lessons are based in this literature, and which are regularly cited in them, so that he appears to teach — at times with surprising bitterness — on his own authority. That is, the charm of the rabbinic literature, with its schoolhouse dialectics and focus on scriptural proof-texts, is replaced here not only by the Matthean Jesus' concision, but also his severity. Nonetheless it is clear that Matthew considers Jesus' audience to be familiar with the style of discourse within the various schools of the Scribes and sages, for Jesus addresses his audience according to this style.

Because in this section of the sermon Jesus offers a number of reproofs and moral injunctions, we might call it "The Proverbs of Jesus." In the first several verses Jesus again speaks in terms of the theology of reciprocity, only now in a kind of "negative" way. Whereas in Jesus' prayer the one who prays asks God to forgive him because he has also forgiven others, in these first several verses Jesus warns against doing certain things to others — such as judging them — so that others do not also do these things to you. What underlies Jesus' thinking here is the understanding that everyone has faults and so everyone should be concerned first with his own faults rather than another's. That is, it is best not to accuse others of what it is that ails you.[1] In verse 5 he calls the one who does such things *"hupocrita"* — "hypocrite" or "impersonator" — after which, in verse 6, he warns that one should be careful about what one teaches and to whom. Those who are not worthy of the teaching will pervert the wisdom it contains.

In verses 13–14 we encounter Jesus in the role of gatekeeper to the Kingdom of Heaven. Here he offers advice on how to gain admission into the kingdom, or states what it is that will leave one outside it. Jesus appears to be the only one who has this knowledge.

In spite of the demanding exhortations found throughout, the overarching theme in all of the rabbinic literature is the hope found in the unconditional love of God for Israel. That is, while the concept of "measure for measure" is taken seriously in this literature, it is mitigated by the notion that God will never abandon his people. The Rabbis often posed problems concerning God's relationship with the Jews. Scriptures appeared to be inconsistent on the matter. They usually resolved these difficulties by claiming that although individuals *qua* individuals may be judged harshly, God will never abandon his people but will forgive them time and again. Hence, collective religious interaction will always be answered with grace and love.[2] And so prayer offered in the framework of collective membership has much merit. By phrasing his prayer in the plural (using "our," "us"), Jesus, in Matthew's eyes, does not separate the individual from the nation and his theology, at the surface level, seems to be close to that espoused by Rabbis. However, this first impression needs to be examined in greater detail as Matthew's anti-Israel rhetoric increases as the Gospel progresses until he intimates that Israel will be replaced by another.

"Do not judge, so that you will not be judged." (v. 1)

The word "judge" here means to articulate a private estimation of another's character. As is made clear in verse 5, Jesus is actually addressing his critics here and not the wider audience, reminding them of their own teachings and their own failings. As he points out, they are not qualified to judge him. Be that as it may, it is difficult to reconcile what Jesus says here with the language he uses to describe the Jewish religious leaders, calling them at times "hypocrites" (7:5) and at times "vipers" (23:33).

What guides Jesus' thinking here is again the widely held principle of "measure for measure," though at first he begins with a sweeping statement about judgment, that one simply should not judge. He does not say here what he suggests following, that in order to be judged kindly one must judge kindly in return.

According to a text from *b. Ta'an.* 8a, the Rabbis considered it presumptuous for anyone to judge himself as righteous. The text reads:

Rabbi Ami taught: Whoever holds himself as being fully righteous in the earthly realm will be held liable according to the full standard of justice in the heavenly realm. And so Scripture teaches, "Truth (more properly: *full righteousness*) springs up from the earth, and justice (*tsedek*) looks down from the heavens" (Ps. 85:11).

> *"For in the judgment with which you judge you will be judged, and in the measure with which you measure out — it will be measured out to you." (v. 2)*

In *b. Šabb.* 127b it is said that the one "who judges benevolently will be judged benevolently" (the text of *Otsar Midrashim*, p. 162, adds: "and one who judges maliciously will be judged maliciously"). And in 'Abot R. Nat., version A (8:5) something similar is said: "Just as you judged me favorably so God will judge you favorably."

Klausner points out that many of the sayings of Jesus also appear in the rabbinic literature, but in a somewhat different form,[3] but yet there are some sayings of Jesus that appear in that literature almost word for word the same. The saying of Jesus here is found word for word in *m. Soṭah* 1:7, with the difference that (and this is a significant difference) in Matt. 7:2 Jesus is addressing his critics, so that the last word in the saying is directed at them — "in the measure with which you measure out — it will be measured out to *you*" — whereas in *m. Soṭah* the Rabbis are simply stating a rule, so that the last word in the saying here is directed at an anonymous "him" — " in the measure with which a person measures out — it will be measured out to *him*."

> *"Why do you see the speck in your brother's eye, but you do not notice the beam in your own eye? Or how can you say to your brother, 'Let me remove the speck from your eye,' while look — there is a beam in your own eye?" (vv. 3–4)*

The rabbinic version of what Jesus says here appears in both *b. B. Bat.* 15b, though here the speck is said to be in a man's "teeth," and *b. 'Arak.* 16b. Ruth 1:1, which reads literally, "And it was in the days of judging those who judged…," introduces the tradition from *b. B. Bat.*, giving it a judicial setting not found in the tradition from *b. 'Arakhin*. The tradition from *b. B. Bat.* reads:

> If the judge said to a man, "Take the splinter [tiny fault] from between your teeth," he would [justifiably] retort, "Take the beam [large fault] from between your eyes."

People are quick to find faults in others but not so quick to see their own. In this text the man who "retorts" to the judge may indeed have faults but he is aware that the judge has even more serious faults than he. In the same way here Jesus is in the position of the one who has been told that he has faults, to which he now responds by pointing out how much larger are the faults of his critics; for as I say at this point in the sermon Jesus is addressing the more learned sages who have undoubtedly rebuked him and his followers. Jesus answers in the way that the Jewish narrative expects him to. Without knowing the Jewish sources in the background here we would not hear the bitter tones.

The following story is instructive in showing that judges ought not ask of others what they themselves were guilty of. The example shows how the Rabbis, realizing that judges were putting themselves above the law, interpreted the Torah in such a way as to point out that only honest judges would be appointed.

Midrash Tanḥ. Deut. Shoftim 3.
"Judges and [i.e. who are] officers (Deut. 16:18)" tells us that the judges must be vigorous in their good deeds. …It is told of Rabbi Hanina ben Elazar that he had a tree, which while planted on his property, had limbs that stretched over into an adjourning property. One day a litigant came [with his neighbor] to complain to him that his neighbor's tree was overhanging his own property. Then [remembering his very situation] the judge asked him to leave and return the next day. He retorted that the judge was being unfair since he adjudicated the cases of all the others who came before him on the spot while this case he pushed off to the morrow. But what did Rabbi Hanina need to do first? He sent workmen to remove the tree that was on his property and whose branches encroached upon another's. Then the following day the neighbors returned to him for a judgment. He ordered the defendant, "You must remove it!" That one replied — Why so, your own tree has branches that encroach on another's property!" The judge replied, "Go and see for yourself — whatever you see has been done to my property you will have to do to your own." He immediately went and did so.

"Impersonator, first remove the beam from your eye, and then you will be able to see clearly to remove the speck from your brother's eye.
(v. 5)

The word "impersonator" here actually refers to those hypocrites who would criticise others for faults they themselves have. It is here in this verse that we discover that Jesus is addressing his adversaries in this brief section of the sermon (vv. 1–6). It is the first time in the sermon that he actually tells us to whom his remarks are being addressed. Prior to this it was, as Matthew has told us, the crowds and his disciples whom Jesus was addressing. Here Matthew allows Jesus to explicitly address his audience.

> *"Do not give what is holy to the dogs, nor throw your pearls before pigs, lest they trample them under their feet, turn around and attack you."*
> (v. 6)

The word "holy" in this verse is almost certainly a mistake. The Aramaic *qadashin* means "rings" (*Targum Onqelos* to Num. 31:50, singular *qedasha*, a "ring"),[4] but the translator must have confused it with the similar but different *qadishin*, "holy things" (*Targum Onqelos* to Lev. 11:44, singular *qudsha*, "something holy"). Both words could be spelled in the same way, yet pronounced somewhat differently. The proper reading of the verse, then, should be: "Do not give *rings* to the dogs, nor throw your pearls before pigs," which is corroborated by the Syriac rendition of this verse. Our retroversion of the Greek into what must have been the Aramaic original here seems to indicate that at least a part of the sermon in Matthew is based on an Aramaic tradition.

In this verse Jesus offers the Jewish teachers of his day their own advice, which is more fully explained in *Kallah Rab.* 5:3 (which tradition also explains the cryptic saying in the *baraita* called *Kinyan Torah* [now printed as *m. 'Abot* 6:2]):

> "Anyone who does not take to heart their Torah study is called 'needing rebuke,'[5] as the verse says, 'As a golden ring in a swine's snout, so too is a beautiful woman who has turned from sound reason' (Prov. 11:22)" (*m. 'Abot* 6:2). [Commentary]: "Golden [ring]" refers to Torah. ... "(In the nose of a) pig" — refers to one who reads it on rare occasions. God says, "What purpose is there in casting [my Torah] before a pig? Look — my Torah is beautiful and I made it to be meditated upon [constantly], but this one does not constantly meditate upon it to the extent that he wipes out [its purpose]."

While it is tempting to think of "dogs" and "pigs" as the terms used by the Jews to deprecate their non-Jewish enemies, it was in fact the case, as this tradition makes clear, that the Rabbis themselves used these words to refer to those Jews who neglected the Torah. And so here Jesus asks that those whom he has just called "hypocrites" recall their own advice, which is that one should not "sully the Torah."

Jesus' address to his critics ends here. Like all populist leaders, Jesus mocks the current leadership of his day and treats its members as "enemies" while at the same time espousing most of their values. For him it is not so much what they teach that is wrong; it is rather that they do not abide by what they teach.

> *"Ask, and it will be given to you; seek, and you will find; knock, and it*
> *will be opened up to you." (v. 7)*

Now Matthew continues his address, picking up from where he left off in Matt. 6:34. The Rabbis accepted that prayer was always heard.[6] In a tradition from *b. Bek.* 44b, in which this belief is maintained, Deut. 7:14, or at least a part of it, read in a most creative way, is the proof-text. Deut. 7:14 reads literally: "There will not be in you a barren (masc. sing., *aqar*), or a barren (fem. sing., *aqarah*), and, in your cattle." The tradition reads:

> Rabbi Yehoshua ben Levi said, "or a barren (fem. sing.)" means that your prayer will not be barren before God. [The tradition interprets the conjunction "and" to mean, "namely."] When will this occur? When you make yourself (as simple, guileless) as cattle.[7]

There is an ancient tradition preserved in *b. Meg.* 6b for which the Rabbis endeavored to find a context. Rabbi Isaac suggested that it had to do with success in Torah study, but the statement has the mark of a popular saying and in form it resembles Matt. 7:7. The text reads:

> Rabbi Isaac said: If someone says to you, "I took the steps but I did not find" — do not believe. "I did not take any steps but I did find" — do not believe. "I took the steps and I found" — believe. The saying refers to learning Torah.

That God answers prayers is also a common-place in the Hebrew Scriptures (Ps. 20 and 37:4; also Isa. 55:6).

> *"For everyone who asks receives, and the one who seeks finds and it*
> *will be opened to the one who knocks." (v. 8)*

In the Book of Esther, Mordecai is said to be "ben (son of) Kish" (Esther 2:5). A tradition in *b. Meg.* 12b wonders why he was called this when his father was called Yair, the answer to which contains a fairly close parallel to what Jesus says here.

> "Son of Kish (i.e. 'the knocker')": [Mordecai] would knock on the gates of mercy and they would be opened to him.

"For what person among you, when his child asks for bread, will give him a stone? Or if he or she asks for a fish, will give him a snake? If then you who are wicked know how to give good gifts to your children, how much more will your heavenly father give good things to those who ask him?" (vv. 9–11)

Here Jesus makes the argument that God gives to people what they ask for. The argument runs as follows: Human beings have the ability to be cruel yet still they give to their children what they ask for. *Human beings are God's children. God has no evil within him, so how much more does he give to human beings what they ask for.* The argument is in the typical rabbinic style, called "kal vehomer," that is, from the lesser to the greater. A text from *Lev. Rab.* 34:14 contains a similar sentiment in the same argumentative style:

> [During a drought] Rabbi Tanhuma raised his face to the heavens and said, If a person of cruel flesh and blood who owes nothing to his divorced wife but when he sees her naked and in great pain will feel pity for her and provide her requests, we who are the children of your renowned ones, Abraham, Isaac and Jacob, and you are responsible for our food, how much more so [will you provide our requests]. At that very moment rain fell and the world was replenished.

"All things, therefore, which you wish people to do to you, so do also to them. For this is the Torah and the Prophets." (v. 12)

This teaching — the Golden Rule — is very ancient and is found in various ancient texts. The version of the rule attributed to Hillel in *b. Šabb.* 31a — "What is hateful to you, do not do to your neighbor" — is fairly close to the version of the Rule found at the beginning of *Didache*, which reads: "Love your neighbor as yourself (Lev. 19:18), and do not do to another what you would not want done to you." But the version of the Rule attributed to Hillel ends with the advice that "this is the whole Torah, while the rest is the commentary to it; go and learn."

In light of Hillel's version of the Rule, it is reasonable to assume that the Matthean Jesus means here that the whole of Scripture is for the sake of teaching people the Golden Rule; that is, that every law in it furthers that goal. This can only be the meaning of the phrase: "For this [rule] is the Torah and the Prophets." The similarity between this phrase from the Matthean Jesus here and the phrase "This is the whole Torah" from the version attributed to Hillel can only mean that they are not unrelated. After stating his version of the Rule, and then claiming that it is, in essence, the whole of the Torah, Hillel concludes with the exhortation that one should "go and learn it." As I have pointed out, the Gospel writers never show (except for

Matt. 9:13) Jesus exhorting anyone to study Torah (they may even have removed this exhortation, if it was known to them).[8]

This is the culmination of the part of the sermon concerning righteousness. From here on Jesus assumes the role of the righteous preacher of the coming apocalypse.

> *"Enter through the narrow gate, for wide is the gate and broad is the road which leads to destruction, and many are they who travel upon it. Narrow is the gate and crowded the road which leads to life, and few are they who have found it." (vv. 13–14)*

A saying with a similar rhythm and a somewhat similar meaning revealed in a similar way — through an obvious metaphor (or metaphors) — is found in *m. 'Abot* 2:15: "The day is short, the work is great, the workers are lazy, the reward is great, and the Master of the house presses." There are echoes of this rabbinic text in a later saying of Jesus in Matt. 9:37–38): "The (work of) harvesting is great and the workers are few. Ask the owner of the harvest to bring (more) workers for the work of the harvesting."

Here the Matthean Jesus describes the two ways one might go, either down the wide road, which takes one towards certain "destruction," or down the narrow road, which takes one towards "life." To get to the wide road one must simply follow the crowd; the other, narrow, road, must be sought out and only a very few of those who seek it will find it. That is, only a select few will ever gain eternal life. Jesus' teaching here is exclusive and elitist. It holds little encouragement for the masses. We need give pause here for Matthew allows Jesus to disown his later stance (9:13) that he has come to open up the kingdom to sinners, tax collectors, and gluttons.

> *"Look out for false prophets, who come to you dressed in sheep's clothing, but inside they are violent wolves." (v. 15)*

Here Jesus warns against those who say that little is required for one to gain eternal life. These are the false prophets who seem as benign as sheep but are in fact as destructive as hungry wolves. It is unlikely that Jesus is speaking here of the Scribes and/or Pharisees, but rather of those who say that they are the true prophets of the coming kingdom, or else, perhaps, wonder-workers of some sort.

The Rabbis also warned against false prophets and the rewards they promised to those who might break God's laws. A tradition from *Pesiq. Rab Kah.* 24:15 reads:

A certain Ahab the son of Koliah and a certain Zedekiah the son of Maaseiah were false prophets. They used to seduce the wives of their friends — in the way that these verses relate. ["Thus says the Lord of hosts, the God of Israel, concerning Ahab the son of Kolaiah, and Zedekiah the son of Maaseiah, who prophesy a lie to you in my name. Look, I will deliver them into the hand of Nebuchadnezzar King of Babylon, and he shall slay them in front of your eyes. And because of them a curse shall be current in all the (areas of the) Captivity of Judah in Babylon, saying, "The Lord make you like Zedekiah and Ahab, whom the king of Babylon burned in the fire."] This is because they have done dishonorable things in Israel, committing adultery with their neighbors' wives, [and speaking lies in my name, which I have not commanded them. Indeed I know, and am a witness, says the Lord.]" (Jer 29:21–23). And what did they do exactly? One of them would go to the wife and tell her, I have had a prophetic vision that when my colleague came into you, you gave birth to a prophet in Israel. One would pimp for the other.

"By their fruits you will know them. Are bunches of grapes gathered from thorns, or figs from thistles?" (v. 16)

Jesus begins an argument here which culminates with his assertion in verse 19 that those who are not good shall be cut down, which is very like what John the Baptist says in 3:10. As we mentioned earlier, "fruits" are deeds (see the commentary to 3:10).

"So the good tree bears good fruit, and the rotten tree bears rotten fruit." (v. 17)

The idea that the good person does good deeds and the evil person does evil deeds is standard in the Jewish wisdom literature. For instance, Prov. 11:30 tells us that: "The fruit of the righteous person is a tree of life, and he who is wise secures human lives." And from 1Sam. 24:13 we are told that: "As the proverb of the ancients says, 'Out of the wicked comes forth wickedness.'"

"A good tree is not able to bear rotten fruit, nor is a rotten tree able to bear good fruit. Every tree that does not bear good fruit is cut down and thrown into fire. Therefore, you will know them by their fruits."
(vv. 18–20)

Trees with edible fruit could not be cut down even for reasons of national defense. "Only the trees which you know are not trees for food you shall destroy and cut down" (Deut. 20:20). Again the threat is made here that for those whose deeds are found wanting perdition awaits.

"Not everyone who says to me, 'Lord, Lord,' will enter the heavenly kingdom, but rather the one who does the will of my heavenly father."
(v. 21)

Here Jesus warns those who have accepted him as their teacher that the power of his name alone is not enough to save them from perdition. His message here is that it is not faith that saves but works.

"Many will say to me on that day, 'Lord, Lord, did we not prophesy in your name, and in your name cast out demons, and in your name do many powerful deeds?' Then I will publicly declare to them, 'I never knew you. Depart from me, you who perform iniquity'" (Ps. 6:8). (vv. 22–23)

Matthew's source here indicates a wariness of miracle-workers. Of course the Gospel tradition makes plain that Jesus himself performed many miracles.

The Rabbis warned against those who healed in Jesus' name (apparently it was a common enough phenomenon for there to be such warnings). A tradition from *t. Ḥul.* 2:22–23 reads:

It happened that Rabbi Eleazar ben Dama was bitten by a serpent. Then Jacob of Kephar Sama came to cure him in the name of *Jesus ben Pandira* but Rabbi Yishmael did not permit him to do it. He said: "Ben Dama, you are not permitted!" He replied: "I will bring you a proof that he may heal me!" But he died before he managed to produce his proof. Rabbi Yishmael said, "Blessed are you, ben Dama, for you have departed in peace and have not violated the commandments of the sages!" For lasting punishment comes on anyone who breaks through a fence of the sages, as it is written, "A serpent shall bite him who breaks through the fence" (Eccles. 10:8).

"Everyone who hears these words of mine and does them is compared to a thoughtful person, who built his house on the bedrock. The rain fell, the rivers came, and the winds blew and struck against that house, but it did not fall, for its foundation was upon the bedrock. And everyone who hears these words of mine and does not do them is compared to a stupid person, who built his house upon the sand. And the rain fell and the rivers and came and the winds blew and struck against that house, and it fell, and its fall was great." (vv. 24–27)

The sermon ends differently than one might expect. There is, first, a promise of security for those who adhere to what Jesus has said in it, followed by the threat of destruction for those who do not.[9]

So it happened, that when Jesus finished these sayings, the crowds were dumbfounded at his teaching, for he was teaching them as one having authority, and not as the Scribes. (vv. 28–29)

According to the text, Jesus taught with "authority," whereas the Scribes did not (see also Mark 1:22). The problem is to determine just what kind of authority Jesus had when he taught that the Scribes did not. With regard to the meaning of "authority," a number of popular ideas are sometimes taught in theological colleges, such as that he spoke like the prophets of old with divine authority, or that he did not cite sources, biblical or otherwise, while he taught. One Jewish reader suggested that "authority" means "allegory" (Syriac translates here as *mashalta* which, besides the sense of authority, also can mean parable) since he spoke in parables (Chajes, cited in Klausner).[10] Or perhaps it is the case that Matthew was not concerned about what it meant that Jesus taught with "authority," only that he taught with it, whereas the Scribes did not. Luke too points out that Jesus taught with "authority," but he does not say along with Matthew that this was in contrast to the Scribes when they taught. He does say, however, that an effect of Jesus' "authority" was that he could even command "unclean spirits" (4:32; 4:36). And so "authority" here might mean something like "the possession of a palpable and awesome power." The rabbinic term that describes the extent of the power and/or authority of a court or a rabbi is *koah*.[11]

Perhaps the best way to understand "one having authority" is to see in it the Aramaic (and Syriac) term *rishana*, "one possessing authority." Rashbam explains "*rishtai(n)hi denashim kashpaniot* in *b. Pesah.* 10a as "mistress of sorceresses—one who commands them with authority to teach them." She instructs the women under her commanding control in the secret arts of sorcery. For Matthew, Jesus' style as a teacher was not technical but rather charismatic, confident, and commanding. This is not to say that the underpinnings of his sermon were other than exegetical, just that the overt exegetical style of preaching was not his style. The Gospel writer intends for us to understand that Jesus' audience likely already knew much of what he said in the sermon, but that the manner in which he said it was surprising. Jesus commanded obedience according to his own authority as if he were free to teach his opinions as binding rules; he did not cite other teachers for support. For Matthew, Jesus' manner of teaching throughout the sermon, especially in this chapter, must have amazed or even confused his audience, but what he said did not.

NOTES

[1]   *B. B. Meṣ.* 59a.

[2]   In *b. Taʻan.* 8a Shmuel the teacher considers the issue and explains that those teachers who teach that God's anger is difficult to assuage are seemingly contradicted by Ps. 78:36–37: "But they flattered him with their mouths; they lied to him with their tongues. Their heart was not steadfast toward him; they were not faithful to his covenant." But then the Psalm states in the next verse: "Yet he, being compassionate, forgave their iniquity and did not destroy them; he restrained his anger often and did not stir up all his wrath."
He explains that there is no contradiction. The teachers speak about how God attends to the prayer of the *individual*, requiring him (in his private prayer) to repent fully or be punished, while the Psalm discusses the way God deals with the prayers of the assembly which may not be completely sincere. Still, God loves Israel and will always forgive her people.

[3]   Klausner, *Jesus of Nazareth*, 385.

[4]   Fitzmyer, in his book, *A Wandering Aramean*, 15, points out that in 11Qtg Job 38:8, from Qumran, the very same word — *qedasha*, "ring" — also appears.

[5]   One of the methods used by the Rabbis to explain texts (or items in dreams) is called in the Greek *notorikon*. In this method the first two letters of the first word in a phrase is joined to the last letter of the last word in the phrase. Then the three letters are read as a new word that is meant to shed light on the phrase as a whole. In our case "NZM (ring) B'F (in the nose)" yields "NZF." "NZF" is a strong word signifying one who deserves extreme rebuke, to the point even of being ostracized from the community. The message is that anyone who treats the Torah casually sullies it and becomes an object of censure himself.

[6]   See Strack/Billerbeck, 450–58.

[7]   The first use of the word "barren" — *aqar* — in the biblical text, which is masculine and so meant to refer to a man, was (also) taken by the Rabbis to refer to a male student who was uncommitted to his Torah studies. The second use of the word "barren" — *aqarah* — in the text, which is feminine and is meant to refer to a woman, was (also) taken by the Rabbis to refer to the feminine singular for prayer — "*tefillah*" — and so a barren, unanswered prayer. The reason the Rabbis found meaning in the verse beyond the traditional one has to do with their notion of biblical economy. The shortest way to express the idea that no one would be barren is to say, "No one will be barren." Why then does the biblical text say what it does and not mention the word "people"? The Rabbis assume in such cases that there is another meaning to be found in these seemingly extravagant wordings of the verse.

8   Torah study was the supreme value in the first century. Both Philo (*Legat.* 31) and Josephus (*Ag. Ap.* 1:60 and 2:204) note that Jewish children were immersed in this study from a very early age.

9   See *Sipre Deut.* piska 342 for the basis of sermons ending on a note of comfort as a general rule.

10   Klausner,. *Jesus of Nazareth,* 265 n. 35.

11   See, e.g., *m. Ketub.* 11:5 and *b. Qidd.* 60b.

INTRODUCTION

Chapter 7 ends with the listeners of Jesus' sermon expressing astonishment at the authority with which Jesus teaches, which is so unlike the Scribes. Now in chapter 8 we see other manifestations of his authority, whether in his ability to heal (and in this chapter he heals many), or in his ability to control the elements. Also, from time to time in the sermon Jesus speaks reprovingly of the Gentiles, pointing out, for instance, that their prayers are too wordy, or that they only love those who love them. But now in chapter 8 Jesus, although he heals far more Jews than Gentiles, nonetheless seems to privilege the Gentiles over the Jews, claiming in the story of the healing of the centurion's servant that it will be they rather than the Jews who will have a place in the kingdom.

With regard to this story it is noteworthy that whereas in Matthew the centurion comes to speak to Jesus himself (8:5), in Luke (and in the sources he used, which were likely known to Matthew) the centurion sends the well-respected "elders of the Jews" to speak for him (7:3). Moreover in Luke the elders make it clear that the centurion has been a friend and benefactor to the Jews, whereas in Matthew the centurion seemingly has no connection with the Jews at all. And whereas in both Matthew and Luke the centurion is said by Jesus to be superior in his faith to every Jew in Israel, it is only in Matthew that Jesus goes on to say that it will be the Gentiles and not the Jews who will dine with Abraham, Isaac, and Jacob in the kingdom. The differences in these accounts are startling, especially since many scholars consider Luke to be a Gentile and Matthew to be a Jew.[1] Does it not stand to reason that

Matthew's presentation of this story shows him to be either a Gentile or at the very least a Jew-turned-Gentile?

In this chapter we also encounter the first of what are known as the hard sayings of Jesus, responses of his to others which make him appear insensitive, even cruel. To the student who says to him that he is ready to become one of his followers, if only he might first bury his father, Jesus replies, "Follow me, and leave the dead to bury their own dead!" (Matt. 8:22). Although the harshness of this saying is obvious, its meaning is not. Just who are the "dead" who, according to Jesus, should be "burying their own dead"? According to some, these "dead" are hedonists or unbelievers who, because of this, are already dead to God, since they lack an immortal soul.[2] Others suggest that the "dead" are those of the old, dying order.[3] E. P. Sanders believes that this is an authentic saying of Jesus, since it would be hard to imagine anyone in the early church inventing such a saying and attributing it to Jesus.[4] However it may be the case that the saying can only be properly understood if the word "dead" is held to be a mistranslation of a word from the saying in the original Aramaic.[5] That is, the word "dead" might very well be a mistranslation of an Aramaic word meaning "waverers," "gravediggers," or "townsfolk."[6]

Mack and Robbins list and comment on some of the plausible meanings of the saying:

> If the statement means "let the real dead do it," it is probably a paradoxical way of saying "that business must look after itself." If it means "let the spiritually dead do it," it implies that those who do not follow Jesus have missed the life associated with the kingdom. If it means "let the gravediggers do it," it implies that the obligation of following Jesus requires a person to leave tasks that would otherwise be his to fulfill. Any which way it is unsettling.[7]

It is worth noting that in Matt. 4:19 Jesus also speaks a kind of hard saying, though here, as I have pointed out, it is in the form of a pun. That is, Jesus says to Peter and Andrew that if they follow him, he will make them "fishers of men," but by this he means too, of course, that they must abandon their father. It may be that we have a pun in the notice that the dead are to bury their dead since "dead" can also refer to the townsfolk with a slight change of intonation in Aramaic. In this case some of the various suggestions to explain "dead" as "spiritually dead" may still find their place figuratively, while literally the ostensible meaning is that the townsfolk should be charged with supervising the burial.

In this chapter we also encounter two terms that are very important not just for Matthew but for the other Gospel writers as well — the "Son of God" and the "Son of Man" (Greek: *huios tou anthropou*). The former term refers to an earthly figure who shares in God's powers. The meaning of the latter term — which in the synoptics, as Geza Vermes points out, is only ever spoken by Jesus, and this more than four dozen times — is the subject of a massive literature.[8] Though no one knows for certain what the term means,[9] many scholars see that it likely refers to a kind of heavenly apocalyptic figure such as the one spoken of in Dan. 7:13–14 (though this understanding of the term is not without problems, I too accept that the term "Son of Man" is a title for a heavenly apocalyptic figure):

> I saw in the night, visions, and behold, *with the clouds of heaven there came one like a Son of Man,* and he came to the Ancient of Days and was presented before him,[10] and to him was given dominion and glory and kingdom, that all peoples, nations, and languages should serve him; his dominion is an everlasting dominion, which shall not pass away, and his kingdom one that shall not be destroyed (Dan. 7:13–14).[11]

The problem in determining the meaning of the term in Matthew's Gospel is that Matthew uses it to refer to a number of different beings. For instance, in 25:31–46 the "Son of Man" is said to be a kind of divine Judge in company with angels. But at 8:20 Jesus uses the term as a kind of pun. That is, although in the messianic framework Jesus is the "Son of Man" — Lord of all, even the Sabbath (12:8) — he uses the term here to refer to a figure that is even less privileged than the animals and man. And so the term here refers to both a "thing and its opposite" — a messiah, but a messiah who is far more burdened than any other creature. That is, the term embodies the ambiguity of the saying in which it appears. For as Jesus says at 8:20: "If you want to be a disciple of the Son of Man, you must first give up every comfort known to animal or man." The ambiguity in the meaning of the term highlights the ambiguous status of Jesus, who exists in a kind of liminal space between the realm of human authority and the realm of the divine.

As for the Rabbis, a tradition in b. Sanh. 98a makes plain that they also identified the "Son of Man" figure with the Messiah (though the idea that the "Son of Man" possessed divine attributes such as the ability to absolve sins was antithetical to them and to the Scribes):[12]

> Rabbi Alexandri said: Rabbi Yehoshua [reconciled] two contrary verses: it is written, "And behold, with the clouds of heaven there came one like a Son of Man" (Dan. 7:13) and [contrariwise] it is written, "[Behold, thy king cometh unto thee ...] lowly, and riding upon an ass!" (Zech 9:7). [There is no contradiction.] If they are meritorious, [the Messiah comes] "with the clouds of heaven," but if they are not [then he comes] "lowly and riding upon an ass."

Moreover in *y. Ta'an* 2:1 the Rabbis warn against anyone falsely claiming to be the "Son of Man," that is, the Messiah:

Said Rabbi Abbahu, "If a man should tell you, 'I am God,' he is lying. If he says, 'I am the Son of Man,' in the end he will regret it.

When he came down from the mountain, many crowds were following him. Suddenly, there was a leper approaching him, who knelt before him, and said, "Lord, if you were willing, you are able to make me pure." (vv. 1–2)

No sooner has Jesus finished his sermon than he is again engaged in healing. It was on the determination of the priest that someone was pronounced a "leper" (Lev. 13:3); it was also on the determination of the priest that the leper was declared clean again (Lev. 13:17). Lev. 13 also says that the leper lived apart from others, wore "torn clothes," and cried aloud as he walked, "Unclean, unclean" (13:45–46).

And stretching out his hand, he touched him, saying "I am willing. Be purified." Immediately, his leprosy was purified. (v. 3)

"Be purified" is not so much a prayer for healing as it is a command for the leper to become pure. Healing through touch was well known among the Rabbis. A tradition in *b. Ber.* 5b says that while conversing with the ill Rabbi Yohanan, Rabbi Hanina reached out and, touching him, cured him (the words "raised up" in the tradition mean "cured," as they do in Matt. 9:7: "Being raised up, [the paralytic] went into his house").

"Do you attach importance to suffering?"
He replied, "Not them and not their reward."
He told him, "Give me your hand."
He gave him his hand and he raised him up.

The story of the healing of the leper by Jesus, with slight variations, is found in all the synoptic Gospels (Mark 1:40–44, Luke 5:13–14) and so must have appealed to the early church. The variations are interesting. Both in Matthew and in Luke nothing is said about what Jesus felt toward the leper. However in most of the texts of Mark (1:41) it is said that Jesus was "moved with pity" for the leper, while Codex Bezae and some Latin versions of Mark say that Jesus was actually "moved with anger."[13]

Now in touching the leper Jesus would have acquired a degree of impurity which, though it was not a sin, still meant that he would have had to have purified himself before entering the Temple again or else touching priestly gifts. Perhaps Jesus is said to have felt anger for the leper in Codex Bezea and in a number of Latin texts of Mark because he knew that in touching the leper he would have acquired a minor degree of impurity.[14]

Finally, while the Gospel writers tell us miracle stories to show us both the singular power and authority of Jesus, there remain a considerable number of passages suggesting Jesus feared being known solely as a magician and exorcist. His message was not to be related to his miracle working. However, the synoptic Gospels never quite declare what unique message he intended to convey. As I say, for Jesus' audience there was nothing really new in the sermon although the way it is phrased and constructed makes it an eternal masterpiece. Jesus' real message seems to lie buried in his parables but their obscurity, except in a few well-known cases, prevents them from gaining wide appeal. One might speculate that Gospel tradition has only hinted (since the writers and audience were Roman citizens, unlike Jesus) that Jesus might have been seen, at an earlier stage in the telling of the Jesus story, as subversive to Roman rule and that earlier traditions spoke of messianic pretensions more openly.

Jesus says to him, "Say nothing to anyone, but go and show yourself to the priest, and bring the offering Moses commanded as a testimony to them." (v. 4)

The word "testimony" here means a "statute" for the Israelites. According to the provisions of the law of lepers, the offering the cleansed leper would have brought to the priest would have been a "sin" offering (Lev. 14:19). Presumably the crowds have gone now, or else Jesus has moved away from them, and he does not want anyone to know that he has cured the leper, for as a matter of law only the priest's declaration that the leper is pure, as I have pointed out, renders him pure.[15] Plausibly, Jesus shunned crowds because he was worried that his cures might not work, since he knew they were dependent on the strength of the faith of those being healed or, more likely, he worried about Rome's views of his activities. It was dangerous for holy men to attract crowds in Roman Palestine because they would have been considered as rebels and rebels might rouse mobs against the Romans.

When he entered Kfar Nahum, a centurion came to him, beseeching him: "Lord, my houseboy is laid in bed at home, paralytic and terribly tormented." He said to him, "I shall come and cure him." The centurion answered him, "Lord, I am not worthy to have you enter under my roof, but only say the word, and my houseboy shall be healed. For I am a person representing authority, and I have soldiers under me, and I say to one, 'Go,' and he goes, and to another, 'Come,' and he comes, and to my slave, 'Do this,' and he does it." (vv. 5–9)

It is in the story of the healing of the centurion's servant that the theme of the greater faith of the Gentiles over against that of the Jews first appears in the Gospel of Matthew. Toward the end of the Gospel another centurion will remark that Jesus is truly a Son of God (27:54). Centurions were commanders in the Roman army and so representatives of Roman power. Recognition by the centurion of the power of Jesus is an act of submission by one who knows that his temporal power is as nothing compared to the power of the divine.

Jesus, hearing this, marveled, and said to those who were following him, "'Amen,' I say to you, never have I found such faith in anyone in Israel. I say to you that many will come from the east and the west and they will recline at the table with Abraham and Isaac and Jacob in the heavenly kingdom." (vv. 10–11)

Here Jesus says that it will not be the Jews but rather the Gentiles who, because of their greater faith, shall gain a place in the Kingdom of Heaven. It is because of such statements as this concerning the exclusivity of the Gentiles over against the Jews that I find it difficult to accept that Matthew (and also the other Gospel writers) was Jewish.

"But the children of the kingdom will be thrown into the outer darkness, where there will be wailing and the grinding of teeth."[16] (v. 12)

Jesus says here what is implied above. Those who think they will inherit the kingdom, that is, the Jews, will instead be eternally damned.

Jesus said to the centurion, "Go; let it be done as you trusted it would." And his houseboy was cured in that hour. (v. 13)

Most likely "in that hour" means "at that very moment." The Hebrew *hahu sha'ah* means "in that very instant," although *sha'ah* technically means "hour."

*Jesus came to Peter's house, and saw his mother-in-law lying in bed
and feverish. He touched her hand, and the fever left her, and she arose
and brought him food. (vv. 14–15)*

Again we see a cure effected by touch.

*When evening came, they brought to him many who were possessed
by demons, and he threw out the spirits by speaking, and he healed all
who were ill. (v. 16)*

Here we are told that Jesus casts out demons through speech alone. In
general, nothing is attributed to God; all of the healing is done under his own
authority. This is the power of the holy man.

*Thus was fulfilled what had been spoken by Isaiah the prophet, "He
took our weaknesses and bore our illnesses" (Isa. 53:4). (v. 17)*

Here we have another fulfillment text, this one based on Isa. 53:4. The text as
it appears here is not from the extant LXX, which reads: "He bears our sins
and suffers pain for us." It is in fact much closer to the Masoretic Text, which
reads: "Indeed, he bore our illnesses and carried our pain."

*Jesus, seeing the crowd around him, ordered them to go across to the
other side. (v. 18)*

It is tempting to think that "the other side" here means only "the other side
of the Sea of Galilee." But Jesus' command to go to "the other side" may also
be an indication of his discomfort and/or unwillingness to be followed by the
masses as we have said above. That is, Jesus was acting on the awareness that
holy men of this period ran the danger of being arrested for sedition if they
gathered crowds about them.[17]

*A certain scribe approached and said to him, "Teacher, I will follow
you wherever you go." (v. 19)*

The word "scribe" here means a follower of those who taught piety and
good works based on the written Torah, and who also prescribed methods
of interpretation of the oral traditions and customs either produced and/or
enacted by them or earlier Scribes. What Matthew's source suggests here is
that such people did not see in Jesus anyone other than the kind of teacher

they normally esteemed. The response of Jesus toward the scribe, who expresses admiration for him, is startling.

> *Jesus says to him, "Foxes have dens and birds nests, but the Son of Man has no place to lay his head." (v. 20)*

What the scribe says to Jesus here resonates with what Ruth says to Naomi in Ruth 1:16: "Don't urge me to leave you or to turn back from you. Where you go I will go." Jewish tradition considered this statement as tantamount to an act of conversion to Judaism on the part of Ruth, which Naomi then tried to discourage her from doing (*y. Yebam.* 47b). Here the scribe wants to become a follower of Jesus and, like Naomi with Ruth, Jesus tries to discourage him (and presumably does). For the first time in Matthew Jesus uses the term "Son of Man" and, whatever this term might mean elsewhere (see the introduction to this chapter for a longer discussion on the usage of the term), here by placing the "Son of Man" in contrast with animals and birds, Jesus is using the term as a type of pun.[18] Animals and birds have homes, and so are able to do certain things in them, that the "Son of Man," because he has no home, cannot do.

> *Another of the students said to him, "Lord, allow me first to go and to bury my father." But Jesus says to him, "Follow me, and leave the dead to bury their own dead."[19] (vv. 21–22)*

Jesus' radical insistence that his followers must renounce the cares of this world is based on his understanding that the demands of the spirit must override the demands of one's society. This understanding is not shared by the Rabbis.

Together verses 21–22 form a concise and well-designed unit. The student says two things to Jesus and Jesus in turn, harshly and enigmatically, reverses both. We analyze the structure of and the implication of certain words in this unit:

"Allow me first to *go* (to leave the crowd, but not to come to you first), and to *bury*[20] my father (to act according to the demands society places on me)."
"*Follow* me (leave the crowd, but come to *me*), and leave the dead to *bury* their own dead (ignore what society asks of you)."

The purpose of the scene as a whole (vv. 18–22) is to make clear what discipleship means for Jesus — total separation from the crowd. To the scribe Jesus says that a disciple of his must live in a kind of homeless state in which no comfort or rest can be found. And to the student he says that to live in a homeless place is literally to be homeless, which means also to be society-less, and so whatever the demands of the home or of the society, they are to be discounted. And so to be a disciple of Jesus means to be a follower not of the crowd but rather the lone, kindred spirit who would follow him without expectation of any comfort. The scene reminds one of the calling of Peter and Andrew (4:18ff.), in which Jesus says to the brothers, "Follow me," after which here too Jesus makes a clever play on words.[21]

The overall content of 8:1–22 is perplexing, because it shows Jesus as both a pious Jewish holy man but also as someone who condemns the Jews (while at the same time esteeming the Gentiles).

When he got into the boat, his students followed him. Suddenly, a great storm came upon the sea, so that the boat was covered by the waves, but he was sleeping. They approached and woke him up, saying "Lord, save us! We are perishing!" (vv. 23–25)

Apparently it was the students who approached him rather than the other people on the boat.

But he says to them, "Why are you afraid, you of little faith?" Then, arising, he commanded the winds and the sea, and there was a great calm. (v. 26)

Why when they turn to him for help in this situation Jesus says of his students (and this is a harsh saying too) that they are of little faith is puzzling. Was Jesus angry because they woke him, when instead they should have trusted that all would be well since he was on the boat with them? But if this was the case, then why did he command the sea and the winds to become calm? The Gospel writers include this story to suggest that even over the elements Jesus has authority. In *b. B. Bat.* 73a a story is told of sailors using divine names to save themselves from disaster.[22]

The people were amazed, saying, "What sort of person is this, that the winds and the sea obey him?" (v. 27)

It is the people on the ship who were amazed, not the students, and again they were amazed at his authority.

When he came across to the region of the Gadarenes (Gadara), two demonically possessed people met him from the tombs, so fierce that no one was strong enough to pass by that road. (v. 28)

It seems the region of the Gadarenes was populated by Gentiles and here again Jesus does not shy away from healing Gentiles. Matthew seems to be telling us here that demons inhabited areas in which the tombs were found and, once the two Gadarenes had become possessed, they were driven to one of these areas of the Gadarenes by the demons, since they could no longer live in civilized society. A tradition in *b. Sanh.* 65b states that it was forbidden to starve oneself and then to spend the night in a cemetery waiting for a demon to visit (apparently this practice was common enough to draw the attention of the Rabbis). It seems this practice allowed one to do supernatural feats or else gain supernatural knowledge.

Suddenly they called out, "What do we have to do with each other, Son of God? Have you come here to torture us before the proper time?"
(v. 29)

Apparently the demons possessing the Gadarenes thought they would reign unchallenged until the End of Days. The demons knew, of course, as did Satan in the Temptation scene, that Jesus shared divine power, which meant that he had the power to exorcize them, hence their addressing him as "Son of God." Though in the coming kingdom demons will have no power, in the temporal world they enjoy immense power, for which reason they chastise Jesus for challenging them before the kingdom has come.

There was a herd of many swine being fed far away from them.

Jews did not raise swine and the demons were aware of this. (v. 30)

The demons urged him, "If you throw us out, send us into the herd of swine." (v. 31)

Jesus did as they asked. As a Jew he had no sympathy for swine. It seems the demons wanted a little amusement before being forced to flee from that region. Scholars are not sure what locale the Gospels might have had in mind.

*He said to them, "Go." They departed and went into the swine.
Suddenly the entire herd rushed down the slope into the sea and died
in the water. (v. 32)*

Apparently it was enough for a holy man to simply to say "Go" in order to exorcize a demon. In *b. Me'il.* 17b there is a recounting of an exorcism performed by Rabbi Shimon bar Yohai on the emperor's daughter. "He said: 'Ben Tamalion, go. Ben Tamalion, go!' And when [the demon] was called, he left." Josephus speaks of exorcism as being an ancient art and also mentions having seen a certain Eleazar perform an exorcism (*Ant.* 8:46–48).

*The ones who were feeding the swine fled, and, coming into the city,
they reported everything, especially about the men who were being
possessed. Suddenly the entire city went out to meet Jesus, and when
they saw him, they urged him to depart from their territory. (vv. 33–34)*

The Gadarenes can not have been pleased that their livestock was destroyed as a result of a bargain Jesus had made with the demons. Almost certainly Jesus would not have preached to the Gadarenes anyway — they were not of the "lost sheep of the house of Israel" — and so he departed once more for Kfar Nahum (Capernaum).

NOTES

1   Nowhere is this point better expressed than in Jules Isaac's *Jesus and Israel*, 190–94. Isaac points out that in Matthew's account of this story there is the promise of the salvation of the faithful Gentiles, typified by the anonymous centurion, coupled with the promise that there shall be no salvation for the Jews. This passage echoes the condemnation of the Jews by John the Baptist in Matt. 3:9. On the other hand, he notes, Luke presents the centurion as a "God-fearer" and friend of the Jews and Jesus castigates none but those Jews who are full of iniquity but accepts that many other Jews are righteous and need no rebuke. Isaac shows word by word the subtle changes in Matthew from Luke's more congenial account. For the rabbinic portrayal of those "half-converts" called God-fearers or heaven-fearers see *Midr. Deut. Rab.* 2:24. and the references to Roman authors in Stern, ed., *Greek and Latin Authors on Jews and Judaism*, 2:382–84.

2   This and similar views are espoused by Clement of Alexandria (second century), Cyprian (third century), Ambrose (fourth century), and Augustine (fourth–fifth century), and also more recently by M. Hengel in his *Nachfolge und Charisma*, 8.

Calvin (sixteenth century) suggests that those who keep up appearances of custom before people are themselves like dead people preoccupied in the funeral customs of burial of the dead removed from life and the needs of the living. In his *Jesus and Judaism*, E. P Sanders suggests a meaning akin to Calvin's and stresses Jesus is serious when he says "leave your father" (252–53). See also Sanders and Davies, *Studying the Synoptic Gospels*, 317.

3   W. F. Albright and C. S. Mann, in their commentary to Matthew 8:22, tell us that this saying should be read: "Follow me, and let the dying bury the dead." By "the dying" he means those who are of the old order that is passing away, and who will have no share in the coming kingdom. Because they are the dying they can bury their own dead. The living are to proclaim the kingdom for the living. See Albright and Mann, *Matthew*, 95–96.

4   Again in *Jesus and Judaism* (252–54), Sanders takes the statement to mean what it literally says, that Jesus expects the student to "follow him rather than bury his father." In other words, at least here, according to Sanders, Jesus is saying that to be a follower of his means that one must utterly disregard an especially important social and religious requirement. Sanders also refers to Hengel here, who claims that refusing to bury to a parent in the Greco-Roman world was, as in the Jewish world, the gravest of ills.

5   Black, Perles, Shwarz, Lachs, and Basser have all made suggestions as to the way it might originally have read.

6   See also Klemm, "Das Wort von der Selbstbestattung der Toten."

7   See Mack and Robbins, *Patterns and Persuasion in the Gospels*.

8   Vermes, *Jesus in His Jewish Context*, 89ff. Also see Burkett, *The Son of Man Debate*. In John the term "Son of Man" is used almost a dozen times and in a way that is similar to the way the term "Son of God" is used in other Gospels. Elsewhere in the New Testament the term is found in Rev. 1:13 and 14:14, and also in Acts 7:56, which reads: "[T]he Son of Man sits at the right hand of God in heaven." Note the passage that reflects this description of the Messiah as an angelic heavenly being in *Midrash Psalms* (ed. Buber) 18:29. "Rabbi Yuden said in the name of Rabbi Chama: In the Future to Come, the Holy One will seat King Messiah at his right hand, 'And God said to my Lord, "Sit at my right hand, until I may make your enemies your footstool"' (Ps. 110:1)." A verse from Psalm 20 seems pertinent as well: "Now I know that the Lord saves his anointed (Hebrew: his *messiah*); he proclaims him from his holy heaven, with the saving power (Heb. *Yesha*, nearly equivalent to *Jesus)* at his right hand" (Ps. 20:6). Because the "Son of God" is a title given to an earthly figure, he who bears it has limited divine power. In contrast, the "Son of Man" is a title given to a heavenly figure, and so he who bears this title has much greater abilities.

9   In some cases the term may even refer to a figure known as "Metatron." See my discussion of this figure further in 11:19. The name of the angel who led the Israelites through the desert (Exod. 23:21) is said to have been "Metatron," and

in the Hebrew apocalypse known as *3 Enoch,* or *Sefer ha-Heikhalot,* he is the angelic form of Enoch. In the Ethiopic Book of *1 Enoch* (37–71) "Son of Man," "Righteous One," "Messiah," and "Chosen One" are all titles of the angelic Enoch. See Vanderkam, "Righteous One, Messiah, Chosen One, and Son of Man in I Enoch 3–71." Many year ago Dr. Alan Unterman suggested to me that we should see *t-tr* in M*etatron* not as [me]*tatr*[on] but as [me]*tetr*[on] (Greek: "four") as in *tetragrammaton,* the four-letter name of God which is said "to be in him," that is, the angel leading the Israelites in the wilderness (Exod. 23:21). So the angel's name literally contains God's name — the prefixed letter *m* (= from), plus *tetra,* and the suffix "on" (an angelic name ending as in "Sandelfon"). In *3 Enoch* it is said that he sits at the right hand of God (S. Lieberman, in Gruenwald, *Apocalyptic and Merkavah Mysticism,* 235–41, understands the name to mean "beside The Throne"), and also that God's name is in him. The connection with the title "Son of Man" in the synoptics need not be dismissed out of hand. The descriptions are somewhat similar. Unterman's derivation is certainly as plausible as the myriad explanations given for the name "Metatron" and for the "Son of Man" in *1 Enoch* (Enoch having been a person who was taken into the heavens, [Gen. 5:24]). It is sometimes argued that this section of *1Enoch* is later than the Gospels and so the author of it borrowed the term from them. Scholars note that no evidence for the section called *Similitudes* in *1 Enoch,* where Son of Man is mentioned, was found in any Semitic version (somewhat fragmented and partial) of Enoch recently unearthed at Qumran. In sum, no one knows where the term came from and what it means.

10   The apocalyptic colorings of Dan. 7:13 are also found in Matt. 24:29–31: "Immediately after the tribulation of those days shall the sun be darkened, and the moon shall not give her light, and the stars shall fall from heaven, and the powers of the heavens shall be shaken: And then shall appear the sign of the Son of Man in heaven: and then shall all the tribes of the earth mourn, and they shall see *the Son of Man coming in the clouds of heaven with power and great glory.* And he shall send his angels with a great sound of a trumpet, and they shall gather together his elect from the four winds, from one end of heaven to the other."

11   In another passage in Daniel (7:26–27) the apocalyptic aspect of the term is defused: "And the kingdom and the dominion and the greatness of the kingdoms under the whole heaven shall be given to the people of the saints of the most high One; their kingdom shall be an everlasting kingdom, and all dominions shall serve and obey them." This passage may undermine the force of the *Son of Man* being a title for anything more than the people of the saints.

12   We shall have occasion to return to this theme in our introduction to chapter 9 and not without some puzzlement.

13   The case for Jesus having felt "anger" (*orgistheis*) towards the leper rather than "compassion" (*splanxnistheis*) has been made by M. A. Proctor in *The "Western" Text of Mark 1:41: A Case for the Angry Jesus,* Ph.D. diss., Baylor University, 1999.

14 When Miriam, Moses' sister, was stricken with leprosy, he prayed, "Please God, heal her now!" (Num. 12:13). He did not touch her.

15 See Lev. 14:2ff. for a description of the process of the purification of the leper.

16 Compare Matt. 13:42, 50.

17 Josephus reports that the death of John the Baptist was a direct result of his popularity. My comments on 8:4 are applicable here as well.

18 In Dan. 4:10–12 there is a description of a tree under which the "beasts of the field found shade" and in whose branches lived the "birds of the air". The point is that animals manage in nature. But Jesus lives in a liminal space between kingdoms and is not of the natural order. His supernatural characteristics are being shown more and more.

19 See my comments to 6:34.

20 To bury someone is to walk behind him to the grave. In *b. Ber.* 18a it is said that: "Whoever sees a dead person (funeral procession) and does not follow after it transgresses Prov. 17:5: 'He who mocks the poor [dead-man] taunts his Maker.'" And in *Mekhilta of Rabbi Yishmael* to Exod. 18:20: "And you shall inform them of the way in which they will go," the word *go* refers to *burying the dead* (because one follows after the dead to the gravesite).

21 In 4:18ff the two sets of brothers Peter and Andrew, and James and John each abandon their fathers to become disciples of Jesus. I once thought, and still think it possible, that in 8:22 there is a play on the Aramaic words for "city" — "mata" — and "dead" — "meta" — so that the phrase in the original Aramaic would have read: "let the city bury their own dead." However it is uncertain whether in first-century Galilean Aramaic "mata" was still understood to mean "city," as it did in Imperial Aramaic and also in the eastern Aramaic dialects, including Syriac. See the comments of Goldenberg, "Retroversion to Jesus' *Ipsissima Verba* and the Vocabulary of Jewish Palestinian Aramaic": While I do not claim we have Jesus' exact words anywhere I do claim that we can establish that Jesus is making a pun as he enjoins the disciple to "follow him" (8:22). In a similar way at 4:19 Jesus is making a pun when he says "fishers of men" after saying, "Follow me." Whatever the phrase "fishers of men" means, it is clearly a pun of some type.

22 See my comments to this text and other similar ones in "The Rabbinic Attempt to Democratize Salvation and Revelation."

CHAPTER NINE

INTRODUCTION

We begin our discussion of this chapter by comparing the accounts of the healing of the paralytic in Matthew, Mark, and Luke. In Mark (though silently) and Luke, the Scribes and Pharisees wonder how it is that Jesus can say he has the power to forgive sins, a claim that to them is blasphemous. Jesus understands their concerns over this and proceeds calmly to allay them. That is, in the original synoptic account of this story Jesus deals civilly with the Scribes and/or Pharisees as they do with him. The fact that they wonder about the rightness of the claim Jesus makes indicates that they do not see him as a heretic but rather as a pious Jew (this also holds true for them when they ask how Jesus can dine with sinners (Mark 2:16; Luke 5:30; but also Matt. 9:11), since it was commonly thought that people were judged by the company they keep (*m. 'Abot* 1:7). However in typical fashion Matthew has reshaped the story so as to create hostility between the Scribes and Jesus. For in Matthew the Scribes are said to be "wicked in heart," for which reason Jesus upbraids them. Finally, Matthew omits the question that in both Mark and Luke the Scribes and/or Pharisees ask of Jesus: "*Who can forgive sins but God alone?,*" an important fact to which we shall return in my comments to 11:19. Apparently Exod. 23:21 intimates that a lesser divine figure could remit sins if he chose to.

Mark 2:5–12:

And when Jesus saw their faith, he said to the paralytic, "Son, your sins are forgiven." Now some of the Scribes were sitting there, questioning in their hearts, "Why does this man speak like that? *He is blaspheming! Who can forgive sins but God alone?*" And immediately Jesus, perceiving in his spirit that they thus questioned within themselves, said to them, "Why do you question these things in your hearts? Which is easier, to say to the paralytic, 'Your sins are forgiven,' or to say, 'Rise, take up your bed and walk?' But that you may know that the Son of Man has authority on earth to forgive sins" — He said to the paralytic — "I say to you, rise, pick up your bed, and go home." And he rose.

Luke 5:20–26:

When Jesus saw their faith, he said, "Friend, your sins are forgiven." The Pharisees and the teachers of the law began thinking to themselves, "*Who is this fellow who speaks blasphemy? Who can forgive sins but God alone?*" Jesus knew what they were thinking and asked, "Why are you thinking these things in your hearts? Which is easier: to say, 'Your sins are forgiven,' or to say, 'Get up and walk'? But that you may know that the Son of Man has authority on earth to forgive sins...." He said to the paralyzed man, "I tell you, get up, take your mat and go home." Immediately he stood up in front of them, took what he had been lying on and went home praising God. Everyone was amazed and gave praise to God. They were filled with awe and said, "We have seen remarkable things today."

Matthew 9:2–7:

Suddenly they brought to him a paralyzed person laid upon a bed. Jesus, seeing their faith, said to the paralyzed person, "Take courage, son, your sins are forgiven you." Suddenly, some of the Scribes said among themselves, "*He blasphemes!*" Jesus, seeing their design, said, "Why do you think wickedness in your hearts? What is easier, to say 'Your sins are forgiven,' or to say, 'Get up and walk'? But so that you may know that the Son of Man has authority to forgive sins upon the earth" — then he says to the paralyzed person, "Be raised up, and take your bed and go to your house."

That Jesus was a faith-healer was well known by this time in his career, for which he drew no criticism. Indeed a tradition in *b. Ber.* 60a, which is attributed to Rabbi Yishmael, grants people the authority to heal, for it was felt that at least in this respect God was willing to share his authority.[1] But as I say the concern for the Scribes was not in the healing but rather in Jesus' claim that on his own authority he could forgive sins, for this was understood to be something that only God could do (see, for instance, Exod. 34:7: "He extends mercy to thousands [of generations] forgiving iniquity, sin and wrongdoing"; Ps. 32:2: "Fortunate is the man to whom God does not attribute sin"; and Ps. 130:4: "For with you is forgiveness that you may be feared"). This is the reason they ask him why he claims to forgive the sins of the paralytic instead of simply healing him — to which question Jesus gives a shocking reply. He makes this claim in order to show off. Let me explain.

Jesus' argument for saying that he can forgive the sins of the paralytic is that in so doing he can prove that he is the Son of Man. But this is not altogether clear because the argument itself has actually been truncated in the accounts of this story. With the help of the following typically rabbinic argument from *b. B. Qam.* 34b we can see what is missing.

> Why did the Torah talk about an animal which gored other animals three times in three days [Exod. 21:36]? Was it to [make its punishment] harder or easier [than a first-time offender]? You must admit it is to make its case harder. Now, if in the harder case of a repeat offender one pays only for the amount of the damage and nothing extra, should this not the more so be true in the case of the [first time offender] that usually has an easier punishment.

According to the form of this argument, there are two ways of interpreting Jesus' argument (vv. 5–7). The first way is to see that Jesus begins his argument by making the weaker claim, which is that he has forgiven the sins of the paralytic, and not the harder claim, which is that he can cure the paralytic, and which is something, moreover, the Scribes are willing to believe. Of course the problem with interpreting what Jesus says here in this way (as it is with the second way) is that there is no way to confirm that the paralytic's sins have been forgiven.

> "[Why did I say, 'Your sins are forgiven'?] What would be easier — to say [the mere words] 'Your sins are forgiven,' or to say [the empirically verifiable], 'Get up and walk'? [Did I offer the easier case or the harder? You must admit — the easier. Now if in the harder case of curing the paralytic you will believe me, should you not believe me all the more so when I make the easier claim that I can forgive sins?] But [I said "Your sins are forgiven" for rhetorical purposes only] that you may know that the Son of Man has authority to forgive sins upon the earth." Then he says to the paralyzed person, "Be raised up, and take your bed and go to your house."

The second way of interpreting what Jesus says here is to see that he begins his argument with the harder claim, which is that he can forgive sins, and not the easier claim, which is that he can cure the paralytic.

> "[Why did I say, 'Your sins are forgiven'?] What would be easier — to say [I have authority to pronounce], 'Your sins are forgiven,' or to say [I have authority to pronounce], 'Get up and walk'? [Did I offer the easier case or the harder? You must admit — the harder. Now if in the harder case of forgiving sins I actually

> have authority to do this, should this not the more so be true in the case of curing the paralytic?] But [I said "Your sins are forgiven" for rhetorical purposes only] that you may know that the Son of Man has authority to forgive sins upon the earth." Then he says to the paralyzed person, "Be raised up, and take your bed and go to your house."

Again, confirming that the sins of the paralytic have been forgiven remains a problem. Although the logic of the argument fails as it is written in either case here, nonetheless the form of it is traditional. Given these problems in understanding the argument, we can appreciate why the Gospel writers cut it short, leaving the heart of it unstated thereby. It is probable that Jesus' argument in full equated sins with spiritual sickness (see 9:12: "Those who are strong have no need of a doctor, but only those who are ill"). Yet what is clear here is that whereas before this Jesus worried about making his divine powers known, now he is prepared to show them off.

As I point out, Matthew's version of this story lacks the question, "Who can forgive sins but God alone?," which in Mark and Luke follows the statement of the Scribes and/or Pharisees that Jesus blasphemes by claiming that he can forgive sins. Nowhere in any of the Gospels does Jesus answer the charge of blasphemy directly. In the several accounts of this story he simply sidesteps the matter by saying that as the "Son of Man" he has the authority to forgive sins on earth. Yet in Mark and Luke, as I say, this is not the concern of the Scribes and/or Pharisees. Rather it is the fact that the creature is comparing himself with the Creator. But if this is how the Scribes defined blasphemy (as being akin to idolatry, that is; see *b. Ker.* 3b–4a),[2] then Jesus has offered no defense of the accusation, not even a rhetorical one. At any rate, at a loss to understand Jesus' argument (as were Mark and Luke too), Matthew simply left it as he found it. He also must have been at a loss to see how anything Jesus said contravened any contemporary understanding of what blasphemy was in the legal sense (i.e., reviling, cursing, or disparaging God). By removing the definition of blasphemy in his version of the story — that is, by removing the question about God alone being able to forgive sins — the truncated argument in Matthew is not as jarring as it is in Mark and Luke.

The Rabbis too inveighed against the doctrine of two authorities, which they called "*shetei* reshuyot." A fairly late text from *b. Ḥag.* 15a, which explains how Elisha ben Avuyah became the heretic later known as Aher, makes this plain:

> He [in his journey to the heavens] saw authority was granted to Metatron to sit and write down the merits of Israel.[3] ... [Then he thought,] "Perhaps there are two authorities..." Permission was granted to him (Metatron) to strike out the merits of Aher.[4]

Whereas this text shows us that the Rabbis understood the danger inherent in the Son of Man theologies, the story of the healing of the paralytic in the Gospels shows us at what an early date this danger was known.

In this chapter we also hear the two blind men call Jesus "Son of David" (9:27). "Son of David" is the term the Rabbis preferred when referring to the messianic redeemer.[5]

This chapter contains reference to Jesus as the "bridegroom" and refers to the "members (or sons) of the bridal chamber" (9:15). The reference appears to refer to some mythic, mystical construct where the Son of Man and Wisdom (Sophia) are both hypostatic emanations of the Godhead. The union of Son of Man (from below) and Wisdom (from above) signifies the restoration of the "spiritual and divine" realm immediately *below* God intimating the impending unification of all into the divine realm. On the identity of Wisdom and Jesus the arguments of Ben Witherington III in his *Jesus the Sage* and the Gospel of Matthew's references to "Wisdom" and "Son of Man (i.e. Jesus' heavenly identity)" have much merit.[6] The Gnostic Gospels (witnessed by J. M. Robinson's collection of texts, *The Nag Hammadi Library in English*) show their own mythic imagery which extends some philosophic/ mystic conceptualizations (identified by Witherington) within the circle of normative Jewish imaging of God through his personified authorities or attributes: wisdom, power, glory. So the Gnostic text, "Exegesis of the Soul,"[7] suggests Jesus is both brother and bridegroom of Sophia. (Wisdom) — both hypostatic children of God joined in a divine union:

> From heaven the father sent to her her man, who is her brother, the firstborn. Then the bridegroom came down to the bride...she cleansed herself in the bridal chamber. But then the bridegroom came down to her in the bridal chamber which was prepared...before Christ's appearance came John, preaching the baptism of repentance.

Here is a citation concerning the rational soul seeking God (authoritative teaching VI, III — 33).[8]

> She came to rest in him who is at rest. She reclined in the bride-chamber. She ate of the banquet for which she hungered.

To the Gospel of Philip II, chap. 3 (68–70), Robinson discusses how spiritual separations are to be repaired in the Bridal Chamber.[9] In sum it says that the Holy of Holies is the Bridal Chamber. Baptism and Resurrection (the holies) together with Redemption (the holy) take place in the Bridal Chamber, a spiritual realm more than a physical realm. The final paragraphs of this Gnostic Gospel are illuminating. The passage refers to the image of the rending of the veil recorded by Matthew (27:51) to have occurred while Jesus was on the cross:

> The holies of the holies were revealed, and the bridal chamber invited us in...If any one becomes *a son of the bridal chamber,* he will receive the light...And none shall be able to torment a person like this even while he dwells in the world.[10]

I sum up the matter by abridging the words of Pirjo Lapinkivi:

> Gnostics believed that their souls were brides of angels, they saw their entrance into the world beyond as wedding-feast. When Sophia receives Christ the bridegroom, they also receive their bridegrooms — the angels. ...man is drunk and only the call of the redeemer can wake him up.[11]

Lapinkivi traces the motif here to ideas evident in Sumerian, Hellenistic, and Jewish (still extant in kabbalistic sources) writings. While the image of the "bridal chamber" seems to shift in meaning somewhat from tract to tract, there can be no question that the words refer to some kind of anti-chamber where the spiritual worlds and human souls are prepared for entry into the Kingdom of Heaven. The reference in all synoptic Gospels to this "chamber" testify to its early usage in Christian doctrine.[12]

Boarding a boat, he crossed and came to his own city. (v. 1)

The city is Kfar Nahum (Capernaum, see 4:13), which had a tax office (see 9:9).

Suddenly they brought to him a paralyzed person laid upon a bed. Jesus, seeing their faith, said to the paralyzed person, "Take courage, son, your sins are forgiven you." (v. 2)

The text here is clear — Jesus is moved to heal on account of the faith of those who have brought the paralyzed man to him. I have discussed Jesus' shocking affirmation to the paralytic that "your sins are forgiven you" in the introduction to this chapter.

Suddenly, some of the Scribes said among themselves, "He blasphemes!"
(v. 3)

In chapters 5 through 7 Jesus' authority as a teacher is made plain, and confirmed by those who have heard him teach (7:29). In chapter 8 Jesus' authority manifests itself in his ability to heal and to control the elements.

Now here in chapter 9 Jesus claims to have the authority to forgive sins. For the Scribes to condemn such authority as "blasphemy" presents a special problem. The biblical law concerning "blasphemy" is referred to in Lev. 24:16: "He who blasphemes the name of the Lord shall be put to death." It is difficult to see how Jesus has contravened this law by anything he has done here. It may be that what is called "blasphemy" is a more general term that suggests Jesus does not openly give God due credit for the supernatural feats he performs allowing for others to conclude perhaps that he is some kind of god himself, even stronger than God. The usages vary. For instances, an expanded usage is found in 2Kings 19:6: "Be not afraid of the words which thou hast heard, with which the servants of the king of Assyria have blasphemed me." Apparently the blasphemy is found in 2Kings 18:32: "[D]o not listen to Hezekiah, when he leads you astray, saying, 'The Lord will deliver us.'" "Blasphemy" may refer to words that imply that one has independent power equal to or greater than God's. I have discussed the matter more extensively in the introduction to this chapter.

Jesus, seeing their design,[13] *said, "Why do you think wickedness in your hearts?"* (v. 4)

It is difficult to know what "design," means here. Does it mean that the Scribes think ill of Jesus? Are they thinking to accuse him of usurping divine authority to lead people astray? This text begins to prepare the reader, if only with a scene of dark whisperings, for the denouement of the Gospel trial narrative.

"What is easier, to say 'Your sins are forgiven,' or to say, 'Get up and walk'? So that you may know that the Son of Man has authority to forgive sins upon the earth," then he says to the paralyzed person, 'Be raised up, and take your bed and go to your house.'" *Being raised up, he went to his house.* (vv. 5–7)

Here Jesus calls himself the "Son of Man" and proclaims that, though human, still he is in possession of divine authority. It is the first time in the Gospel that he has used this title to confirm his authority (in 8:20, as I say, he used the term as a kind of pun).[14] The logic behind Jesus' answer to the Scribes' accusation of blasphemy remains somewhat enigmatic. The problems have been analyzed in the introduction to this chapter.

I include here again (as I did in my comments to Matt. 8:3) the tradition from *b. Ber.* 5b, in which Rabbi Hanina cures Rabbi Yohanan by touch: "He told him, 'Give me your hand.' He gave him his hand and he *raised him up.*"

The Aramaic (*ve-oqmeih, af'el* of *qum*) is crucial here to appreciate that the phrase "raised up" in the Gospel text is an aramaicism which means "cured," as I have already pointed out that it does in *b. Ber.* 5b. In Mark's version (5:41) of the story of the healing of Jairus' daughter, Jesus says to her, "*talitha qum(i)*" — "Child, arise."

> *When the crowds saw this, they were afraid, and they glorified the*
> *God who gave such power to human beings. (v. 8)*

In glorifying God the crowds likely recited a blessing much like the one the Rabbis said was to be recited while witnessing the majesty of a king: "Blessed is the One who shares his glory with human beings [or to those who fear him]" (*b. Ber.* 58a). The Rabbis created blessings for every occasion based on the wording of 1Chron. 29:11: "Thine, O Lord, is the greatness, and the power, and the glory, and the victory, and the majesty..." One rabbi — Rabbi Shila — proclaimed, "Blessed is the Merciful One who has given [power of] kingship on earth just as his [power] of kingship is in heaven" (*b. Ber.* 58a). The crowds do not think Jesus has usurped power and even if he did not attribute his miracles to God, the crowd does.

> *When Jesus was going along from there, he saw a person sitting at the*
> *tax office, by the name of Matthew. He says to him, "Follow me," and,*
> *standing up, he followed him.*[15] *When he was reclining in the house,*
> *look, many tax collectors and sinners came and were reclining with*
> *Jesus and his students. (vv. 9–10)*

The word "reclining" here means "dining" and is frequent in the ancient Jewish literature (Hebrew: *meisav, mesubin*). It was the general custom for people in the Hellenistic period to recline on couches while eating their meals.

The tax collectors were known as robbers and reprobates. Because their money was ill-gained it was not fit for trade or alms (*m. B. Qam.* 10:1). There may a hint of the Gnostic motif mentioned in the introduction to this chapter that the spiritual knowledge of "drunken" souls waited for the redeemer to make them sober and call them to their true origins.

> *Seeing this, the Pharisees said to his students, "Why does your teacher*
> *eat with tax collectors and sinners?" (v. 11)*

Many Pharisees were concerned about dining with those whose presence at table might cause their food to be defiled (the general rule was that people dined with their peers or their apprentices).[16] But more than this, apparently the Pharisees considered Jesus to be a teacher like one of their own, for which reason they are perplexed here as to why he would dine with reprobates and sinners. With respect to such people the position of the Pharisees is found in *m. 'Abot* 1:7: "Nittai the Arbelite said: Avoid an evil neighbor; do not associate with the wicked; and do not surrender your faith in divine justice." There is no condemnation in their question to Jesus, just puzzlement.

Writing about the same time as Matthew, Josephus (*Ant.* 13:294–97) says of the Pharisees that they "are lenient in the matter of punishments and that they pass down certain regulations which were handed down to them by their ancestors. These laws were not recorded in the Torah of Moses…which are derived from the tradition of the fathers and the Pharisees have the masses on their side."

> *When he heard this, he said, "Those who are strong have no need of*
> *a doctor, but only those who are ill." (v. 12)*

This first part of Jesus' answer is perfectly civil. He says he is in company with sinners because he wants to bring them to repentance.[17] He has nothing to offer those such as the Pharisees, who are already pious and kind. Matthew follows his sources here.

> *"Go, learn what it means, 'I want mercy and not sacrifice' (Hosea 6:6).*
> *For I did not come to call righteous people, but sinners." (v. 13)*

Neither Mark's nor Luke's version of this story contains this saying of Jesus to the Pharisees in which he cites Hos. 6:6. Often Matthew cannot speak of the Scribes or Pharisees without adding some kind of negative or hostile comment about them, but this is not the case here. The phrase "Go, learn" is the anglicized form of the Aramaic *zil gemor*, which is found, for instance, in *b. Šabb.* 31b — "and the rest [of Scriptures] is commentary, Go, learn" — and of the Hebrew *tsei ulemad*, which is found in *Num. Rab.* (*bamidbar*) 5:9 — "to know why the sons of Kehath died, Go and learn from this verse…" That is, the phrase is used to encourage one to study the Scriptures and to apply its various lessons to the appropriate situations. And so Jesus tells the Pharisees here that if they want to know what he means by saying that he "did not come to call righteous people, but sinners," they can go and learn it from the Scriptures, in this case Hosea 6:6. In their own idiom, and by way of their own method, Jesus is pointing out to the Pharisees here that he has every justification in dining with tax collectors and sinners.[18]

Yet by saying that he is there for sinners, and by justifying his presence with them by quoting from Hosea, Jesus sidesteps the matter of his actually dining with them. In any case, the Pharisees seem to accept his answer (but see Matt. 11:19: "[T]hey say, 'Look, a person who is a glutton and a drunkard, a friend of tax collectors and sinners'").

Now some students of John the Baptist come on the scene and they ask a more serious question than did the Pharisees, which concerns not only the practices of the Pharisees but also that of John the Baptist, the comrade-in-arms, so to speak, of Jesus.

> *Then students of John came to him, saying, "Why do we and the Pharisees fast, but your students do not fast?"* (v. 14)

While Matthew writes elsewhere that John was openly hostile to the Pharisees (3:7–10), here we discover that he actually followed Pharisaic practice, at least when it came to fasting. John may have been quite sympathetic to the Pharisees, his antagonism toward them in the Gospel being an invention of Matthew's. John's disciples are not speaking here of the Pharisaic fasts one reads of in the *Didache*, chapter 8 (i.e., those they engaged in on the second and fifth day of the week), but rather of the mourning fasts prescribed for Jews in memory of the catastrophes that befell Judah in the last days of the Davidic Monarchy. These fasts (still observed by Jews) are listed in Zech. 8:19: "Thus says the Lord of hosts: 'The fast of the fourth month, the fast of the fifth, the fast of the seventh, and the fast of the tenth shall be joy and gladness and cheerful feasts for the house of Judah. Therefore love truth and peace.'" Their precise dates are a matter of dispute in a *baraita* in b. *Roš Haš.* 18b.

> *Jesus said to them, "How can the sons of the bride-chamber mourn so long as the bridegroom is with them? The days will come when the bridegroom will be taken away from them, and then they will fast."*
> (v. 15)

The statement that "the sons of the bride-chamber do not mourn so long as the bridegroom is with them" seems to be drawn from a collection of first-century laws. In Jewish law those who attend the bridegroom are called *bnei hupah*; the Greek *huioi tou nymphōnos* is a literal translation of this term. A tradition in *t. Ber.* 2:10 exempts the *bnei hupah* from certain obligations during the wedding festival, such as putting on phylacteries and the saying of the prayers. For this same seven-day period, a tradition in b. *Sukkah* 25b exempts the *bnei hupah* from the obligations of Sukka, that is, of "living in booths," since this obviously would prevent them from celebrating with the bridegroom.

The question of the bridegroom's exemption from the fasts is a matter of some dispute. Rabbis wondered if there was a way to derive the teaching one way or another from extant post-Temple traditions preserved by Rabbis. Apparently, both practices (fasting and not fasting) were current in Jewish communities. According to the eighteenth-century Rabbi Hayyim Yosef David Azulai (*Birchei Yosef,* 686:6), the author of the Responsa *Beit David* (responsum 476) suggests that during the time of the bridal festivities a bridegroom did not and still should not fast on any of the four prescribed fast days, while the thirteenth-century Rabbi Yom Tov ben Ashbili, in his commentary to the Talmud (end of *b. Ta'anit*), says that the bridegroom was always and still is obligated to fast. With regard to the fasts themselves in Jesus' day, it seems that at times during the Second Temple period observing them was voluntary.[19] Jesus' position concerning them, at least in the absence of the bridegroom, was likely more stringent than that of many Jews of his day.[20] It is said here that the Pharisees and the disciples of John did observe the fasts. We might note here that, according to Matthew, John's disciples identify themselves and Jesus also with Pharisaic practice, at least in the matter of observing fasts.

Jesus suggests here that the "bridegroom" will soon die. The early Gospel writers (both canonical and extracanonical) seem to have expressed positions sympathetic to being stringent about observing fasts which they mixed with a kind of gnosis of "bridal-chamber" mysticism[21] to defend a leniency in fasting rules in regards to Jesus' own practices. We cannot be certain of the full import of this mystical imagery; suffice it to say that Jesus is already in some way already married to his divine "Bride" and resident in her "kingdom." The wedding imagery of the Song of Songs is likely at the root of the vocabulary here although who the bride was supposed to be is never made clear.

Be that as it may, what I mean is that here Jesus alludes to mystical notions as outlined in the introduction to this chapter. He suggests his disciples are to observe the law concerning fasts as they apply to the bridegroom and his party. The terminology here reflects the mindset of "sacred bridal chamber" unions of the gnostics. The point is that the disciples are not to fast so long as the "bridegroom" is with them. By "bridegroom" the Gospels may well be utilizing hypostatic concepts of mystical traditions, both Jewish and Gnostic. Jesus insists that all others should properly observe the laws regarding fasts, as also his disciples are to do when they find themselves no longer attending to him. His answer concerning the behavior of his own disciples specifies their quasi-membership in his own supernal, celestial, divine circle which he embodied and their earthly membership in the House of Israel which they embody. In so framing matters he also highlights the incongruence of the two overlapping kingdoms (of Rome, God's enemy, and of Heaven) that Jesus occupies — the kingdom of the future redemption, where there are no fasts but feasts only as God promised Zechariah (18:19: "Thus says the Lord of hosts, 'The fast of the fourth, the fast of the fifth, the fast of the seventh and the fast of the tenth [months] will become joy, gladness, and cheerful feasts for the house of Judah; so love truth and peace'"), and the present kingdom of subjugation and mourning and fasting as God commanded Zechariah (above). This insight helps to reveal what Jesus means in the following sayings about sewing new cloth onto old and the pouring of new wine into the old wineskins. The two kingdoms are incongruous and only overlap in the liminality of the "bridal chamber" (the entrance to the new kingdom). Once the bridegroom is gone, the disciples will be part of the old kingdom and the fasts will again be obligatory for them.

In chapter 8 of *Didache* it is noted that Christians are to fast on Wednesday (Jesus' arrest) and Fridays (the day of his crucifixion), unlike the "hypocrites" who fast on Mondays and Thursdays. Luke 18:12 gives us a parable about a Pharisee who boasts, "I fast twice a week." There is a tradition (*b. Ta'an.* 12a citing the last passage in the scholian to *Megillat Ta'anit*) that these optional fasts existed before the year 66 and that *Megillat Ta'anit*, likely composed that year, obliquely alludes to them.[22]

> *"No one attaches a patch of unshrunken cloth on an old cloak. For its fullness takes it up from the cloak, and a worse rip is made. Neither do they pour new wine into old wineskins. If they were to do so, the skins would burst, and the wine would pour out, and the skins are ruined. But they pour new wine into unused wineskins, and both are preserved." (vv. 16–17)*

Undoubtedly Jewish, these proverbs nicely illustrate Jesus' point about the impossibility of grafting one kingdom — the present world of suffering — onto the other — the coming kingdom of salvation.[23] Jewish sources preserve a saying concerning the difficulty of trying to mix the old with the new: "One who studies Torah as an old man, to what is he compared? To ink written on blotted paper" (*m. 'Abot* 4:21).

> *While he was saying these things to them, suddenly one of the leaders came and knelt before him, saying, "My daughter has just now died; but if you come and lay your hand upon her, she will live." (v. 18)*

Mark 5:22 identifies the man who approaches Jesus here as one of the "leaders" of the synagogue, Jairus by name. The exact title is *rosh hakenesset* (*t. Ter.* 2:13 speaks of the *rosh hakenessat* of the synagogue of Keziv). A leader of the synagogue was one of the leaders of the community. The other leaders of the community were the custodians of the city (*hazanei ha'ir*) and the administrators of the city (*parnassei ha'ir*), both of which are mentioned in *b. Ketub.* 8b.

> *Jesus rose and followed him, and his students also. Suddenly, a woman who had been bleeding for twelve years approached from behind him and touched the hemmed-tzitzit of his cloak. (vv. 19–20)*

On his way to the place where the young girl lies, Jesus is approached by a woman who, though Matthew does not say so, is almost certainly Jewish. Owing to purity concerns the woman does not touch Jesus directly but merely the fringes of his cloak.

The Greek *kraspedon* (lit. hem) was the term used by the Jews to translate the Hebrew *tsitsit* — the ceremonial fringes or tassels that hung from the corners of one's outer garment (see Num. 15:38) — in the biblical texts that were meant for popular consumption, such as the Aramaic *Targum Onqelos*: *krusped* and *kruspedin* (Num. 15:38–39, Deut. 22:12). This use of the term was current in very early times, as the LXX testifies (Num. 15:38, Ezek. 8:3, Deut. 22:12, Zech. 8:23).

> *For she said to herself, "If only I touch his cloak, I will be made well."*
> *(v. 21)*

Such was the woman's faith in the holiness of Jesus that she believed it extended even to the cloak he wore. It is clear she feels that simply by touching it she can be made well.

> *Jesus, turning and seeing her, said, "Daughter, your faith has saved you." And the woman was saved at that very hour. (vv. 22)*

Again the Gospel points out that the operative factor in Jesus' healing was the degree of faith either in the one needing to be healed, as here, or else in those asking that another be healed.

> *When Jesus came to the house of the leader, and saw the flutists and the crowd being stirred up (v. 23)*

It was common for flute players (*halilim*) and female mourners (*meqonenot*) to accompany funeral processions in order to draw out the emotions of the crowds. The Rabbis insisted that accompanying the funeral processions of even the poorest of Jews there should be no less than two of each (*m. Ketub.* 4:4). It is likely that in the time of the Gospels those of the middle and upper classes covered these expenses.

> *He said, "Depart, for the girl has not died but she is sleeping." And they laughed at him. (v. 24)*

Certainly to others the girl appeared to be dead, but Jesus seems to indicate otherwise. Has she in fact died, or is she merely asleep?

> *When the crowd had been put outside, he went in and took her hand, and the girl was awakened. (v. 25)*

For the terms "sleeping" and "waking" used together, we refer to Dan. 12:2: "Many of those who sleep in the dust of the ground will awake."

Resurrecting the dead was something a "Son of God" — someone who had been given certain divine powers — was able to do. 1 Kings 17:22–23 tells us that Elijah too, with God's help, was able to revive the dead. "The Lord heard the prayer of Elijah; the life breath returned to the child's body and he revived. Taking the child, Elijah brought him down into the house from the upper room and gave him to his mother. 'See!' Elijah said to her, 'your son is alive.'" For Matthew, Jesus has come to possess all the divine attributes that God had shared with Moses and Elijah. This is confirmed in the story of the Transfiguration, when Moses and Elijah appear together with Jesus (Matt. 17:3).

> *This report went out to that whole land. (v. 26)*

Again we read that, once Jesus has performed a miracle, a report of it immediately goes out far and wide.

> *When Jesus passed by from there, two blind people followed, calling out and saying, "Have mercy on us, Son of David!" (v. 27)*

For the Jews the Messiah is expected to restore the national pride of the people of Israel, along with the independence of the land, as David had done, for which reason, besides lineage, he is called "Son of David."

And when he entered the house, the blind people came to him, and Jesus says to them, "Do you trust that I am able to do this?" They say to him, "Yes, Lord." Then he touched their eyes, saying, "According to your trust, let it be done to you." (vv. 28–29)

Again the faith of those who ask to be healed is the key to Jesus' ability to heal.

And their eyes were opened. Jesus sternly ordered them, "See that no one comes to know this!" When they went out, they spread it around that whole world. (vv. 30–31)

From these blind men he has cured Jesus asks for secrecy but this they refuse, as did others he cured (see 8:4). The Gospel uses an Aramaicism. When it is said in Aramaic that the blind are cured, the word "*itpatah*" is used. For instance in *Lev. Rab.* 22:4 it is said that "the one who was blind was cured (*itpatah*, literally 'opened')."

When they had gone out, suddenly they brought to him a mute person possessed by a demon. When the demon was thrown out, the mute spoke. The crowds were amazed, saying, "Never has such a thing ever appeared in Israel." (vv. 32–33)

The amazement of the crowds in response to the miracles of Jesus is a recurring topos in the Gospel. Throughout the crowds act somewhat like the chorus does in Greek drama, providing a kind of commentary on the acts of Jesus.

But the Pharisees said, "He casts out demons through the ruler of demons." (v. 34)

In Matthew's day it was commonly thought that Jesus had been a magician, a sorcerer (*b. Sanh.* 43a), and that it was because he had access to the world of demons that he was able to perform miracles.[24] For this reason the Pharisees do not deny that Jesus cast out the demon here, but they do claim that it was only because he had access to demons that he was able to do this. This is typical of early Christian polemic. The point is that the authority of the Pharisees could be undermined by such miraculous displays of Jesus, though in fact their authority was based on their expertise in interpreting the Scriptures and the oral tradition, not on their ability to perform miracles.

May the Lord, the God of the spirits of all flesh, appoint a man over the congregation who shall go out before them and come in before them, who shall lead them out and bring them in, that the congregation of the Lord may not be as sheep that have no shepherd. So the Lord said to Moses, "Take Joshua the son of Nun, a man in whom is the Spirit, and lay your hand on him."

Sipre Num. piska 139 explains the verse "That the congregation of the Lord may not be *like sheep that have no shepherd*" (Num. 27:17) with reference to Song of Songs 1:7, 8.

"Tell me, O one whom my soul loves, how you pasture your flock, how you make it lie down at noon's heat; for why should I be like one who is *swept away*[26] [from beside the flocks of your companions?] (Song of Songs 1:7)" — according to its usage in the verse, "And he shall *sweep away* the land of Egypt as *a shepherd sweeps away* his cloak of vermin, and he shall go away from there in peace (Jer. 43:12)." [Moses asked:] For why should I be like one who is *swept away* [from beside the flocks of your companions?] — [which means] "beside the flocks of Abraham, Isaac and Jacob." Now Go and see what the Holy One replied to him, "If you do not know, O fairest amongst women..." [O Moses,] most eminent amongst the prophets... "Go follow the trackers of the sheep..." The trackers I will ordain to help them... "and pasture your lambs [by the tents of the shepherds]" (Song of Songs 1:8). From where can you say that God showed Moses all the leaders who in the future would attend Israel from the day they would leave the desert until the day the dead would live? As it said, "Go follow the trackers of the sheep" (Song 1:8).

The point of verse 36 seems to be that, despite having preached and healed as much as he has, still Jesus feels that he has done so little of what needs to be done for the people of Israel. The suffering of the Jews in the first century under Roman occupation, which led to the disastrous revolt against Rome in 66 C.E., was severe. And of course while under it there was no opportunity for the official Jewish leadership to institute programs of national renewal. During this period of occupation many diverse groups arose, including Christianity, which by the time of Matthew professed no message of national renewal at all. There seems to be an admission by Jesus here that he did not see himself as being able to address this problem by himself.

Then he says to his students, "The harvest is plentiful, but the workers are few. So beseech the lord of the harvest to send out workers for his harvest." (vv. 37–38)

For Jesus to say that the "harvest is plentiful, but the workers are few" is to say metaphorically that the need for teachers and healers far exceeds those who are engaged in doing these things. A similar saying, previously mentioned and to be mentioned again in comments to Matt. 13:27, is attributed to Rabbi Tarfon in *m. 'Abot* 2:15, only the need here is for teachers of the Torah:

> Rabbi Tarfon says — the day is short and work plentiful and the workers are lethargic; but the reward is great and the householder is eager.

The lord of the harvest must be God, while in 13:27 it is the Son of Man. That the metaphors are used differently in different places suggests that the image of a master of harvest was a commonplace predating the Gospel and open to a variety of usages.

NOTES

[1] The proof-text for this tradition is Exod. 21:19: "If one [who was injured by another] gets up and walks around outside on his own support the other who inflicted the injury is not liable but shall pay for missed work and what it took to have him cured." At the end of this verse in Hebrew the root for "cured" is written twice, for which reason the Rabbis said, "From here [the doubling] we learn that authority is given to a healer to heal" (*b. B. Qam.* 85b).

[2] The biblical law concerning "blasphemy" is referred to in Lev. 24:16: "He who blasphemes the name of the Lord shall be put to death." It is difficult to see how Jesus has contravened this law by anything he has done here. Yet "blasphemy" seems to be a fluid term with a considerable range of meaning. In the Gospels its usage may lie in the fact that in their accounts Jesus does not openly give credit to God for the healings he performs. So, perhaps the problem lies in allowing others to think that he is some kind of god himself. This is something like the expression "the creature is comparing himself with the Creator." On the other hand we see usages of "blaspheme," which aim to mock God's power and say, "My powers are greater than God's." This is the meaning of the term as it is used in 2Kings 19:6: "Isaiah said to [Hezekiah's servants], 'Say to your master, 'Thus says the Lord: Be not afraid of the words which thou hast heard, with which the servants of the king of Assyria have *blasphemed* me [by saying that I, God, am unable to deliver the people of Judah from his hand (2Kings 18:32)]." That is, the king of Assyria assumes here that he is more powerful than God, for which reason God says that he has blasphemed against him. He has also mocked God's name openly, an act which could encompass the definition of blasphemy of Lev. 24:16.

[3] That is, Metatron is said here to be a heavenly scribe which, according to the apocalyptic literature, is the same position held by Enoch in heaven once he was taken up to it. Moreover, there is reason to see in the image of these heavenly

Scribes the *Son of Man* figure of Daniel (in some texts Enoch is called "Son of Man"). See n. 6 below. See further my comments to 11:19.

4   I omit the part of the story in which Metatron is severely flogged for having misled Aher into thinking that there are two authorities in heaven.

5   The term appears over one hundred times in the rabbinic literature, including *Kallah Rab.* 2:4 and 7:4, *b. Yoma* 10a, *b. Sukkah* 52a, *b. Meg.* 17b, *b. Yebam.* 62a, *b. Sanh.* 38a, 97a–98b, *y. Sukkah* 5:1, *y. Ta'an.* 1:1, 4:5, *y. Qidd.* 4:1, *Gen. Rab.* 97:9.

6   Witherington, *Jesus the Sage.*

7   Robinson, *The Nag Hammadi Library in English,* 168

8   Ibid., 310.

9   Ibid., 149–51.

10   Ibid., 159–60.

11   Pirjo Lapinkivi, *The Sumerian Sacred Marriage in the Light of Comparative Evidence,* vol. 15 of *State Archives of Assyria Studies* (Helsinki, 2004), 172.

12   We must also note the protest of Irenaeus, who notes the abuse of the Gnostic doctrine among some Christians to seduce women in the name of spiritual union. I quote now from chapter 23:6 of *Against Heresies* of Irenaeus (based on the Old Latin), from *Ante-Nicene Fathers,* vol. 1, *The Apostolic Fathers, Justin Martyr, Irenaeus,* ed. Alexander Roberts and James Donaldson (Edinburgh, 1867; reprint, Grand Rapids, Mich.: Eerdmans, 2001). The added notes in the following text set in square brackets are by A. Cleveland Coxe:

> *For they affirm, that because of the "Redemption"* [Grabe is of opinion that reference is made in this term to an imprecatory formula in use among the Marcosians, analogous to the form of thanksgiving employed night and morning by the Jews for their redemption from Egypt. Harvey refers the word to the second baptism practiced among these and other heretics, by which it was supposed they were removed from the cognizance of the Demiurge, who is styled the "judge" in the close of the above sentence.] *it has come to pass that they can neither be apprehended, nor even seen by the judge. But even if he should happen to lay hold upon them, then they might simply repeat these words, while standing in his presence along with the "Redemption": "O thou, who sittest beside God,* [That is, Sophia, of whom Achamoth, afterwards referred to, was the emanation.] *and the mystical, eternal Sige, thou through whom the angels (mightiness), who continually behold the face of the Father, having thee as their guide and introducer, do derive their forms* [The angels accompanying Soter were the consorts of spiritual Gnostics, to whom they were restored after death]. *from above, which she in the greatness of her daring inspiring with mind on account of the goodness of the Propator, produced us as their images, having her mind then intent upon the things above, as in a dream, — behold, the judge is at*

hand, and the crier orders me to make my defense. But do thou, as being acquainted with the affairs of both, present the cause of both of us to the judge, inasmuch as it is in reality but one cause. [The syntax in this long sentence is very confused, but the meaning is tolerably plain. The gist of it is, that these Gnostics, as being the spiritual seed, claimed a consubstantiality with Achamoth, and consequently escaped from the material Demiurge, and attained at last to the Pleroma.] *Now, as soon as the Mother hears these words, she puts the Homeric* [Rendering the wearer invisible.] *helmet of Pluto upon them, so that they may invisibly escape the judge. And then she immediately catches them up, conducts them into the* bridal chamber, *and hands them over to their consorts.*

Sige (the name might be related to that of a Sumerian goddess), according to Gnostic texts, refers to the primordial Silence who existed at the Creation. She gave birth to Sophia, the Gnostic's divine Mother, who seems to have been the "mother" of the Divinity and his "consort" as well. See Campbell, *Myths to Live By*, 12. We might take note the term "sits beside God" (which is equated with Sophia in the text) and think of the Jewish Metatron (sitting beside God) who is, I think, to be equated with Matthew's "Son of Man." In full circle, we come back to the work of Witherington who sees, in the canonical Gospels (apart from John) allusions to the lower Jesus, the heavenly Sophia, and the intermediate Son of Man as various forms of the *Logos or Memra*. A comprehensive list of works discussing Jesus and Sophia can be found in Deutsch, "Wisdom in Matthew." We will have occasion to return to these themes when we discuss Matt. 11:29.

¹³ The Greek noun *enthumeseis* means "thought," "idea," "imagination," and the verb *enthumeomai* means to "think," "ponder," "reflect." It is therefore roughly equivalent to the rabbinic term "*hirhur* (n), *leharher* (v)" that can mean anything from "silent *shema* meditation" (*m. Ber.* 3:4) to "thinking impure thoughts" (*b. 'Abod. Zar.* 20b) to adopting an accusatory and suspicious stance toward another's words and actions (*Tanḥ. Exod. pikudei* 11) to devising a plot (*Midrash Abba Gurion* [ed. Buber] to Esther, chap. 3). This last passage discusses how the Persian king plotted to preoccupy Mordecai from rebuilding the Temple by supporting Haman, his enemy, to thwart the rebuilding. The same passage discusses Haman's plot to rise to power by wresting Esther's privileged position (*proskope*) from her. I suggest this is the sense of Matthew's formulation here. Jesus understands that the Scribes are harboring suspicions and conspiring against him. He perceives their design. This midrash text seems to fill in the missing sentences from *Esther Rab.* 7:4 which is obviously cut short since the text mentions "many *hirhurim* (plans)" and not even one of them is fully described. The use of Greek *pro[s]kope* in the Buber text and the attribution to Rabbi Yehuda suggest the tradition is relatively early. Evidence for my supposition concerning the relationship between words denoting "conspiring" and "thinking" is found in Gen. 37:18, "And they saw him afar off, and before he came near unto them, *they conspired* against him to slay him." The Aramaic *Targum Onqelos* provides: "[T]hey reflected about him."

14 D. Flusser (*Jewish Sources in Early Christianity*, 56) traces the title from Daniel 7 to Enoch 37–71 to Testament of Abraham (son of Adam or Abel) who sees him as the final judge in the End of Days.

15 This Matthew, who is a Jew, is not to be identified with the author of the Gospel of Matthew. There is no evidence for such identification, although it is strange that he is named and that the scene is recorded. What is significant is that Jesus has said "follow me" to those he wishes to be his disciples (See 4:19, 8:22). That he says, "Follow me," to Matthew suggests that he wishes that he too should become a disciple of his. In *b. Sanh.* 43a a disciple of Jesus is referred to as "Matthai" (i.e., Matthew; the Syriac name of Matthew is Matthai).

16 Concerning this matter, see the works by Westerholm, *Jesus and Scribal Authority*, 62–67, and Sanders, "Jesus and the Sinners."

17 A tradition from *Lev. Rab.* 34:13 shows that the Rabbis also understood the importance of visiting the poorly educated masses to teach them better ways. Purity considerations were not an issue. "'*And the impoverished poor you should bring into the house*' (Isa. 58:7). This refers to the Disciples of the sages who frequently enter the houses of the ignorant masses (*umei ha'arets*) to nourish them from the words of the Torah…and teach them to do the will of their Father who is in heaven."

18 In his *Mishneh Torah* ("Laws of Festivals," 6:18), Maimonides records a law — not found in the Talmuds — which states that on the festival day one is obligated to feed the stranger, the orphan, and the widow (Deut. 16:11), among other less fortunate people; otherwise the festival sacrifice has no meaning for God. In support of this law he cites Hosea 9:4 — "Their sacrifices are as bread of mourners to them, All eating it are unclean: For their bread is for themselves" — and Mal. 2:3 — "And have scattered dung before your faces, Dung of your festival sacrifices." It is noteworthy that Maimonides says nothing here about dining with sinners, which is a different thing than dining with the poor.

19 See *b. Roš Haš.* 18b: "When there is peace they (the fast days) will be for joy and gladness; if there is persecution there will be fast days; if there is no persecution and yet no peace, then those who desire to fast may fast and those who do not need not fast."

20 Even though today the fasts are obligatory, nevertheless some authorities permit exemptions for a bridegroom during the seven days of his rejoicing in the bridal chamber (the name given to the new abode of the couple after their wedding).

21 Much of the Gnostic *Gospel of Philip* is based on such mystical utterances that defy ready explanation. For example consider 2.3: 72 "In this world the slaves serve the free. In the Kingdom of Heaven the free will minister to the slaves; the Sons of the Bridal-Chamber shall serve the Sons of Marriage. The Sons of the Bridal-Chamber have [a single] name among them, the repose occurs among them mutually, they are made to have no needs. The contemplation [of the

imagery is aware]ness in greatness of glory. [Truly there is immortal]ity within those in the [Holy Bridal-Chamber, who receive] the glories of those who [are fulfilled]. (Cf. Robinson, *The Nag Hammadi Library in English*, 153.)" I have discussed these mystical notions at some length in the introduction to chapter 9.

22   See further Schremer, "The Concluding Passage of *Megillat Ta'anit* and the Nullification of Its Halakhic Significance during the Talmudic Period." Also see Avneri, "Megillat Ta'anit," 350, for textual variants.

23   For Jews the coming kingdom means a worldly kingdom governed by a messianic figure in which the dead are resurrected and in which relief from all persecution is to be found. Prior to the advent of this kingdom there may be upheavals and wars and terror (three generations preceding the "Days of the Messiah"). See *Sipre Deut.* piska 318. Also see Scholem's "Toward an Understanding of the Messianic Idea."

24   See Smith, *Jesus the Magician*.

25   See Klausner, *Jesus of Nazareth*, 272, also see Penney and Wise, "By the Power of Beelzebub." The name seems to be equivalent to Satan in Matthew. Also see Geller, "Jesus' Theurgic Powers."

26   And so will die and leave the flocks of Israel unattended.

It is noteworthy that when later in the Gospel the Pharisees hear that Jesus has healed another demoniac, they say again what they say here, only this time they call the "ruler of demons" by name — "Beelzebub": "But when the Pharisees heard this, they said, 'It is only by Beelzebub, the prince of demons, that this fellow drives out demons'" (Matt. 12:24–27; compare Luke 11:15). In relation to the word Beelzebub 2Kings 1:15–16 tells us that:

> The angel of the Lord said to Elijah, "Go down with him [the third captain of the fifty]; do not be afraid of him." So he arose and went down with him to the king [Ahaziah]. Then he said to him, "Thus says the Lord, 'Because you have sent messengers to inquire of Ba'alzebub, the god of Ekron — is it because there is no God in Israel to inquire of His word? — therefore you shall not come down from the bed where you have gone up, but shall surely die.'"

In other words, the name "Beelzebub" seems to have been derived from Ba'alzebub, the "god" of Ekron. Its use by the Pharisees in this text suggests that they see Jesus here as a false prophet who intends with his healings to lead Israel after false gods, such as are spoken of in Deut. 13:1ff. For the Pharisees, Elijah was the true divine healer and not Jesus, who heals in the name of a demon bearing the name of a false god.[25]

Jesus went around all the cities and all the villages teaching in their assemblies and proclaiming the good news of the kingdom and healing every disease and every weakness. (v. 35)

The verse provides a kind of summary of Jesus' activity as a preacher and healer in the various local synagogues of the Galilee. The verse calls to mind Isa. 52:7: "How beautiful upon the mountains are the feet of him that brings good tidings, that announces peace; that brings tidings of good, that announces salvation; that says to Zion, 'Your God reigns!'"

Seeing the crowds he had compassion for them, because they were troubled and dejected, like sheep that had no shepherd. (v. 36)

Though Jewish tradition claims that God will never abandon Israel and that he will ever-provide firm leadership for its people, Jesus says here that that leadership was weak in his day. The content of this verse is similar to Isa. 51:18: "There is none to guide her [Jerusalem] among all the sons whom she hath brought forth; neither is there any that takes her by the hand of all the sons that she has brought up."

In Num. 27:16–18, just after being told by God that he is about to die, Moses worries aloud to him about the future leadership of his people.

in *b. Bek.* 29a. Also his suggestion to his apostles that they "be cunning as serpents and pure as doves" (v. 16) is likewise found almost verbatim in Song of Songs Rab. 2:30. As well, his saying that it "is sufficient for a student to be like his teacher, and [it is sufficient for] the slave to be like his master" (v. 25a) is found word for word in many places in the rabbinic literature, for example in *b. Ber.* 58b. Also of interest, but in this case because of its form (this also applies to the saying above), is Jesus' saying, "If they slandered (literally "named") the master of the house [calling him] 'Beelzebub,' how much more will [they so slander] the members of his household" (v. 25b), for the form of this saying adheres exactly to a complex legal argument that appears in *b. B. Bat.* 111a.[4] I include the rabbinic parallels in the appropriate sections of the commentary to chapter 10.

Also of interest in this chapter is Matthew's advice to the Christian missionaries of his own day, which he put into the mouth of Jesus at the time of the commissioning of his apostles, for it tells us of the court activities that were carried out in the "synagogues" (which may or may not refer to the places of prayer of the same name) of his day: "Be on guard against people, for they will hand you over to councils, and they will whip you in their assemblies" (v. 17). Not only does this saying reflect what is said about public flogging in *m. Mak.* 3:12, but also Jesus' mention here of "assemblies" and what happens in them suggests that these "assemblies," or "synagogues," were institutions that housed courts that oversaw community affairs, including the pronouncing and administering of punishments. Josephus confirms this when he says of the synagogue at Sardis that it was a "place" in which the Jews could "decide their affairs and controversies with one another" (*Ant.* 14:235).[5]

The final point that needs to be addressed before we begin our commentary to chapter 10 is the implication from Matthew's citation of Jesus' words in verse 25 that people referred to him as "Beelzebub." With regard to this we must first recall what Matthew claims the Pharisees said of Jesus once he healed the dumb man possessed of a demon: "He casts out demons through the ruler of demons" (9:34). Next we must also consider Matt. 12:24, in which the name of this ruler of the demons is said to be Beelzebub. "But the Pharisees, having heard [it], said, 'This one does not cast out demons, but by Beelzebub [some mss. "Beelzeboul"], ruler of demons.'" That is, at least for the words claimed of the Pharisees, Jesus is said to have cast out demons by the power of Beelzebub, the prince of demons. But what understanding could lie behind these sayings of the Gospel Pharisees? According to Abaye in *b. Ker.* 3a and *b. Sanh.* 65a, the term for summoning a *shed* (an evil spirit) is *mekater le-shed*. Now some think that this means to give an offering, f incense (from *qtr, heqter*: "to place on a smoking altar"), to the order to summon him to one's aid thereby.[6] Alternatively, *mekater* may refer to a process of mystical "binding" (*qshr*)[7] by the recitation of a magical name. That is, angels or demons might be conjured and bound to do one's bidding by the use of a magical name.

The conjuring (*melahashim* and *hover havarim* using Ps. 58:6 — "the spell of conjurings, the enchantment of the most skilled of magicians") about which Abaye speaks in *b. Ker.* 3a and *b. Sanh.* 65a is done by the one hoping to bind the *shed* to his will, so that he might then do the conjurer's bidding. Now if Jesus was really claimed to have been conjuring the power of Beelzebub, then it stands to reason (at least for Matthean tradition) that over time he may have been called by that name himself. Whom would demons listen to if not to Beelzebub, their king? And so perhaps Jesus came to be seen as Beelzebub, that is, not merely a conjurer but in fact the demon himself.

In ways such as this — that is, having the Pharisees associate Jesus with Beelzebub — Matthew sets the stage for his attack on the Jews, that is, on those who witnessed the miracles of Jesus and shut their eyes to his claims. That attack is the substance of chapter 11.

Calling his twelve students, he gave them authority over impure spirits, to be able to cast them out[8] and to heal every disease and every weakness. (v. 1)

Jewish sources indicate that the Rabbis knew that faith healing was being done in Jesus' name (after his demise). Indeed, the apparent popularity of the Jewish-Christian missionaries troubled the Rabbis (perhaps more for social considerations than "letter of the law" reasons) for which cause they forbade their followers to avail themselves of those who healed in his name. The Rabbis did not want Jews lending credibility to the Christian movement. The aforementioned tradition from *t. Hul.* 2.22–23 (also *y. 'Abod. Zar.* 2:2),[9] in which we read that Rabbi Yishmael prevented Jacob of Sama from curing Eleazar ben Dama in the name of Jesus, was likely told to make Jews aware of the dangers involved in seeking healing from those who healed in Jesus' name. For at the end of the story it is said that because Eleazar died without the name of Jesus being pronounced on him no evil would befall him in the world to come.

The number twelve here is taken by many commentators, without much evidence, as an obvious reference to the twelve tribes of Israel, descended from the twelve sons of Jacob, and representing the entirety of the people. The following verse seems to suggest Gospel writers want us to avoid such speculation. The number, for these writers, is not symbolic but "historical."

The names of the twelve students are these: first, Simon, called Peter, and Andrew his brother, and Jacob the son of Zebediah and John his brother; Philip and Bartholomew, Thomas and Matthew the tax-collector, Jacob the son of Alphaeus, and (Lebbaeus, whose surname was) Thaddeus. (vv. 2–3)

The inclusion of "Lebbaeus,[10] whose surname was" before the name "Thaddeus," which is found in some manuscripts, appears to be the more original reading. Since "Thaddeus" alone is what is written in Mark 3:18, it is likely that in their copying of Matthew some Scribes simply skipped over the words "Lebbaeus, whose surname was" and wrote only the single name "Thaddeus," as Mark has it. "Todos" is a known Jewish name from this period, for example, "Todos of Rome" (*t. Beṣah.* 2:15). And the name "Todah" appears in the Talmud as the name of one of the disciples of Jesus (*b. Sanh.* 43a).

Simon the Cananaean and Judas the Iscariot, who betrayed him moreover. (v. 4)

It may be that *Cananaean* here refers to someone who was a "Qanai." "Qanai" appears as a rabbinic term for "zealot" (*'Abot R. Nat.,* end chap. 6),[11] that is, for someone who was a member of that group, which was aligned with the Pharisees but whose members differed from them in their willingness to use violence as a way of resisting the Roman occupation of Judah and especially of the Galilee. It is more likely, however, that the designation *Cananaen* in relation to Simon means that Simon came from the town of Cana in the Galilee. In the same way, the designation "Iscariot" means that Judas may have come from the town of Kariot (Josh. 15:25). If so, the name "Iscariot," then, would be a Greek rendition of the Hebrew "ish Kariot," that is, "a person of Kariot" (much as Todos of Rome, whom we mentioned above, was called in the rabbinic sources Todos "ish Romi").

Jesus sent out these twelve, commanding them, "Do not go out into the way of the Gentiles, and do not enter into a Samaritan city." (v. 5)

When Jesus "sent out" (*apesteilen* in Greek = *shalah* in Hebrew/Aramaic) his disciples, he sent them out to act on his behalf. That is, no longer were they to be simply his disciples. Now they were to be his "apostles" or "*shelihim.*" "*Shelihim*" is a Jewish legal term that refers to those agents or "apostles" who have the authority to carry out the wishes of the one who sent them, as though it were the sender himself who was carrying them out. Later in this chapter (v. 40) we are told not only that the twelve were apostles of Jesus, but that Jesus was also apostle to God.

The status of the Samaritans (Heb.: *kutim*) as converts to Judaism was a matter of some confusion for Jewish authorities during this period, and it remains so to this day, although the Samaritan community is now negligible in size and is in fact on the verge of dying out altogether.

"Go rather to the lost sheep of the house of Israel. (v. 6)

By having Jesus instruct his disciples to go only to "the lost sheep of the house of Israel," Matthew is in effect setting up the Jews so that he can then knock them down. That he does so is made especially clear at the end of the Gospel where he shows the Jews willingly accepting responsibility for Jesus' death, and not just at that time, but for all time (Matt. 27:25–26). For Matthew the Jews were presumed to be the chosen people but Jesus, though he directed his ministry toward them, was ultimately rejected by them. Instead it was the Gentiles who, though Jesus did not seek them out, showed such faith in him that in the end he called them to be his disciples (Matt. 28:19)[12] rather than the Jews (Matt. 21:43).

It is likely that this chapter dates from a period after the Christians and the Jews had gone their separate ways and while the Christian mission to the Jews was being met with stiff resistance, for the divide between Christians and Jews is clearly indicated throughout it. For example, Matthew says here that Jesus commands his disciples to stay away from the Gentiles as they go about healing the Jews and raising their dead, but he also warns them that the Jews will scourge them, and even hand them over to gentile kings to be killed (10:17ff.). For in fact the "lost sheep of the house of Israel" are wolves (see v. 16), whereas it is the apostles Jesus sends out who are the "sheep" (though as yet no one in the Gospel has raised a finger against either Jesus or his disciples). It would seem that for Matthew the Jews hated the mere name of Jesus and, since his apostles will speak and act in his name, they too will be hated. It is because of statements such as the one Jesus makes here (vv. 16ff.) that I am inclined to believe that Matthew was not Jewish. I suspect he was not a self-hating Jew (although it is arguably possible he was a Jew-turned-Gentile) and would posit he was likely a Gentile.

As I say, here in this chapter a sharp turn is made. Indications of this turn have appeared before (see 8:11–12), but from now on Matthew will begin more clearly to indicate the divide between the Jews and Jesus and the tension that exists between them because of it.

"As you go, proclaim, 'The Kingdom of Heaven is at hand'." (v. 7)

"The Kingdom of Heaven is at hand" were the first words Jesus said as he began his ministry (4:17). This was also the message of John the Baptist (Matt. 3:2). What is different here is that when Jesus tells his disciples to go about proclaiming that "the Kingdom of Heaven is at hand," he does not tell them to preface this message with the word "Repent!" as both he and John reportedly did when they proclaimed it. While Matthew is careful to show that repentance and the confessing of sins were central to the ministry of John, he does not make either of these the central pillars of the ministry of Jesus, despite Jesus' initial proclamation that all repent and some later references to that call. Very likely in Matthew's day the Christian evangelists were having little success in Palestine, although their threat was felt in the Jewish communities. Repentance was preached by the Jews, so there was no need for this to be reinforced either by Gentile-Christians, or by the suspect Jewish-Christians whose communities were being overshadowed by those of the Gentile-Christians who by Matthew's day likely populated the majority of the churches. Under pagan influence the understanding of what the "Kingdom of Heaven" was changed so that for the Christians at least it came to refer to a kind of inner mystical domain rather than an external reality.

"Heal the weak, raise the dead, purify lepers, cast out demons. You received for free, so give for free." (v. 8)

All the miracles that up to this point in the Gospel Matthew has shown Jesus doing are now to be done by his students as well.

Raise the Dead: The ability to raise the dead was considered rare and special during both the period of the prophets and the period of the Second Temple. However by the time Matthew was writing his Gospel, sometime after 70 C.E. apparently, this ability was said to belong not only to certain holy people but also to their students, at least according to a tradition in *Lev. Rab.* 10:4. For here it is said that even the least of the disciples of Rabbi Yehuda the Prince was able to raise the dead. Moreover the tradition relates that one of Rabbi Yehuda's disciples was sent to heal a certain slave of Antoninus, a Roman ruler, who was on the verge of death. When the student approached the slave and asked him why he was lying down instead of working, the slave immediately quickened and began to work again.

Jesus tells his disciples that as they go about teaching and healing they are not to take any fees. The Jewish sources indicate that this was standard practice. A *baraita* (a teaching of the *Tannaim* not included in the Mishnah) in *b. Bek.* 29a states:

> "See, I have taught you statutes and laws as the Lord my God commanded me to do so" (Deut. 4:5). Just as I [taught you] for free so you also [teach] for free."

> *"Do not acquire gold or silver or copper coins in your belts; nor a bag for the road, nor two shirts, nor sandals, nor a staff. For the worker is worthy of his food." (vv. 9–10)*

Jesus' point here is that since God provides the wages for those doing his work, there is no need for his disciples to take anything with them as they go about doing it. In relation to this, the Rabbis taught: "For all who labor in the Torah his food is provided by the Torah and he gains wealth and success in his quests" (*Tanḥ. Exod.* [*Ki Tissa*] 29).

> *"Whatever city or village you enter, search for whoever in it is worthy, and stay with them until you leave." (v. 11)*

Offering hospitality to travelers and strangers was a paramount duty for Jews, as was asking after their welfare and offering them blessings of peace. Both *b. Šabb.* 127a, in which it is said that "offering hospitality to strangers is greater than communication with God," and *Midr. Tanḥ. Num., Pinhas* 1, in which it is said that "[w]hen someone arrives from the road — they ask after his peace — and likewise in the morning they inquire after his peace and at evening they inquire after his peace."

> *"When you enter into the house,*[13] *greet it. If the house is worthy, let your peace come upon it, but if it is not worthy, let your peace turn back to you." (vv. 12–13)*

Here Jesus tells the apostles that they are to offer blessings of peace upon those in whose homes they are invited to stay (the Hebrew idiom is that blessings "come upon" people and things, e.g.: "The giver of kindness — blessing will *come upon* him" [minor tractate *'Abot R. Nat.*, A, chap. 41]). He then says that if those living in these homes are "worthy," the blessings the apostles offer them will indeed fall upon them, but if they are not worthy, then the blessings that they offer them will instead fall back upon the apostles. That is, at no time will the blessings offered by the apostles ever be free of recipients, for which reason they need have no fear in offering them. The tone of Jesus' instructions to his apostles here is somewhat harsh and it will get harsher.

Jewish sources state that even if the recipient of another's hospitality does not return this hospitality with a blessing, still the giving of hospitality itself causes blessing to come upon the one who gives it.

"Whoever will not receive you, nor listen to what you say, shake the dust from your feet when you leave that house or that city." (v. 14)

Isaiah 52:2 also speaks of the shaking off of dust, only here it is God who commands Jerusalem to do this: "Shake yourself from the dust; be quick and sit down, O Jerusalem. Free yourself from the shackles of your neck, O captive daughter of Zion." The point here is that in shaking itself free of the dust Jerusalem is at last freeing itself from its period of captivity in Babylon so that it can return in freedom to its rightful home. So too are the apostles to free themselves from the oppressive atmosphere of hostile cities.

"'Amen,' I say to you, it shall be more bearable for the land of Sodom and Gomorrah on the day of judgment than for that city." (v. 15)

In having Jesus declare that the punishment awaiting those who reject his apostles is to be far worse than the sulphur and fire that God rained down on Sodom and Gomorrah (Gen. 19:24), Matthew makes plain his antipathy for the Jews who rejected him and his movement. According to the Rabbis, the chief sin of the people of Sodom and Gomorrah was their inhospitality to strangers (*b. Sanh.* 109a [see also *Gen. Rab.* 49:6]).

"Look, I am sending you out like sheep in the midst of wolves, so be cunning as serpents and pure as doves." (v. 16)

Matthew's language reporting Jesus' instructions to his disciples here to be both "cunning as serpents" and "pure as doves" is likely of Jewish origin. A tradition in Song of Songs Rab. 2:30 tells us that in commenting on Song of Songs 2:14 Rabbi Yehuda remarked, in the name of Rabbi Simon: "God said to Israel: In respect to me, 'be' [text emended from 'they are']14 pure as doves but with the nations of the world ['be'] cunning as serpents."

"Be on guard against people, for they will hand you over to councils, and they will whip you in their assemblies." (v. 17)

The councils (*synhedria*) are the Jewish courts. It would seem that Matthew presumes here that the Jews would forbid anyone to preach Christian doctrines in public. As I say, it is probable that by the time Matthew was writing his Gospel the split between the Christian and Jewish communities had occurred. Moreover by this time the Christians understood the Torah to be antiquated and had replaced its teachings with their own.

It may be that "assemblies" here refers to actual synagogues, and perhaps it was the case that when floggings were carried out — and this by the designated official known as the *hazan hakenesset* (*m. Mak.* 3:12) — they were carried out adjacent to the synagogues. Those flogged in public were those who had transgressed laws that concerned the well-being of the community, whether from an internal (transgression of law concerning Jewish matters only) or external (transgression of laws meant to safeguard coexistence with Rome) point of view. The courts decided if one was guilty of a breach; they would also decide the punishment to be administered. If the punishment was public flogging, then the courts would also decide the number of lashes to be administered (in any case, never more than thirty-nine). It is unlikely that in the time of Jesus any legislation existed pertaining to those in his movement for which flogging was the punishment, since Christian doctrine had yet to be formulated, though there may well have been legislation that, broadly speaking, forbade anyone to incite crowds against Rome (especially by predicting that a Davidic king had come to overthrow the empire). It is more reasonable to assume that Jesus' warning to his disciples here represents an anachronism, in that it speaks of the dangers that Christian missionaries faced in Matthew's day rather than in Jesus' day.

> *"You will be led before rulers and kings for my sake, as a witness to them and to the Gentiles." (v. 18)*

During the time of Matthew, we might suspect that Rome treated Christian missionaries somewhat harshly. This is so in general at a slightly later period judging from the Pliny-Trajan correspondence, this is dated c. 110–111, a little later than Matthew. Tacitus mentions Nero's persecution in Rome in 64 that was sporadic and local.[15] It may well be that some of those who were accused by Rome of being Christian at that time willingly died for their faith.

Behind a number of verses in this chapter lie texts from Isaiah 51–52. We have seen that behind verse 16 lies Isa. 52:2. Behind both this and the previous verse lies Isa. 51:7: "Listen to me, you who know righteousness, the people in whose heart is My law; have no fear of the scorn of people, nor should you fear their abuse."

"But when they hand you over, do not worry about how you should speak or what you should speak about; for what you should say will be given to you in that hour." (v. 19)

Likely behind this verse lies Isa. 52:15: "So shall He sprinkle many nations; the kings shall shut their mouths at Him. For that which had not been told them shall they see, and that which they had not heard shall they consider."

"For it is not you who are speaking, but the spirit of your Father who is speaking in you." (v. 20)

That the spirit of God speaks through another is often commented on in the rabbinic literature. For instance, a text from the *Mekhilta of Rabbi Yishmael* to Exod. 19:19 *(bahodesh, yitro* 4) states that Rabbi Akiva said to Rabbi Eliezer:

> *Vadai* (in the realm of the mysterious *absolute*),[16] the matter is such that the Torah reports that "Moses would speak [and it would be God answering in the voice (Exod. 19:19)]." The point is taught that God placed his strength and power in Moses and God would support him with His/his voice. And with the very melody that Moses would hear in Him/him, he would inform Israel.

Another relevant text, this one from *Midrash Aggada* (ed. Buber), Num. 24:2, says of the evil Balaam: "'And *the spirit of God* was upon him (Num. 24:2)' — this refers to *the Holy Spirit* that fell into his mouth and said all the words that Balaam spoke."

"A brother will hand over brother to death and a father his child, and children will rebel against parents and kill them." (v. 21)

See further Matt. 10:35–36, where Jesus says that these betrayals will in fact be his doing. This text flies in the face of the report that John the Baptist was to fulfill the role of Elijah, who before "the great and terrible day of the Lord" was to come so that he could unite fathers with their sons and sons with their fathers (Mal. 4:5). Rather, it seems to indicate the utter depravity of that generation, which will be the last before the Messiah comes.

A text from *m. Soṭah* 9:15 confirms that among the Rabbis too it was believed that the period before the coming of the Messiah was to be marked by depravity and corruption.

> In the footsteps of the Messiah, arrogance will increase...the border people will wander from city to city and none will show them compassion; the wisdom of authors will stink; sin-fearing people will be detested; truth will be missing;

young men will humiliate the elderly; the elderly will stand while the young sit; sons will revile their fathers; daughters will strike their mothers, brides will strike their mothers-in-law; and a man's enemies will take over his house. The face of the generation is like the face of a dog! Sons have no shame in front of their fathers. And so, on whom do we depend? — Only upon our Father in heaven.

"You will be hated by all on account of my name, but he who endures
to the end, this one will be saved." (v. 22)

That certain motifs from Isaiah 51–52 lie behind this section of the chapter does not mean for Matthew that the Second Isaiah's prophecies are now being fulfilled. Matthew does not offer a list of events here, each of which must come to pass before the end-time can begin. Rather the art of storytelling requires him to describe the degenerate nature of the time just before the end, with the motifs from Isaiah functioning somewhat like background music does in a film, enhancing the mood of the scene. Lying behind this and also, perhaps, the next verse is Isa. 52:5: "'Now therefore, what have I here,' says the Lord, 'that My people are taken away for nothing? They that rule over them make them to howl, says the Lord,' and My name continually every day is blasphemed.'"

"When they persecute you in this city, flee to the other. 'Amen,' I say to
you, you will not have completed all the cities of Israel before the Son
of Man comes." (v. 23)

The implication here is that no matter what city or town they enter, Jesus' disciples will almost certainly be rejected. Be that as it may, before they can be rejected for a final time Jesus in his capacity as the Son of Man will arrive to usher in the new kingdom, and save his apostles thereby.

The prophet Malachi foresaw that on the day of the coming of the Lord, God would judge, among others, those who had refused to offer aid to travelers: "And I have drawn near to you for judgment, And I have been a witness, Making haste against…those turning aside a sojourner, And who fear Me not" (3:6).

"A student is not above his teacher, nor a slave above his master. It
is sufficient for a student to be like his teacher, and the slave like his
master. If they call the master of the house 'Beelzebub,' how much more
will [they so slander] the members of his household!" (vv. 24–25)

The members of the household (Heb., *bnei bayit*; see Gen. 15:3) are the servants, the slaves, and the attendants. "It is sufficient for a slave to be like his master" was a popular saying that appears over a dozen times in the rabbinic literature (Sipra Lev. [parashat 3] *Behar* ch. 4, *b. Ber.* 58b, *Gen. Rab.* 49:2 [ed. Theodor-Albeck], as well as the near parallels in. *Exod. Rab.* 42:5, and *Tanh. Gen.* (*lekh lekha*) 23). Here Jesus uses this saying, but in the form of a well-known legal argument ("sufficient" meaning "ample" for legal argument). Technically the argument is called, literally, "an argument of sufficiency to discover an unknown premise that will be clarified from a known premise" (in Heb., *dayo lavo min hadin lihiot kenidon*). A tradition from *Sipra Baraita de Rabbi Yishmael* 1:3 (and *b. B. Bat.* 111a) shows us how the argument was used by the Rabbis:

> How should we apply the principle of *kol vehomer*?[17] [We need to consider] *"And God said to Moses: If her father had spat in her face* [an exaggerated way of saying if a woman's father was totally annoyed with her behavior] *would she not carry her shame for 7 days?"* (Num. 12:14a). All the more if the Shekhinah was totally annoyed with her should she not be locked away for 14 days? [But God indicated to Moses] that conclusions based on comparing punishments of greater and lesser cases are sufficiently cogent to warrant punishments no more severe than those applied to the original cases [and so he told him] *Let* [Miriam] *be shut out of the camp seven days and afterwards she may be brought back* (Num. 12:14b).[18]

The logic of what Jesus says in Matt. 10:24–25 is as follows: because it is beyond any reasonable expectation that a student should ever be shown more respect than his teacher, then if it should happen that a teacher is besmirched, it can only follow that his student is besmirched the more. The limit of least respect shown to a teacher marks the limit of greatest respect that could ever be shown to his student. That is, the sufficient limit of least respect shown the teacher is also the limit of greatest respect shown the student. And so what Jesus means to says here is: "They are referring to me, your superior, [at their maximum level of insult] as 'Beelzebub' [see also 12:25], therefore how much more will they call you that (at the minimum level of insult)."

"So do not fear them, for nothing is hidden which will not be uncovered, nor secret which will not be known." (v. 26)

In the end all will be revealed, according to Matthew's report of Jesus' words. Again, a text from Isaiah 51–52 lies behind this verse, in this case 52:10: "The Lord has made bare His holy arm in the eyes of all the nations; and all the ends of the earth shall see the salvation of our God."

"What I say to you in the darkness, speak in the light, and what you hear whispered in your ear, proclaim upon the rooftops." (v. 27)

According to a tradition in *y. Beṣah* 1:11 (see also *Gen. Rab.* 3:4), some Rabbis actually did the opposite; for in this tradition we are told that Rabbi Yudan said: "Just as I received (the teaching) in a whisper (assuming it to be esoteric) so I transmit it in a whisper." But this certainly was not always the case. A tradition preserved in *b. Ber.* 22a informs us that Nachum of Gamzo whispered a teaching to Rabbi Akiva, who whispered it to Shimon ben Azzai, who then went and taught it aloud in the market place.

"Do not fear those who kill the body, but they are not able to kill the soul. Fear rather the one who is able to destroy both the soul and the body in Gehenna." (v. 28)

The one who is able to destroy both the soul and the body in Gehenna is, of course, "the evil one" — "Satan."

"Aren't two sparrows sold for a mere assarion? But not one of them falls to the earth apart from your Father." (v. 29)

Though sparrows are of little worth, still God watches over them, Jesus says. The same point is made in a tradition preserved in *y. Šeb.* 9:1, in which we are told of Rabbi Shimon bar Yohai's flight from the Romans. According to this tradition, Rabbi Shimon while in flight found a cave in which to hide. Finally deeming that it was safe to come out he

> saw a hunter of birds spread a trap [to catch them]. [When he spread it for the first time] he heard a heavenly voice saying *demos*, "reprieved!" and the bird escaped. [When he spread the net for a second time he heard a heavenly voice say *spekula*, "sentenced," and the bird was caught.]

The conclusion of this story is found at verse 31, where Jesus too concludes what he has to say about sparrows and their worth in relation to human beings.

"And even all the hairs of your head are numbered." (v. 30)

A brief aside in which Jesus makes clear that God is attentive to even the very minutest of things in the world. A tradition in *b. B. Bat.* 16a states that God provides each hair with its own follicle for a specific reason.

"So do not fear. You are more valuable than many sparrows."
(v. 31)

The tradition concerning Rabbi Simon from *y. Šeb.* continues like this: He thought—if a mere bird, unless heaven will it, cannot be trapped—how much more a man [who is infinitely more valuable] cannot be trapped.

"Everyone who acknowledges me before people, that one will I acknowledge before my heavenly Father. But whoever denies me before people, that one will I deny before my heavenly Father. Do not think that I came to cause peace upon the earth. I did not come to cause peace but a sword." (vv. 32–34)

The Rabbis too spoke of great wars that were to occur just before the coming of the Messiah (*b. Sanh.* 97a). What Jesus says in verse 34, and then in verses 35–39, is difficult to reconcile with what he says elsewhere about love and forgiveness. If the sayings of Jesus in these verses are not original to him, we can only wonder who would have put them in his mouth.

For I have come to turn a son against his father, and a daughter against her mother, and a daughter-in-law against her mother-in-law. And a person's enemies will be the members of his own family (Micah 7:6). (vv. 35–36)

"For the son dishonors his father, the daughter rises up against her mother, the daughter-in-law against her mother-in-law, and a person's enemies are those of his household" (Micah 7:6). Scripture speaks of the breakdown of society, with the younger generation sassing the older, as a horrible evil, but even so, one can trust God. Rabbinic literature expanded the theme of the same social breakdown in portraying the last generation before the arrival of the Messiah. For example, the widely cited *baraita* mentioned in *b. Sanh.* 97a ("the generation when Son of David comes") and the text found in *m. Soṭah* 9:15 show extreme reversals and cite Micah 7:6. But these passages show us a society so broken that only the Messiah can fix it. Perhaps Rabbis are describing their own generation and holding out some hope. The Gospel, on the other hand, shows us it is Jesus himself who will break down society and all its social relationships. It is instructive to consider these societal reversals as signaling losses of old structures and the creation of the new society in the coming kingdom, a purposely vague notion that can only be known on its arrival.

Liminal periods, perceived as a period between one mode of being and another, are often marked by social breakdown such as the reversing of structures of hierarchy. In his "Liminality and Communitas," Turner points out. "recognizably in the liminal period, is of society as an unstructured or rudimentarily structured and relatively undifferentiated *comitatus*, community, or even communion of equal individuals who submit together to the general authority of the ritual elders."[19]

"Whoever loves father or mother more than me is not worthy of me, and the one who loves his son or his daughter more than me is not worthy of me. And whoever does not take his cross and follow me, he is not worthy of me." (vv. 37–38)

Gen. Rab. 56 to Gen. 22:6 informs us that the phrase "taking one's cross" was a known idiom and so independent of any association with the crucifixion; therefore it could, perhaps, have been used by Jesus without reference to it.

"The one who finds his life will destroy it, and the one who destroys his life on my account will find it." (v. 39)

Paradox was very much a style of the early teachers. For instance, a tradition in *b. Tamid* 32a tells us that they asked: "What shall a man do that he may live? — Kill himself. And what shall a man do that he may die? — Give himself life." And a tradition from *m. 'Abot* 1:13 says that the "one who extends his name destroys his name."

"The one who welcomes you welcomes me, and the one who welcomes me welcomes the one who sent me." (v. 40)

In a dozen places or more the Talmuds make the claim that the messenger is the equivalent of the one who sent him. In the *Mekhilta of Rabbi Yishmael* to Exod. 12:6 the Rabbis, in discussing the commandment in this verse, which states that the whole assembly of Israel is to slaughter the lamb chosen for the Passover sacrifice, wonder how this can be done. Is literally everyone in the community supposed to participate in the slaughter? What the Rabbis conclude is that the purpose of the commandment in the verse is to make known to the community that one's messenger is equivalent to the one — or in this case to the many — who sent him. And so, when the slaughterer in slaughtering the lamb keeps in mind that he is performing the sacrifice in the name of the many who sent him, the many also receive the reward for having fulfilled the command that "they shall slaughter it" (Exod. 12:6).

> *"He that receives a prophet in the name of a prophet, shall receive*
> *a prophet's reward; and he that receives a righteous man in the name*
> *of a righteous man, shall receive a righteous man's reward." (v. 41)*

Whoever serves the prophet or the righteous man becomes like the one he serves and receives the same reward. For without receiving help, both the prophet and the righteous man would have to concern themselves with earning their own livelihoods instead of serving God. It is for this reason that those who help them deserve to receive the rewards of either the prophet or the righteous man, as the case may be. A tradition from *Gen. Rab.* 72:5 is of interest here:

> From whom did Issachar manage to gain glory in Torah learning? From Zebulun. The latter worked in business and supported Issachar who was a great scholar. …Hence when Moses came to bless the tribes [with their deserved rewards] he gave precedence to Zebulun (the generous donor) over Issachar (for enabling the scholar).

> *"And whosoever shall give to drink to one of these little ones a cup of*
> *cold [water] only in the name of a disciple, verily I say unto you, he*
> *shall in no wise lose his reward." (v. 42)*

Whoever gives a drink to a student with the intent to help the student learn better, that one shall share the student's reward.

NOTES

1   It should be pointed out, however, that although there is this remarkable degree of correspondence between texts in the Gospel and rabbinic literatures, nevertheless with respect to certain matters there are significant differences between what Jesus and the Rabbis say about them. For instance, Jesus' point of view concerning divorce as it is presented in the Gospels is not that of certain Rabbis of the School of Shammai as is sometimes claimed. For whereas concerning divorce these Shammai-school Rabbis show a complete adherence to the Mosaic law, Jesus makes it clear that for him the Mosaic law concerning divorce is too lenient (19:3–9; 5:31). As well, it is not the case that Jesus' statement in the Gospels that the "Son of Man is lord of the Sabbath"

(Matt. 12:8; Mark 2:28) means the same as the rabbinic statement, *b. Yoma 85b*, to the effect that "the Sabbath was made for man, not man for the Sabbath." In fact these sayings have nothing in common at all.

2   See the *Review of Biblical Literature* 22 (August 2007).

3   See Eco, *The Limits of Interpretation*, 21.

4   In the commentary proper to this chapter I shall point out many more remarkable correspondences between Gospel texts and texts that come from the later — in some cases much later — rabbinic literature.

5   1 Macc. 14:28 may also be suggesting that the synagogue assembly can refer to a court rather than a prayer hall: "At Saramel, in the great congregation of the priests, and people, and rulers of the nation, and Elders of the country, were these things notified unto us." Also see R. A. Horsley, "Synagogues in the Galilee and the Gospels," in *Evolution of the Synagogue in the Diaspora*, ed. H. C. Kee and L. H. Cohick (Harrisburg, Pa.: Trinity Press International, 1999), 96ff.

6   See the commentary of Rashi to *b. Ker.* 3a and *b. Sanh.* 65a.

7   See Epstein, "Glosses Babylo-arame'ennes," 33; also Gruenwald, *Apocalyptic and Merkabah Mysticism*, 6 n. 135. In *b. Ker.* 3a and *b. Sanh.* 65a Abaye says: "in order to enchant him (the demon)." I suggest *qatar* means to recite an incantation of an angelic (or demonic) name, equivalent to *amar shem*, in order to accomplish a supernatural feat. My proof derives from a comparison of the text of paragraph 20 in "Ma'aseh Merkabah" (in Scholem, *Jewish Gnosticism, Merkabah Mysticism, and Talmudic Tradition*, 111) — "QATAR [= enchanted] *a crown for his master that it might rise*" — and the text in *b. Ḥag.* 13b: "AMAR SHEM [= uttered a divine name] *for the crown that it might go and rest.*"

8   The Greek says "*ekballow*," "force out," "drive out."

9   It once happened that Rabbi Elazar ben Dama was bitten by a snake, and Jacob of Kefar Sama came to heal him in the name of Jesus son of Pantera, but Rabbi Yishmael did not allow him. He said to him: 'You are not permitted, Ben Dama!' He said to him: 'I shall bring you proof that he may heal me', but he did not have time to bring the proof before he dropped dead. Said Rabbi Yishmael: 'Happy are you, Ben Dama, for you have expired in peace, and you did not break down the hedge erected by sages. For whoever breaks down the hedge erected by sages eventually suffers punishment, as it is said: "He who breaks down a hedge is bitten by a snake"' (Eccles. 10:8). (Translation from Schremer, "What Is Midrash Torah?")

10   Possibly the Hebrew name "Lev" — "heart" — which was a common name in the Middle Ages and later but not attested in the early sources.

11   For the Zealots, see Josephus' *Ant.* 18:23ff.

12   See chapter 2, n. 1, and also see chap. 12, verses 15–17 in this book.

13   That is, the house of your hosts.

14   The simple emendation allows us to understand the preface of the statement — God is commanding Israel. I conjecture *Heh-vav-yodh* (be) was confused for *heh-mem* (they) by a careless scribe.

15   Tacitus' *Ann.* 15:44 (composed c. 116) relates: "Consequently, to get rid of the report, Nero fastened the guilt and inflicted the most exquisite tortures on a class hated for their abominations, called Christians by the populace. Christus, from whom the name had its origin, suffered the extreme penalty during the reign of Tiberius at the hands of one of our procurators, Pontius Pilatus, and a most mischievous superstition, thus checked for the moment, again broke out not only in Judaea, the first source of the evil, but even in Rome, where all things hideous and shameful from every part of the world find their center and become popular. Accordingly, an arrest was first made of all who pleaded guilty; then, upon their information, an immense multitude was convicted, not so much of the crime of firing the city, as of hatred against mankind. Mockery of every sort was added to their deaths."

16   The word *vadai* literally means "assuredly" and it may signal that the meaning of the statement that follows it refers to a supernatural event. This usage is found in the Zohar, but it appears to operate in this sense in the Tannaitic literature as well. For its use in Zohar, see Matt, "New Ancient Words," 203–4.

17   *Kal vehomer* (literally "light and heavy") arguments draw conclusions based on the effects of items which are quantitatively different. A leniency permitted in a "heavy" (e.g., capital) case can often be argued to be at least equally permitted in a "light" (civil) case.

18   *B. B. Bat,* 111a and its commentators analyze the problems associated with this statement.

19   Turner, "Liminality and Communitas," 96.

CHAPTER ELEVEN

INTRODUCTION

This chapter shows us that the previous chapters have been designed to allow the argument that Jesus has been teaching and performing miracles for the Jews with little appreciation from them. From prison John the Baptist now sends word to Jesus asking him if he is really the promised redeemer. Obviously, both Jesus' own failures to gain wide acceptance and John's disappointing career, ending in imprisonment and imminent execution, are cause for concern. By way of the words of a children's chant in a certain kind of parable that he tells, Jesus shows the Jews that they really do not know what a redeemer figure looks like. The Jews find every reason to ignore the possibility that either Jesus or John might be the figure the prophets and all Jewish teachers have been talking about for hundreds of years.

Curiously, Matthew says here on the one hand that, in contrast to pagans, all Jews are irredeemable. Yet further along in the chapter, on the other hand, amidst what are perhaps veiled references to the haughtiness of the Pharisees, he also says that even they are excused from their failure to recognize Jesus as God's servant, since God has in fact withheld from them his true identity. In the end, however, Matthew will come down on the side of the pagans, declaring that they will become the true believers, once they learn about Jesus. "Go, therefore, make disciples of all the nations" (Matt. 28:19).[1]

In this chapter reference is also made to Wisdom or Logos theology, a Middle Platonist/Stoic mystical view of the world based on the figure of a demiurge or agent creator. In this theology Wisdom/Logos (*Wisdom of Solomon* already presupposes the link) has two associates or Powers (to use Philo's terms). Depending upon the text of Matthew, either the acts of Wisdom are vindicated (i.e., Jesus as Wisdom), or the Children/Powers of Wisdom are justified (i.e., John and Jesus). The Powers seem to be related to the various names of God in Scripture (Y-H-W-H and E-L-O-H-I-M). The Rabbis saw these powers or "*midot*" as either benevolent or strict. Thus chapter 11 tells us that Jesus appeared to the people as a friend of sinners (as indeed mercy is), while John appeared to the people as just the opposite (as sternness is).

Breaking with my usual pattern, I refrain in this introduction from discussing the complex exegetical problems (including speculations on the redaction of certain passages) involved in the understanding of this chapter. Rather, I will discuss these matters at length in the commentary proper to avoid unnecessary repetitions.

> *When Jesus finished commanding his twelve students, he left from there to teach and to proclaim in their cities.* (v. 1)

Chapter 11 deals with Jesus' failure to appeal to the Jewish people, despite his almost unceasing activity as a preacher and healer among them. In this chapter we also see Jesus chastise the crowds for failing to recognize John's eschatological role and so, by implication, his own.

> *John, hearing in prison about the deeds of the Christ sent word through his students.* (v. 2)

According to Josephus, John was arrested by Herod Antipas for gathering crowds about him and preaching to them of the imminent arrival of the Kingdom of God. Having heard of "the deeds of Christ" while in prison, John sends a number of his disciples to Jesus to inquire of him concerning what role he is to play in the coming final act of history. The reason John sends more than one disciple to Jesus is twofold: first, it was not the custom in those days for people to travel alone; second, so that there would be more than one witness to report back to John what Jesus says in response to his query (Matt. 11:4).

According to the overwhelming testimony of manuscript evidence, there is no doubt that for Matthew Jesus was the messianic redeemer, as is made plain here in his reference to Jesus as "the Christ," that is, "the Messiah" though it is true that in some early manuscripts, at least according to the commentaries of Matthew by both Origen and Chrysostom, "the deeds of Jesus" is read here, and not "the deeds of Christ."

> *And said to him, "Are you the one who is coming, or shall we expect*
> *another?" (v. 3)*

John wonders if the reports he has heard about Jesus indicate that he is the Messiah. He refers here to the expected Messiah as "the one who is coming," echoing what is said of the divine messenger in Mal 3:1.

> *Jesus answered them, "Go, tell John what you hear and see. The blind*
> *receive sight, and the lame walk, the plagued with leprosy are cleansed,*
> *and the deaf hear, and the dead are raised, and the poor have good*
> *news proclaimed to them … " (vv. 4–5)*

Without saying, "Yes, I am the one" to John's disciples in response to John's question concerning whether or not he is the Messiah, Jesus offers testimony with which John will only be able to conclude that he is indeed the one. Though Jesus is reluctant here to reveal his divine/messianic identity (yet he has already revealed it over and again by offering signs and proofs), he overcomes this reluctance in verse 27.

Up to this point in the Gospel, Jesus has performed all the miracles about which he speaks here, save the restoration of hearing to the deaf, though a story that tells of him doing this occurs in Mark 7:31–37 (it is clear that the source that both Matthew and Luke used here [7:22] contained traditions known to Mark). He has cleansed a leper (8:2–3), cured a paralytic (9:6), resurrected the dead (9:25), and given sight to the blind (9:27). This list of miracles, which is almost word for word the same in Luke 7:22, also corresponds, at least in part, to the lists of miracles that also appear in a number of Jewish sources — the Hebrew Bible, documents from Qumran, and rabbinic prayers. In these other sources the miracles are said not only to be divine attributes of mercy, but they are also related to the period of the final redemption. The similarity of the lists that appear in these other sources suggests that Matthew is drawing on a pan-Israelite tradition here.

What follows are excerpts from these other Jewish sources, each of which in speaking of the good news of the redemption includes a list of at least some of the miracles Jesus speaks of here, though only the document from Qumran includes the statement concerning the proclaiming of the "good news to the meek [i.e., the poor]."

Say to those who have an anxious heart... "He will come and save you." Then the *eyes of the blind shall be opened,* and the *ears of the deaf unstopped;* then *shall the lame man leap* like a deer, and the tongue of the mute sing for joy... but the redeemed shall walk there. And the *ransomed* of the Lord shall return and come to Zion with singing; everlasting joy shall be upon their heads they shall obtain gladness and joy, and sorrow and sighing shall flee away (Isa. 35:4–6, 9–10).

[The Lord...] executes justice for the oppressed, *gives food to the hungry.* The Lord *sets prisoners free;* the Lord gives *sight to the blind.* The Lord *raises up those who are bowed down,* the Lord loves the righteous. The Lord *protects the stranger,* sustains the orphan and the widow, but thwarts the way of the wicked. The Lord shall reign forever your God, Zion, through all generations! (Ps. 146:7–10).

[F]reeing prisoners, *giving sight to the blind, straightening out the twisted.* Ever shall I cling to those who hope. In his mercy he will jud[ge,] and from no-one shall the fruit [of] good [deeds] be delayed, and the Lord will perform marvelous acts such as have not existed, just as he sa[id], for *he will heal the badly wounded* and *will make the dead live,*[2] he will proclaim good news to the meek, give lavishly [to the need]y, lead the exiled *and enrich the hungry* [4Q521 2 II 8–13 (DSST 394)].

[The Great God...] remembering the pious deeds of the forefathers, who, in love, will bring a redeemer to their children's children for his Name's sake. ...You, O Lord, are mighty, *the reviver of the dead,* You perform great deeds to save the world, sustaining the living with much loving-kindness, *supporting the fallen,* and *healing the sick, freeing the prisoners,* and keeping your promise to them that sleep in the dust. Who is like You, master of mighty deeds, and who resembles You who is the king, who brings death but resurrects the dead, and causes salvation to spring forth? [Opening lines of the central rabbinic prayer of Eighteen Blessings].

"And blessed is the one who finds no offense in me." (v. 6)

While some might think that the miracles Jesus has performed are not his work but rather the work of demons and/or dark powers, he refutes this by saying that providence is on the side of those who resist such thinking. He is not a charlatan, nor is he allied with demons. It is understandable, however, that many would take offense at Jesus who, while performing miracles as a holy man, also kept company with those of ill repute.

As they were leaving, Jesus began to speak to the crowds about John: "What did you go out to the desert to look for? A reed shaken by the wind? So what did you come to see? A person dressed in soft things? Look, the ones who wear the soft things are in the houses of kings. So what did you come to see? A prophet? I say to you, Yes, and more than a prophet." (vv. 7–9)

Three times in this text Jesus asks the crowd what they have come out to see. After asking the first time, he dismisses the charge that John is in any way aligned with such haughty figures as the Pharisees. Of interest here is a tradition in minor tractate *Derekh Eretz* 7:1 (other texts 8.1), in which it is said that the one who is humble in spirit is like the soft reed which bends with the blowing wind. He is not like the hard reed which, because it lacks pliability, does not bend in the wind but is shaken by it, and so does not endure as it encounters what is greater than itself.

After asking the crowd what they have come out to see the second time, Jesus dismisses the charge that John is in any way aligned with royalty. How could this be, for he is humble, a man of plain dress? Finally, after asking the third time, Jesus states that John is that messenger who precedes the Messiah, that messenger of whom Malachi speaks. Indeed, he is Elijah the prophet (though again he does not yet clearly state this), whose purpose is to be the forerunner of the Messiah. In fact, in his new incarnation as the Baptist, Elijah is now greater than any prophet; he is the harbinger of the messianic kingdom.[3]

Properly speaking, this passage continues at verse 14. The following verse provides the proof that Elijah was indeed to be forerunner of the Messiah, a claim we have dealt with at length in chapter 2. Verse 10 also offers a further explanation of John's role in relation to Jesus, for at least part of it is drawn from Exod. 23:20, in which God promised Moses that a messenger would accompany the Israelites into the promised land a full forty years before it happened.

"This is the one concerning whom it has been written, 'Look, I am sending my messenger before your face [Exod. 23:20], who will prepare your way before you' [Mal 3:1]." (v. 10)

The introductory formula here is rare, though it also occurs in the Lucan parallel (7:27). In fact, it appears to be a rendering of two formulae, one in Hebrew, *zehu [mah] shekatuv,* and the other in Aramaic, *al da kativ.* This would explain its unusual form: "This is the one (Heb., *zehu*) concerning whom (Aram., *al da*) it has been written." The purpose of the formula is to summarize a list of claims by appealing to the authority of Scripture (Exod. 23 and Malachi 3). Jesus' curing of the blind and the sick, etc. (vv. 5–6a), testifies to his being the Son of Man (see below the comments to v. 19); while it is John who is to prepare the way for Jesus. It is likely Jesus who is meant to be speaking here rather than the narrator, and it says in verse 7 that he is speaking about John.

With regard to the quotation itself, lying behind it are parts of two biblical texts — Exod. 23:20, as I say, and Mal. 3:1. "This is what is written, *'Look, I am sending my messenger before your face'* [Exod. 23:20]" (which is identical to the reading in the LXX except LXX begins with "And"), which is then followed by a proof of the claim that John is greater than the prophets. "Concerning this it is written, *'He will prepare the way before me'* [Mal. 3:1]." That is, John will prepare the way for Jesus. In the process of editing, the two texts were conflated into a single text (which looks very much like the whole of Mal. 3:1). The texts that have been conflated here anticipate the identification of Wisdom's children in verse 19. To see that in this text two introductory formulae have been conflated into one, as have also two proof-texts, provides a much more elegant solution to the problems inherent in this verse than those proposed by J. B. De Young.[4]

> *"'Amen,' I say to you: No one has arisen from those born of women*
> *greater than John the Baptist. But the least in the Kingdom of Heaven*
> *is greater than he." (v. 11)*

In a tradition in *b. Šabb.* 88b, it is said that once Moses arrived in heaven to receive the Torah, the angels complained to God that no one born of a woman (in relation to them a sign of inferiority) should ever be found among them. Almost always when the Rabbis use the phrase "born of a woman," they use it to contrast angels with someone of the stature of either Moses or Jacob.

I assume "Kingdom of Heaven" here refers to the actual experience of redemption and the ensuing witnessing of God's glory. Of interest here is the rabbinic claim that even the lowliest maidservant who witnessed the splitting of the Red Sea saw God (i.e., the Glory) in a way that the greatest of the prophets did not (*Mekhilta of Rabbi Shimon* 2:15 and parallels).

> *"From the days of John the Baptist until now the Kingdom of Heaven*
> *has suffered violence, and violent people besiege it." (v. 12)*

This text cannot logically be part of the narrative of Jesus' life, for John is still alive at this point in the Gospel story. It can, however, be seen as a kind of footnote concerning the Kingdom of Heaven. The liminal gap between the time of John's ministry, which inaugurated the expectations of the coming of the kingdom, and the time of the writing of the Gospel, by which time the kingdom had yet to arrive, troubled or confused many who were impatient for its arrival. The text likely refers to the events of 66–70 C.E., during which time numerous prophets and zealots in Israel were expecting God to actively intervene on behalf of Israel against Rome for the sake of its redemption. A tradition in *Song Rab.* 2 to *Song* 2:7 expands on a popular motif of those who failed to force the redemption through violent means (*dahku al haketz*) by naming them or their time periods. Both Matthew and the Rabbis saw such activity as being counterproductive and against the divine plan.

"for all the Prophets and the Law till John did prophesy" (v. 13)

The precise time of the arrival of the kingdom, and also the way in which it will be manifested once it has arrived, are unknown in this post-Johannine age. For according to Jesus, no prophet has ever foretold what one should expect at this time. A tradition in *b. Ber.* 34b points out that the prophets prophesied only up until the turbulent period of the Messiah (*yemot hamashiah*), which is to precede the future kingdom (*Olam ha-Ba*). After that no one knows, except God, what is to happen. The digression begun at verse 10 ends here and now we return to Jesus' discourse on the living John.

"and if you are willing to accept [it], he is Elijah who was to come" (v. 14)

While not everyone in the very early church accepted that John was an incarnation of Elijah (see John 1:21), Matthew certainly did.

"Whoever has ears should listen." (v. 15)

This phrase introduces a wisdom teaching that will take some effort to understand and Matthew uses it in connection with his parables (13:9, 13:43). Compare Prov. 22:17: "Direct your ears and listen to the sayings of the wise; apply your heart to what I teach."

Jesus now offers the teaching that lies at the heart of this chapter (vv. 15–20). Why is it that he and John have not succeeded in bringing about a change in the people of Israel as a whole, so that they repent for their sins? Using a rhetorical device known as a *mashal,* Jesus tries to explain why he and John have failed in this regard. A *mashal* is a type of allegory or parable used to compare actions of people involved in an often unusual or even extraordinary situation with the actions of the characters involved in a similar but much more mundane situation in the *mashal* itself. The purpose in telling the *mashal* is that, once the reasons for the behavior of the characters in the *mashal* are understood, the behavior of the people in the actual situation, and the reasons for it, also become clear. The *mashal* ends with an explanation concerning the relationship between the people involved in the actual situation and the characters spoken of in the *mashal*. This is known as the *nimshal*. Before we comment on the *mashal* in our Gospel text, let us first consider a *mashal* found in *b. Ber.* 11a, the purpose of which is to highlight the seemingly spiteful behavior of Rabbi Yishmael that so frustrates Rabbi Eleazar, who is telling it.[5]

> I shall give you a *mashal*: to what can this issue be compared? It is like someone who was told, "You have a beautifully grown beard," and this other replied "[Yuk] — Let it befall the razors." [Now the *nimshal*:] So too are you [Rabbi Yishmael], who, whenever I stood erect, you bent forward and whenever I bent forward you stood erect."

Finally, before we comment on the *mashal* here one more thing need be said. Matthew 11:15–20, in which the *mashal* is found, forms a complete unit. It also may well be a commentary on Deut. 32:4–5, for in this text too mention is made of a perverse generation. "He is the Rock, his *work* is perfect: for all his ways are judgment: a God of truth and without iniquity, just and right is he. It has acted corruptly with Him; their blemish is not *His sons'*, A generation perverse and crooked! they are a perverse and crooked *generation*."

> *"To what shall I compare this generation? It is like children sitting in the marketplaces who call out to each other. They say, 'We played the flute for you, but [you say this is abnormal, so] you did not dance; we sang a dirge, but [you say that is abnormal too, so] you did not mourn.'"*[6] *(vv. 16–17)*

The *mashal* Jesus uses here to explain the failure of himself and John with respect to their own "perverse" generation is confined to the behaviors illustrated in the sing-song words that children call out to each other in the market-places: "We played the flute for you...." The characters, actions, and setting of the *mashal* — the children's chant casts blame upon the merchants for ignoring the cues they have set up — are used by Jesus to compare the failures of himself and John in their ministries to a situation that, though similar, is much more mundane. The following verses illustrate this; in them is given the *nimshal,* or key to the meaning of the children's words.

> *"So [gar] John came neither eating nor drinking, and they say ['you (pl.) say' (Luke, 7:31)], 'He has a demon.'"* (v. 18)

John, as Matthew has already told us (3:4), was an ascetic living on locusts and wild honey. John behaves one way (dirgeful) and is belittled.

> *"The Son of Man came eating and drinking, and they say ['you (pl.) say' (Luke 7:31)], 'Look, a person who is a glutton and a drunkard, a friend of tax collectors and sinners.'"* (v. 19)

Jesus acts the opposite way and is belittled. Luke's "you say" makes much more sense in relation to the "*you* did not dance" and the "*you* did not mourn" of the children here. John came to stir up lament among the people but got no response from them, save the accusation that he was mad. Jesus came to play the flute, thereby announcing the good news that the world was on the edge of redemption, but, like John, he got no response from the people, save the accusation that he was a reprobate who kept bad company.

The *mashal* ends with Jesus' comment about Wisdom that makes plain that with it he means to critique his, and John's, generation. The *mashal* renders intelligible the behavior of those who do not respond to the message of Jesus. However that may be, in the end, because of this failure to respond, the people will be punished. The self-identification of Jesus as Son of Man reinforces his supernal status in the spiritual world. How ironic that he should be called a "glutton" and a reprobate by those he has come to serve.

> But Wisdom is declared righteous by her children [*teknon,* majority reading] / by her works [*ergon,* reading in Nestle-Aland edition].

If we look at Deut. 32:4–5 cited above, both "work(s)" and "children" are mentioned in it. In *nuce:* "his *work* is perfect"; and: "their blemish is not *His sons.*" It seems, then, that we have a true variant. Both "works" and "children" are equally plausible here and there is no way to decide on the better reading.

Wisdom, the *logos* or active element of the Godhead, is spoken of here as a designation of God's creative powers.[7] God created the world through the medium of "wisdom," which is akin to the platonic "demiurge." The divine activity both in the beginning-time and now in the end-time is referred to as "wisdom." Wisdom is also considered the maker of heaven and earth in some traditions in rabbinic thought. For example, in *Midr. Tanḥ. Gen.* (ed. Buber) 16, the Rabbis state:

> "These are the generations of the heavens and earth when they were created on the day the Lord God fashioned the earth and the heavens (Gen 2:4)" — which is explained by Prov. 3:19. "The Lord through Wisdom founded the earth and established the heavens with Understanding." So you find that through *Wisdom* the Holy One created the heavens and the earth.

The "children of the generation" of Jesus and John are doomed, for aside from the two of them it is made up largely of those who are not God's children. Only Jesus and John recognize that God is righteous and just and that his work is perfect. They also understand that, in spite of the contrariness of those of this generation, still redemption will come. Wisdom's "children" will be vindicated. Creation will find its completion. The respective missions of John and Jesus will end with the coming together of heaven and earth.

We again make note of the title "Son of Man" which, for the Rabbis, as I have previously said, refers to the angelic figure later known as "Metatron." This figure is mentioned in *b. Hag.* 15a, though the Talmud here absolutely rejects any thought of him as being a second god, which can perhaps mean that at some point he was thought of in this way. In his book *Kabbalah*, Scholem says of the Karaite scholar Jacob Qirqisani (flourished c. 930) that he was able to read in his version of the Talmud that Metatron was "the lesser YHVH."[8] *B. Sanh.* 38b understands that a reference is also made to Metatron in Exod. 23:21. According to the Rabbis, he is the "him" in whom God says in the verse that his name resides: "Be on your guard before him and obey his voice; do not be rebellious toward him, for he will not pardon your transgression, *since My name is in him.*" Note here that the Rabbis must also have seen that Metatron had the power to forgive sins, a power that Jesus also claimed for himself. In the same tradition from *b. Sanh.* 38b Rabbi Idith explains that in Exod. 24:1 it is written that God said to Moses, "Come up to *the Lord*, you and Aaron, Nadab and Abihu and seventy of the elders of Israel, and you shall worship at a distance," and not "Come up to *Me*," because it is actually Metatron who said this and not God. As well, the pseudepigraphic *Apocalypse of Abraham* says of the angelic figure Jahoel, whose attributes, according to Scholem, were later attributed to Metatron,[9] that he also "has the tetragrammaton in him." *B. Hag.* 15a, as we have seen, would have none of this. In this latter text, Metatron is said to be only a heavenly scribe with no real power of his own. It seems that "Sophia/Wisdom" typologies stood behind the image of Metatron (perhaps *meta-thronios*, the one who sits next to the Throne of Glory).[10]

> *Then he began to reprimand the cities in which most of his miracles had occurred, because they did not repent. (v. 20)*

This verse ends the unit in which Jesus' failure to effect change among his hearers so that they might repent in preparation for the end is emphasized. Repentance is the dominant theme in John's ministry, and it carries over into this very pro-John section of the Gospel. In speaking of his miracles here, Jesus speaks of that about him which above all demonstrates his divine election.

> *"Woe to you, Chorazin! Woe to you, Bethsaida! Because if in Tyre and Sidon had been done the mighty works that were done in you, long ago in sackcloth and ashes they would have repented; but I say to you, to Tyre and Sidon it shall be more tolerable in a day of judgment than for you." (vv. 21–22)*

Here Jesus makes final condemnation against Israel while at the same time offering praise of the Gentiles. As he says, were even the most wicked in the pagans cities of Tyre and Sidon (Joel 3:4–7) to have witnessed the miracles of Jesus that the Jews of Chorazin and Bethsaida have witnessed, then, unlike the Jews in these cities, they would certainly have repented. It is for this reason that in the end the Gentiles will be saved but the Jews will not. According to the Rabbis, only Jonah prophesied among the people of the city of Nineveh; they then donned sackcloth and repented (Jonah 3:3–8). But many prophets came to the Jews and they would not repent so then they were sent into exile (*Midrash Eicha Rab.,* Proem 31) According to Matthew, Jesus, like the midrash, had no reservations about condemning the Jews for by their works they condemned the Jews. For Matthew, Jesus' mission has proved to be a failure not only among the Jewish priestly and political elite, but among all Jews. In the end, as far as Matthew is concerned, Jesus will find his followers from among the Nations.

> *"And you, Capernaum, will you be raised up? Unto Hades shall you be brought down, because if in Sodom had been done the mighty works that were done in you, it would still be standing to this day." (v. 23)*

Even the sinful people of Sodom would have been moved to repent had they witnessed the miracles Jesus performed in Capernaum, but the Jews of that city, because they have failed to take notice of them, are, according to Jesus, even more reprehensible than the sinners of Sodom, for which reason their punishment will be eternal. That is, even the notorious people of Sodom will be judged more favorably in the end than the people of Capernaum.

> *"but I say to you, to the land of Sodom it shall be more tolerable in a day of judgment than to you." (v. 24)*

The source, which both Matthew and Luke shared and which contained these several verses (11:20–24 in Matthew; 10:13–15 in Luke), gives us the words of a gentile polemicist at his most vitriolic, who also knows that in Tyre and Sidon there are many who have become followers of Jesus. In fact, Jesus and John did not fail in their mission to the Jews; it was rather that their mission to them was impossible. It is not they who should be blamed for their lack of success: it is the Jews who are to blame. The polemic in these several verses is unmistakable. To my mind it remains very doubtful that any Jew (save perhaps a Jew-turned-Gentile) could have written these words.

> *At that time Jesus, answering, said, "I do confess [thank] to You, O Father, Lord of the heavens and of the earth, that you concealed these things from wise and understanding ones, and did reveal them to babes." (v. 25)*

It is likely that this section is dependent on a Semitic original, and so a few comments on the semiticisms here, and when elsewhere they appear, are in order. "Answering" (Heb., *"anah"*) really means "to praise" (*"anta"* means "praise," "song" — see *Tanḥ. Gen.* [ed. Buber], *Vayera* 22). Also, rather than "I do confess," this phrase in the original probably read something more like *Modim anaḥnu lakh*, as in the following text from *y. Ber.* 1:1: "We thank you, O Master Of All Creatures, Lord Of All Praises… *that you*…"; or else *modeh ani lefanekha*, as in the following text from *t. Ber.* 6:16: "[When he entered (the town) peacefully he said,] '*I thank you*, O Lord My God, *that* [= *because*] *you* brought me in with peace so may it be well pleasing before thee, O Lord My God, that you bring me out in peace…" That is, although according to Matthew Jesus says "I confess to you," what he means to say is "I thank you…that (on account of)…"

Jesus says here that the meaning of the events of the present time and of his miracles remains hidden from the Wise (*hakhamim*), that is, the scholars or Understanding Ones (*bunim*), but has been revealed to those who are thought to be unwise. The rabbinic tradition that equates *bunim* (scholars) with *banim* (children) comes to mind here. At the conclusion of *b.* Talmud tractates *Berakhot, Nazir, Yevamot,* and *Keritot,* the initial letters of each of which, when put together, form an anagram spelling BNYK (*banayik*), or "your children." Here is the early tradition that was appended to these tractates:

> Rabbi Eleazar said in the name of Rabbi Hanina, "Torah scholars (*hakhamim*) increase peace throughout the world, for it says, 'All your children shall be taught by the Lord, and great shall be the peace of your children [*banayikh*]' (Isa. 54:13)."

The tradition tells us that we are to read "children" (*banim*) here to mean "Understanding Ones" (*bunim*).[11] In light of Jesus' words (allegedly reported by Matthew above) we might see a reversal (in the Talmudic passage) of Jesus' implied interpretation of Isa. 54:13 children (*banim*) were taught by God of the coming kingdom, but the sages (*bunim*) were not. Hence, for the Gospel's Jesus, the "Era of Peace" is for the children alone.

In contrast with the harsh rhetoric above in which Jesus condemns the Jews by comparing them unfavorably with the men of Sodom, his tone here is comparatively mild. Here Jesus simply points out that the sages are not to blame for their refusal to expound his message to their followers, for God has deliberately hidden this message from them for his own purposes but has revealed it to the children (i.e., the uneducated peasants). In relation to this, nothing more can be said than that such was God's will. Klausner remarks on the change in temperament in Jesus from his harsh condemnation of the Jews of Capernaum and Chorazin above to his much milder reproof of the wise here and would have us believe that both are original to the historical Jesus.[12]

"Yes, Father, because it was well-pleasing before you." (v. 26)

The semitic construction that lies behind the phrase "well-pleasing before you" (*ratzon milefanekha*) is used here for the sake of protecting God's honor. That is, distance is created between God and his feelings by way of the prepositional phrase "before you."

"All things were delivered to me by my Father, and no one knows the
Son except the Father, nor does any know the Father except the Son,
and he to whom the Son may wish to reveal him." (v. 27)

The mystical tone of the passage indicates that Jesus has some kind of divine status.

*"Come to me, all you belabored and burdened ones, and I will give
you rest; take up my yoke upon you, and learn from me, because I am
meek and humble in heart, and you shall find rest for your souls"*
(vv. 28–29)

What we seem to have here is an implied contrast between the haughty
Pharisees (Matt. 16:11) and their doctrines, and the much more humble Jesus
and his teachings. "Rest for your souls" seems to mirror *"nahat ruah"* (e.g.,
b. Hag. 16b), which often carries a sense of religious fulfillment and spiritual
accomplishment. The term is used to express the emotion felt by someone
underprivileged by the prevailing rules when a rabbinic authority grants
them what had been (or could have been) denied them.

To "take up the yoke upon oneself" (Heb., *mekabel ol*) means to
commit oneself to a unique way of life that marks one's identity. Usually the
acceptance of such a "yoke" requires dedication and discipline. In relation
to this, in *Sipra Behar* 5 (to Lev. 25:35–38) the Rabbis state: "Whoever takes
upon himself the yoke of usury laws takes upon himself the yoke of heaven."

"for my yoke [is] easy, and my burden is light." (v. 30)

It is not clear if Jesus means to say here that his yoke and burden are lighter
than other leaders whose burdens are heavy, or whether he means to say here
that his yoke and his burdens are his doctrinal teachings of the end-time that
are both inspiring and full of hope for redemption, making the burdens of
life under Rome more bearable.

NOTES

1   See the introduction to chapter 2, n. 1, and also see chap. 12, vv. 15–17.

2   Compare *Sipre Deut.* to Deut. 32:39, "I put to death and I bring to life, I have
wounded and I will heal," which is taken to mean the one upon whom God
has brought death he will later revive and the one he has wounded he will later
heal. *Sipre Deut.* explains that the logic of the verse suggests a reversing of the
order of it so that its meaning becomes clearer: "God wounds and heals (the
same person who was wounded) and puts to death and bring to life (the same
person who died)."

3   Morris M. Faierstein, ("Why Do the Scribes Say That Elijah Must Come First")
argues that this was not a current popular belief at the time. However, Jesus'

disciples challenged Jesus and asked in Matt. 17:10 "Why Do the Scribes say that Elijah must come first" (and Jesus explains that he has already come). They wondered if Jesus could be the Messiah since Elijah has not yet appeared and they politely intimated this is all wrong." Teachers are challenged in Jewish culture by asking: but did not you teach us…?" (pointing out a general teaching that was well known). The answer points out that the question is misplaced to one who knows the facts of the current situation. (e.g., *m. Ber.* 1:1 or 2:7). But more to the point. Malachi 3 must be taken to mean that Elijah will come back on the Great Day — but when? Before the Messiah or after the Messiah. The Scribes taught "before." The disciples, who apparently followed their teachings, queried how Jesus could be the Messiah since he had to follow after Elijah. Jesus explains John and Elijah are the same. Since the New Testament knows the Scribes taught he would come before the Messiah and the Talmudic Rabbis of a much later era taught the same thing (*b. 'Erub.* 43b) we should see a line of tradition from the pre-Christian Jewish Scribes passing to the Talmud, even if the available evidence is sparse in between them. Ginzberg (*An Unknown Jewish Sect*, 251) does well to interpret the available evidence in this light since there is no reason to doubt the accuracy of the Gospel's assertions that the Scribes taught Elijah would come first. We also note that in chapter 3:11, "I immerse you in water for repentance, but the one coming after me is stronger than I, whose shoes I am not worthy to carry. He will immerse you in holy spirit and in fire." There is an idea that John is Elijah and Jesus the Messiah.

[4] De Young, "The Function of Malachi 3:1 in Matthew 11:10."

[5] Maurice Simon's translation (Soncino edition, 1952, ed. I. Epsein) of *b. Ber.* 11a is as follows:

> Our Rabbis taught: Beth Hillel say that one may recite the *Shema* standing, one may recite it sitting, one may recite it reclining, one may recite it walking on the road, one may recite it at one's work. Once Rabbi Yishmael and Rabbi Eleazar b. Azariah were dining at the same place, and Rabbi Yishmael was reclining while Rabbi Eleazar was standing upright. When the time came for reciting the *Shema*, Rabbi Eleazar reclined and Rabbi Yishmael stood upright. Said Rabbi Eleazar b. Azariah to Rabbi Yishmael: Brother Yishmael, I will tell you a parable. To what is this [our conduct] like? It is like that of a man to whom people say, You have a fine beard, and he replies, Let this go to meet the destroyers. So now, with you: as long as I was upright you were reclining, and now that I recline you stand upright! He replied: I have acted according to the rule of Beth Hillel and you have acted according to the rule of Beth Shammai.

[6] There is a *mashal* from the rabbinic literature, found in *Yalkut Shimoni*, v. 12, 876, which also has bearing on the one in our Gospel text. Taken from the section on Ps. 119:52, it is meant to explicate problems where the inconsistency between dirge and song is at issue in Psalm 8.

"I equate for you a] *mashal:* to what can this issue be compared? It is like a king who became angry at his son and chased him away. Then the king sent his tutor after him. He went and found him crying and singing. 'If you cry why do you sing?'"

7   Compare *Sipre Deut.* piska 307, which, in discussing Deut. 32:4–5, speaks of the "rock (*tsur*)" as both designer and creator (*tsayar, yatsar*), and says that the creator's ways of reward and punishment are perfect.

8   Scholem, *Kabbalah,* 377–78.

9   Ibid., 378

10   See further, Idel, *Ben.* Most pertinent for our purposes are Idel's discussions in the introduction, chapter 1, and the appendix.

11   Following the translation of R. Gordis, "Increasing Peace in the World."

12   Klausner, *Jesus of Nazareth,* 410.

INTRODUCTION

In this chapter the deep revulsion Matthew feels toward the Pharisees and their legal system is made plain. However that may be, the primary Gospel traditions are not absolute in their condemnations of the Jewish sages and their legal systems; indeed. the layers of Gospel traditions we have show us a Jesus who adheres to and is adept in that legal system.

It is by way of Matthew's additions to the narrative that we are able to discover the overall plan of his Gospel. In it, Jesus inaugurates the *eschaton* by first defeating the Pharisaic power structure — and this by disregarding Pharisaic law — so that he can justify the apparent violations of his disciples (it would seem, perhaps, that even sacrifices are to be suspended, if they hamper the exercise of mercy and justice).[1] Matthew portrays the sort of ongoing debate between Jesus and the Pharisees in his Gospel as a debate between the scribal legal system and God's era of mercy and peace. Ultimately Matthew's Gospel is the story of Jesus versus the Pharisees. For him, Jesus represents kindness and mercy, the Pharisees and their legal system a burdensome yoke. And so chapter 12 is a continuation of chapter 11, in that chapter 12 is a kind of extended interpretation of Jesus' claim in 11:30 that he is the "light yoke" and the promise of spiritual satisfaction at the close of this chapter.

Matthean additions to the Gospel story found by comparing Matthew to Mark and Luke show us that the Matthean Jesus sees the final movement of human history as the complete salvation of the gentile nations and the defeat of the prevailing Jewish hierarchies. All of this comes to the fore in this chapter. With great skill, Matthew has interpolated his own views into the basic themes of the received Gospel tradition. He has one purpose here: to stress how Jesus struggled to show the Jews how much more significant are the matters of mercy and justice;[2] in so doing he shows Jesus downplaying the values of the prevailing structures of the oral legal system of the Jewish sages.

Jesus' major speeches and actions as reported by the early church were understood by Matthew to be prophetic fulfillment of the final act of world history. The next act would belong to the kingdom. Matthew's understanding of the enigmatic stories he heard from the Gospel tradition were informed by Isaiah's vision (chap. 42) of the *eschaton*, the opening verse of which (Isa. 42:1) he quotes at Jesus' Baptism (3:17) and again at the Transfiguration (17:5), and also in this chapter 12 (v. 18). This vision of Isaiah is presented by Matthew, with some license, as the key to understanding the Pharisaic obstruction of brotherly love, the vindication and victorious judgment of the Gentiles (of whom Matthew must have seen himself as its chief scribe).[3] The meek and humble Jesus has already contrasted himself with these haughty teachers who will be judged to the flames, opening the door to the final kingdom, the arrival of which is imminent.

Richard Beaton has rightly seen the redacting hands of Matthew manipulating his story at every turn so as to give this lesson which was not lost on the Church Fathers and Christians up until modern times.[4] The medieval Rabbis (not unlike Christian clerics) also accepted the view that Jesus was a renegade who disparaged rabbinic law and teaching while claiming to be divine; they also accepted the idea that Jesus was killed because he blasphemed God and disparaged Jewish authorities. Beaton shows how Matthew repeatedly portrays Jesus as one who shows a deep concern for the outcasts who are his followers, while the Pharisees treat with haughty contempt any of their followers who neglect even the minutest of their rules. His work should be read as an introduction to this commentary.

The underlying story of Jesus in the synoptic Gospels presents him as someone whose arguments are closely aligned to and in sympathy with Pharisaic teaching as we know them today. It is to great extent Matthew's skill as a writer that has widened the gulf separating Jew from Christian and further opened the door for enmity and strife between the two.

As the chapter opens, Jesus has finished his preaching (end of 11), and now he and his disciples are wandering through fields of grain on the Sabbath. The episode leads to controversy. The dialogue in the argument that follows between Jesus and the Pharisees is contrived but the style and content of it are well within the parameters of typical Jewish debate forms. We will keep our eyes open for Matthean additions and interpretations of the controversy as Matthew presents his version of the events that ensue.

We now need to take stock of the setting of the story. According to both Mark and Matthew, Jesus confined his preaching to the Galilee (Mark 1:38, Matt. 4:23), while Luke indicates that he preached in Judea as well (Luke 4:43). In chapter 11 Matthew suggests that Jesus preached to the Jews alone and allegedly only about the coming of the kingdom. "Preaching" in Jesus' day (as it still does) meant giving sermons based on biblical texts and oral traditions, the telling of stories and parables, and the reciting of proverbs. Now Jesus, if he really did preach, delivered his sermons in the authorized synagogue style and not like a student-scribe of the sages of his day (Matt. 7:29). And while some in Jesus' day might have been surprised at the Gospels' reported control of the material in his name, we should not be. For had it been otherwise, why would anyone have paid attention to him? Undoubtedly he spoke the same language and used the same methods current with the official synagogue preachers of his day. So while we lack direct evidence for the bulk of his sermons in the synagogue and so can only assume he gave them in the accepted manner of first-century Jewish sages, we can demonstrate that what we have of his reported legal teachings, generally not concerning the news of the kingdom, was said in the manner now preserved in the literature of the Rabbis. Those legal teachings are what we shall examine here in their Matthean form.

The Gospels provide us with a number of accounts of debates Jesus purportedly entered into with groups of Pharisees of his day, who complain about his disregard of the oral laws instituted by sages throughout the Second Temple period. These laws, while not divinely given, were held to be sacred on account of their antiquity. The Gospels show us a Jesus who, although he respects and honors these laws, is not above educating his critics as to the legal possibility of overriding them when he feels this is warranted.

Here follows a short schema of what intra-Jewish debate forms looked like. These debate forms, which appear in conflicts with "heretics" in the rabbinic literature, follow well-set formats:

    A. a statement of complaint:
    B. a statement of practice (from the opponent's point of view) analogous to that complained about seeking the opponent's approval. This justifying practice phrased as a question: Do not you also…?
    C. a conclusion, usually argued from an "all the more so in our case" construction: So we can now both agree that your complaint is groundless.

A text from *m. Yad.* 4:6 provides the following example:

A. The Sadducees said: We object to you, Pharisees, when you say, "The Sacred Scrolls defile the hands but the [profane] Scrolls of *Homoros* do not defile the hands."

B. Rabbi Yohanan Ben Zakkai said: And why should this be the only complaint against the Pharisees, after all, they [Pharisees] say: the bones of a donkey [Hebrew: *hamor* resonates with *homoros* and both are pure for Pharisees] are inherently pure, but the bones of the High Priest Yohanan [beloved of the Sadducees] defile? They [Sadducees] replied to him: According to their preciousness is their defilement determined for otherwise [and God wanted to safeguard against this eventuality] a person may make the bones of his father and mother into spoons.

C. He [Rabbi Yohanan Ben Zakkai] said to them: It is the very same in the case of the Sacred Scrolls. According to their preciousness is their defilement determined [and Pharisees wanted to safeguard against their misuse]. But the Scrolls of *Homoros* are not precious, so they do not defile the hands [and so no one cares how they are treated].

In short, one would not expect reasonable people to state that sacred Scriptures would defile the hands that touch them (and so enact legislation that would prevent this). Yet the Pharisees did state this and were challenged by the Sadducees for it, as the tradition indicates. Rabbi Yohanan ben Zakkai, the chief Pharisee, answered according to the Sadducean method of reasoning, in order to demonstrate to them their misunderstanding. He pointed out to them that the example of the sacred texts is not the only example in which an esteemed thing causes "defilement." The analogous example he gives is that of bones. Finally Rabbi Yohanan then uses the Sadducees' reply to respond to their first claim and says that defilement is also used as a safeguard in the proper handling of books. The Sacred Scrolls deserve special handling; therefore they cause defilement of the hands.

Now let us turn to Matt. 12:1–8 (with variants in Mark 2:23–28; Luke 6:1–5):

At that time Jesus went through the grain-fields on the Sabbath; his disciples were hungry and they began to pluck the ears of grain and to eat [rubbing them in their hands (Luke's version)]. But when the Pharisees saw it, they said to him, "Look, your disciples are doing what is not lawful to do on the Sabbath." He said to them, "Have you not read what David did, when he was hungry, and those who were with him: how he entered the House of God and ate the Show Bread, which it was not lawful for him to eat nor for those who were with him, but only for the priests? [Or *have you not read in the law how on the* Sabbath *the priests in the Temple profane the Sabbath and are guiltless? I tell you something greater than the Temple is here, and if you had known what this means, "I desire mercy and not sacrifice"* (Hosea 6:6),[5] *you would not have condemned the guiltless* (Matthew's version)]. And he said to them, ["The Sabbath was made for man, not man for the Sabbath (Mark's version alone — 2:28)]. For the Son of Man is lord of the Sabbath."

At this point I state that everything I have ever said about this passage in Matthew I now repudiate and begin anew. Previously when I have spoken of this passage I failed to take into account the rhetoric that guides its structure. I deal here with Matthew's text since his Gospel is what I comment on in this work, though I suggest here that the other Gospels have omitted what Matthew includes here because they did not understand their sources, just as Matthew did not completely understand them either and even edited them (unless a copyist did it). What strikes one in this passage is the story of the *hungry* disciples allegedly profaning the *Sabbath*. Jesus' defense of his disciples' behavior lies in the cumulative effect of two biblical texts. A *hungry* David and his men eating the bread, without condemnation, that was not lawful for anyone to eat save priests alone, and priests in the *Temple* desecrating the *Sabbath*, without condemnation. What Jesus suggests here is that hunger can excuse unlawful behavior and that the presence of the Temple can excuse Sabbath desecration. Since Jesus is greater than the Temple, his presence excuses Sabbath desecration that were he not present could not be condemned in any event because hunger is involved.

Commentators have been perplexed by the story in 1Sam. 23:1–5. How could David have eaten the Show bread? According to an ancient tradition found in *b. Menaḥ.* 96a and *Yalkut Shimoni* 1 Samuel section 130, David was stricken by a disease brought about by near-starvation and so had no choice but to eat it; that is, had he not eaten the Show bread he may well have died. There was no other food available for him at this time. It is a principle of Jewish law that to save one's life overrides all laws, including the law which forbids one from eating the bread consecrated for priests alone.

While this answer was sufficient for the Rabbis' understanding of David's action here, how did the Gospel writers understand this story of David eating the bread and how did they relate it to the case of the disciples of Jesus? And where is the "all the more so" argument that gives shape to these kinds of texts? Note what Matthew has Jesus say in 12:12: "How much more valuable is a man than a sheep! Therefore it is lawful to do good on the Sabbath." The problems inherent in this story of David eating the Show bread have produced an enormous amount of scholarly speculation. As well, we do not know where the law tells us that priests who profane the Sabbath are to be held blameless. Matthew likely assumed it referred both to the daily sacrifice, and also the special sacrifice performed on the Sabbath, prescribed in Num 29:9–10: "On the Sabbath day you shall offer two unblemished yearling lambs, with their cereal offering, two tenths of an ephah of fine flour mixed with oil, and with their libations. Each Sabbath there shall be the Sabbath holocaust in addition to the established holocaust and its libation." Thus Matthew can cite Hos. 6:6 to say that sacrifice is of less importance than mercy, so if sacrifice pushes aside Sabbath guilt, then kindness to the hungry will also.

In fact, only the arguments concerning Sabbath desecration (for sacrifices) in the Temple being blameless or Jesus being greater than sacrifices and the Temple seem to lead somewhere. The story about David being hungry and presumably eating forbidden food may be included here (though this seems a stretch to say), simply to add to the preponderance of evidence to excuse the hungry disciples and was taken on its own to have served as a sufficient argument (as in Mark and Luke). However, being "lord of the Sabbath" does not fit the story of David where there is no mention of the Sabbath in the Gospel account at all; it plausibly fits the story of the Temple precincts permitting Sabbath desecration. When we hear that Jesus is greater than the Temple, and the Temple exempts priests for Sabbath violations, then it follows that Jesus also is above any laws pertaining to the Sabbath. This fits Matthew's assertion about the Temple priests but nothing in the other Gospel accounts. So I assume Matthew's text is the more complete. I also assume the inclusion of Hos. 6:6, in which it is said that mercy trumps sacrifices, is meant as a direct challenge to the Pharisees whom Matthew sees as being obsessed with ritual concerns (the trivia of the law). However all this may be, I cannot follow the logic of the arguments. If the story of David's exemption from ritual concerns on account of hunger was the point here, then the Gospels should have said: "Just as David and his men were permitted to eat forbidden food to assuage hunger, so should my disciples." But the argument is never concluded in this way. Of the following account in Matthew we are left to consider this question: "If the priests were enjoined to offer sacrifices on the Sabbath and so prepared and offered burnt offerings, how does this exempt the disciples from plucking grain on the Sabbath who were obviously not commanded to pluck grain on that day?" Furthermore, where does the law say that the priests who profane the Sabbath in the Temple are blameless? Offering a sacrifice that has been commanded for the Sabbath cannot qualify as profaning the Sabbath. I suspect it is the lack of an answer to this question that accounted for the statement being dropped in the source followed by both Mark and Luke. The whole passage in Matthew remains an enigma that requires some technical elucidation.

Let us briefly examine the synoptic use of Jesus' saying "have you not read" introduction for polemic purposes to refute accusations of wrongdoing. He says it three times in Matthew, three times in Mark, and once in Luke. It always comes to produce a counterexample, as if introducing some kind of sermon based on Scriptures to establish the divine law. It occurs twice in Matthew 12 (vv. 3 and 5); once at 19:4, to forbid divorce; and at 22:31, to establish the doctrine of resurrection. It also occurs in Mark 12:10 to establish his authority, Mark 2:25 to speak of David's eating Show bread, Mark 12:26 to establish the doctrine of resurrection, and in Luke 6:3 to speak of David's eating Show bread. In our passage is it used to excuse a one-time infraction of a commandment. Further, in Matt. 12:11 the analogous question begins, "Which person among you...will not lay hold of it and lift it out?"[6] In other words, in this case we get a clear argument based on a practical analogy and not an exegesis or sermon. Furthermore, in Matthew 12 no biblical text is cited verbatim which breaks the set form of the other usages. I draw no conclusions from these observations except to say that we either have a highly contrived unit or else a badly garbled rendition of something that once made sense.

We might have to be satisfied that the argument is purely sarcastic rhetoric using the argument from analogous case which is the standard form to argue these complaint debates. "Leave me alone and better complain about David and Temple priests!" On the other hand, the double argument (from the actions of both David and the priests in the Temple) suggests that there were two different traditions concerning what Jesus answered here. If so, the final saying of Jesus here is truly enigmatic: "The Son of Man is Lord of the Sabbath." What does this mean here?

I suspect we have a complicated development in the tradition. Since it is unlikely that we are to think of the disciples as thieves, I assume the Gospel story originally envisioned them eating what has been "left for the poor," as Lev 19:9–10 prescribes:

> When you reap the harvest of your land, you shall not be so thorough that you reap the field to its very edge, nor shall you glean the stray ears of grain. Likewise, you shall not pick your vineyard bare, nor gather up the grapes that have fallen. These things you shall leave for the poor and the alien. I, the Lord, am your God.

Some Pharisees wonder how they could profane the Sabbath by plucking the grain left for the poor. Jesus reminds them about David's hunger. A more sophisticated argument ensues and this time it is in proper form and to the point. The argument concerns Sabbath rules that did not apply in the Temple.

Neither argument really addresses hunger on the Sabbath, though together they seem to. The second argument is very sophisticated and seems to be original since all Gospels contain a line that is relevant to it alone.

Let us try to imagine what the objection in the Gospel might be. It might be that the disciples have contravened the law of God and Jesus seeks to exonerate them. I have no doubt that this is how the Gospel writers understood their sources. But there is another possibility, which is that it is the Pharisaic law that has been contravened and not God's law. In my opinion, every case in Matthew where the Pharisees accuse Jesus and his disciples of Sabbath infringement concerns Pharisaic or scribal laws. If this is so, then we must understand the tradition behind Matthew 12 to have read: "Do you *not know* [rather than "not read"] how the priests in the Temple profane the Sabbath[7] and are blameless…" In joining the Temple pericope to the tradition concerning David the editor repeated the words "have you not read" from the David introduction to introduce the Temple tradition. If this was the case, then Matt. 12:5–8, concerning Pharisaic law and not biblical law, is entirely consistent with Matt. 12:10–12: A question of soliciting agreement on a contemporary practice that seems to break the scribal prohibitions (do not you rescue animals on the Sabbath?) and then using an "all the more so" argument (are not people more valuable than animals?) that addresses the issue at hand.

So far so good. Now for the particulars. Nowhere does the law state that priests who profane the Sabbath in the Temple are blameless. The argument, when phrased as in the way that it is — "Do you not know how on the Sabbath the priests in the Temple profane the Sabbath[8] and are guiltless?" — corresponds to a known rule. Priests may profane scribal laws (*shevut*) in the Temple on the Sabbath, since they will keep watch of one another and fear the sanctity of the Temple. So the disciples may all the more profane scribal law as it pertains to the Sabbath when need be since they are in the presence of the Son of Man, the fear of whose watchfulness is even greater than what priests experienced in the Temple. No other Gospel argues from this premise, and it seems likely that Matthew's version is a parallel to the widespread Gospel tradition: "have you not read [in Scripture] what David did…" and attempts to explain the meaning of the passage concerning David, although weakly.

When people pluck grain on the Sabbath, then push out the kernel of wheat, which is an unusual way of harvesting (normally wheat is harvested in large amounts with a sickle), they do not violate any biblical laws that pertain to the Sabbath.[9] However the Scribes, to protect the spirit of Mosaic laws, banned "abnormal" Sabbath acts, which were allowed biblically. Ears of grain were not normally plucked from the fields one by one, as opposed to the more common harvesting and threshing methods in use at the time. *B. Šabb.* 103a[10] records a very early tradition that specifies the types of plants that are forbidden by biblical law to be plucked (by hand) and ears of grain are not mentioned (since they are normally harvested with a sickle). Deut. 23:26 specifically mentions a method of plucking off the tops of the wheat to get to the kernels by hand in an unusual way when eating in another's field. The normal methods of reaping and threshing are bypassed. The activity in this New Testament passage mirrors that unusual method which was not forbidden by biblical law. Furthermore this New Testament tradition notes that in fields not belonging to the one plucking the wheat one would not transgress the further prohibition of clearing fields. Another source, *b. Beṣ.* 13b, contains examples of the rabbinic rules of *shinui* (change from regular manner) to show specifically that rubbing kernels of ripened grain to eat was unusual (as we find in Luke's version). It was not considered a biblical prohibition in regards to the Sabbath. It follows that what is described in the Gospels would be forbidden by a scribal prohibition but not by a biblical one. Thus room for leniency might be found, as the Scribes left loopholes in their rulings for various circumstances when their rulings would not apply. If there were reason to know that particular circumstances prevented the disciples from actually profaning the Sabbath while they were engaged in separating the sheaves or kernels, they acted blamelessly.[11]

Let us review the details of the above argument. Matthew's addition citing Hos. 6:6 as antithetical to Temple sacrifice shows us how he has manipulated his source. He purposely confuses the Sabbath sacrifices prescribed by the Torah with his source's reference to certain scribal rules called *"shevut,"* which indeed were suspended in the Temple.[12] In this way he introduces again the notion that the Pharisees neglect mercy and are obsessed with rituals that God abhors. The real force of his source is to show the point that the Scribes assumed the Temple authorities would be careful that no biblical rules would be infringed.[13] So this example shows that scribal laws can indeed be infringed where there is watchfulness (the awe of the Temple itself provides such). In Matthew's original source, it seems most likely, Jesus argues that the Son of Man is greater than the Temple, which must mean his own presence provides more watchfulness than the presence of Temple authorities in the Temple would. Thus, the *scribal infringement* would not apply in this case had it happened in the Temple. Plucking by hand and rolling out the kernal was a *"shvut"* (since it was so unproductive and unusual a way to prepare the grain for consumption) purely of a scribal nature. Just as the Temple safeguarded the Sabbath, so the Son of Man did so and he might be called "the lord of Sabbath" who ensured that every law pertaining to it was observed to the last detail.

This saying of Jesus here in Matthew makes sense in terms of the idea that Temple priests are not bound by scribal rules while in the Temple. I would argue that Matthew's source is, if not the more original, at least a text that explains the David pericope. To end the passage by saying the Son of Man is lord of the Sabbath makes no sense if it is to be the conclusion of an argument based on David transgressing a Levitic law by eating sacred loaves at the sanctuary in Nob. So that in itself cannot be the argument. The Gospel defense that uses David's eating of bread in Nob is truly baffling and, to make matters more confusing, all synoptic traditions record it, so it cannot be easily dismissed as extraneous. Let us examine the details and speculate upon them.

According to an ancient tradition found in *b. Menaḥ.* 96a and *Yalkut Shimoni* 1 Samuel section 130, as I have pointed out, David was stricken by a disease brought about by starvation and ate the Show bread because he would have died if he had not eaten it. There was no other food available to him at that time. The Jewish tradition cites the story of David to justify the general principle that only the possible saving of life can override the Sabbath laws. It is not claimed in the Gospels that the disciples were on the verge of starving to death. So what has this story in 1 Samuel to do with the question of permitting scribal Sabbath laws to be broken? I am inclined to leave this answer as one of rhetoric and not of legal substance.

Still, it is not clear in Matthew that the Pharisees who engaged Jesus were pleased with the answer he gives them, that no real Sabbath desecrations would occur,[14] but they have been assured by the type of argument that the infringement is of a scribal nature and that there was supervision to see that no biblical laws were violated. Again, there would be little warrant here for any condemnation save that the Pharisees would not have accepted Jesus' claim that his presence would guarantee no laws would be broken. Similarly, *b. Šabb.* 29b refers to the upper chamber of the house of Nithza in Lod (noted in many places, e.g., *b. Sanh.* 74a) as the place where the supreme court of elders decided many problematic issues. Here the elders did not protest Rabbi Yehuda's trespass of a rabbinic enactment as the Sabbath approached. The circumstances somehow obviated the law. In his commentary to *m. Shabbat* chapter 2, Maimonides explains that the sages of the court who met here were alert, watchful, and vigilant so as to guarantee no biblical laws would be broken in those Sabbath sessions (probably lectures), which were held under their auspices in this particular place.[15] Therefore the reason for the enactment (i.e., suspected negligence) did not apply and they said nothing about the laxity.[16] In short, there is nothing at all to learn from these Jesus/Pharisee debates, if seen out of their later literary contexts. Originally, they might have been preserved to show Jesus' mastery of Jewish law and humane application of it. About which cases of healing the majority of sages in the first century C.E. would have ruled leniently and which ones they would have ruled stringently is a matter of speculation, since the rabbinic evidence shows a variety of approaches where there is no danger to life or limb and not too much pain. If laying on of hands was considered medicinal or not also seems to have been an issue, but this constituted no more than a *shevut* category infringement. At any rate, the cases the synoptics report that Jesus used as the point of departure for his arguments are confirmed as consonant with scribal law and it may well be that his arguments would have been acceptable for him, but probably not endorsed, given the wide latitude that was available for dealing with scribal enactments. No divine laws, written or oral, were threatened by the kinds of faith healings that Jesus was said to have performed. There could be little cause for unhappiness with these approaches.[17] The Gospels present a Jesus whose vocabulary and reasoning in these passages and his knowledge of technical laws devised by Rabbis to enhance the observance of the Sabbath match the systematic workings peculiar to rabbinic Sabbath law in minute detail. So it appears that we have traces of traditions that intended to highlight his fulfilling the minute details of laws that his interlocutors had overlooked. But in the end these traces dissolve in the overwhelming hostility of the Gospels' anti-Jewish stance so evident in chapter 11.

We can now look at the next passages in chapter 12, which illustrates the same Jewish A-B-C debate form we noted above.

Matthew 12:10–12 (Luke 14:3–5)

A. (10) Looking for a reason to accuse Jesus, they asked him: "Is it lawful to heal on the Sabbath?"
B. (11) He said to them, "If any of you has a sheep and it falls into a pit on the Sabbath, will you not take hold of it and lift it out?
C. (12) How much more valuable is a man than a sheep! Therefore it is lawful to do good on the Sabbath.

The earliest extant specific teachings concerning an animal stuck in a pit on the Sabbath[18] are found in the *Damascus Document*[19] and may well relate to the problem humanely addressed by scribal decrees that are found in the Tosefta. The Tosefta says that if an animal falls into a pit from which it cannot get out on its own but in which there is water, then one should feed it food while it is there but not extricate it (*t. Šabb.* 14:3). The Babylonian *amoraim* (masters of Mishnah in the rabbinic academies) thought that this meant if the animal could stay comfortably in the pit, then one should feed it there, but if it would cause the animal pain to be left there, then it could be removed even though this would entail infringing upon a minor scribal decree.[20] The Babylonians apparently followed the reasoning that any animal in pain had to be relieved of it by Torah decree, and this Torah injunction could override some scribal prohibitions of the Sabbath.[21] Although we have no tannaitic statements like this, the force of Babylonian Amoraic tradition is borne out by the New Testament. The practice of alleviating pain for animals stuck in pits dates to Second Temple times although the written Jewish sources are attested relatively late.

A NOTE ABOUT SCRIBAL TRADITION

The Mishnah and Tosefta record many Sabbath rulings that were prohibited by Scribes but not considered prohibited by Torah law. The Tosefta discusses the origins of scribal *"muktseh"*-type prohibitions.[22] Since these types of decrees discuss Temple practices, the firm Palestinian and Babylonian traditions claiming these decrees date to Second Temple times are warranted. These laws are manmade, and each of them had a rationale and a hierarchy of importance in the total scheme of things, for example, to protect people from mistakenly transgressing biblical laws. Certain priorities of urgency can override scribal rules in certain circumstances. These rules were circulated and practiced but not frequently discussed.[23] New Testament writings, such as the expression found in Matt. 12:11 — "seizing and lifting" — would seem to confirm the impression of the antiquity of these laws.[24]

Scribal law was accorded deep respect and not easily disregarded. Thus even when certain rules were overridden, they were overridden in ways commensurate with scribal priorities. Relax this minor law rather than another. The principal reasons adduced by the majority of authorities to suspend scribal laws forbidding either the lifting and/or moving of animals or nonprepared utensils were for the sake of enabling important good deeds such as Sabbath Torah study, Sabbath hospitality, easing pain to animals, calming people about loss of belongings.

Animals are categorized as "non-Sabbath items" and thus are not to be moved on that day.[25] Since the New Testament uses the expression "lay hold of and lift," we see the problem is one of scribal *muktseh* — "animals are not set aside for Sabbath use" — and so must not be taken and lifted. The Scribes prescribed that *muktseh* items are not to be taken and lifted. In the need to justify a teaching, the Babylonian Talmud reveals there could be a rule of *hefsed meruba* (substantial loss).[26] The Talmud posited that if something was of small value it could not be rescued by overriding scribal law.[27] This is said to be the idea behind *m. Šabb.* 24:1. We now infer that where something was of great value it could be rescued and, if necessary, even at the expense of scribal law.[28] But that is not the issue at hand in Matthew. The passages dealing with alleviating the pain of an animal can be found in *b. Šabb.* 128b and this is the sole issue. That scribal prohibitions are overridden in cases of doing important good deeds is discussed in *m. Šabb.* 18:1 and the commentaries of the Talmuds on it. Jesus is not saying anything very radical here.

We must point out that the alleviating of pain for animals is a most complicated issue.[29] There were two schools of thought on the matter and the first two *amoraim* (teachers of Mishnah, *ca.* 215 C.E.) offered different opinions. Shmuel held the more lenient view and Rav the stricter view. Both agreed that severe pain had to be alleviated, but even in doing so measures to protect rabbinic laws had to be reasonably enforced. The two Rabbis differed sharply on how to apply these principles. It is correct to state that scribal laws are worked out for animals in fine detail in the fifth chapter of *m. Šabb.* If need be, there would be no reason not to extend these very leniencies to humans. However, the Rabbis had traditions more direct than arguing from rules concerning animals to permit various categories of healing on the Sabbath. It might well be that the questioners of Jesus (as reported in the Gospels) were not aware of the full range of possibilities within the scribal legal framework. At any rate, it should not be thought that arguments stated in the Talmuds were unknown before the Talmudic period. The Gospels, like those under present discussion, show us that at least some arguments found in the Talmuds do predate the Talmuds, since they evidence the same differences of opinion. In general, we find that the rules that the Gospels report Jesus puts forth as the basis of his arguments are known from rabbinic literature. Quite often, the specific arguments in the Gospels (based on well-known data) seem unique to Jesus. The arguments are sufficient but usually unnecessary to establish the leniency. The Rabbis in many cases had used more specific arguments to make the same points.

SUMMARY

Jesus' argument with the Pharisees in the synoptic healing passages may best be seen as assuming the tenets of scribal law. For Matthew, if Jesus does not accept scribal law, he will not convince his opponents and also the rhetorical features of these passages will make no sense. So Jesus argues from scribal premises. The question put to Jesus is: In cases where there is no immediate threat to health and no immediate unbearable pain, how can you permit healing? The accusation against Jesus' healing on the Sabbath must be in the light of scribal law. The Scribes forbade elective healing, lest one think one could pound herbs and drugs to cure a person *whose life or limb or organ is in no danger* and come eventually to permit "grinding herbs" in such cases (which were considered biblical prohibitions).[30] To cure a sick person *whose life or limb or organ may be in danger* is not only permissible on the Sabbath but mandatory.

In every case, Jesus permits the overriding of Sabbath laws by using the *a fortiori* hermeneutic operation of *"kal vehomer."* In Matthew and Luke this generally means "you permit forbidden things in cases of animals, so all the more so you are to permit forbidden things in cases of humans."

For Matthew, these exchanges with the Pharisees lead further into the story of conflict between Jesus and the Jewish teachers of his day. Below, in verse 19, we find another of Matthew's fulfillment Scriptures and again from the Book of Isaiah. But it is not he who will fulfill the text but those who will keep his secret of who he is. Jesus simply warns them to be quiet. The Isaiah text begins by suggesting the Gentiles will be judged and at the end notes that they will emerge victorious. The Gentiles gain salvation through the name of the servant.

The narrative proceeds, hinged on the wrath of the Pharisees and the mercy of Jesus toward his followers. This hinge heightens our grasp of the biased understanding of the legal issues that Matthew brings to interpret the debate scenes.

14. But the Pharisees plotted against him, how they might destroy him.
15. Jesus, knowing this, departed from there, and many crowds followed him, and he healed all of them,
16. And he warned them not to expose him,
17. So that what was spoken through Isaiah the prophet might be fulfilled:
18. *"Look, my servant whom I chose; my beloved in whom my soul is pleased. I shall place my spirit upon him, and he will proclaim a judgment for the nations.*[31]
19. *"He will not quarrel nor will he cry out, nor will anyone hear his voice in the streets.*[32]
20. *"A crushed reed he will not break, nor extinguish a smoking wick, until he brings the judgment to victory.*[33]
21. *"And in his name, the nations will hope."*[34]

As the rest of the chapter and the Gospel follow suit, I would dub this chapter "A study in dualism," for in it the world is divided in two: Jesus and his followers and the Gentiles who do good things, Satan and everyone else who do evil. Two articles need be mentioned here. The first is "The Gentile Bias in Matthew" by

Kenneth Clark. Clark argues that Matthew at all times consults a Greek Bible which is like our LXX. It differs from it in some instances where it has been corrected against a Hebrew text which better approximates our Masoretic Text. Clark argues that Matthew was rather ignorant of Hebrew and his facility with biblical texts was no greater than many gentile Christian biblical scholars of his day who used Greek texts. The evidence for this assertion is moderately persuasive but until we find such Greek texts I remain skeptical that Matthew knew no Hebrew, although I do think he was Gentile. Clark, as have many others, finds many Cynic motifs in Matthew, although I am inclined to account a portion of these to Christian Gnostic motifs. As for Matthew's dismissal of Jews as being doomed and having their promise of final salvation transferred to the Gentiles, he cites 8:12, 12:21, 21:34, 21:43, 22:1–14, 25:31–46. Furthermore, Matthew's real "Christ-of-faith messiah" is not the just the humanoid "son of David (son of Abraham) messiah," as shown from birth to death, but in the end is revealed as the divinoid "Son of Man" figure.[35] As for the gentile membership of Matthew's church, he shows us 23:37–39 and 24:45. He mistakenly points out how Matthew mocks Jewish *tefillin* mentioned in 23:5 using the Greek *phylakterion* (pagan good-luck charms) and in general mentions hardly any Hebrew or Aramaic terms even where Mark or Luke do. The article mirrors many of my own thoughts concerning the gentile identity of Matthew. Nevertheless, as I said, he is wrong about Matthew's usage of *phylakterion*. Jews could also refer to them by the term "*kameia*," amulet and Rabbis (*y. Ber.* 2:3 and its variants elsewhere) noted some hypocrites donned their fringed cloak and phylacteries to pretend to be pious and defraud the gullible. The Rabbis complained, "Why do they [the masses] treat them [*tefillin*] laxly? Because of the hypocrites."[36]

The second article that should be mentioned is Maarten J. J. Menken's "The Quotation from Isaiah 42:1–4 In Matthew 12:18–21: Its Textual Form." In this article Menken also argues for Matthew using a revised LXX and himself introducing very minute changes to his text for the sake of smoothing out or sharpening a point. All Matthew's quotations seem to come from the same type of pre-Matthean Greek Bible. The citation from Isaiah in this chapter addresses the Pharisees' plot to destroy Jesus, his silence, his healings, and his command that his miracles be kept secret. Right now Jesus' identity must be kept secret. His death and resurrection stand at the center of the meaning of this Gospel to the Gentiles who will experience his justice, as the Pharisees will get their just end. The citation from Isaiah is cited with an omission that is incompatible with the passion and death and what is to be realized then. The main point of interest to us in this article will be discussed in the comments to 12:21. The LXX followed by Matthew gives us "the Gentiles who will hope in his name." Clearly LXX is referring to God's name while Matthew likely understands the reference to be to Jesus' name. Yet all Hebrew texts have "hope for his Torah." The issue will be taken up in the commentary proper.

> *At that time, Jesus went on the Sabbath through the fields of grain.*
> *His students were hungry and began to pick the ears of grain and eat.*
> (v. 1)

Presumably Jesus has finished teaching his Sabbath lesson but no one has provided him or his students with food for the day. It is difficult to see how this could have happened since Jesus should have had the foresight to prepare food for himself and his students for the Sabbath, or at least to have arranged for himself and them to be guests at a Sabbath meal, as was the rule (*m. Pe'ah* 8:7). How it happens that Jesus is out of the city and walking in the fields is also somewhat puzzling. Since it is doubtful the disciples were stealing the grain, one must assume they were taking what of the grain harvest the Torah commanded be left in the field for the poor (Lev. 19:9–10). It is possible the Gospels tradition considered these fields to be ownerless.

> *The Pharisees who saw it said to him, "Look, your students are doing*
> *what is not permitted to do on the Sabbath. (v. 2)*

The Pharisees are not being confrontational here but simply drawing Jesus' attention to the actions of his disciples. The Pharisees are presuming that Jesus would be concerned enough about what his disciples are doing to tell them to stop doing it. If the Pharisees had been interested in creating trouble for Jesus they could have done so; as witnesses to the Sabbath violation his disciples were committing, they could have issued a sterner warning. Penalties for flagrant Sabbath violation were fairly severe, as the violation was understood to be a denial of God.

> *He said to them, "Have you not read what David did when he and*
> *those with him were hungry? How he entered the house of God and*
> *they ate the bread of the offering, which was not permitted for him to*
> *eat, nor those with him, but only for the Priests." (vv. 3–4)*

The argument here is preposterous, for with it one could justify every violation of the law. The Pharisees would not have been impressed with such an argument, and the Gospels writers, and Jesus, too, if he actually said it, would have been easily mocked for it. I have discussed this matter at length in the introduction to this chapter.

> *"Or have you not read in the law that on Sabbath, the Priests in the*
> *Temple profane the Sabbath and are blameless?"* (v. 5)

The words "have you not read in the law" may have been original to Matthew's source, or else he may have inserted them here to act as a kind of parallel to the "Have you not read what David did" from above. Given what Jesus says next, it would seem that he is not talking here about prohibitions spoken of in the law, but rather prohibitions instituted by the Scribes to safeguard that which might lead to real Sabbath violations. Because of an understanding of the greatness of the Temple, it is certain that the priests would have taken extra care in their handling of the prescribed sacrifices on the Sabbath (Num. 28:9–10), for which reason the scribal laws pertaining to these matters would have been set aside for them. Thus what Jesus says next makes perfect sense.

> *"I say to you, something greater than the Temple is here.* (v. 6)

That is, because the Son of Man is even greater than the Temple, scribal laws that can be set aside in the Temple can also, of course, be set aside in his presence.

> *"If you had known what it means to say, 'I want mercy and not sacrifice'*
> *[Hos. 6:6], you would not have condemned the blameless."* (v. 7)

Matthew seems to have misunderstood the argument in his source. He assumed that the priests (v. 5) were said to be blameless on the Sabbath because they were performing the Sabbath sacrifices, which God had commanded them to do. So he compares sacrifice to Sabbath and mercy to eating. Hence Jesus' disciples, as he understood it, who have taken food to eat on the Sabbath in a way that is in violation of it, should likewise be thought of as blameless.

Matthew has divided verse 6 from verse 8 in his source, which together form a complete thought, so that this interpolation can act as a kind of footnote to the argument in his sources. Interpolations such as these can act as footnotes in the rabbinic literature as well.

> *"For the Son of Man is Lord of the Sabbath."* (v. 8)

Likely "Lord of the Sabbath" means something like "Guardian of the Sabbath" (in Heb., *ba'al/adon ha-shabbat*). By his presence, Jesus guards the Sabbath as if it were an extension of himself. That Jesus is "Guardian of the Sabbath" does not mean that he is free to place himself above the Sabbath, but that as a divine figure he is the one in charge of Sabbath observance.

Having departed from there, he went into their assembly. (v. 9)

Jesus is now back in the synagogue, within the Jewish community of the Pharisees.

And look, there was a man with a withered hand. They asked him, "Is it permitted to heal on Sabbath?" so that they might have some grounds to accuse him. (v. 10)

In giving us the motive for the question the Pharisees ask Jesus here Matthew makes clear the Pharisees are enemies of Jesus. In the near parallel in Luke (14:3–6) it is Jesus who asks the Pharisees this question.

He said to them, "Which person from among you who has a [single][37] sheep, would not grasp it and lift it out, should it fall into a pit on the Sabbath?" (v. 11)

The point here is not that the act of rescuing a sheep in distress on the Sabbath is forbidden, as non-Pharisee texts found at Qumran and the Cairo Geniza suggest (CD 11:13), but that one would rescue it anyway. The point is not, but might have originally been, that as abiders of the law the Pharisees would follow the more prevalent teaching that permits the rescue of an animal on the Sabbath if it is in distress, though not if it is not in distress (*b. Šabb.* 128b; *t. Šabb.* 15:1). "Grasp and lift" (in Heb., *tiltul*) is the twofold act referred to in the scribal prohibition. Biblical law has nothing to say about not rescuing a sheep on the Sabbath. According to the Talmud, when an animal is in distress on the Sabbath one must rescue it in a prescribed way so, that even though the ruling of the sages is recalled through this way, their restriction is set aside. Apart from the rhetoric of the Gospel, the words of Jesus and Talmudic teaching are compatible.

"Now, how greatly does a human being surpass a sheep! So it is permitted to do good on the Sabbath." (v. 12)

I have already dealt with the pertinent issues found here in the introduction to this chapter and in the introduction to this book. The "all the more so" argument is standard in these debate forms.

Then he says to the man, "Extend your hand." He extended it, and it was restored, healthy as the other one. (v. 13)

Satisfied with the argument and presumably his critics are as well, Jesus is now said to have wholly cured the man's hand.

But the Pharisees going out, plotted against him, how they might destroy him. (v. 14)

Here again we have reference to a plot to destroy Jesus. The plot to destroy Jesus stands at the center of Matthew's focus on issues of conflict, or of duality, in this unit: Jesus against the Pharisees, Gentiles against the Jews, Jesus against the Satan, Jesus' followers against his nonfollowers, trees bearing good fruit against trees bearing bad fruit.

Jesus, knowing this, departed from there, and many crowds followed him, and he healed all of them, and he warned them not to expose him, so that what was spoken through Isaiah the prophet might be fulfilled (vv. 15–17)

With his use of the following fulfillment text from Isaiah (unique to his Gospels), specifically Isa. 42:2, Matthew shows Jesus warns others and this warning fulfills the text. That is, everyone is to remain silent, Jesus intends, about the deeds they have seen him do. This text from Isaiah is enigmatic. Matthew must have understood the text as a precondition for Isa. 42:4, which concerns the hope of salvation for the Gentiles.

Generally fulfillment of these texts in Matthew, as I have argued earlier, depends upon an almost too-literal reading of them. Here we see that for this text from Isaiah (42:2) to be fulfilled by others, Jesus must ensure his voice and actions are not the subjects of public declarations. Jesus will perform his deeds as softly as the sound a reed makes when it breaks, or a wick makes when it smolders. That is, what Jesus is saying here is that he can only perform miracles so long as his true identity remains concealed.

"Look, my servant/son[38] whom I have chosen; my beloved with whom my soul is well pleased. I will put my spirit upon him, and he will proclaim judgment/ justice to the Gentiles" (Isa. 42:1). (v. 18)

The choice here of "Gentiles" to translate the word *ethnesin* in the text instead of the alternative "nations" (the two terms were essentially synonymous in the first century), has been guided by my sense of the anti-Jewish tone of the chapter. The RSV also has "Gentiles" here.

Twice elsewhere in his Gospels Matthew cites Isa. 42:1, though in neither of these other cases does he use it as a fulfillment proof-text. Rather in these other cases Matthew says of it that it is a direct word from God, to mark either Jesus' initiation into "sonship" at the Baptism (Matt. 3:17), or to mark his graduation into "divine partnership" at the Transfiguration (Matt. 17:5).[39] Matthew uses Isa. 42:1–2 here as a fulfillment text of a kind (Jesus is to fulfill Isa. 42:1; as for Isa. 42:2, see v. 19, he acts in such a way that others will fulfill it too), but he also continues to quote from Isaiah 42 as far as verse 4. This is for polemical reasons rather than for the sake of including the full fulfillment proof-text itself, which requires him to quote only as far as Isa. 42:3.

"He will not wrangle or cry aloud, nor will anyone hear his voice in the streets" (Isa. 42:2). (v. 19)

Jesus wants the reports of his miracles to be silenced. "He" and "his voice" in this text, as I say, are somewhat strained to refer to his own actions as well as his audience's compliance. Perhaps it is best to see the fulfillment of the verse in Jesus warning the crowds not to broadcast reports of his miracles in public. Elsewhere in the text the pronouns and pronominal adjectives are all understood to refer to Jesus himself. That is, if Matthew really intends to break up this text here and refer the fulfillment solely to his audience, would he not have done it in a clearer way? In Isaiah itself the third-person-singular pronoun in this text always refers to the servant. Moreover, later in the chapter the fact that the generation to whom Jesus has preached has failed to listen to him and has spoken beyond his wishes, becomes an issue, which perhaps fits with what the text is saying here. See also what Menken says in n. 47 below.

"A crushed reed he will not break, or quench a smoldering wick, until he brings judgment/justice to victory.[40] And upon his name, the Nations/Gentiles will have hope" (Isa. 42:3–4). (vv. 20–21)

Concerning this text from Isaiah more should be said. First, however, I quote Isa. 42:1–4 from the text of the MT followed by the same text from the LXX.

Masoretic Hebrew text:
Look, my servant, whom I support; my chosen, [in whom] my soul is pleased;
I have put my spirit upon him: he shall bring out judgment/justice to the Gentiles.
He shall not cry out, nor lift up, nor cause his voice to be heard in the street.

A bruised reed he will not break, and the smoking flax he will not quench: he will bring forth judgment unto truth. He will not grow faint nor be discouraged, until he has set judgment/justice in the earth: and [even the furthest] shores will hope for his law [*torato*].

LXX:

"Jacob, my child, I shall help him; Israel, my chosen. My soul has received him; I have laid my spirit upon him, he will carry out a judgment for the nations. His voice will not cry out, nor lift up, nor be heard outside. A broken reed he will not crush, and a burning wick he will not extinguish, but he will carry the judgment to the truth. He will shine brightly, and not be discouraged, until he puts a judgment upon the earth, *and upon his name [onomati] the Nations/ Gentiles will have hope*."

Matthew's version of Isa. 42:1–3 is closer to what is found in the received Hebrew texts, but his version of Isa. 42:4 is closer to what is found in the received texts of the LXX. Matthew sees that Jesus is the servant/son (see n. 42 below) and not Israel, as the LXX does. But he also stresses that the *Nations/Gentiles* will learn justice from Jesus and so will derive hope from the power of his name, which has been given to him by God.

It is of interest that in the MT this text ends with the phrase "and [even the furthest] shores will hope for his law," whereas in both Matthew and LXX the text concludes with the phrase "and upon his name the Nations/ Gentiles will have hope."[41] The stability of the Hebrew reading of "his law" is confirmed by the Isaiah Scroll from Qumran, column 35:13. However, in this text it is said that the furthest shores "will inherit [*NHL*] his Torah" (or at any rate this is the common translation, but "bequeath" is grammatically better), and not that the furthest shores "will hope for [*YHL*] his Torah." This must be an error, since the phrase "will hope *for* his Torah" makes much better sense than "will bequeath *to* his Torah." It would seem then that our text from LXX — "and upon his name [*onomati*] the Gentiles will have hope" — cannot have been the original reading in LXX. Most likely *YHL*, "will hope for his Torah," was the parent reading.

In any event, all manuscripts of LXX Isa. 42:4 read *onoma* and the word must somehow refer to Torah in this text, as it does elsewhere in LXX (although it is true that in the Gottingen edition of LXX Isa. 42:4 reads "hope for his law, *nomos*," the editors emended the text so that this reading would make sense).[42] Menken points out that there are places in the LXX that translate "Torah" by *onoma* and places that translate "name" by *nomos*, or, to be more precise, as Dale Allison once informed me, there are fragments and fuller texts that show how frequently these terms interchange with each other (Allison pointed me to versions of Exod. 16:4; 2Chron. 1:9, 6:16;

Ps. 58 (59):12, and elsewhere).[43] It is not likely that we have copyist mistakes in all these places. Therefore we must conclude that these two words could, at times, be interchanged, but for reasons that were theological rather than linguistic, as Menken says. It must also be admitted, however, that the verb "will hope for" — *elpiousin* — seems to imply the expectation of the arrival of a potent force rather than the arrival of a document or oral instruction.[44]

In light of all this, I can only conclude that Matthew does follow LXX for 42:4 (although as I say his reading of Isa. 42:1–3 is closer to what is found in the Masoretic Text, but this may be due to his particular version of LXX). Moreover, we should also understand that the word *onoma* in this verse in LXX means "Torah." According to the context of the narrative at this point the addition of Isa. 42:4 in Matthew is not warranted at all. Yet, he included Isa. 42:4 here because in it he found a prophecy in which it is said that the Gentiles would find hope "in his [Jesus'] name" (in the literal sense of the Greek). In Matthew's vocabulary, I suspect, *nomos* and *onoma* are never interchanged, so he happily used this text from LXX to suit his needs. If he was aware of the Hebrew text, he either ignored it as being irrelevant or else as having been corrupted by Jews. Given the fact that, strictly speaking, Matthew quotes from Isaiah 42 more than he needs, the polemical nature of the text as he uses it stands out all the more.

Matthew's use of LXX for this verse alone shows us that it had special meaning for him. His use of it is also an indication to me that Matthew and his audience were Gentiles. It is the Gentiles who will be the ones to trust and have faith in Jesus' name. Matthew is looking forward to the end of the Gospels here when Jesus, who while alive preached only to the "lost sheep of Israel," after his death and resurrection calls on his disciples to turn toward the Gentiles so that they might be the ones to carry forth his teachings (Matt. 28:19).[45] This is clearly the message of Matthew 12:42–45. Isaiah 42:4 is not meant to be a proof-text for Jesus' insistence that no one may broadcast the news of his miracles. The citation, as Matthew understands it, serves to introduce the idea that the Gentiles are worthy of salvation while the Jews are not.

Then there was carried to him a blind and mute person possessed by a demon and he healed him, so that the mute person could speak and see. (v. 22)

Incredibly here Matthew ignores the preceding narrative in which Jesus makes known that he wants no report of his miracles to spread. The healing is followed by another debate between Jesus and the Pharisees that is similar to those we have seen before, in which the Pharisees challenge Jesus over the propriety of his healings. See my comments to 11:5 above, which cite Isa. 35:5: "Then will the eyes of the blind be opened and the ears of the deaf unstopped."

> *And all the crowds were beside themselves, and said, "Is not this one the Son of David!" (v. 23)*

"Son of David" is another term for Messiah in rabbinic literature. The Messiah is envisioned as the descendent of King David, who saved Israel from the hands of its enemies.

> *The Pharisees, having heard, said, "This one only casts out demons by the name of Beelzeboul, the Prince of Demons!" (v. 24)*

The Pharisees want to defuse the messianic aura surrounding Jesus the healer, for which reason, according to Matthew, they offer another explanation for his ability to heal, by which means too they are able to castigate him. For the Rabbis as well Jesus was thought to be a sorcerer, at least according to a tradition in *b. Sanh.* 43a (uncensored editions): "Jesus practiced sorcery and corrupted and misled Israel."

Both the Syriac and the Vulgate offer "Beelzeboub" for Beelzeboul" here in Matthew. In T. Sol. 6:1–4, "Beelzeboul" is said to be the name of the "prince of the demons." About himself in this text Beelzeboul says: "I bring destruction by means of tyrants; I cause the demons to be worshiped alongside men; and I arouse desire in holy men and select priests. I bring about jealousies and murders in a country, and I instigate wars."

> *He knew what they were thinking, and said to them, "Every kingdom divided against itself is made barren, and every city or every house divided against itself will never be established." (v. 25)*

Again here we have the motif of Jesus' being aware of the nefarious intentions of the Pharisees toward him. I have discussed this motif in note 13 to chapter 9. Matthew introduces Jesus' diatribe by putting into his mouth a saying similar to the saying the later Rabbis used to introduce traditions concerning Hosea 10. Minor tractate *Derekh Eretz* 37:7 provides an example:

> "Their heart is divided, now they will be found sinful" (Hosea 10:2): The upshot is that being at peace is deemed precious, while division is deprecated. What are the examples? *A city in which there is division — it is destined to be made desolate.*

For the Rabbis have stated division in a house is [destined to bring wretched]
vileness... division in a court is [destined to bring] the desolation of the world.

"If the Satan casts out the Satan, he is divided against himself. How
then will his kingdom be established?" (v. 26)

Jesus' argument is this: If he were the Satan, the king of demons, and he were
casting out demons, then it would follow from what he has said above that by
doing this he would be dividing his own kingdom, thereby preventing it from
being established. So if his purpose were to establish the kingdom of Satan,
why would he divide his "own" kingdom by casting out demons? Hence he
cannot be working for Beelzeboul.

"And if I cast out demons by the name of Beelzeboul, by whom do your
people cast them out? Therefore they will be your judges." (v. 27)

Jesus knows that certain of the Pharisees also cast out demons and so now he
asks them why they think that by casting out demons he is in league with the
prince of demons, but the Pharisees who do the same are not? Should it not
follow that they are in league with Beelzeboul too? Let them — that is, those
of their own people — declare if demons are cast out by Satan or by God.

"But if I cast out demons by the Spirit of God, then God's kingdom has
already come upon you." (v. 28)

But in fact, Jesus says here, he casts out demons by the agency of the divine
Spirit. Moreover, since he has this power to cast out demons, then where he
is is where God's kingdom is, too. It should be noted that Jesus does not say
this explicitly, but by using an "if-then" construction, he leaves the matter for
the listener to decide rather than to make the case outright for his rulership
in God's kingdom.

"How can anyone enter a strong person's house and seize his things,
unless he first binds the strong person? Then he robs his house." (v. 29)

Here the discussion concerning Jesus' being in league with Beelzeboul (or
even being him) draws to a close. Yet what Jesus says here is perplexing. Just
how a weaker person can bind the stronger is not made clear. Nor is it made
clear who the weaker one is here and who the stronger. It is doubtful that
Jesus is suggesting that he is the weaker one in relation to Satan who is the

stronger, and whom he yet must somehow bind. It is more likely that he is saying that the God-given will in the body is the stronger one, and Satan the weaker. In the Book of Job (4:18–19), the human body is said to be a house: "He charges His angels with error; how much more those who dwell in houses of clay, whose foundation is in the dust." The use of the word "bind" here suggests the casting of a spell. In casting a spell, the Satan casts a spell on a person's will to do good and then takes control of the body (or house). The point is that Satan then takes possession of that person, or anyway a demon does so in his name, by ridding him of his will. It is Jesus who can free the person from possession of the demon by casting the demon out.

The use of "bind" to mean "possess" is found in Jewish mystical contexts. There are glimpses of this use of the word "bind" in normative rabbinic texts as well. Consider this tradition from *b. Šabb.* 81b:

> How does magic work? It is similar to the story of Rabbi Hisda and Rabba who were traveling on a boat. A Roman lady said to them, "Let me sit between you." They did not let her. She uttered an incantation (*mlta*) and bound (*asra* — literally "tied" or "bound") the boat [with a spell, which presumably froze the boat's travel]. They said *M-L-T* and released the spell.[46]

This confrontation then is between the Satan, who robs the body (house; see also v. 44 below) by tying up the moral "will" and Jesus, who frees the strong man (will). In some ways, the imagery is very close to Gnostic typologies. However, a distinction must be made: in Gnosticism the body is *ab initio* evil, not so here, where the body is possessed by Satan but is not inherently evil. No longer can this figure of Satan in Matthew be seen as the accusing and testing angel of the Lord, but rather as the king of that evil realm that opposes God's rule. We have here complete and utter dualism — the war between the divine and Satan.

> *"The one who is not with me is against me, and the one who does not*
> *gather with me scatters." (v. 30)*

The extreme dualism is now articulated. Either one is with him, Jesus says, or one is against him. There is no middle ground. One is reminded here of the words Elijah spoke at the contest on Mt. Carmel between God and Baal: "If the Lord is God, follow him; if Baal, follow him" (1 Kings 18: 21).

The acts of gathering and scattering stand in opposition to each other. Jesus says that one who does not gather with him scatters. In relation to this, an early teaching of the Rabbis, found in *y. Ma'as.* 3:1 (also *t. Ma'as. Rishon* 2:17), states:

One found grain in a field. What had been gathered into piles (intentionally) is forbidden [to be taken] since it would become stolen property. What remained scattered is permitted since it would not be stolen property.

The point here is that the gathered grain, the result of productive labor, belongs to the owner, for which reason to take it is to steal from him; whereas what has remained scattered belongs to all, so that, so far as the owner of the field is concerned, there is no theft in the taking of it, nor does it matter to him who takes it. But according to what Jesus says here, however, indifference is tantamount to scattering (i.e., removing from God's domain and control) the fruit of Jesus' labor. In this unit, the world is divided between the followers of Jesus and all the rest.

"Therefore I say to you, every sin and blasphemy will be forgiven people, but the blasphemy against the Spirit will not be forgiven." (v. 31)

Sipre Deut., piska 328 (end) has a similar saying: "For every [sin] the Holy One forgives people; for desecrating his name he exacts immediate punishment."

"And whoever speaks a word against the Son of Man, it will be forgiven him, but whoever speaks against the Holy Spirit, it will not be forgiven him, neither in this World nor in the World to Come." (v. 32)

The Hebrew idiom for the last part of the saying here is unmistakable: *lo ba'olam hazeh velo ba'olam haba.* For example, *Tanḥ. Gen.* (ed. Buber), *Vayera* 11, states:

"Far be it from you, far be it from you!" (Gen 18:25) that you do not forgo justice for all individuals, not in This World and not in the World to Come. Thus the doubling in Scripture [signifying that justice due in both worlds will not be ignored] of "far be it from you."

For Matthew, even if other sins may be set aside, blaspheming against God's name is a sin punishable twice over.

"Either make the tree good and its fruit good, or make the tree rotten and its fruit rotten, for the tree is known by its fruit." (v. 33)

Here and in the next verse the duality is heightened — good trees and the good fruit they produce as opposed to rotten trees and the rotten fruit they produce. The image of fruit in association with deeds is that of Jer. 17:10, as is made clear in a tradition in *Midrash Panim Aherim* (ed. Buber) to Esther, version B, parasha 6:

> For the Holy One judges each person according to his deeds, as it is said, "I the Lord search the heart and test the kidneys to give every man according to his ways, *according to the fruit of his deeds*" (Jer. 17:10).

Verses 12:31–37 concern blasphemy and evil speech, so this verse in which Jesus speaks of the quality of the fruit resembling the quality of the tree when considered in context also refers also to what one says. Speech is a deed and one will be judged for what one has said.

> *"Offspring of poisonous serpents, how are you able to speak good things, being evil? Out of the abundant things of the heart the mouth speaks." (v. 34)*

Again here the duality is clear and the anti-Pharisaic rhetoric rises to a pitch. The tone and content of this verse is not unlike that of Isa. 57:3: "But draw near hither, you children of the sorceress, the seed of the adulterer and the harlot." Matthew refers to the serpent here to highlight the treachery of the Pharisees, which is not unlike the treachery of the serpent in the Garden. What Jesus means here is that although the Pharisees can make sound good whatever they say, still they say it with evil intent. The harsh rhetoric here is meant to demonize Jesus' interlocutors and their leaders. A near parallel to the last part of the verse can be found in *Midrash Psalms* (ed. Buber), Ps. 28:4: "for what is in the heart comes into the mouth."

> *"The good person brings out good things from his good treasury, and the evil person brings out evil things from his evil treasury." (v. 35)*

Again we encounter a dualism, this time of a good person as opposed to the evil person. 1Sam. 24:13 contains a similar sentiment: "As the proverb of the ancients says, *'Out of the wicked comes forth wickedness.'*"

> *"I say to you that for every careless word which people say, they will have to give an account for it on the Day of Judgment." (v. 36)*

A tradition recorded in the medieval *Sefer Orhot Hayyim* purporting to be what Rabbi Eliezer the Elder said to the sages who were visiting him on his sickbed (quoted here from Eisenstein's *Otsar Midrashim*, p. 29, vol. 1, paragraph 9) gives this advice:

> "And do not make your mouth impure or utter even a word in jest for in the future judgment you will have to give an account [even] on words between you and your wife…and do not make room for evil thoughts in your heart for thinking will them bring to deed."

Rendering accounts on judgment day for every word and deed is a commonplace in the extensive moral literature of the Jews.

> *"For by your words you will be declared righteous, and by your words you will be condemned." (v. 37)*

Sipre Deut., piska 307 tells us that every act will be paraded before one at the final judgment, and then one will be forced to recall that "such and such you did on this day." Speech is also an act.

> *Then some of the Scribes and Pharisees answered him, "Teacher, we wish to see a sign from you." (v. 38)*

In Matt. 10:24 *didaskalos* (in Heb., *moreh, melamed*) is used to signify a teacher, while in 10:25 *kyrios* (Heb., *adon*) signifies the master of a slave. In minor tractate *Sem.* 12:13 we find *moreh* and *melamed* in exact parallel. *Mori* seems to have been the term used in direct address and is, in this late text, overshadowed by *Rabbi.*[47]

The "sign" the Pharisees ask for is of course a miracle but instead Jesus takes the word to refer to himself as teacher who in that role condemns his interlocutors. While they treat him with respect he responds with taunts and sarcasm.

> *He answered them, "An evil and adulterous generation seeks a sign, but no sign will be given to it except the sign of Jonah the prophet. For just as Jonah was in the stomach of the giant fish for three days and three nights, so too will the Son of Man be three days and three nights in the heart of the earth." (vv. 39–40)*

Jesus' mention here of his coming to rest in "the heart of the earth" for three days and three nights, just as Jonah spent the same number of days and nights in the belly of the fish (Jonah 1:17), is not, strictly speaking, what happened to him, according to the Gospels record. Jesus was only in the tomb three days and two nights. For the Gospels tradition, the story of Jonah's being in the belly of the fish for three days provides a direct foretelling of the three days (and two nights) that Jesus spends in the tomb between his death and resurrection (see Matt. 27:63–64 and 28:6). The point is that, for Matthew, biblical stories are seen as signs portending events in the life of Jesus. Christian interpretation, from its earliest times to the present, has understood the Hebrew Bible to be a collection of signs pointing toward the life, death, and resurrection of Jesus. This method of reading the biblical text has often been compared to *pesher*, a method of interpretation practiced by the Qumranites, in which biblical texts were read in light of that group's own situation. However, the form and intent of *pesher* is only broadly suggestive of this particular type of Christian exegesis, whose rules are not nearly as formal as those that governed *pesher*.[48]

"The Ninevites will awaken in judgment with this generation and condemn it, because they repented at Jonah's proclamation, and look, something greater than Jonah is here." (v. 41)

The point is that although Jonah did not preach repentance among the Ninevites but merely warned them of impending destruction, still they repented (Jonah 3.5). On the other hand, although Jesus, who says of himself here that he is greater than Jonah, has preached repentance among the Jews of this generation, they have not repented. Because the Jews of this generation have refused to repent, they will be condemned by those of a nation once sinful that did repent.

The obvious sense, as many commentators note, is that at the time of the last judgment, when the dead are to be resurrected, the people of Nineveh, who because they repented were saved from destruction, would by their own example serve to condemn the rebellious generation of the Jews in Jesus' day.

This view fits well with the Jewish idea of condemnation by example at the last judgment. A text from *b. Yoma* 35b includes a story of the final judgment concerning those who did not study Torah. Or rather this text contains three stories, the first two of which speak of those who did not study Torah; while the third, though in its redacted form does appear to do so (but this is only because it is included with the others), in fact does not. Moreover, only the third story relies on proof-texts, which shows it to be different in structure from the other two. The point of the third story is that the wicked are condemned by Joseph's refusal to be wicked, even though he was faced with severe temptations. I suspect it was the original prototype of the whole text, which was later reworked by the Rabbis to include also the stories about those who did not study Torah.

The Rabbis taught: In the World to Come, when (a poor man, a rich man, and) a wicked man[49] come[s] to the judgment — (when the poor is asked, "Why have you not studied Torah?" if he answers: "I have been poor, I had to earn my bread, and had no time," they answer him: "Were you poorer than Hillel the Elder?" Of Hillel the Elder it was said: Every day he went to work, and earned a Tarpeik. Half he gave away to the attendant of the college, to let him in, and on the other half he and his family lived. Once it happened he did not earn anything, the attendant did not let him in. He ascended the roof where there was an opening, and listened to the words of the living God, from the mouths of Shemaia and Avtalian. It was said: That day was a Friday, and in the season of Teveth [Dec/Jan], and he was covered in snow. When it became dawn time, Shemaia said to Avtalian: "My colleague, every day it becomes light at this time, and now it is dark. Is it such a cloudy day?" They raised their eyes, and saw the figure of a man. When they went up, they found on him a layer of snow three cubits thick. They took him down, washed him, dressed him with oil, placed him before a fire, and they said: "For such as this, it is proper that the Sabbath should be violated for him."

When the rich man is asked: "Why have you not studied Torah?" if he answers: "Because I was a rich man, and had many estates, and had no time to study," they answer him: "Were you richer than Rabbi Eleazar ben Harsum?" Of him it was said: His father had bequeathed to him a thousand towns on land, and a thousand ships on the sea, and he himself used to take a bag of flour on his shoulder, and wander from town to town and land to land to study Torah. Once his own slaves found him, and put him to hard labor. He said to them: "I pray you, let me go to study the Torah." They replied: "We swear, by Rabbi Eleazar ben Harsum's life, we will not let you go before you work." Thus, as long as he lived, he did not attend to his affairs, but studied Torah all day and all night.)

(When) the wicked man is asked: ("Why have you not studied Torah?") [reconstructed: Why have you sinned?], if he replies: "I was handsome, and was tempted by my sins," they answer him: "Were you more handsome than Joseph?" It was said of Joseph the Righteous that every day Potiphar's wife used to try to seduce him by her talk. The clothes she used to put on in the morning (to attract his attention) she did not put on in the evening, and vice versa, and her refrain was always: "Listen to me; do what I ask of you." He answered: "No." She said: "I will imprison you." He replied: "The Lord frees prisoners" (Ps. 146:7). She then said: "I will bend your loftiness." His reply was: "The Lord raises up those who are bowed down" (Ps. 146:7). She said to him: "I will blind you." He answered: "The Lord causes the blind to see" (Ps. 146:8). She gave him a thousand talents of silver. He was averse to her, or "to lie with her, or to be with her" [Gen. 39:10]. "To lie with her" in This World, "to be with her" in the World to Come. — *From here we see that* (Hillel condemns the poor man, Rabbi Eleazer ben Harsum the rich, and) *Joseph [condemns] the wicked (b. Yoma 35b).*

It is also noteworthy that in *y. Sanh.* 11:5 the point is made that God will severely punish Israel because they did not repent whereas the Ninevi tes did.

> *"The Queen of the South will awaken in judgment with this generation and condemn it, because she came from the ends of the earth to hear the wisdom of Solomon, and look, someone greater than Solomon is here. (v. 42)*

The queen here is said to be "Queen of the South's," several of whose ancestors may be referred to in Gen. 10:7, 25:3. While most scholars see that an actual kingdom is being referred to here which was geographically to the south of the Jewish homeland, it is possible that something else was meant by this designation which is now unknown to us. For some reason rabbinic tradition equated the south with wisdom (e.g., *b. B. Bat.* 25b: Rabbi Isaac said: He who desires to become wise should turn to the south [to pray]). However that may be, there can be little doubt that Matthew speaks of the queen here as "of the South" rather than "of Sheba" in order to show how very far she had to come to hear Solomon's wisdom. That is, Matthew makes plain how much effort the queen made in order to hear the wisdom of Solomon while Jesus, of far greater wisdom than Solomon, is ignored by the Jews. The argument of condemnation is the same as in the previous verse which speaks of the Ninevites. The reason Matthew includes the story of the Queen of the South's devotion to wisdom is so that he can say that not one but two witnesses will rise against Israel to condemn it at the judgment.

1 Kings 10:6–9 tells of the Queen of Sheba's visit to Solomon.

> And she said to the king, "It was a true report that I heard in my own land of your deeds and of your wisdom. However I did not believe the words, until I came, and my eyes saw it: and, behold, the half was not told me: your wisdom and prosperity exceed the report which I heard. Fortunate be your people, fortunate be your servants, who stand continually before you, and who hear your wisdom. Blessed be the Lord your God, who delighted in you, to set you on the throne of Israel: because the Lord loved Israel for ever, therefore he made you king, to do judgment and justice."

The theme of God delighting in the king who performs judgment and justice echoes that of Isa. 42:1–4, cited above in reference to Jesus.

And again echoing what is said in Isa. 42:4, both the Ninevites and the Queen of the South are examples of Gentiles who either repented or else sought out and/or received wisdom, unlike the Jews, for which reason they will be condemned by them. Unlike the prophets of Israel, Matthew's Jesus proclaims that the Jews are doomed and does not foresee their return to God and his Torah.

"When the impure spirit has left a person, it travels through waterless places to seek rest, but it does not find it." (v. 43)

Now Jesus explains why this generation will never be able to repent. Demons rushed to water in chapter 8 when Jesus performed an exorcism and by extension it is claimed here that they cannot rest if they do not find water. This is not the case in Matthew 17. Ironically, Matt. 8:28–32 shows us the demons in the form of swine charging headlong into the Sea of Galilee only to drown because they are in swine form. The Rabbis instituted "a ban on pouring impure water on the ground" (when that water had been used to wet the hands at a meal's close). A tradition in *b. Hull.* 105b states:

> At first I thought the reason you cannot pour *after waters* on the ground was because of the *grease*, but Mar told me it was because of the *evil spirit*.

Demons (impure spirits) are the forces that inhabit a person to incite his passions to rebel and sin. The exorcist can remove the demon but not for long. For the Rabbis, a person does not sin unless a "strange spirit" enters him.[50]

"Then it says, 'I shall return to my house where I came from.' And when it comes it finds things vacant, swept, and put in order. Then it goes and brings along with itself seven other spirits more evil than itself, and enters and settles there, and the last things of that person are worse than the first. So will it be with this evil generation."
(vv. 44–45)

When the evil desire has been purged it finds seven allies to come and capture the person's body (house) again and take it over. I do not know if seven is anything more than a symbolic way of saying "a magical, potent host of demons" here (and also in Luke 8:2: "Mary, called Magdalene, from whom seven demons had come out").

While he was speaking to the crowds, look, his mother and his brothers and sisters stood outside, seeking to speak with him. Someone said to him, "Look, your mother and your brothers and sisters are outside, seeking to speak to you." He answered the one who spoke to him, "Who is my mother and who are my brothers?" Extending his hands to his students, he said, "Look, my mother and my brothers and sisters. Whoever does the will of my heavenly father, that one is my brother and sister and mother." (vv. 46–50)

The final few verses of this chapter do more than reflect the theme of the ideological group insisting that its adherents make a clean break from their families, for it is now the members of the group who are family to the adherents. Jesus' language here concerning the disowning of the family goes beyond the rhetoric of the Cynics, in that it also implies a division of past from future, Jew from Gentile. The one who is God's child, Jesus says, is his sibling, whatever his ethnicity. In relation to this, *y. Qidd.* 1:7 (*Midrash Tannaim* to Deut. 14:1, commenting on Prov. 4:3: "For a son I have been to my father") states:

> When Israel does the will of the Holy One they are called "children" and when Israel does not do the will of the Holy One they are not called children.

The text's location at the close of this chapter on dualities highlights this message of breaking with the past, and also the destruction of the final generation of Jews, but in particular their leadership.

The next chapter will continue the theme of those who are inside and saved and those outside and doomed.

NOTES

[1] The Gospel will frame the issue as one of mercy and kindness to portray the Pharisees as heartless and unaccommodating where they should be the opposite. However, the point is rhetorical as no legal system can simply overlook its inner dynamic to accommodate all who are at some point disadvantaged by it. It would be difficult to argue that all the prophets wanted to uproot the practice of sacrifice which brought atonement when people failed to behave properly.

[2] See Matt. 23:23: "Woe to you, Scribes and Pharisees, hypocrites! For you tithe mint and dill and cumin, and have neglected the weightier provisions of the

law: justice and mercy and faithfulness; but these are the things you should have done without neglecting the others." About which weighing Rabbi Judah the Prince remarks (*m. 'Abot* 2:1) that one should be as careful with a light precept as with a weightier one.

3 Whereas in the Christian understanding of the *eschaton* it is the Nations who are victorious while Israel is condemned, in the Jewish understanding Israel emerges victorious from the final judgment and the Nations are condemned. *Midrash Tanḥ. Lev. Emor* 18 (cf. *Lev. Rab.* 30) explains the carrying of palm branches on the festival of Sukkot as emblematic of the outcome of the final trial of history where Israel and the Nations are judged.

> Compare it to two who went before a judge. For a time, we cannot know the outcome... whoever emerges carrying date fronds in his hands then signals he is the victor. So it is with Israel and the Nations as they pass before the Lord for judgment on the Day of Atonement: For a time, we do not know who is victorious. God told them to take palm fronds in their hands so all can know they were victorious in judgment. Thus did David say: Then shall the trees of the wood sing for joy, before the Lord — *when did this happen?* — when He came to judge the earth *on* the Day of Atonement. (We note the interpolations into 1Chron. 16: 33.) So Israel waits another five days so all can know that Israel was victorious. For this reason is it written, "And you shall take for yourselves on the first day" (Lev. 23:40).

4 Beaton, "Messiah and Justice: A Key to Matthew's Use of Isaiah 42:1–4?"

5 In Matthew Jesus will always criticize the Pharisees for lack of compassion. In mentioning sacrifice, Matthew adds that the Pharisees neglect compassion, but that is not central to the argument here. It is an aside.

6 These expressions translate the Hebrew *NTL* — "seize and raise (lift)" — the scribal transgression of handling certain items like animals on the Sabbath.

7 That is, "*mehallelim et hashabbat*," desecrating the Sabbath according either to biblical law or Pharisaic law. "Blameless" here means from the usual recriminations administered for transgressing the Sabbath rules of the sages.

8 Priests did not have to keep all the customary Sabbath rules of *shevut* in the Temple to safeguard against infractions of biblical Sabbath law. The fear and reverence of Temple priests within the confines of the Temple precincts guarded them from taking laxities there.

9 See *b. Šabb* 128a. In Mark we must assume that the text reads "plucking" and "rubbing" of the kernels to show the kernels were hard and taken from the field in an *ad hoc* way. See *t. Šabb.* 14:12 which permits *kotem* and *molel*, plucking and rubbing. The idea here is more the idea of plucking out the kernel from the ear and then rubbing it, which might be the idea in Luke (rather than uprooting the whole ear of grain as might be suggested in the other versions).

10 Compare *t. Šabb.* 9:14–16.

[11] To fully appreciate the point one needs to know that the law of sages is divided into two areas — infractions that in themselves can lead to physical or moral harm and infractions that protect people from getting involved in harmful physical or moral activities, While driving across a street against a red light might be dangerous, police officers may ticket drivers proceeding through yellow lights although they are in no real danger in doing so. Likewise safety margins on job sites and building codes must be observed even if these in and of themselves would not matter if ignored. At certain times these safeguard measures might be suspended if the need were pressing. Pharisaic law introduced safety legislation into Sabbath laws that were intended simply as safety measures but in and of themselves when transgressed are not subject to the penalties of real Sabbath violations. The rabbinic category for these safety infractions was "*patur aval assur*" (exempt from Sabbath law punishment but nevertheless forbidden by rabbinic decree). When some people saw Jesus and his disciples relaxing the safety measures they queried Jesus for his reasons and he supplied them.

[12] David Hill has noted that Matthew has edited this passage. See his "On the Use and Meaning of Hosea 6:6 in Matthew's Gospel."

[13] See *b. Beṣ.* 11b and *Šabb.* 20a.

[14] The Gospel is useful here in providing the scribal thinking behind "*eyn shevut bamikdash*" and "*kohanim zrizim hem,*" which are principles applied by later authorities to early laws. The Gospel evidence shows the aptness of these applications.

[15] It is unlikely that the idea of permitting laxity in that place was the invention of the Talmud's editors. The whole idea of such laxity runs counter to the thrust of Talmudic civilization and proves embarrassing in its permissive attitudes. The very next line in the Talmud criticizes the elders in the upper chamber for remaining silent in the face of one taking liberties with scribal laws. Rabbi Moses Feinstein, in his *Dibrot Moshe* commentary to *b. Šabb.* 29b, cannot accept the words as given in the Talmud without his positing very unlikely circumstances to account for the permissive attitude. The oddity attests to its originality. No one would invent it. It likely reflects actual ancient scribal notions concerning relaxing nonbiblical legislation. It seems obvious that the Scribes, open to the accusation that they were hypocrites by enacting rules and then exempting themselves, would have later abolished this questionable practice. But the vestiges of such exemptions (in places of vigilant authority) are preserved in the Talmudic version of the Tosefta and in the Gospels.

[16] This passage is similar to *t. Šabb.,* chap. 2, which however lacks mention of the vigilance of the court. The Tosefta may be an edited version since the old idea that rabbinic rulings might in some cases be suspended is nowhere else to be found except here. The language of the Palestinian teaching in the Talmud is also suspect as it utilizes Babylonian Aramaic. The reading in the commentary of Rabbi Hannanel is superior and it is likely that there was some such teaching in early times which fell out of the Tosefta. Similarly we find cases where certain

rabbinic laws are suspended both for priests since they are diligent; and also among the groups at Passover sacrificial meals where people are watchful. We note certain rabbinic laws may be suspended in these cases but never biblical laws.

17   Especially since he administered no medicines or herbs.

18   Aside from New Testament sources.

19   CD 11:13. The point seems to be that it is forbidden to extricate the animal on the Sabbath but we do not know the parameters governing this law.

20   See *b. Šabb.* 128b.

21   See *b. B. Meṣ.* 32b. Exod. 23:5 concerning an animal under stress states, "You shall surely help."

22   That is, utensils scribally forbidden to handle on the Sabbath. *T. Šabb.* 14:1 is discussed in *b. Šabb.* 123b, which mentions that both the Palestinian and Babylonian authorities dated the laws of "muktseh" to Second Temple times.

23   This "public silence" as to when rabbinic law might be mitigated was justified on the basis that divine honor was at stake. See *b. Šabb.* 153a.

24   The prohibition of "*muktseh*" is that of seizing and lifting ("*tiltul*") objects which are in categories that preclude normal handling on the Sabbath.

25   See *b. Šabb.* 128b and *t. Šabb.* 15:1.

26   Permission to override scribal Sabbath law where an object is of great value to its owner.

27   See *b. Šabb.* 154b.

28   See *b. Šabb.* 153a.

29   See *b. Šabb.* 53a.

30   See *b. Šabb.* 53b and 108b. This is spelled out clearly in Luke 13:14 where a woman was crippled for eighteen years here and the healer is told to come back on a weekday and do the cure. The condition was not worsening and presumably the pain was by this time quite habitual and not severely felt.

31   LXX Isa. 42:1 "Jacob, my child, I shall help him; Israel, my chosen. My soul has received him; I have laid my spirit upon him, he will carry out a judgment for the nations."

32   LXX Isa. 42:2: "His voice will not cry out, nor lift up, nor be heard outside."

33   LXX Isa. 42:3: "A broken reed he will not crush, and a burning wick he will not extinguish, but he will carry the judgment to the truth."

34   LXX Isa. 42:4: "He will shine brightly, and not be oppressed, until he puts a judgment upon the earth, and upon his name the nations will have hope."

35 See Matt. 22:41–46: While the Pharisees were gathered together, Jesus asked them, saying, What do you think of "messiah"? Whose son is he? They say to him, "The son of David." He says to them, How then does David by the Spirit call him "Lord," saying, "The Lord said unto my Lord, "Sit on my right hand, till I make your enemies your footstool"? If David then calls him "Lord," how is he his son? And no man was able to answer him a word, neither dared any man from that day on to ask him any more questions.

36 See Tigay, "On the Term 'Phylacteries' (Matt 23:5)."

37 I argue in the introduction to the volume that Matthew's source actually meant "a sheep."

38 "Son" is undoubtedly the meaning Matthew is thinking of if he is using a Greek text here. But a slave was also a "son" to his master.

39 For more on this, see Beaton, *Isaiah's Christ in Matthew's Gospels*. This work is devoted to the citations of Isa. 42:1–4 in Matthew.

40 A part of the text from Isaiah, — "He will shine brightly, and not be discouraged, until he puts a judgment upon the earth," — has been omitted, suggesting that what Matthew includes after the omission is intentional and operates as a direct message for what the narrative is meant to imply, which is spelled out in Menken's article on Isaiah 42.

41 It is possible LXX readings of this text have been influenced by Matthew's citation.

42 See Pietersma and Wright, eds., *A New English Translation of the Septuagint*. Moisés Silva translated Isaiah (Esaias) in this work and on the first page of his introduction to it he notes that he has diverged from J. Ziegler (Ziegler, ed., *Isaias*, 2nd ed., Septuaginta: Vetus Testamentum Graecum 14 [Göttingen: Vandenhoeck and Ruprecht, 1967]) in sixteen places and Isa. 42:4 is listed among them. Silva (p. 856) has followed the LXX manuscript readings and gives us here "name," as does Matthew. In balance, it does not seem likely, although it remains possible, that the mss were corrupted by the Matthean reading. The stronger argument here is that Matthew followed LXX here because it was convenient for him and it is likely this was the reason for his choosing to find a fulfillment text in way that did not typically call for one, since Jesus is not fulfilling any prophecy here.

43 Menken, "The Quotations from Isaiah 42, 1–4 in Matthew 12, 18–21," 45, and notes.

44 Menken points out that Isa. 26:8 in our Hebrew texts has "name" and "mention" as parallels, whereas in the same verse in Qumran 1QIsa "name" and "Torah" are given as parallels (ibid.). The interchange is likely theological, as Menken suggests. Although he does not tell us this, we should note that for the Rabbis God created the world through Torah, and in *b. Sukkot* 53b it is told how David created the space of the Temple by tossing a shard with "God's name" into the

Tehom, which suggests Gen. 1:2 — "the spirit of God hovered over *Tehom*." The thirteenth-century kabbalists say outright that Torah and the Divine Name are one and the same and again what is thought of in the thirteenth century indicates what might have been thought in the first. LXX seems to be evidence of this. From his book *On the Kabbalah and Its Symbolism* 40–42, here is Gershom Scholem's description of the phenomenon:

> "To say that the Torah was in essence nothing but the great Name of God was assuredly a daring statement that called for an explanation. … To say that the Torah is a name does not mean that it is a name which might be pronounced as such. … The meaning is rather that in the Torah God has expressed his transcendent being, or at least that part or aspect of his being which can be revealed to Creation and though Creation. [Scholem then goes on to discuss *m. 'Abot* 3:14, *Sipre Deut.*, piska 48, *Gen. Rab.* 1:1 (all of which share much with Plato and Philo [e.g., *Moses* 2:51]), esoteric and apocalyptic works of the Rabbis showing that heaven and earth were created by the Name of God and that Torah does not refer to a physical document but to a pre-existential being [Pseudo Rabad to *Sefer Yetsira* 1:2: "The primordial Torah is the name of God."] There were kabbalists for whom the conception of the Torah as the Name of God meant simply that it was identical with God's Wisdom … "

45   See chapter 2, n. 1.

46   Apparently there are two texts. Our printed editions have MLTA "a [counter] spell." Rashi assumes her spell was that she uttered the name of a demon and their spell was that they uttered a divine name. But the reading MLT (no A) is also said in Hassidic oral lore to be an original reading where the Talmud abbreviated the verse M[echasheifa] L[o] T[ehayeh], "You shall not allow a witch to live" (Exod. 22:17), as a word play on her *mlta*, which they counteracted by summoning this verse concerning witches.

47   See *b. Ta'an.* 20b: "Peace upon you, Rabbi, Rabbi; Mori, Mori." He said to them, "Whom are you calling 'Rabbi, Rabbi'?"

48   The rules are illustrated in my article, "Pesher Hadavar."

49   To be consistent the text should have read "handsome man" here. The questions are always of the sort: "Were you poorer than Hillel?" etc., but here we get: "Were you more handsome than Joseph?" instead of: "Were you more wicked than X?" This is the form we would need to have consistency. This section of the text in which Joseph represents the ideal of behavior must at one point have been independent from the others. In substance, it is closer to the meaning of what Jesus says here in Matthew: "The Ninevites will rise up in judgment with this generation and condemn it, because they repented at Jonah's proclamation."

50   See *b. Sotah* 3a and my article, "The Meaning of 'Shtuth,' *Gen. Rab.* 11 in reference to Mt. V: 29: 30," 148–51.

CHAPTER THIRTEEN

INTRODUCTION

In this chapter we will find an array of parables, which are supposedly meant to confuse the listener so that Scripture might be fulfilled asking that Israel be instructed in such a way as to close them from repentance. At least, that is the message of the Gospel's take on the passage. Parables, that is, analogies, yield abstract lessons that are expressed in terms of familiar scenes recognizable to the listener. In these familiar scenes there is always something peculiar that draws our attention, suggesting the meaning of the scene is not the familiar motif we expected at first glance. The parable requires we exchange the peculiarities for items that are required to render the scene intelligible. The scene that was familiar yet unintelligible requires the master to bring the decoded message into focus.[1] He must explain the required exchanges or substitutions that satisfy the listener as to the deeper meaning of the parable. Without the key to solve the parable, the untutored listener is forced to feel defeat; with the key, the listener values the revealed lesson.

In chapter 13 we will find the three types of parables that have their counterparts in form in rabbinic literature:

1. A series of analogies tied together in one scene, usually based on a reading of biblical verses (Matt. 13:18–23).[2]
2. Sometimes simply a story to illustrate a point, often enhanced by linkage to a biblical verse which has been read creatively to suggest the given parable.[3]

3. And other times, simply an analogy drawn from experience which is somewhat rare but testifies to an event that is within the realm of the possible now, and so by an inductive stretch could be normal at some time in the *eschaton* at the end of days (Matt. 13:33).[4]

Of the several parables found in Tanak we might note the failed vineyard that had been tended very carefully (Isa. 5:1–6) and its meaning: Israel failed to live the life required by its sacred covenant despite all the trouble God took to tend to Israel's needs. This motif was a favorite of the Tanḥuma cycle of midrashim which created its own parables around a king who had a vineyard.

The first parable in Matthew 13 provides us with the key to the parable by citing a text much like LXX Isa. 6:9–10 (cf. Mark 4:12; Luke 8:10). In this text the people are told that because they refused to listen they will be punished.

> By hearing, you will hear, but never understand, and looking, you will look, and you will never see. For this people's heart has thickened, and they hear slowly with their ears, and they have closed their eyes, so that they might never see with their eyes, nor hear with their ears, nor understand with their heart, and repent, and I shall heal them.

But the Hebrew of the Masoretic Text suggests that the prophet is to prevent the people from understanding so they will not repent and be redeemed. Repentance is to be denied to them.

> Hear indeed but do not understand; see indeed but do not perceive. Make the heart of this people calloused; make their ears dull and close their eyes. Otherwise they might see with their eyes, hear with their ears, understand with their hearts, and repent and be healed.

Those who have understanding already are able to gain more.

The Gospel tradition, in its pristine form, seems to solve a problem in the Isaiah verses. Who hears but does not understand? — the one who is robbed by Satan. Likewise, who sees but does not perceive? — the one ensnared by a parched soul. And for those who might have escaped Satan, anxieties and materialism thicken the heart to rebel and so dull the ears and blind the eyes from understanding. Only those already saved who are thereby guarded from Satan will repent and be healed of all ills. Matthew's editorial has a Gnostic tinge in his explaining that only the saved can be saved. This explanation of Matthew to make sense of Jesus' use of parable is actually embedded in the solution to the parable of the sower.

The style and form of the Gospel tradition explains the parable in the way that Qumran pesher explains its codes, and the biblical Joseph explained dream scenes he had heard: Item A stands for item B.[5]

In Jesus' first parable in this chapter he describes a farmer sowing seeds, of which those near the trodden path are snatched away by birds (Luke 8:5 "trod underfoot"); others land in stony areas with no soil (Luke 8:6 "no moisture"); others on thorn-bushes that smother the seeds; and others on good soil that yield high proportions.

Matthew 13:19–23 relates (Matthew uses singulars which I have rendered as "some" to better fit the English idiom. In the text of the chapter proper, which follows the introduction, I have given a more conventional rendition):

> Some people in hearing the word of the [entrance exam into the] Kingdom, and not understanding — [are disposed to let] the evil one come, and grab away that which was sown in the heart — this is [the meaning of the image of] what is "sown by the path."
> Further, [as for the image of] what is "sown on the rocky places" this [means] some who in hearing the word get it and immediately rejoice but it has only a temporary root in them. So when affliction and persecution come on account of the (enemy of the) word, they immediately are snared [by Satan].
> Yet [as for the image of] that sown in the thorn-bushes, — this [means] some who in hearing the word, and [are entrenched in] the anxiety of The Eon [of This Generation], and the seduction of riches, which [both] smother the word, until it [the word] is rendered fruitless.
> And [as for the image of] that sown on the best ground: this [means] some who in hearing the word, and [getting] understanding, indeed bear fruit, and [so] produces [more and more] — indeed [these yield] a hundredfold, then sixty-fold, then thirty-fold.

We can see here a series of analogies tied together by one common setting. The analogies are: a) Just as a bird snatches seeds from areas where crowds travel (and drop food) so Satan snatches away the understanding from those whose commitments are formed while traveling the road of the masses. b) Just as seeds on rocky terrain even in some growth are easily plucked up by passing winds, so the early understanding of one whose commitment is shaky will be uprooted by persecution until utterly dashed by Satan. c) Just as seeds fallen among thorns are smothered by them from growing, so one's growing understanding when based on a commitment subject to temptation from materialism and worry, will be choked by them. d) Just as seed grown on fertile, well cultivated ground will thrive and produce seed-bearing plants, so one's growing understanding, when based on a well-cultivated and firm commitment, will grow productively and increase to grand proportions. The parable ties the four analogies into a single scene.

In contrast, when the Rabbis (*m. 'Abot* 5:12) spoke of four types of student aptitudes, they categorized them somewhat differently from the Gospels: "Quick to hear, quick to lose." This has little merit but its opposite has considerable merit: "Slow to hear, slow to lose." Of greatest merit, is "Quick to hear, slow to lose" — this is the wise [person's lot]. And they pronounced, "Slow to hear, quick to lose — this is the worst lot (for a student of God's Torah)." The Rabbis did not lay the blame on Satan but on the disposition of the student.

In order to locate the thinking behind the parable it is useful to realize that the Jewish worldview has two models to locate what lies at the center of the world and what lies at the periphery. One model is that of the Holy Temple/Tent sanctuary, where divine revelation and holiness are concentrated in the center of three camps, each one with decreasing sanctity until the periphery and the excluded *tameh* are on the outside. Here the priests are the central focus of divine blessing, and through them and through their service the world is sustained. The Gentiles are at the edges.[6] The other model is that of Sinai/Torah where revelation and well-being are centered in the teaching and interpreting of the Holy Torah through its scholars and their houses of learning. The learned are in the inside, while the ignorant are distant, and the nations removed far to the edge. While initially the two models were largely conceived as coinciding with each other such that priests were teachers and the Great Sanhedrin was situated near the Temple's altar, in point of fact the two models, ritual intercession versus Torah learning, competed with each other and finally culminated in a bitter rift, the *Hassid-mitnagid* controversy in the eighteenth and nineteenth centuries.

So, too, the Gospels located two centers in their scheme of the world, Temple/priest and Pharisee/scribal teacher. In both models the Gospels will revel in the fall of these central institutions and reverse the insides and outsides of the worldview scheme. In Matt. 21:42–45 (Mark 12:10–13, Luke 20:17–19) Jesus will proclaim in the Temple that the people of Israel are to be replaced as well as their leaders, 1) intercessor-priest and 2) the guardian-of-Torah Pharisee. They will be displaced by Gentiles. In Matthew's "Great Commission" (Matt. 28:18–20) the Scribes/teachers will be displaced by those of the gentile nations. The two central models of Jewish life are to fall and in their stead completely reverse models are to arise. Israel and her leaders will be at the darkest outer region while the Gentiles will be in the center of the kingdom.[7]

This binary reversal has its echoes in the parables in Matthew 13. The ones at the edge of the field are under the sway of Satan and are kept in the dark; the ones closer to the center progressively find enlightenment. This is the model of the new kingdom: those so endowed by virtue of their being untainted by the worldviews of Temple/Torah will occupy the center and have open ears to hear the message; those at the edges of the kingdom cannot hear it at all. The Jews therefore miss the point; the Gentiles do not. Even Jesus' disciples cannot find their way without their teacher revealing to them the new setup. They too have been raised on the worn-out, sterile models. The orientation of the sacred cosmos has been turned completely inside out, the first are now last and the last are now first.

The parable of chapter 11 has now come full circle. Those, at the old center, who refused to listen to Jesus and John the Baptist are now not able to listen at the new center. They have migrated to the edges and will soon be cut off and destroyed in the fullness of time. And so the interpretive keys of the parables allow the suggestions of the oppositions of the worthy and the worthy. However, the key breaks down with the mustard seed and leaven in the dough parables, where another key is called for, the key of "much from little." The parables in chapter 13 find their realization in narrative events within chapters 13–14: a) those deaf to Jesus' teachings and b) small amounts of food increasing to feed multitudes. One must be careful to examine each parable on its own merits. It seems that the style and message of the parables come in pairs.

On that day, Jesus left the house and sat by the seashore. (v. 1)

It seems the text is disjointed and refers to some day when other things happened, which Matthew does not preserve. The sentence is strange because the previous chapter seems to have taken place on the Sabbath. So are we now to assume in this day, in addition to hiking through fields and debating Pharisees, that he addresses huge crowds? In chapter 12 the crowds were already there. In the Hebrew Bible the phrase "that day," or "that night" sometimes signals "a certain day" where simple events in a story begin to turn toward the climax. It might not mean literally that it was the same day in which prior events occurred. That "turn" has to do with his seeking those who are tuned to him and weeding out those who are not. His leaving his private space to go to the public area seems to suggest he went looking for an audience to address.

Many great crowds gathered to him, so he got into a boat and sat there,
and the whole crowd stood on the beach. (v. 2)

While the substance of the Jesus parables usually hinges on the deafness of most of his audience, it seems here the storyteller seeks a place for himself from which he can address the waiting crowds. Yet, what he has to say is both obscure and, if understood, rather demeaning.

> *He told them many things in parables: "Look, the sower went out to sow…" (v. 3)*

The use of "look" suggests the biblical language of dream as in Gen. 41:1. "[And it was at the end of two full years that] Pharaoh had a dream — namely, *'look*, he was standing at the River….'" Judges 7:13, "Look — I had a dream — a loaf of barley bread was tumbling into the camp of Midian," Isa. 29:8. "It will be like when a hungry man dreams, and *look*, he eats; but he awakes." The term, in dream or prophetic context, usually introduces an unexpected turn of events and portends something of profound consequence. In the passage that unpacks the parable (vv. 19ff) we discover that the seeds of instruction all fall on the ground of the heart, that is, the mind. The psychic site of the person represents the degree of distraction that hinders the growth of understanding (absorption and germination of the seed) in the mind.

> *And in the process of sowing, some seeds fell alongside the path, and the birds came and ate them. Others fell upon the rocky ground, where there was not much soil, and they grew up suddenly, on account of not having deep soil. When the sun rose, they were scorched, and they withered, because they had no root. Still others fell upon thorn-bushes, and the thorn-bushes grew up and smothered them. Others fell upon good soil and bore fruit, once a hundred, then sixty, and then thirty. Whoever has ears should listen. (vv. 4–9)*

Only those with unencumbered spiritual understanding will grasp the sense. Not all have eyes to see or ears to hear the message. We saw this expression earlier in chapter 11 to introduce the parable contained in the children's chant.

> *The disciples came and said to him, "Why do you speak to them in parables?" (v. 10)*

The irony is that they, who should grasp the meaning clearly, are troubled by this method of preaching — hiding more than is revealed. If they cannot fathom the message, how will others manage to appreciate the messages of Jesus? The point seems to be that if Jesus is complaining that he and John are being ignored by the masses, why does he teach in such an inaccessible form without including the key to his parables?

He answered, "Because to you it has been granted to know the mysteries of the Kingdom of Heaven, but to them it has not been granted." (v. 11)

"You already know my teachings, and are eager to learn so you have no need to be stimulated to hear more. But there are others, whose spirits are alive but inadvertently sleep. Hearing my words in parables, their ears awaken, and by watching, their eyes will awaken, for their spirit will envision that they are the subject of my parables. You are already awake." The Gnostic dualism that delineates the saved and the damned is discernable in these passages.

"For whoever has, it will be given to him, and it will be abundant; but whoever does not have, whatever he has will be taken from him." (v. 12)

Only the saved will gain rewards; the others will be deprived of all. In the next verses we hear that the people of Israel are the ones who are the unsaved, blind and deaf. The clear implication is that non-Israel, the Gentile, is to know the mystery of the Kingdom of Heaven.[8] The masses are not meant to understand. That is his point. No one should try to see the sayings of Jesus as being consistent with each other. At times it will seem the Jewish leaders are guilty of ignoring Jesus, at other times it will seem they are not guilty but so it has been ordained. At times it will seem the advent of the Son of Man is imminent and at others that Jesus himself is unaware of the time for his advent.

"Thus I speak to them in parables, because 'Looking, they do not look, and hearing, they do not hear, nor do they understand.'" (v. 13)

Much of the background necessary to grasp the sense of the following verses has already been explained in the introduction to this chapter.

The prophecy of Isaiah is fulfilled for them, "By hearing, you will hear, but not understand, and looking, you will look, but not see. For this people's heart has thickened, and they hear slowly with their ears, and they have closed their eyes, so that they might never see with their eyes, nor hear with their ears, nor understand with their heart, and repent, and I shall heal them (Isa. 6:10). But blessed are your eyes, because they see, and your ears, because they hear." (vv. 14–16)

Jesus remarks that the disciples are not of Isaiah's sinful, ignorant Israel but of the kingdom's saved. And the parable of the sower is precisely about those who understand the secret of salvation and those who do not.

*"'Amen,' I say to you, many prophets and righteous people yearned to
see what you see, and they did not see it, and to hear what you hear,
and they did not hear it." (v. 17)*

The very sentiment that the disciples are privileged to see what greater
prophets did not see is echoed in many passages in rabbinic literature — the
disciples are glimpsing the heavenly revelation of the Coming Age.
This is not unlike the tradition that the lowliest maidservant, at the time
when the Israelites were crossing the Red Sea, saw more than Isaiah and
Ezekiel (who gazed on angels and the divine throne) ever saw (*Mekhilta
of Rabbi Yishmael* to Exod. 19:11). Ordinary people witnessing miracles at
the time of redemption is a higher form of knowledge than prophecy. The
Rabbis took note that the events of the *eschaton* and the Coming World
were unseen and unheard by the greatest of visionaries. The language and
sentiment reveals that Matthew, using similar language, is making a claim
here of the redemptive process reaching historical realization at this point
in time:

Job 13:1 relates, "My eyes have seen all this, my ears have heard and
understood it." Yet, as for the Coming World, the Talmud notes:

And Rabbi Hiyya bar Abba said in the name of Rabbi Yohanan: "All the prophets, bar none, only envisioned [up to] the Days of the Messiah [preceding the
advent of the Messiah] but as for the [actual] Next World" *From of old no [ears]
have heard or given ear, [no] eye has seen, O God, except for you, what He will
make happen for those who hope in him* (b. Ber. 32b).

The italicized citation is from Isa. 64:3 which in its targumic (Aramaic)
form reads as follows:

*From of old no ear has heard the Mighty sound, not listened to the Awesome
utterance; the eye has not seen* — [including] what your people already
witnessed [in seeing] the glorious divine Shekhina, for there is no other
but you! — [*they wonder*] *that You in the future are to make happen for your
nation of saints who from time immemorial have been hoping in your [ultimate]
redemption.*

The Septuagint version is phrased as "we have not heard nor have our eyes
seen any God besides you and your works which you will do for those who
hope for your mercy." The switches from second to third persons in Isaiah
are perplexing. The Targum seems to echo the outlook of the Septuagint, and
Matthew's Jesus relates that the experience of the disciples signals the onset
of the new era.

Jesus now tells his disciples that only to them have the secrets of the future kingdom been shown. And since they have the eyes and ears to see and hear they will grasp his parables. The chapter now relates more parables, but Matthew in the meantime inserts a footnote containing the sense of the parable of the sower. The disciples, having prepared hearts, are able or should be able to discern the message.

"You, then, hear the parable about the sower." (v. 18)

The expression "hear" may signal a further tradition in the early Gospel corpus where we have the parable decoded. Parables about sowing were a commonplace in apocalyptic sources.[9]

"When anyone hears the message of the Kingdom and does not understand, the evil one comes and seizes what has been sown in his heart; this is what was sown alongside the path." (v. 19)

All messages that come into the heart are subject to the condition of the mind — is it spoiled by conforming to the popular ways of the times? The introduction to this chapter has dealt with the pertinent issues here.[10] It is worth noting the style here is different from the rest of the decoding passages. Everywhere else in that exercise we are given a sentence and then its commentary but here the commentary comes first and then the sentence it interprets (i.e., *"What was sown along the path"*). I think the point is that what needs to be stressed is that those at the edges of society, the marginals, have the best chance to receive the vision of the kingdom. It is not the mainstream Jews of the generation who stand at the entranceway. The question must be asked here: why does the listener not understand? Is that because they have some defect, moral or intellectual? It would seem the heart cannot absorb the message because this heart has been hardened by crowds who have well-set ideas to the contrary. The message that was sown in the heart is not familiar enough to be processed into understanding without lengthy effort. Intermediary teachers obstruct the heart from being able to directly grasp the message and hence aid Satan's work. The evil tempter is now easily able to confuse the hearer so he forgets about messianic teachings.

The message of the kingdom seems to refer to those teachings that enable one to enter the kingdom. One must prepare the heart first and then the kingdom will appear. The form of first message and then symbol makes this opening statement the operative key to the parable from which the other symbols derive meaning. Seeds give birth to produce what comes of their own; God has designed the seeds to do so. The same is true of teachings. In themselves they do little but they are catalysts in the prepared heart to give birth to new eyes and new ears to see the kingdom. Those who have ears are already of the kingdom since they can grasp the intent of what is transpiring in the historical present. The meaning of the parable leaves open the question of whether the unprepared hearts are so because these hearts belong to Satan or whether unhappy circumstances are the cause. The latter seems to be the case and Satan merely takes advantage of this turn of events. In the next parable, Satan plants unbelievers in the world.

"The one sown upon the rocky ground, this is the one who hears the message and takes it with joy right away. But he does not have a root in him, and he is temporary, so when trouble or persecution comes on account of the report, he stumbles. The one sown among the thorn-bushes, this one is the one who hears the message, and the anxieties of the world and the deceitfulness of wealth choke the message and it becomes fruitless. The one sown upon the good soil, this is the one who hears the message and understands, who indeed bears fruit and produces once a hundred, then sixty, then thirty."
(vv. 20–23)

It might seem that the next parable suggests that once those who are prepared are in place there needs to be a separation of those will enter and those who will not. But the next parable is a variant of this one, where those who reject Jesus are creatures of Satan. It is Satan who has placed the unworthy among the worthy. The final destruction of Satan's weeds (those who follow the Jewish leaders) is assured to happen at the appointed time. Patience is required. Why wait? The next parable explains why matters are delayed.

He gave them a different parable: "The Kingdom of Heaven is compared to a person who sows good seed in his field." (v. 24)

Who does enter the next world and who does not is the subject here.[11] The "kingdom" means events concerning the entrance to the Future World. The dualism here is good-seed/bad-seed. This parable requires no code as the previous one did. The method of interpretation in these cases follows a form we might call *pesher* that was a commonplace in the decoding of allegories.[12] Of course, not all parables are allegories where there are specific codes in place that assign a reference for each noun in the story; sometimes the story transcends the details.

> *"While he was sleeping, his enemy came and sowed poisonous weeds in the midst of the wheat, and left." (v. 25)*

The image is close to the generic myth of the Gnostics. Satan has created his own soulless creatures in this world of Creation. They are noxious weeds. No one is aware that he has done this but God. At the end a divine messenger, Jesus, will redeem the spiritual children of God (the wheat). The noxious poisons are of Satan. The Pharisees (or, perhaps more widely, the Jews) are the tools of the Devil to pollute God's world and must be eradicated. These teachings and their images have had a toxic effect on Christendom's treatment of Jews from early times through the twentieth century.

> *"When the plants sprouted and bore fruit, then the poisonous weeds appeared as well. The slaves of the householder came and said to him, 'Master, did you not sow good seeds in your field? Then, where did these poisonous weeds come from?'" (vv. 26–27)*

The story now names the person who did the sowing as "the householder" — a figure used by Jews to refer to God in their parables (*m. 'Abot* 2:15: "Rabbi Tarfon says: The day is short, and work is plentiful, and the workers are lethargic, but the reward is great and the householder is eager"). Matthew will tell us that the householder, in such images, refers to the "Son of Man" rather than God as Jewish tradition has maintained.[13]

> *"He said to them, 'A person who is my enemy did this.' The slaves said to him, 'Do you wish us to go out and gather them?'" (v. 28)*

Satan, the enemy of God is responsible for planting the weeds. The slaves must be the attending angels and this is confirmed later in the decoding of the parable in verse 39.

> *"He said, 'No, for when you gather the poisonous weeds, you will uproot the wheat with them at the same time.'" (v. 29)*

Hence the parable shows delay is required. The evil ones and the good ones might not be distinguishable until the time when the evil are completely ugly and the good completely beautiful.

> *"Leave them both to grow together until the harvest, and at harvest time I will ask the harvesters, 'Gather first the poisonous weeds and bind them into bundles in order to burn them, and gather the wheat into my barn.'"* (v. 30)

Now at the end of time, the apocalyptic separation of the saints and the sinners will occur and the evil ones will be destroyed. This image has been used in chapter 3 where John threatens the Pharisees and Sadducees. My comments to 3:1 show that the parable here has a biblical referent. Here end the parables drawing distinctions between the chosen and the damned. The harvesters are heavenly beings who have this task.[14] The interpretation of this parable is given further down in verses 36ff. Also see my comments to Matt. 3:10. Gathering can be used of inanimate objects or of people: "A time to scatter stones and a time to *gather* them" (Eccles. 3:5). Also note: "I will *gather* you and I will blow on you with my fiery wrath, and you will be melted inside her. As silver is melted in a furnace, so you will be melted inside her, and you will know that I the Lord have poured out my wrath upon you" (Ezek. 22:21–22). And "[T]hen they will know that I am the Lord their God, for though I sent them into exile among the nations, I will *gather* them to their own land, not leaving any behind" (Ezek. 39:28).

> *He gave them another parable: "The heavenly kingdom is like a mustard seed, which a person took and sowed in his field."* (v. 31)

This mustard parable is not really a substitution-coded parable like the others we have seen, but an example, a sample, of what is now possible that reflects the World to Come. The point of the mustard-seed teaching is to show that plants have been known to grow, although rarely, to very large sizes. The future is a present possibility, not an eruption and miraculous change of the present world order. The present has partial characteristics of the future. The style of parable is different from above and the message is different. It is not an allegory and is not to be interpreted as such.

Seder Eliahu Rab. chap. 3 (ed. Friedmann, 14) presents similar teachings about good fortune in the *eschaton* in parable form:

> They gave a parable, to what can the thing be compared. ... This is how it will be at The End in the Future World while a part of it is reality today.

Matthew's words here echo the beginning of Luke 13:19: like a mustard seed, which a person takes and sowed (Luke too has past tense) in his garden.

"It is the smallest of all the seeds, but when it grows it is the greatest of the garden plants, and becomes a tree, so that the sky's birds come and nest in its branches." (v. 32)

There is a puzzle here. This sentence mirrors Mark 4:32, "becomes [Mark too uses present tense] the greatest of all the garden plants and puts out large branches, so that the birds of the air can make nests in its shade." The conclusion is unavoidable that our texts of Matthew conflate the forms of Luke and that of Mark. Although the tenses are completely inconsistent, no attempt has been made to harmonize them.

Compare the following traditions where the abundance of the Messianic Era is noted as evident in our world. The difference is not one of substance but of degree. What is sometimes evident now will be normative in the New Era.

Sipre Deut. piska 316–17:

A: In the Eschatological Age every grain of wheat will be like two kidneys of a big ox, weighing four Sephorian liters.
B: And if this surprises you then consider the case of the turnip heads, for it once happened that one weighed thirty Sephorian liters. And it happened that a fox made a nest in the head of a turnip. It once happened there was a mustard stock with three twigs and one of them fell off and they covered a whole potter's hut with it. They struck it and they found in it nine kabim of mustard. Rabbi Simeon bar Halafta reported: A cabbage stalk was in the middle of my house and I could go up and down on it like a ladder...
C: You will not be wearied by treading or harvesting the grape but you will bring it in a wagon and stand it in a corner and it will constantly renew the supply that you may drink from it as from a jug.[15]
The Church Fathers cite Pappias who quoted John of Asia Minor in the name of Jesus:
C1: The days will come in which vines shall spring up and each grape when pressed shall yield five and twenty measures of wine
A1: Likewise also a grain of wheat shall cause to spring up...ten pounds of fine, pure flour. And so it shall be with the rest of the fruits and seeds and every herb after its kind.[16]

He told them another illustration: "The Kingdom of Heaven is like yeast, which a woman took and hid in three measures of flour until the whole of it was leavened." (v. 33)

Once again the parable stresses that what is now visible is a taste of the future. The word "parable" here means "an illustration" of what will be. Here "Kingdom of Heaven" refers to the changes in nature that will occur in the

Future. The mustard and yeast parables have the same message: much from little and find fulfillment in 14:17–20. The narrative "proves" the meaning of the parable. Of the four parables in this chapter the first two show anger against a group that rejects Jesus while the last two show the abundance of what is in store for those who accept him. They form two doublets.

> *Jesus said all these things in parables to the crowds, and except for parables, he told nothing to them. (v. 34)*

So we learn that he left it such that those to whom his message was directed would understand while others would not. The parables have messages that separate the worthy from the unworthy and that the reward of the worthy will be great, even in material and physical terms.

> *Thus was fulfilled what was spoken through the prophet, "I will open my mouth in illustrations, I will proclaim what has been hidden from the foundation of the world" (Ps. 78:2). (v. 35)*

Illustrations are parables. In the introduction to the next chapter I discuss that the parables of the weeds and mustard seed are more than parables — they are prophetic images awaiting fulfillment.

> *Then, leaving the crowds, he went into the house. His students came to him, and said, "Explain for us the parable about the poisonous weeds of the field." (v. 36)*

It is remarkable that they ask for explanation but since the parable of the sower has been decoded and this parable is a variant with a different mind-set, it needs to be spelled out.

> *He answered, "The one who sows the good seed is the Son of Man." (v. 37)*

We might have thought it to be God.

> *"The field is the world, and the good seeds are the kingdom's children. The poisonous weeds are the children of the evil one." (v. 38)*

Here the radical dualism is spelled out. This Satan is not merely a tempter, he is the ruler of the Kingdom of Evil and his children are likely meant to be Jews (as Gnostic myth often related.)

> *"The enemy who sows them is the devil, and the harvest is the culmination of the world, and the harvesters are angels." (v. 39)*

He speaks of the End of Days—the period preceding the coming of the kingdom.

> *"So just as the poisonous weeds are collected and prepared for fire, so will be the culmination of the world." (v. 40)*

This style of comparison is completely Jewish in style: "Just as…so…" Note the following explanations of poetic biblical verses which speak of Israel as comparable to sand (Hosea 2:1) and stars (Gen. 22:17) utilizing this type of rhetorical device:

> "In the messianic era they [Israel] are compared to sand—*just* as sand *grinds the teeth so* Israel will destroy all the nations." Israel is compared to stars—*just* as in the case of stars one is able to burn up the whole world so to the righteous [as Elijah could bring down fire through his word (2Kings 1:10)]. (*Num. Rab.* 2:13)

Of course, in the Gospel, it is sinful Israel that is meant to suffer extinction, not the sinful Gentiles.

> *41. "The Son of Man will send his angels, and they will collect from his Kingdom all the offenses and all who do lawlessness, and they will throw them into the furnace of fire. There will be wailing and the grinding of teeth." (vv. 41–42)*

Note how the same image of *grinding of teeth* occurs in *Num. Rab.* 2:3 above and v. 42.

> *"Then the righteous will shine like the sun in their father's kingdom."*
> (v. 43a)

The passage prefigures the Transfiguration scene in Matt. 17:2 (recalling Exod. 34:29): "And he was transfigured before them, and his face shone like the sun." The image of "shining" is an image of sharing in the divine, Next World, Consider the imagery in *'Abot R. Nat.*, A chap. 1 where it is said the righteous will sit with crowns on their heads and they will be basking from the glow of the Shekhina in the Next World.

Whoever has ears should listen. (v. 43b)

Again we meet with this expression inviting people to hear a parable, more so "to listen." The following parables all contain messages of investment, giving up everything for one single item of overwhelming value and not caring about the other things, which may be ignored. In this way the message is something like the weed parable. Within the decoding of the weed parable is a set of parables, the last one of which is to be decoded in much the same way as the weed parable. Those who are worthy are admitted into the kingdom; the others are cast away.

> *"The Kingdom of Heaven is like a treasure box hidden in the field,*
> *which a person who found it hid, and in his joy he goes and buys that*
> *field." (v. 44)*

He has no interest in the field but only in the treasure. God only cares for his treasured ones and will discard everything else in the field.

> *"Again, the Kingdom of Heaven is like a person in business, who searches*
> *for beautiful pearls. And, when he found one especially precious pearl,*
> *he went out and sold all that he had and bought it." (vv. 45–46)*

God will exchange faithless Jews for precious Gentiles of faith (see further v. 49 for narrative fulfillment).

> *"Again, the Kingdom of Heaven is like a net thrown into the sea, and*
> *all types of things were gathered into it. When it was full, they pulled*
> *it upon onto the shore and, sitting down, they gathered the good things*
> *into containers, and the rotten things they threw outside." (vv. 47–48)*

Only people of value will be gathered at the end. The rest will be discarded.

> *"So, it will be in the culmination of the world. The angels will go out and*
> *remove the wicked from the midst of the righteous. And they will throw*
> *them into the fiery furnace. There will be wailing and the grinding of teeth.*
> *"Do you understand all these things?" They say to him, "Yes." (vv. 49–51)*

In the next few verses the narrator shows us that the Jews have no faith in Jesus — Jesus turns his back on them and so the parable of the weeds finds immediate prophetic fulfillment.

So he said to them, "On account of this, every scribe who has been taught about the Kingdom of Heaven is like a person who is a householder, who brings out of his treasury everything, both new and old." (v. 52)

As is typical in Matthew's reconstruction of Jesus' teaching, he ends with an exhortation. The exhortation seems to be a message to the preachers, the Scribes of all the nations. Here I think Matthew would identify with the message: You are like a householder who needs to use whatever is at your disposal — old teachings to some groups and new teachings to others.

When Jesus finished these parables, he left from there. Coming to his home town, he taught them in their assembly, so that they were amazed, and said, "From where did this wisdom and these miracles come to him?" (vv. 53–54)

The Greek says *patris* — his home province — but it likely reflects the Semitic *medina* which can also refer to his city.[17] What is amazement here ends up as being criticism, sarcasm and dismissive: How can this common man be a teacher and a miracle-worker?

"Isn't this the builder's son? Isn't his mother called Mary and his brothers Jacob and Joseph and Simon and Judah?" (v. 55)

Who is this person who claims to be more than we know him to be — a local boy from a local family and no one more than that.

"And aren't his sisters all with us? From where did all these things come to him?" (v. 56)

"We know his friends and family, oh so well — so fools might believe the stories told of him but we do not." This response to Jesus is likely meant to deal with the question of his rejection. If his miracles were so public, how come few Jews followed him? The answer is because to the Jews of his city and to his family he was just a local boy and no one special. So the Gospels explain how it is that Jesus' own family is not numbered among his disciples.

And they were offended by him. Jesus said to them, "A prophet is not dishonored, except in this home town and in this house." (v. 57)

The sentiment is universally strong and some universities do not hire their own graduates to teach in the institutions that trained them. Yair Chaim

Bacharach in his *Havvat Yair* (Lemberg, 1896; reprinted, Jerusalem, 1987, p. 230b) notes the custom in Worms: "In our community it cannot happen that one homebred (*ben bayit*) will become the city Rabbi." Three years before his death (1701/2) he actually received such an appointment and served as the Rabbi of Worms until his death. The words of Jesus here reflect the same disappointment that Bacharach discusses in his work but the bitter phrasing in the Gospel suggests outright condemnation of the attitude of his former friends. They should be proud and his strongest supporters, not those who think of him as "the kid down the block." However, 14:35 provides the rest of the key. While the Jesus-character seems to be distraught at what is happening, Matthew pushes forward with his subtle narrative.

And he did not do many miracles there, because of their faithlessness.
(v. 58)

One might have expected him to prove himself and dispel all doubts but the Gospel tells us he did not do this.

NOTES

[1]   In rabbinic writing, parables are certainly a common device for explaining concepts. In many cases, they relate abstract concepts to more familiar social dynamics in order to make the abstract concepts more understandable, more believable. In Matthew (and Luke) the message of the parable is often purposely blurred for the casual reader/listener.

[2]   See my discussion in *Midrashic Interpretations of the Song of Moses*, 132–37.

[3]   *Y. Ber.* 2:8:

> When Rabbi [A]bun the son of Rabbi Hiyya passed away [while young] Rabbi Zera came to deliver the eulogy. He decoded the allegory of the verse in Eccles. 5:11/12: "Sweet is the *shenat* of the laborer…" and pointed out the verse did NOT say "sleep" but DID say "*shenat*" (on the surface it does mean *shenah* — sleep but its deeper meaning is, *shanah*, "year." And in this light we read the continuation of the verse) "If of few (years) he consumed as much as if of many." To what can the situation of Rabbi [A]bun be compared? To a king who hired many laborers amongst whom was one who accomplished more [than his daily share] What did the king do? He took him out to stroll about the long and short paths with him. When evening came the laborers went to collect their wages. He paid this one equally with the others. The laborers complained, "We have toiled the

whole day, while this man has toiled only two hours. Should he be given the same wages as we earned?" The king said to them: "Why are you angry? He accomplished more in toiling two hours than you accomplished in the entirety of a whole day."

So Rabbi [A]bun accomplished more [and will be rewarded as such] in his twenty-eight years [shanah] than a diligent student might accomplish in one hundred.

The idea of equal pay for late adherents to the teaching of Jesus together with the original members of his [Jewish?] followers is the point of Matt. 20:1–16. While the parables look similar, the messages are not at all alike. The title of the above might be "the good die young: equal reward for equal accomplishment" while the title of the next one might be "last come first served: equal pay for all members notwithstanding unequal efforts or work done."

> For the [notion of reward in the] Kingdom of Heaven is comparable to a householder, who went out early to hire workers for his vineyard. When he negotiated with the workers for a rate of a denarius per day, he sent them into his vineyard. When he went out three hours later he saw others standing idle in the marketplace. He said to them, "Get yourselves to the vineyard, and I will give you whatever is right." They left. Again he went out around the sixth and ninth hour, and did the same. When he went out around the eleventh hour he found others standing and said to them, "Why have you stood here all day idle?" They say to him, "Because no one hired us." He says to them, "Get yourselves to the vineyard!" When evening came the lord of the vineyard says to his foreman, "Call the workers and pay them their wage, beginning with the last up to the first." When the ones hired around the eleventh hour came they took each a denarius. And when the first one came, they thought that they would receive more, but he gave to each a denarius — even to them. When they took it, they murmured against the householder. These last worked one hour, and you have made them equal to us, who suffered the burden and the heat of the day. He answered one of them, "I did not treat you unfairly. Did not you negotiate a denarius with me? Take what is yours and go. I wish to give to the last as I gave to you. Am I not permitted to do what I wish with what is mine? Or is your eye wicked because I am good?" So will the last be first and the first last.

4   *B. Šabb.* 30b claims that in the Future Era women will give birth to large numbers of children and nature in general would produce food abundantly. The analogy is provided: Even today chickens lay eggs daily and some trees can produce more than one type of fruit. These samples are a parable for the *eschaton*.

5   See my "Pesher Hadavar."

6   See Josephus, *Ag. Ap.* 2:8; 103–9. The model of the Temple shows the world hierarchy from center to periphery. In prayer, the Temple axis remains the

central fixed point to locate the divine (*b. Ber.* 30a). *M. Hor.* 3:8 preserves the Temple Hierarchy but shows that Torah knowledge trumps everything.

7   The message is hardly new at this point. See Matt. 8:10–12:

> Jesus, hearing this, marveled, and said to those who were following him, "'Amen,' I say to you, never have I found such faith in anyone in Israel. I say to you that many will come from the east and the west and they will recline at the table with Abraham and Isaac and Jacob in the heavenly kingdom. But the children of the kingdom will be thrown into the outer darkness, where there will be wailing and the grinding of teeth."

8   Acts 28:26–28 has Paul interpreting Isa. 6:9–10: "Saying, Go unto this people, and say, Hearing ye shall hear, and shall not understand; and seeing ye shall see, and not perceive: — For the heart of this people is waxed gross, and their ears are dull of hearing, and their eyes have they closed; lest they should see with [their] eyes, and hear with [their] ears, and understand with [their] heart, and should be converted, and I should heal them." Be it known therefore unto you, that the salvation of God is sent unto the Gentiles, and [that] they will hear it.

9   Compare 4 Ezra 9:31 "I sow my law in you."

10   Some scholars assumed Matthew has taken a Gospel parable from his source and affixed to it his own interpretation. Some introductions to the New Testament still state it as a fact. Be that as it may, we deal here with Matthew who provides the meaning of the figures and we leave it at that. See Kee, *Understanding the New Testament*, 142. Kee accepts J. Jeremias' (*The Parables of Jesus*, 81–85, 224–27) assertion that the interpretations of parables in Matthew are the evangelist's creations and were never affixed to the original parables attributed to Jesus. The vocabulary is purely Matthean, according to Jeremias. There is no point for a commentator to Matthew's Gospel to decide this particular issue since the commentary is meant to explain the Gospel of Matthew that assuredly does contain these interpretations.

11   Compare 4 Ezra 8:41: "For just as the farmer sows many seeds upon the ground...not all that were planted will take root."

12   I have discussed this form at length in my work, "Pesher Hadavar."

13   See Matt. 9:37–38 for the parallel.

14   *The Rule of the Community*, 1QS columns III and IV, draw similar distinctions between the saved and the damned. The task of uprooting these latter falls to the Angels of Destruction.

15   A/C forms a single unit, introduced in A by "In the Eschatological Age," and its theme is found in the Second Apocalypse of Baruch, 29:5–8 (post 70 c.e.) but may well be prior to it. B interrupts this unit. Such interruptions are not uncommon in the Talmuds and midrashim of the Rabbis, and tend to signify

what we might call "notes." They are rarely scribal interpolations. B shows us an unaffected expectation of prosperity since such abundance is even evident, although rare, in the present era. The examples of B are not of wheat or wine but of cabbages and turnips and mustards. *B. Ketub.* 111b has variants of these themes.

16   J. Klausner (*Jesus of Nazareth,* 401), cites the passage at length. Nevertheless, since the teaching of physical bounty in the Kingdom reported by Pappias flies in the face of the post-Jesus spiritualization of God's Dominion, we might well accept this declaration was suppressed from the Gospels by those who preserved Christian tradition. However, what escaped suppression (and likely did so because of its ambiguity) was preserved in the Gospels, namely, I suggest, the mustard seed parable.

17   Luke 4:16, in reporting the city name, tells us it is Nazareth which was the city where Jesus grew up.

<hr>

CHAPTER FOURTEEN

<hr>

INTRODUCTION

This chapter, marking the halfway point in the traditional chapter division of the Gospel of Matthew, is a fitting point to end this volume. Matthew, early in the Gospel, portrays how Jesus' mission was revealed to him at the time of his meeting with John the Baptist (chapter 3). Subsequently, Matthew presents John and Jesus as highly unsuccessful in their efforts to create meaningful change on the historical stage of their lifetimes (chapter 11). Indeed, neither figure looms large or even at all in the writings that have been preserved from the first half of the first century. Nonetheless, it might be gathered from the late first-century writings by Josephus (*Ant.* 18:118–19) that John was loved by the people and feared by the authorities. Jesus also left his mark in that his cult following continued to grow in the first century. The writings of Paul, Acts, Didache, and Barnabas show us the growth of churches and their organization.

In this chapter, we get historical flashbacks showing us the senseless execution of the saintly John. The plot of Herodias and her daughter manipulate the Tetrarch to utter a rash oath. The machinations of those in power, feeling threatened by his message of impending salvation from tyranny and his loyalty to Jewish law, risked antagonizing the masses by making a martyr of him. In near parallel, at the end of the Gospel, those in power felt Jesus' threat to them was equally strong and execute him. While no curse is attached to those who murdered John, in the most straightforward reading of his narrative Matthew will expand the blame for the spilling of Jesus' blood to all Jews living at the time of Jesus and to their children who are to descend after them (Matt. 27:25).

The gruesome beheading of John ends the historical setting of the events of the chapter. What follows is Matthew's ingenious structuring of the theological setting of the chapter. Just as Jesus went into the desert alone after his first encounter with the Baptist, so, too, did he after the Baptist's death. Whereas in the early scene Jesus refuses to demonstrate his divine powers proving his entitlement to the title "Son of God," here he demonstrates them fully.

The scene has shifted; historical time has ceased. In this twilight desert scene, between two worlds, present existence is at the threshold of change. Everyone present now stands at the entrance to the kingdom. The disciples fail to grasp they have entered a spiritual space. The meaning of the parable of the mustard seed of chapter 13 and the leavening is suddenly, starkly realized. The crowds are huge, a dozen thousand or more, including women and children. Morsels of food give rise to not only enough to fill the crowds but also the leftovers will fill twelve baskets. Abundance is everywhere. The disciples failed at first to grasp the change in scene and would have dismissed the usual followers who sought Jesus' cures. There is one other place (chap. 21) where historical time stops and huge crowds stand at the entrance to the kingdom. While the model of the narrative might be based on 2Kings 4:41–43, the Gospels use of the motif, feeding many from little, serves a completely new Gospel function: entering the time tunnel of *eschaton*. In chapter 21 Jesus enters Jerusalem as throngs proclaim his glory. In this chapter, the Jewish leaders and the Jews as a whole are told they will be deserted by God who will chose another nation and so the parable of the weeds of chapter 13 is now brought to reality in that scene.[1] In a similar way, 21:9 find the crowd reciting Ps. 118:26, "Blessed be the one who comes in the name of the Lord." A few chapters later in 23:39 we read: "For I say to you, You will not see me from this time till you say, *Blessed be the one who comes in the name of the Lord.*" The fulfillment of the later verse occurs two chapters earlier. Furthermore, in Matt. 21:9 the crowds welcome Jesus as he rides his messiah-charged animals to Jerusalem, but in the next verse, 21:10, we read, "And when he came into Jerusalem, all the town was moved, saying, Who is this?" The people in the Temple have no idea who he is until informed by the followers from the previous scene. We have two episodes viewed through an interstitiary forward movement of donkey canter, prayer, and rejoicing — then backwards to old conflict scenes. Time is divided between now and future expectancy. The symbols here mark the ambiguity in the narrative. Time moves between historical present and the entrance to the kingdom in the future. Chapter 14 shares the same ambiguous time switches (and parable fulfillment) with the scene in chapter 21 portraying Jesus' entrance to Jerusalem. The halfway point is a kind of marker at the center of the Gospel that moves the action to its climax: death in historical time, salvation in sacred time.

At that time Herod, the Tetrarch, heard the report about Jesus. (v. 1)

This Herod in chapter 14, also called Herod Antipas, was the stepson of Herod the Great mentioned in chapter 2. As Tetrarch he was ruler of a province, in this case the Galilee.

He said to his slaves, "This is John the Baptist. He has risen from the dead, and on account of this the miracles are accomplished by him." (v. 2)

Up to this point the narrator suggests that Herod Antipas had never heard of Jesus. Now that he had executed John and soon after Jesus appeared on the scene curing invalids, Herod thought that the two men were one and the same.

For Herod had seized John and bound him and put him in prison on account of Herodias, the wife of Philip, his brother. (v. 3)

Herodias was the granddaughter of Herod the Great and the wife of Herod's son Philip until she abandoned him for his half-brother, Herod Antipas. The arrest of John may have been either because she manipulated Herod Antipas to silence John's condemnation of their marriage, or, more likely, because of John's messianic preachings (see below in v. 5), which threatened Rome's authority. The Gospel's account subsequently makes Herod look sympathetic to John.

For John used to say to him, it is not permitted for you to marry her.
(v. 4)

Herodias left Herod's son and then married her husband's half-brother, Herod Antipas, the Tetrarch of Galilee. Even had she been properly divorced by her husband, she was nonetheless marrying her husband's brother, as Jewish law would have it; a brother from the same father, an act considered incest (Lev. 18:16). Only when a man dies without leaving any offspring may his wife enter into a living arrangement with a surviving brother. The law of Deut. 25:5–10 spells out the laws of "*yibum*." Josephus (*Ant.* 18:136), like Matthew, also mentions that for Herodias to marry her husband's half-brother they flouted ancestral laws.[2] He says this was because she parted from a "living husband." I have no idea what is gained by having the word "living" here. The problem to my knowledge would not be any less had Philip died while they had still been married.

*And wishing to kill him, he feared the crowd, because they held that he
was a prophet. (v. 5)*

This verse does not accord well with the previous (v. 3) in which Herod had
arrested John due to the pressure of his wife. Here it says that he wished to
kill him but below in verse 9 it says that he had no such intention and repeats
that Herodias forced his hand. I suspect this verse comes from a variant story
that Herod, Tetrarch of the Galilee, feared that John's messianic speeches
might cause popular uprisings against himself and Rome as Josephus remarks
in *Ant.* 118–19.

*But at the time of Herod's birthday, Herodias' daughter danced in the
middle of the court, and pleased Herod (v. 6)*

In Josephus's *Antiquities* 18.136 it is said that Herodias gave birth in her first
marriage with Philip to a daughter. It is usually assumed that the reference
here, in Matthew, is to that daughter.

*So that he promised her by an oath to give her whatever she asked.
(v. 7)*

Public oaths were serious promises that people were duty-bound to keep.[3]

*She had been prepared for this by her mother: "Give me," she said,
"here on a board, the head of John the Baptist." (v. 8)*

Herodias had plotted the occasion and knew Herod would kill John if he
made an oath in front of others. In the end it was her daughter, Herod's niece,
who actually made the demand. Herod, knowing the vindictive grudges held
by Herodias, would never have offered "whatever you desire" to her. But she
outsmarted him and "set him up" to get her way.

*The king was grieved, but he called for this to be granted, on account
of the oaths and the dinner guests. (v. 9)*

The Tetrarch was also referred to as king. The verse suggests remorse, as
if to say — what else could he do? He acted impatiently and made an oath
that might now create disturbances. The Gospels tradition seems to express
some sympathy for his dilemma — not a bad guy, just a victim of circumstances.

He sent and beheaded John in the prison. (v. 10)

Beheading with a sword was a normal Roman way of doing away with those sentenced to death by Roman courts. The next verse seems to say that the prison was nearby. Events are likely truncated for the sake of keeping the narrative at a quick pace. Josephus' account of John's death differs from Matthew's as I pointed out in the introduction to chapter 4 (discussing v. 4:3).

His head was brought on a board and given to the little girl, and she brought it to her 3mother. (v. 11)

The gruesome act is a brilliant piece of writing that shows us the callousness and wretchedness of those involved. The picture of the girl, whom we might have expected to be gentle and kind, with the severed head of the prophet on her platter, makes us shudder at her vileness. She presents the head to her mother. The two of them appear completely depraved and Herod appears as weak and ineffective. The actions tell the story, not the dialogue at all. It is all done in silence in the narrative. The horror of the scene depends on the rapidity of the five verbs "sent," "beheaded," "was brought," "given," "she brought." The effect shows us one continuous action from Herod's first command until her mother receives the head. What happens then is left open to the imagination as nothing further is said — it would be anticlimatic to say another word. The mother's reaction is left off the page. The words "her mother" would normally sound kind and gentle, but here there is an ironic twist. In verse 8 we are told "her mother" had put her up to having the king order John's death. The daughter was the mother's agent to connive John's murder and finally her agent to deliver his lifeless head to her. The final act shows the daughter again — the mother's hand is unseen but always there behind each of the five verbs.

His students came and took the corpse and buried it, and they came and reported to Jesus. (v. 12)

John is buried and we now get the impression that Jesus is the one who must continue the work of John in spreading the message of repentance and redemption. At the same time, the students likely warn him that the Tetrarch suspects he is a reincarnation of John.

When Jesus heard he left from there in a boat to a desert place by himself. When the crowds heard, they followed him on foot from the cities. (v. 13)

Jesus had not gone so far that he could not be found. Seeking solace, he is pursued by crowds of lame and sick who were somehow able to walk the distance.

Coming out, he saw a great crowd and he had compassion for them, and he healed their sick. (v. 14)

Jesus attends to their needs, performing miracles.

As evening arrived, his disciples came to him: "This is a deserted area and the hour has passed. Discharge the crowds, so that they might go into the villages and buy themselves food." (v. 15)

Mark relates (during the scene depicting the confusion of the stormy sea) that the disciples had not understood the significance of the feeding (and further in Matt. 16 and Mark 8 we learn there are mystical interpretations behind the bread episodes). Luke gives meaning to the event by placing the Transfiguration (a kind of baptism by light) of Jesus in chapter 9, eight days after the miracle of the loaves. John 6, while relating the same events, tells us that Jesus is the true bread and that the manna in the desert was just a sign of Moses to tell us that eventually one will come who will be the bread of everlasting life.[4] Apparently, the Gospels accounts reflect the controversies in the churches to make sense of the miracle. This is the only miracle shared by John and the synoptics. This sharing shows it to have been an ancient tradition. The miracle was understood to mean something more than just another miracle performed by Jesus.

The present narrative makes the reader work and may reflect various subtle changes introduced by the evangelists into an early apostolic tradition. Chapter 14 began with historical time, projecting Herod the Tetrarch's arrest and beheading of John, then forwarding to Jesus' withdrawal to a lonely, deserted place. Incredibly, hordes of people appear to whom Jesus, presumably, preaches about the kingdom and cures their illnesses. Then the narrator reports that in this desolate place it was evening. The disciples remark that the time, the hour, the era has passed — on the surface they seem to be noting that the hour is growing late and the people need to be sent away now. However, that is not what they say — they say, "the time has passed."

Matthew's organization of the passage when compared to Mark's shows us his literary skill in taking highly complex and poetic images and showing us the mystery through subtle shifting and editing. Elsewhere in Matthew (v. 23) (cf. Mark 6 and John 6) evening comes after they have eaten — quite logical, for otherwise the people would have been eating in the dark.[5] We will need to account for Matthew's mention of evening so early in the account. Also, markets closed at dark, and we are told in Matthew the people still have time to get to market on foot from the desolate location. It was clearly not evening yet. So why does Matthew say it is? The intent is to illustrate that they are living in dual time and space — liminal, desert, a twilight zone of historical time and eschatological time. The time of This World is passing through an ontological portal, through the looking glass into the dream reality of the Next World.

> *Jesus said to them, "They have no need to go; you give them something to eat." (v. 16)*

Jesus rebukes them, "Hey guys, wake up — you can supply them. In this vision of the New World there is no difference between much and little." The verse recalls, as the does the entire episode, 2Kings 41–44.

> *But they said to him, "We have nothing here except five loaves of bread and two fish." (v. 17)*

The disciples do not get it. They are stuck in the historical present. Since they are oblivious to the fact that they stand at the entranceway to a new realm, they ask Jesus to have the people return to the markets to purchase food. Jesus, knowing they are at the edge of the *eschaton,* supplies much from little. The parable of the mustard seed and the leaven comes to fruition — the feeding of the thousands is no longer a miracle — it is the norm for the *eschaton,* the new world.[6] The disciples fail to see what they are experiencing, and behave as if all is normal.

> *He said, "Bring them here to me." (v. 18)*

Jesus is not stuck in any particular time frame. He is now in the entrance to the future.

Calling the crowds to lean back upon the grass, he took the five loaves of bread and the two fish, and, looking up to heaven he said the blessing, and, breaking them, he gave the loaves of bread to his disciples, and gave them to the crowds. (v. 19)

Eyes upward toward God, he blesses over the bread with a *berakhah* (blessing), giving thanks to the Lord who sustains. Then he broke (Greek *klasas:* used of breaking bread, precisely like Hebrew *pores* or its equivalent *botse'a*) the bread into pieces to have them distributed to the masses. Everything is as normal — no one says a miracle occurred, no one takes note that such little food could feed the masses and have leftovers. The phrases of "blessing," "breaking," and "giving of the food" have found their way into church liturgy, suggesting the framers of the liturgy understood that the meal was a sign of the future communion of his followers. The verb used here to signify that they should sit for the meal is *"anaklino,"* literally to recline and is equivalent to Hebrew *lehasev* which is "to recline." Meals of the upper classes were customarily eaten on dining couches in Roman times, and the word came to mean simply to "sit at a meal" as here and by extension "to eat a festive, substantial meal."

Early Jews were divided as to whether one should first break the loaves and then bless or the reverse (break first and then bless) before distributing the bread. The Talmud decides that first one should bless and then break the bread. Rashi (*b. Ber.* 47a) neatly summarizes an involved discussion by citing the Talmudic decision of *b. Ber.* folio 39b (eight pages earlier) that the blessing had to be concluded before commencing the breaking: "he would break off a piece and give it to whoever was beside him saying, 'take from the slice of blessing [i.e., one that had already been blessed before being sliced].'"[7] The order of blessing first and breaking afterwards is fixed in Jewish law and we see it to be precisely the order found in the "Last Supper" descriptions in 1Cor. 11:24 and Matt. 26:26.

And all ate and were satisfied, and they took what was left over of the broken pieces, twelve baskets full. (v. 20)

The disciples might be amazed but no one else seems to be — and even the disciples say nothing. The image of eating and being satisfied and having leftovers is found in Ruth 2:14: "And she did eat, and was satisfied, and had leftovers." The mystery of the scene has not been lost on commentators and preachers who have speculated on its illusive and elusive sense. The numbers here may have some allegorical significance, but I will refrain from speculating on such matters in this commentary. The parables of "much which comes from near nothing" are here illustrated in the dramatic events. The reader, as I said in comments to verse 16, might consult 2Kings 4:43–44 for a similar story including the leftovers ("and they [100 men] ate and they left thereof").

The ones who ate were about five thousand men, not counting women and children. (v. 21)

In discussing the 600,000 men who journeyed out of Egypt ("besides young ones") in Exod. 12:37, *Mekhilta of Rabbi Yishmael* (*Pischa Bo* 14) tells us that "besides young ones" means "not counting women and children." The manner of counting those present is decidedly Jewish.

Right away, he compelled the disciples to go into the boat and to go ahead of him to the other side, until he dismissed the crowds. (v. 22)

In quick succession now the action has Jesus pushing the students to get into the boat where they are to be tossed in stormy waves and high winds. The disciples are singled out for a more personal journey to "the other side" of the world. They did not see the dual blurred worlds of the twilight existence (between the past-day and the not-yet-night) that marked the deserted place. So they will now journey into the unknown night until daybreak, where they will have an ascension-like experience over the waters that threaten to drown them. The conquering of the threatening sea, the home of satanic monsters, is a motif of new creation (Isa. 51:9–13), and intimates that a new mode of existence awaits those who are prepared. In the end, and the Gospel primes us now (see v 31), Peter will fail; he will at early dawn (the time of v. 31) deny Jesus (Matt. 26:74). The storytelling here is rich with allusions that prefigure the closing chapters of the Gospel.

He dismissed the crowds and went up to the mountain by himself to pray. When evening came, he alone was there. (v. 23)

Now Jesus is left alone on the mountain and he offers his solitary evening prayer. This is now "true evening" — the world he is in is no longer that of history. He offers his prayer closed away from the others in accord with his dictum to pray in private (Matt. 6:6).

But the boat had already sailed many stadia from the land, and it was being tossed about by the waves, for the wind was up against it. (v. 24)

The disciples have lost control of the boat and seem to be victims of ill winds. The measure of a *stadium* (pl. *stadia*) is approximately 607 feet or 185 meters.

> *In the fourth watch of the night he came to them walking upon the sea.*
> (v. 25)

Likely, the sense is that this event occurred just as dawn was about to break. The night was divided into four watches in the Western empire, while Babylonian and the East held on to the older system, also used in ancient Greece, of three watches. Jews in Judea and the Galilee sometimes used the one and at other times the other. It is of interest to note that while Judg. 7:19 and every version of it reports a three-watch night ("Gideon and the hundred men with him reached the edge of the camp at the beginning of the middle watch, just after they had changed the guard") Josephus, *Ant.* 5:223–28, readjusting one system for the other, takes some liberty by pushing the time forward ("about the fourth watch, Gideon marched forth his army...confusion and panic seized the hapless creatures..."). That time must have been thought to be the time when ghosts and specters are prone to attack people. Hence it would have been fitting for Gideon to have frightened the Midianites at that time. Josephus' audience would have appreciated Gideon's cunning in that context. And so the Gospel finds this to be the auspicious moment to have the disciples imagine they see a "ghost."[8]

> *His disciples saw him walking on the sea, and they were disturbed and*
> *said, "It is a ghost!" And they cried out from fear.* (v. 26)

Because it is the time when phantoms roam and fear rules the world, Jesus has trouble convincing the disciples that they are mistaken. The transition from one world to the next is by faith and belief in Jesus' ability to transform time and place from one world to the next. Jesus needs to persuade them all is well. Ghosts and demons have no rule over those of the Next World.

> *Right away, Jesus spoke to them saying: "Be brave (Deut. 31:6).*
> *It is I (Exod. 3:14). Do not be afraid (Deut. 31:6)."* (v. 27)

The citations from Deut. 31:6 (Moses' farewell address) and Exod. 3:14 (God revealing his name) not only inform the disciples that salvation is at hand, a statement that should be taken to allude to a much larger salvation, but also may be seen to be propitiatory and effective words to calm the raging sea. Similarly, rabbinic literature (*b. B. Bat.* 73a) also reports a story about Jewish seafarers who must confront a stormy sea. They, too, turned to the same Exodus verse alluded to in Matthew.

These Jewish sailors used amulets to save them from apparitions on the stormy seas. Obviously, the experience was terrifying and the delivery from it seen as miraculous.

A certain wave was threatening to sink their boat — it seemed as if bright beams of light were on its crest — so we showed (or beat) it with sticks that had engraved on them, "I am that which I am... *amen amen selah*," and it stopped.

Some further analysis here is called for. Either the disciples recognize Jesus' voice or they do not. If they do, all is fine, but if they do not, "It is I" will not help them. Peter is not completely sure who it is, and will ask for a test to discover the truth. Jesus calms everyone down, and like the amulet, repeats, "It is I" — "I am," the phrase used in Exod. 3:14 to inform the Israelites that the worker of their salvation will save them.

> *Peter, answering him, said: "Lord, if it is you, command me to come to you over the waters." (v. 28)*

Peter still has some lingering doubts concerning the figure's identity and asks to be commanded and so be given power. Jesus' words have authority over nature.

> *He said, "Come," and, getting out of the boat, Peter walked upon the waters and was coming to Jesus. (v. 29)*

The mere command of Jesus is sufficient motivation for Peter to focus his concentration and move into the world of belief, where nature does not impose its normal limitations.

> *But seeing the turbulent wind, he was afraid, and began to sink, and called out, saying, "Lord, save me!" (v. 30)*

Peter experiences the reality of his fear in his disturbed consciousness of time and space frames. The laws of nature are not operative in any disruptive way for those whose belief transmutes them and their world out of the historical present into the realm of the transcendent.

> *Right away, Jesus stretched out his hand and took hold of him, and said to him, "You of little faith, why did you waver?"*
> *(v. 31)*

Jesus castigates him — if Peter cannot see over the edge, who will? With Peter's doubt the portal is shut and historical time returns. The teachings of the kingdom have some more to grow.

When they got back into the boat, the wind stopped. (v. 32)

Jesus imposes his miracle for those in the boat who are not yet ready to experience the world beyond. All is calm.

Those in the boat worshiped him: "Truly, you are the Son of God." (v. 33)

What the tempter in Matt. 4:9 demanded of Jesus at the beginning of his career, Peter gives to Jesus, and Jesus does not flinch to accept. Time, space, and circumstances have changed. The disciples in some sense had crossed into eternal time and now have crossed back. The meaning of "Son of God" here is "one who shares in the divine."[9]

And when they crossed they landed in Gennesaret. (v. 34)

The boat regains balance and all is back to normal — time has resumed its steady pace. Gennesaret Sea or Lake was named after the lush region at its shore which measured some sixteen by five miles (*War* 3:516–21).[10] This city would have kept Jesus safe from Herod Antipas (who feared that Jesus and John were one and the same) for there was no love lost between the two Tetrarchs.[11]

The men of that place knew him, and sent out to that whole region, and they brought him all who were ill. (v. 35)

These locals seem to be mainly Gentiles and unschooled peasants. Josephus (*War* 3:516–52) remarks that after the death of Herod the Great, Herod's son Philip then ruled the area called Gennesaret. That these people are noted to have known him means they knew his powers, and unlike the people of his hometown, believed he could perform miracles. Apparently, Jesus was not keen on agreeing and a compromise was struck.

They urged him so that at least they might touch the fringed-hem of his cloak, and those who touched were healed. (v. 36)

The compromise was that Jesus need not touch them but they would touch the mere fringes of his garment. The Greek *kraspedon* is the Aramaic *keruspad* (pl. *keruspedin*).[12] In the end, the mere trace of a touch of a tassel that he was wearing at the hem of his garment sufficed to bring the ailing person complete health. Jesus' power was extremely strong. On this note, we end this volum.

NOTES

1   For Matthew, the Gentiles are signified in Ps. 118 as the new chosen to replace the Jews. This is the Psalm of victory for Matthew. The Jewish nation, defined as a nation by their teachers and leaders, are not present in the *eschaton* when Jesus will usher in the New Age which, in essence, has already happened in mythic time in 21:42–45. Matthew describes how ancient prophecy is now happening:

> Jesus says to them, "Did you never see in the Writings, 'The stone which the builders rejected, the same has been made the chief stone of the building: this was the Lord's doing, and it is a wonder in our eyes (Ps. 118:22)'? For this reason I say to you, *The Kingdom of God will be taken away from you, and will be given to a nation producing the fruits of it.* Any man falling on this stone will be broken, but he on whom it comes down will be crushed to dust."

And when his stories came to the ears of the chief priests and the Pharisees, they saw that he was talking of them.

2   LXX 25:5–10, like the Rabbis and the Sadducees in Mark 12:19, rules that a child of any sex will suffice to close off the possibility of levirate marriage. Davies, "Inheritance Rights and the Hebrew Levirate Marriage: Part 1," 142 n. 15, suggests that Josephus, in his discussion of marriage laws in *Antiquities* 4, is of the opinion that a son is necessary but his translation of Josephus does not substantiate the claim:

> This is clearly the way in which Josephus (*Ant.* IV. viii. 23) understood the Deuteronomic provision, for in his comment on Dt xxv 5–10 he makes the following remark (I have added the emphasis): "When a woman is left *childless* on her husband's death, the husband's brother shall marry her, and shall call the *child* that shall be born by the name of the deceased and rear him as heir to the estate; for this will at once be profitable to the public welfare, houses not dying out and property remaining with the relatives, and it will moreover bring the women an alleviation of their misfortune to live with the nearest kinsman of their former husbands."

3   We note in this regard that, while under some circumstances it is possible to have private promises remitted, under no circumstances does any Jewish law permit remitting of public promises.

4   John 6:16–35:

> When evening came, his disciples went down to the sea, got into a boat, and started across the sea to Capernaum. It was now dark, and Jesus had not yet come to them. The sea became rough because a strong wind was blowing. When they had rowed about twenty-five or thirty *stadia*, they saw Jesus walking on the sea and coming near the boat, and they were frightened. ... But he said to them, "It is I; do not be afraid." Then they were

> glad to take him into the boat, and immediately the boat was at the land to which they were going. On the next day… "Do not labor for the food that perishes, but for the food that endures to eternal life, which the Son of Man will give to you. For on him God the Father has set his seal." Then they said to him, "What must we do, to be doing the works of God?" Jesus answered them, "This is the work of God, that you believe in him whom he has sent." "Truly, truly, I say to you, it was not Moses who gave you the bread from heaven, but my Father gives you the true bread from heaven. For the bread of God is he who comes down from heaven and gives life to the world." They said to him, "Sir, give us this bread always." Jesus said to them, "I am the bread of life…"

5   Luke 9 omits any mention of evening.

6   See the commentary to Matt. 13:31.

7   James 2:21–22 speaks of Abraham's faith being justified by works when he offered his son Isaac on the altar. Ramban (commentary Gen. 15:6), some twelve centuries later, said the very same thing but provided the scriptural hermeneutic of shared wordings (Gen. 15:5–6 and 22:17) that yields this conclusion. Medieval works are not irrelevant to the study of the New Testament.

8   In *Ant.* 5:213, Josephus remarks that Gideon saw a specter in the night.

9   See my article, "Sharing in the Divine."

10   The name is known to the Targum of Numbers 34:11 and is the same as the Sea of Kinneret (*b. Meg.* 6a). The lush fertility of the area is noted by Josephus (*War* 3:515–21) and *b. 'Erub.* 30a.

11   Philip possessed this area and. I assume Matthew would understand that Jesus did not frequent Herod's territory very much right after John's death for fear of being taken as John *redivivus*.

12   LXX Num. 15:38–39 speaks of the *tsitsit* fringes as"*kraspeda*" while Aramaic *Targum Onqelos* translates these fringes as "*kruspedin.*" The Hebrew *tsitsit* is used to this day and many Jews observe the commandment daily. Obviously, it was part of Jesus' daily attire. Its purpose is to remind Israel to perform their sacred commandments, avoid physical or mental distractions, and to cement their bond with God who redeemed Israel from Egyptian bondage. The Gospel writers do not hide this Jesus from our eyes, from our touch.

BIBLIOGRAPHY

Agnon, S. Y. "According to the Suffering is the Reward." In Ha-Esh Ve-Ha-Etzim (The Fire and the Wood). Jerusalem: Schocken Books, 1962.

Albright. W. F., and C. S. Mann. Matthew. Anchor Yale Bible. New York: Doubleday, 1971.

Allison, D. C. Jesus of Nazareth: Millenarian Prophet. Minneapolis: Fortress Press, 1988.

Allison, D. C. The New Moses. Minneapolis: Fortress Press, 1993.

Allison, D. C., M. J. Borg, J. D. Crossan, and S. J. Patterson. The Apocalyptic Jesus: A Debate. Edited by R. J. Miller. Sonoma, Calif.: Polebridge Press, 2001.

Aus, R. D. Matthew 1–2 and the Virginal Conception in Light of Palestinian and Hellenistic Judaic Traditions on the Birth of Israel's First Redeemer, Moses. Lanham, Md.: University Press of America, 2004.

Avneri, T. L. "Megillat Ta'anit." Hebrew Union College Annual 8–9 (1931–32).

Basser, H. W. "Approaching the Text: The Study of Midrash." In Methodology in the Academic Study of Judaism, ed. Z. Garber, 117–34. Lanham, Md.: University Press of America, 1986.

-----. "A Distinctive Usage of PTH in Rabbinic Literature." Hebrew Studies 20–21 (1979–80): 60–81.

-----. "Derrett's 'Binding' Reopened." Journal of Biblical Literature 104 (1985): 297–300.

-----. "Gospel and Talmud." In The Historical Jesus in Context, ed. A.-J. Levine, D. C. Allison, and J. D. Crossan, 285–95. Princeton, N.J.: Princeton University Press, 2006.

-----. "The Gospels and Rabbinic Literature." In The Missing Jesus, ed. C. A. Evans, 97–125. Binghamton, N.Y.: Global, 2001.

-----. "The Gospels Would Have Been Greek to Jesus." In Who Was Jesus? A Jewish-Christian Dialogue, ed. C. A. Evans and P. Copan, 111–24. Louisville, Ky.: Westminster/John Knox Press, 2001.

-----. "Ideas of Glory and Sonship in Hebrew Scriptures and the Gospels." Approaches to Ancient Judaism, n.s., 15 (1999): 1–8.

-----. In the Margins of the Midrash. Atlanta: Scholars Press, 1990.

-----. "The Jewish Roots of the Transfiguration." Bible Review 14 (June 1998): 30–36.

-----. "Matching Patterns at the Seams: A Literary Study." In From Ancient Israel to Modern Judaism: Intellect in Quest of Understanding, 2:95–118. Atlanta: Brown University, 1989).

-----. "Matthew 21:12: Trading Words, Turning the Tables, Timing the End." In When Judaism and Christianity Began: Essays in Memory of Anthony Saldarini, ed. A. Avery-Peck, D. Harrington, and J. Neusner, 1:3–18. Supplements to the Journal for the Study of Judaism 85 (2004). Leiden: Brill.

-----. "The Meaning of 'Shtuth,' Gen. Rab. 11 in reference to Mt. V:29:30." New Testament Studies 31 (1985): 148–51.

-----. "Midrashic Form in the New Testament: A Study in Rhetoric of Likes and Opposites." Approaches to Ancient Judaism, n.s., 3 (1992): 141–54.

-----. Midrashic Interpretations of the Song of Moses. New York: Peter Lang, 1984.

-----. "Pesher Hadavar: The Truth of the Matter." Revue de Qumran 13 (1988): 389–405.

-----. "Planting Christian Trees in Jewish Soil." Review of Rabbinic Judaism: Ancient, Medieval, and Modern 8 (2005): 91–112.

-----. "The Rabbinic Attempt to Democratize Salvation and Revelation." Studies in Religion 12 (1983): 27–33.

-----. Response to Katz, "Methodology in Basser's Studies." Review of Rabbinic Judaism 4, no. 2 (2001):

-----. Response to Marcus Bockmuehl: A Critical Note," Review of Rabbinic Judaism 7 (2004): 172–75.

-----. Review of D. Rottzoll's, Rabbinischer Kommentar zum Buch Genesis: Darstellung der Rezeption des Buches Genesis in Mischna und Talmud unter Angabe targumischer und midrashicher Paralleltexte. CBQ 57 (1995): 564–76.

-----. "Sharing in the Divine." Bible Review (April 2002): 20–26.

-----. Studies in Exegesis: Christian Critiques of Jewish Law and Rabbinic Responses, 70–300 C.E. Boston: Leiden: E. J. Brill, 2000.

-----. "Uncovering the Plots: The Image of Rabbi Shimon bar Yohai." In The Mathers' Lectures and Other Papers in the Study of Judaism at Queen's University, ed. J. Neusner, 53–56. Binghamton: Global, 2001.

-----. "What Makes a Commentary Jewish or Christian." In The Reception and Interpretation of the Bible in Late Antiquity, ed. L. DiTommaso and L. Turcescu, 37–53. The Bible in Ancient Christianity. Leiden: E. J. Brill, 2008.

Bauckham, R. Jesus and the Eyewitnesses: The Gospels as Eyewitness Testimony. Grand Rapids, Mich.: Eerdmans, 2006.

Baumgarten, A. I. "The Pharisaic Paradosis." Harvard Theological Review 80, no. 1 (1987): 63–77.

Beaton, R. Isaiah's Christ in Matthew's Gospels. Cambridge: Cambridge University Press, 2002.

-----. "Messiah and Justice: A Key to Matthew's Use of Isaiah 42:1–4?" Journal for the Study of the New Testament, no. 75 (1999): 5–23.

Becker, A. H., and A. Y. Reed, eds. The Ways That Never Parted: Jews and Christians in Late Antiquity and the Early Middle Ages. Minneapolis: Fortress Press, 2007.

Bernstein, M. J., and S. A. Koyfman. "The Interpretation of Biblical Law in the Dead Sea Scrolls: Forms and Methods." In Biblical Interpretation at Qumran, ed. M. Henze, 61–87. Grand Rapids, Mich.: Eerdmans, 2005.

Bourke, M. "The Literary Genus of Matthew 1–2." Catholic Biblical Quarterly 22 (1960): 160–75.

Boyarin, D. "A Revised Version of the Translation of a Toledot Yeshu Fragment." Tarbiz 47 (1978): 250ff.

Brown, R. The Birth of the Messiah: A Commentary on the Infancy Narratives in the Gospels of Matthew and Luke. New York: Random House, 1999.

Brown, S. "The Matthean Community and the Gentile Mission." Novum Testamentum 22, no. 3 (July 1980): 193–221.

Buechler, A. "The Induction of the Bride and Bridegroom into Chupa in the First and Second Centuries in Palestine." In Livre d'hommage a la memoire du Dr Samuel Poznanski, ed. A. Friemant, M. Schorr, and D. Simonsen. Warsaw, 1927.

Burkett, D. R. The Son of Man Debate: A History and Evaluation. Society for New Testament Studies Monograph Series. Cambridge: Cambridge University Press, 1999.

Campbell, J. The Hero with a Thousand Faces. Princeton, N.J.: Princeton University Press, 1999.

-----. Myths to Live By. New York: Viking Press, 1972.

Complete ArtScroll Siddur. Brooklyn: Mesora, 1985.

Crossan, J. D. "Virgin Mother or Bastard Child?" In A Feminist Companion to Mariology, ed. A.-J. Levine with M. M. Robbins, 37–55. London: T&T Clark, 2005.

Daube, D. The New Testament and Rabbinic Judaism. London: Athlone Press, 1956.

Davies, E. W. "Inheritance Rights and the Hebrew Levirate Marriage: Part 1." Vetus Testamentum 31, fasc. 2 (1981): 138–44.

Davies, W. D., and D. C. Allison. Matthew 1–7: A Critical and Exegetical Commentary on the Gospel According to Saint Matthew. ICC Critical Commentary Series. London: Continuum International, 2004.

-----. Matthew: A Shorter Commentary: Based on the Three-Volume International Critical Commentary. London: T&T Clark, 2004.

Deutsch, C. "Wisdom in Matthew: Transformation of a Symbol." Novum Testamentum 22, no. 1 (1990): 13–47.

De Young, J. B. "The Function of Malachi 3:1 in Matthew 11:10: Kingdom Reality as the Hermeneutic of Jesus." In The Gospels and the Scriptures of Israel, ed. C. Evans and W. R. Stegner, 66–91. Sheffield: JSOT Press, 1994.

Diest, F. "Appayim (1Sam. 1:5) * Pym?" Vetus Testamentum 27, fasc. 2 (April 1977): 205–9.

Dor, Z. M. Torat Erets-Yisrael be-Vavel (The Teachings of Eretz Israel in Babylonia). Tel Aviv: Dvir, 1971.

Duling, D. C. "The Eleazar Miracle and Solomon's Magical Wisdom in Flavius Josephus's Antiquities Judaicae 8:42-49." Harvard Theological Review 78 (1985): 1–25.

Dunn, J. "John the Baptist's Use of Scripture." The Gospels and the Scriptures of Israel, ed. C. A. Evans and W. R. Stegner. Sheffield: Sheffield Academic Press, 1994.

Eco, Umberto. The Limits of Interpretation. Bloomington: Indiana University Press, 1990.

Elbogen. I. Ha-tefila Be-yisrael Be-hitp'hutah Ha-historit. Tel Aviv: Dvir, 1988.

Elbogen, I., and R. P. Scheindlin. Jewish Liturgy: A Comprehensive History. Philadelphia: Jewish Publications Society, 1993.

Epstein, J. N. "Glosses Babylo-arame'ennes." Revue des Etudes Juives 73 (1921): 33.

Etkes, I. The Besht: Magician, Mystic, and Leader. Waltham, Mass.: Brandeis University Press, 2005.

Faierstein, M. M. "Why Do the Scribes Say That Elijah Must Come First." Journal of Biblical Literature 100, no. 1 (1981): 75–78.

Feldman, L. H., and G. Hata, eds. Josephus, Judaism, and Christianity. Leiden: E. J. Brill, 1987.

Feldman, L. H., and M. Reinhold. Jewish Life and Thought among Greeks and Romans: Primary Readings. Minneapolis: Fortress Press, 1996.

Fine, S. Art and Judaism in the Greco-Roman World: Toward a New Jewish Archaeology. Cambridge: Cambridge University Press, 2005.

Finkelstein, L. "The Development of the Amidah." Jewish Quarterly Review, n.s., 16 (1925–26): 1–4, 127–70.

Fitzmyer, J. A. The Dead Sea Scrolls and Christian Origins, Grand Rapids, Mich.: Eerdmans, 2000.

-----. "The Use of Explicit Old Testament Quotations in Qumran Literature and in the New Testament." New Testament Studies 7 (1961): 297–333.

-----. A Wandering Aramean: Collected Aramaic Sayings. Missoula, Mont.: Scholars Press, 1979

Flusser, D. Jewish Sources in Early Christianity. Tel Aviv: Mod Books, 1989.

Fonrobert, C. E. "From Separatism to Urbanism: The Dead Sea Scrolls and the Origins of the Rabbinic Eruv." Dead Sea Discoveries 11, no. 1 (2004): 43–71.

Fonrobert, C. E., and M. S. Jaffee. The Cambridge Companion to the Talmud and Rabbinic Literature. Cambridge: Cambridge University Press, 2007.

France, R. T. The Gospel According to Matthew: Introduction and Commentary. Tyndale New Testament Commentaries. Grand Rapids, Mich.: Eerdmans, 1985,

Geller, M. "Jesus' Theurgic Powers: Parallels in the Talmud and Incantation Bowls." Journal of Jewish Studies 28 (1977): 141–55.

Geller, M. J. "Early Christianity and the Dead Sea Scrolls." Bulletin of the School of Oriental and African Studies: University of London 58 (1993): 82–86. In Honour of J. E. Wansbrough.

Ginzberg, L. "Die Haggada bei den Kirchenvätern und in der Apokryphischen Litteratur." Monatsschrift (1898): 42, 43.

-----. Legends of the Jews. Philadelphia: Jewish Publication Society, 1948.

-----. An Unknown Jewish Sect. New York: Jewish Theological Seminary of America, 1976.

Goldenberg, D. M. "Retroversion to Jesus' Ipsissima Verba and the Vocabulary of Jewish Palestinian Aramaic: The Case of Mata' and Qarta." Biblia 77 (1996): 64–83.

Gordis, R. "Increasing Peace in the World: A Note on a Talmudic Passage." Jewish Quarterly Review, n.s., 67, no. 1 (July 1976): 44–46

Green, W. S. "Romancing the Tome: Rabbinic Hermeneutics and the Theory of Literature." Semeia 40 (1987): 67–68.

Gropp, D. M. "The Samaria Papyri from Wadi Daliyeh II (Cave 4): Introduction." In Wadi Daliyeh II, ed. D. M. Gropp, J. C. VanderKam, M. J. Bernstein, and M. Brady, 3–32. Discoveries in the Judean Desert 28, pt. 2. Oxford: Oxford University Press, 2003.

Gruenwald, I. Apocalyptic and Merkavah Mysticism. Leiden: Brill, 1980.

Guedemann, M. Naechstenliebe, ein Beitrag zur Erlkaerung des Mathaeus-Evangeliums. Vienna, 1890.

Harrington, H. "Holiness in the Laws of 4QMMT." In Legal Texts and Legal Issues: Proceedings of the Second Meeting of the International Organization for Qumran Studies Published in Honor of Joseph M. Baumgarten, ed. M. J. Bernstein, F. C. Martinez, and J. Kampen, 109–28. Leiden: Brill, 1997.

Hengel, M. Nachfolge und Charisma: Eine exegetisch religionsgeschichtliche Studie zu Mt 8:21f. Berlin, 1968.

Herr, M. D. "The Calendar." In The Jewish People in the First Century, ed. S. Safrai, M. Stern, and D. Flusser. Minneapolis: Fortress, 1976.

Hill, D. "On the Use and Meaning of Hosea 6:6 in Matthew's Gospel." New Testament Studies 24 (1971): 107–19.

Horbury, W., W. D. Davies, and John Sturdy, eds. The Early Roman Period. Vol. 3 of Cambridge History of Judaism. Cambridge: Cambridge University Press, 1999.

Howard, T. L. "The Use of Hosea 11:1 in Matthew 2:15: An Alternative Solution." Bibliotheca Sacra (October–December 1986): 316–20.

Idel, M. Ben: Sonship and Jewish Mysticism. New York: Continuum, 2008.

Isaac, J. Jesus and Israel. Translated by S. Gran. New York: Holt, Rinehart and Winston, 1971.

Jellinek, A. ed., Bet ha-Midrash. Leipzig, 1853-77.

Jeremias, J. The Parables of Jesus. Revised ed. New York: Scribner's, 1963.

Joyce, J. Finnegans Wake. New York: Penguin Books, 1939.

Katz, Steven T. "Methodology in Basser's Studies." Review of Rabbinic Judaism 4, no. 2 (2001): 320–43.

Kee, H. C. Understanding the New Testament. 4th ed. Englewood Cliffs, N.J.: Prentice Hall, 1983.

Keener, C. S. A Commentary on the Gospel of Matthew. Grand Rapids, Mich.: Eerdmans, 1999.

Klausner, J. Jesus of Nazareth: His Life, Times, and Teachings. Boston: Beacon, 1964.

Klemm, K. G. "Das Wort von der Selbstbestattung der Toten: Beobachtungen zur Auslegungsgeschichte von Mt. viii. 22 Par." New Testament Studies 16 (1969–70): 60–75.

Kraus, S. "Church Fathers." Jewish Encyclopedia 4 (1906): 82.

-----. "The Jews in the Works of the Church Fathers." Jewish Quarterly Review 6 (1894): 233–58.

Lachs, S. T. "John the Baptist and His Audience." Gratz College Annual of Jewish Studies 4 (1975): 28ff.

-----. A Rabbinic Commentary on the New Testament: The Gospels of Matthew, Mark, and Luke. Hoboken, N.J.: Ktav, 1987.

-----. "Studies in the Semitic Background to the Gospel of Matthew." Jewish Quarterly Review 67 (1977): 197–99.

Luz, U., and R. Selle. Studies in Matthew. Grand Rapids, Mich.: Eerdmans, 2005.

Mack, B., and V. K. Robbins. Patterns and Persuasion in the Gospels. Sonoma, Calif.: Polebridge, 1989.

Manns, F., E. Alliata, and E. Testa, eds. Early Christianity in Context: Monuments and Documents. Studium Biblicum Franciscanum. Jerusalem: Franciscan Printing Press, 1993.

Martyn, J. L. History and Theology in the Fourth Gospel. 3rd ed. Louisville, Ky.: Westminster/John Knox Press, 2003.

Mason, S. Flavius Josephus on the Pharisees: A Composition-Critical Study. Leiden: Brill. 2001.

Matt, D. C. "New Ancient Words: The Aura of Cecercy in the Zohar." In. Major Trends in Jewish Mysticism, 50 Years Later, ed. J. Dan and P. Schaefer. Tübingen: Mohr, 1993.

Meier, J. P. A Marginal Jew. Vol. 2. New York: Doubleday, 1994.

Menken, M. J. J. "The Quotations from Isaiah 42, 1–4 in Matthew 12, 18–21: Its Textual Form." Ephemerides Theologicae Lovanienses 75 (1999): 35–52.

Milikowsky, Ch. "Josephus: Between Rabbinic Culture and Hellenistic Historio-graphy." In Shem in the Tents of Japhet: Essays on the Encounter of Judaism and Hellenism, ed. J. L. Kugel, 159–200. Journal for the Study of Judaism Suppl. Ser. 74. Leiden: Brill, 2002.

Mintz, J. R., and D. Ben-Amos, eds. In Praise of the Ba'al Shem Tov. Bloomington: Indiana University Press, 1970.

Mirsky, A.."From Midrash to Piyyut to Jewish Poetry." Leshonenu 32 (1967–68): 129–39 (in Hebrew).

-----. Yesodot Tzurot Hapiyyut. Jerusalem: Magnes, 1985.

Mondshine, Y. (aka Mondshain), ed. Sefer Shivhei Habesht, Facsimile of a Unique Manuscript, with Introduction, Variant Versions, and Appendices. Jerusalem, 1982.

Moore, George Foot. Judaism in the First Centuries of the Christian Era: The Age of the Tannaim. Vol. 2. Cambridge: Harvard University Press, 1927.

Neusner, J. Talmud Torah. Lanham, Md.: University Press of America, 2002.

Newman, Hillel L. "The Death of Jesus in the Toledot Yeshu Literature." Journal of Theological Studies 50 (1999): 59–79.

Odeberg, H. Pharisaism and Christianity. Translated from the original 1946 Swedish edition by J. M. Moe. St. Louis: Concordia, 1964.

Penney, Douglas L., and Michael O. Wise. "By the Power of Beelzebub: An Aramaic Incantation Formula from Qumran (4Q560)." Journal of Biblical Literature 113, no. 4 (Winter 1994): 627–50.

Pietersma, A., and B. G. Wright, eds. A New English Translation of the Septuagint. New York: Oxford University Press, 2007.

Puech, E. Qumrân grotte 4, XVIII: Textes hébreux (4Q521–4Q528, Q576–4Q579). Discoveries in the Judaean Desert 25. Oxford: Clarendon Press, 1998.

Rank, O. The Myth of the Birth of the Hero: A Psychological Exploration of Myth. Translated by G.. Richter and E. Lieberman. Baltimore: Johns Hopkins University Press, 2004.

Reed, A. Y. "Rabbinization of Roman Palestine? Depictions of Pharisees from the Gospel of Matthew to the Pseudo-Clementine Homilies." Unpublished paper.

Riffaterre, M. Fictional Truth. Baltimore: Johns Hopkins University Press, 1990.

Robinson, J. M., ed. The Nag Hammadi Library in English. San Francisco: Harper and Row, 1988.

Rosen-Zvi, I. "'Tractate Kinui': A Forgotten Tannaitic Debate about Marriage, Freedom of Movement, and Sexual Supervision." JSIJ 5 (2006), http://www.biu. ac.il/JS/JSIJ/heb/sum5.html.

Rosman, M. "Le-Toledotav Shel Mekor Histori." Zion 58 (5753).

Rosman, M. Founder of Hasidism: A Quest for the Historical Ba'al Shem Tov. Berkeley: University of California Press, 1996.

Safrai, S. The Literature of the sages. Philadelphia: Van Gorcum, 1987.

Sanders, E. P. The Historical Figure of Jesus. London: Penguin Books, 1995.
–––––. Jesus and Judaism. Philadelphia: Fortress Press, 1985:
–––––. "Jesus and the Sinners." Journal for the Study of the New Testament 19 (1983): 5–36.

Sanders, E. P., and M. Davies. Studying the Synoptic Gospels. Philadelphia: Trinity Press International, 1989.

Satlow, Michael L. Jewish Marriage in Antiquity. Princeton, N.J.: Princeton University Press, 2001.

Scholem, G. Jewish Gnosticism, Merkabah Mysticis,m and Talmudic Tradition. New York: JTS, 1965.

-----. Kabbalah. New York: Quadrangle/The New York Times Book Co., 1974.

-----. On the Kabbalah and Its Symbolism. Translated by Ralph Manheim. New York: Schocken, 1965.

-----. "Toward an Understanding of the Messianic Idea." In The Messianic Idea in Judaism and Other Essays on Jewish Spirituality, 1–36. New York: Schocken Books, 1971.

Schremer, A. "The Concluding Passage of Megilat Ta'anit and the Nullification of Its Halakhic Significance During the Talmudic Period." Zion 65 (2000): 411–39.

-----. Male and Female He Created Them: Jewish Marriage in Late Second Temple, Mishnah and Talmud Periods (Zakhar unekevah bera'am). Jerusalem: Zalman Shazar Center, 2003.

-----. "What Is Midrash Torah? Seclusion and Exclusion: Rhetoric of Separation in Qumran and Tannaitic Literature," symposium paper, http://orion.mscc.huji. ac.il/symposiums/8th/adielPaper.html.

Shakespeare, William. Hamlet. Vol. 14 of The Complete Works of William Shakespeare, Harvard Edition, ed. H. N. Hudson. Boston: Ginn and Heath, 1881.

Sigal, P. Halakah of Jesus of Nazareth According to the Gospel of Matthew. Lanham, Md.: London: University Press of America, 1986.

Silva, M. "The New Testament Use of the Old Testament." In Scripture and Truth, ed. D. A. Carson and J. D. Woodbridge, 150–57. Grand Rapids, Mich.: Zondervan, 1983.

Smith, M. Jesus the Magician: Charlatan or Son of God? San Francisco: Harper and Row, 1978.

Soares-Prabhu, G. The Formula Quotations in the Infancy Narrative of Matthew: An Inquiry into the Tradition History of Matt. 1–2. Analecta Biblica. Rome: Biblical Institute Press, 1976.

Steinmetz, D. Punishment and Freedom: The Rabbinic Construction of Criminal Law. Philadelphia: University of Pennsylvania Press, 2008.

Stendahl, K. The School of St. Matthew and Its Use of the Old Testament. Lund: G. W. K. Gleerup, 1954.

Stern, M., ed. Greek and Latin Authors on Jews and Judaism. Vol. 2. Jerusalem: Israel Academy of the Sciences and Humanities, 1974.

Stone, M. "Testament of Naphtali." Journal of Jewish Studies 47 (1996): 311–21.

Strack, H. L., and P. Billerbeck. Kommentar zum Neuen Testament aus Talmud und Midrasch, Erster Band, Das Evangelium nach Mattäus. München: C. H. Beck'sche Verlagsbuchhandlung, 1922.

Swartz, M. D. "Like the Ministering Angels: Ritual and Purity in Early Jewish Mysticism and Magic." AJS Review 19, no. 2 (1994): 135–67.

Taylor, C. The Teaching of the Twelve Apostles, with Illustrations from the Talmud. Cambridge: Cambridge University Press, 1908.

Teppler, Y. Birkat haMinim: Jews and Christians in Conflict in the Ancient World. Translated from the Hebrew by S. Weingarten. Tübingen: Mohr Siebeck, 2007.

Thomas, D. W. Documents from Old Testament Times. New York: Harper and Row, 1958.

Tigay, J. H. "On the Term 'Phylacteries' (Matt. 23:5)." Harvard Theological Review 72 (1979): 46–52.

Tosato, A. "Joseph Being Just Man (Matt. 1:19)." Catholic Biblical Quarterly 41 (1979): 547–51.

Turner, V. "Liminality and Communitas." In The Ritual Process: Structure and Anti-Structure, ed. V. Turner, 94–130. Aldine: de Gruyter, 1969.

Ulrich, E. The Dead Sea Scrolls and the Origins of the Bible. Studies in the Dead Sea Scrolls and Related Literature. Grand Rapids, Mich.: Eerdmans, 1999.

van der Horst, P. W. Ancient Jewish Epitaphs. Kampen: Kok Pharos, 1991.

Vanderkam, J. C. "Righteous One, Messiah, Chosen One, and Son of Man in I Enoch 3-71." In The Messiah: Developments in Early Judaism and Christianity, ed. J. H. Charlesworth, 169–91. Minneapolis: Fortress Press, 1992.

Vermes, G. Jesus in His Jewish Context. Minneapolis: Fortress Press, 2003.

Viviano, B. T. "Beatitudes Found Among Dead Sea Scrolls." Biblical Archaeology Review 18, no. 6 (November/December 1992): 53–55, 66.

Westerholm, S. Jesus and Scribal Authority. Lund: Gleerup, 1978.

Wertheimer, S. A. Batei Midrashot, 4 vols. Jerusalem, 1893–97.

Witherington, Ben, III. Jesus the Sage: The Pilgrimage of Wisdom. Minneapolis: Fortress, 2000.

Yuval, Israel J. Two Nations in Your Womb. Berkeley: University of California Press, 2006.

Zussman, J. "Torah She-Be'al Peh: Peshutah Ke'mashma'ah." In Talmudic Studies: Collected Studies in Talmud and Related Fields Dedicated to the Memory of Ephraim E. Urbach, ed. J. Zussman and D. Rozental, 259–75. Jerusalem: Magnes Press, 2005.

INDEX

Introduction to the Index

In the preparation of this volume I used many editions and versions of various works. I generally consulted the Bar-Ilan Responsa (version 10) data base to check readings. The references are generally to the chapter divisions used in that data base. As well, where English versions were available numbering followed those editions in some places where the standard editions slightly differed. I made extensive use of the following printed editions.

Avot deRabbi Natan (A and B), ed. Schechter, S., 3rd ed. New York, 1967.
Encyclopedia Judaica, eds. Roth, C. and Wigoder, G., Keter, Jerusalem, 1971.
Genesis Rabba, eds. Theodor, J. and Albeck, Ch., 3 Vols, Jerusalem, 1965.
Mekhilta deRabbi Yishmael, eds. Horovitz, S. and Rabin, Y., 2nd ed., Jerusalem, 1970.
Midrash Rabba, ed. Mirkin, M. A., 11 Vols, Tel Aviv, 1987.
Seder Eliahu Rabba, ed. Ish Shalom (Friedmann), M., Vienna 1902.
Sefer Pitron Torah ed. Urbach E. E., Jerusalem, 1978.
Sifra, Facsimile of Venetian 1546 edition (reprinted Jerusalem, 1970).
Sifre Deuteronomy, ed. Finkelstein, L. (*Siphre ad Deuteronomium*), Berlin, 1939.
Sifre Numbers, ed. Horovitz S. (Siphre deVe Rav), Leipzig, 1917.
Tanhuma Facsimile edition, Constantinople 1520–1522. (reprinted Jerusalem, 1971).
Tosefta Kifshuta, S. Lieberman, New York, 5715–33.

Editions of Philo, Josephus.

Colson, *Philo with an English Translation*, translated by F. H. Colson and (vols I–V), G.H. Whitaker, The Loeb Classical Library, 1929–1941.
Thackery, H. St. J., *Jewish Wars* in *Josephus with an English Translation*, Loeb Classical Library, 2nd ed. London, Cambridge Mass, 1957.
-----. *Jewish Antiquities, in Josephus with an English Translation*, Loeb Classical Library, 2nd ed. London, Cambridge Mass, 1957.

Where necessary I availed myself of the translations of Whiston for Josephus and Yonge for Philo as they are not subject to copyright restrictions.

INDEX TO BIBLICAL
AND RELATED WRITINGS

NEW TESTAMENT
Matthew

Mark

EARLY RELIGIOUS LITERATURE
Apocrypha

GENERAL INDEX

Printed in the United States
152882LV00001B/3/P